THE ORIGINS
OF NON-RACIALISM

WHITE OPPOSITION TO APARTHEID IN THE 1950s

THE ORIGINS
OF NON-RACIALISM

WHITE OPPOSITION TO APARTHEID IN THE 1950s

DAVID EVERATT

WITS UNIVERSITY PRESS

Wits University Press
1 Jan Smuts Avenue
Johannesburg
South Africa
http://witspress.wits.ac.za

First published 2009

ISBN 978 1 86814 500 3

Cover image adapted from the Freedom Charter Pamphlet:
Eli Weinberg, UWC Robben-Island Mayibuye Archives

Edited by Pat Tucker
Cover design by Hothouse South Africa
Layout and design by Hothouse South Africa
Printed and bound by Creda Communications

Dedication

This book is dedicated to the loves of my life, my wife Cathi, and my children, Josie and Jonathon.

Table of Contents

Acknowledgements

Books generate debts, and I owe many people far more than I will ever be able to repay. A few, however, deserve special mention.

This book began life as a doctoral thesis in the dark and gloomy days of the 1980s, and I owe my supervisor, the inimitable Stanley Trapido, far more than I knew when we worked together or even fully grasp now. His is one of the many voices in my head.

Secondly, to all the remarkable people who populate the pages of this book, many of whom I had the privilege of meeting, all of whom were unfailingly generous with their time, their private papers, their memories, their gossip and all of whom – from conservative liberal to radical Trotskyist – shared an indefatigable belief in the ultimate triumph of non-racialism over apartheid. Their generosity of spirit and commitment to the ideal of a democratic South Africa taught me more than they will ever know, and all I can offer is deeply sincere thanks and this book.

The original thesis was typed in the days when floppy discs were considered the height of technological sophistication. When I came to re-work the thesis into a book, floppy discs could reduce computers to hysterical laughter – but no more than that. So my thanks to Phindi Hlatswayo who painstakingly re-typed the entire thesis (onto a stiffy disc, as useful nowadays as a floppy disc…).

Raymond Suttner pushed me to publish, and I would never have done so without his prompting. He, Rupert Taylor and Gerry Mare all offered good advice on how to improve the manuscript, for which I am enormously grateful. I even took some of that advice!

And finally, family and friends, the people who have to look politely interested in lengthy mealtime perorations about obscure yet (surely) fascinating moments in the past – my thanks to you one and all. But don't imagine you're getting a free copy in return for listening….

List of abbreviations

AAC	All-African Convention
ADP	African Democratic Party
AES	Army Education Service
ANC	African National Congress
ANCYL	African National Congress Youth League
APO	African People's Organisation
ARM	African Resistance Movement
CC	Central Committee
COD	Congress of Democrats
CoP	Congress of the People
COSATU	Congress of South African Trade Unions
CNETU	Council for Non-European Trade Unions
CPSA	Communist Party of South Africa
CRL	Civil Rights League
CST	colonialism of a special type
DL	Democratic League
FRAC	Franchise Action Committee
FSAW	Federation of South African Women
FSU	Friends of the Soviet Union
LP	Liberal Party of South Africa
MP	Member of Parliament
MRC	Multi-Racial Conference
MYS	Modern Youth Society
NAC	National Action Council
NAD	Native Affairs Department
NCC	National Consultative Committee
NEC	National Executive Committee
NEUM	Non-European unity Movement
NIC	Natal Indian Congress
NNALA	Northern Natal African Landowners' Association
NRC	Native Representative Council
NP	National Party
NUSAS	National Union of South African Students
PAC	Pan Africanist Congress
RDP	Reconstruction and Development Programme

SABRA	South African Bureau of Racial Affairs
SACOD	South African Congress of Democrats
SACP	South African Communist Party
SACPO	South African Coloured People's Organisation
SAIC	South African Indian Congress
SAIRR	South African Institute of Race Relations
SALA	South African Liberal Association
SALG	South African Liberal Group
SL	Springbok League
TIC	Transvaal Indian Congress
UDF	United Democratic Front
UN	United Nations
UNO	United Nations Organisation
UP	United Party

Introduction

We, the people of South Africa, declare for all our country and the world to know:

That South Africa belongs to all who live in it, black and white, and that no government can justly claim authority unless it is based on the will of the people[1]

We, the people of South Africa … Believe that South Africa belongs to all who live in it, united in our diversity.[2]

Among the most consistent threads in the discourse of liberation in South Africa was a commitment to non-racialism. How strong that thread was – unbreakable[3] according to some, distinctly fragile according to others[4] – can be debated. But from the 1955 Freedom Charter to the 1996 Constitution non-racialism has featured significantly in the canon of all anti-apartheid organisations. The same applies internationally.

But it has also become clear since democracy was ushered in, in 1994, that a critical weakness was the failure to *define* non-racialism, to give it content beyond that of a slogan or a self-evident 'good thing'.[5] It made intuitive sense, uniting races where apartheid divided them. But beyond that, what was the meaning of non-racialism? The 1996 Constitution implicitly defined it as a democratic state where the rights of every citizen are equally protected by the law. But is non-racialism the same as formal equality? Is there no more to it than that, nothing to do with the actions or moral base of individuals? Is it a passive or an active state? Are there specific types of action required of a non-racialist, or is it all left to the state or political parties or courts to resolve? For example, should the erstwhile non-racialist follow the advice of Warren Beatty (in *Bulworth*) when he suggested that non-racial democrats should pursue '… a programme of voluntary, free-spirited, open-ended procreative racial deconstruction', by which was meant, he explained, '... everybody just gotta keep fuckin' everybody till we're all the same color'[6]?

If for some reason this fails to appeal, does non-racialism require (some other types of) pro-action on the part of the would-be non-racialist? And if so, what form should this take? Is equity or redress involved, whereby the non-racialist can or should make amends for the racialism of the past? How, and to whom, and for how long? Who decides when enough is enough? And most importantly, how can this be done at an *ethical* level? How do we move beyond repentance and redress – the latter currently the focus of much state activity – and look to building new citizens and a new society on a new moral basis, where individuals are not immediately pigeonholed socially, economically, psychologically, intellectually or morally, by their race? How do we create spaces where citizens can leave behind the trappings of race and engage as fellow South Africans? There are no guidelines for being a genuinely non-racial citizen of the new South Africa.

Worryingly, no one – including the African National Congress (ANC)-led government – seems to know what a 'normal' post-apartheid state looks like, or how we will know when we reach it. South Africa has been in a transition or undergoing transformation since 1994 – overwhelmingly, and appropriately, based on racial redress. But how will we know when South Africa has stopped *becoming* and has arrived?

There is a more compelling philosophical question underpinning the issue, namely is it possible for non-racialism to be realised under a nationalist government? Is non-racialism compatible with nationalism at all? Non-racialism was crafted by the African nationalist resistance movement in response to apartheid, itself a nationalist-fuelled ideology; but it remains questionable whether that same African National Congress is able to throw off the constraints and racial blinkers of nationalism and truly embrace non-racialism. Much of this book analyses the warnings – of radical Marxists, liberals, socialists, humanists and others from the 1950s – that nationalists, in the words of Moeletsi Mbeki (brother of the more famous Thabo), were not militant democrats:

> African nationalism was a movement of the small, Westernised black elite that emerged under colonialism. Its fight was always for inclusion in the colonial system so that it, too, could benefit from the spoils of colonialism.[7]

Ever since the African and Indian congresses formed an alliance, the approach has been 'equality under African leadership'. Post-apartheid experience to date suggests that this is incompatible with non-racialism.

We live in an official non-racial democracy that insists on using the same racial classification system as apartheid in order to measure how far we have travelled *from* our shared, racist past. This is reasonable: disadvantage was created by race, and differentiated by race (Africans had fewer rights than coloureds, who had fewer than

Indians, who had fewer than whites) and we need to measure whether previously disadvantaged people are receiving the democracy dividend. But we lack any pointers showing us *where we are going*, or when – if ever – the need for racial classification will fall away. And with it, when racial pigeonholing (ideologically, socially, inter-personally, discursively) will be sloughed off so that, as Walt Whitman (in *The Mystic Trumpeter*) would have it, it will be 'enough to merely be! Enough to breathe!'

Initially, repentance and forgiveness – symbolised by Archbishop Tutu and President Mandela – dominated the post-apartheid moral and political terrain. But once the Truth and Reconciliation Commission wound up its work, and Mandela stepped down after five years as president, these took a backseat to the aggressive work of developing a national bourgeoisie, the historic task (in the view of many) of the national democratic revolution. Redress is primarily exercised through state-sponsored vehicles such as affirmative action and broad-based black economic empowerment, which seek to ensure that state and some private sector resources are channelled to the emergent black bourgeoisie. The failure to generate sustainable pro-poor growth has resulted in some thirteen million citizens receiving social grants. The predictable white (and Indian and coloured) resentment over 'reverse discrimination' is endemic. The result is that non-racialism has retreated to the realm of the individual and the private, rather than being societal and, by definition, public. Non-racialism has no common pro-active moral content in post-apartheid South Africa.

In his *Preface* to *Humanity: A Moral History of the Twentieth Century*, Jonathan Glover wrote:

> … much English-language writing on ethics is limited by relative insulation from some of the twentieth century's man-made disasters. There must be lessons for ethics in the events of this violent century … thinking about ethics is likely to be enriched by learning what we can about the causes of events we have been lucky to avoid.[8]

This is not a book on philosophy. Nor is it a book about contemporary South Africa. It is a history book. It seeks to help us understand how non-racialism emerged and the various forms it took in doing so in the 1950s, the decade that forged the ANC in its current form. It is primarily concerned with the impact of white participation on the struggle against apartheid. This impact, overwhelmingly, was on the ideologies and discourses of struggle. There were too few anti-apartheid whites to make any numeric impact; but they did have a powerful influence on the nature of the struggle, including ideology as well as the strategies and tactics used – and were visible testament to the non-racialism that all espoused, albeit in different ways and taking different forms.

Like Glover, we too can think about disastrous man-made events such as apartheid – which many of us were unlucky enough to live through – in order to better understand critical issues in contemporary South Africa. The history analysed here leads to questions about fundamental ethical issues that need to be considered by all South Africans living in the post-apartheid state. The intention is not to answer them, but to raise them, and hope that others will take them up.

The ideological associations of non-racialism

Part of the problem is that non-racialism was as undefined in the 1950s as it is now. The language of the time changed during the decade as non-racialism and the issues associated with it – what it meant, as well as how it should be reflected organisationally, the place and function of African nationalism, and so on – were fought out within and beyond the Congress movement.

In the late 1940s and early 1950s multiracial, non-racial, interracial and similar terms were used interchangeably. 'Race relations' was the core focus of white liberals associated with the South African Institute of Race Relations (SAIRR) in particular, but the term was widely used in progressive circles. All these terms, at that time, referred to formal equality between the races – very similar to the way the 1996 South African Constitution resolved the issue – although not necessarily substantive equality.

There was a common goal of equality under the law, but many paths to achieving it, as well as different ways of defining it. By the time the Second World War ended the African National Congress was campaigning unequivocally for full equality and increasingly used extra-parliamentary methods such as passive resistance campaigns in support of their struggle. White liberals – academics and professionals linked to the SAIRR, the Hofmeyr Society and other small organisations, elected Native Representatives and others – overwhelmingly supported a qualified franchise for 'civilised' natives and insisted on this being attained through gradualist, constitutional, parliamentary means.

Other white activists – members of the Communist Party of South Africa (CPSA), non-CPSA Marxists and socialists, as well as a new, younger generation of white liberals and social democrats radicalised by the Second World War and the ideals they had fought for – supported the demand for full, immediate equality for all and were happy to use extra-parliamentary methods. As the decade unfolded the demand for full equality became common to liberals and radicals alike.

But what was less clear was how African nationalism and non-racialism would commingle – both in the struggle and later in a democratic state. While the ANC led the struggle for freedom it insisted on separate, race-based congresses, led by the ANC and joined under what was to become known as the Congress Alliance (referred to in this book also as Congress or the Alliance). This was multiracialism – racially distinct congresses allowing all races to participate in the struggle for freedom, but under African and ANC leadership. Whites were not allowed to join the ANC until the late

1960s, and could not sit on the National Executive Committee until 1985. The United Democratic Front (UDF), which spearheaded legal internal resistance to apartheid in the 1980s (while the ANC was banned and exiled), retained the multiracial approach of the Congress movement.

Multiracialism was one approach. The Communist Party – in both its pre-1950 CPSA and post-1953 South African Communist Party (SACP) forms – had a non-racial structure, where people of all races belonged to the same organisation. The Liberal Party was organised in the same way. Many whites sitting in the South African Congress of Democrats (SACOD), the white wing of the Congress Alliance, were deeply uncomfortable with their racial structure, and the ANC stricture that their task was to organise whites, the community to which they supposedly had easy access. (Many white activists, of course, were ostracised by other whites, who had no interest in their 'communist' message or 'kaffirboet' lifestyles.) As we see throughout this book, many white liberals and leftists wanted little or nothing to do with their fellow white citizens – they wanted to identify with, be seen with and work among black South Africans – 'the path of least resistance', ANC–CPSA stalwart Moses Kotane labelled it.

Marxists and socialists not in the SACP also resisted the whites-only basis of SACOD and the Congress Alliance more broadly, arguing that the struggle for equal rights for all races was obscuring the 'real' struggle, which was class-based and aimed at substantive equality for all. Non-racialism, in other words, was not merely a different way of structuring an organisation or political party but had (or obtained) distinct ideological overtones.

Over time the race-based structure of the Congress Alliance became a highly politicised issue. Liberals and Africanists saw the multiracial structure of the alliance as a vehicle designed by (white) communists through which they were able to exert overweening influence over the ANC. Lacking any significant numeric base, the argument went, white communists were still able to lead Congress by the nose via its multiracial structure, which gave them seats on the co-ordinating structures at the apex of the Alliance, regardless of their tiny numerical base. Non-SACP Marxists attacked multiracialism and the ANC for elevating national liberation above class struggle and socialist revolution; since 1928 the CPSA had supported the need for initial national liberation preceding a class-based struggle.

The dispute heated up throughout the 1950s and, as a result, people became more sensitive to the terms they used and what the different terms actually meant. By the end of the decade, 'interracial' had largely disappeared. 'Race relations' had largely returned to the Institute named after it. Multiracial referred to the way the Congress movement was organised, while non-racialism was both the way the SACP and the Liberal Party were organised *and* the stated goal of all anti-apartheid forces. Unless quoting from the time, this is the way in which these terms are used in this book.

Nationalism, socialism, liberalism, communism ... and whites

But if terminology had become more precise the same could not be said of the understanding of how non-racialism would be realised under African nationalist leadership. In part this was because beneath the disputes about the structure of the Congress Alliance lay a deeper set of competing ideologies, whose differences were fought out over the multi-racialism versus non-racialism debate. In the face of an increasingly vicious apartheid state and security apparatus, moreover, blurry 'non-racialism' had a much-needed feel-good factor and was a rallying cry for all those opposed to the implementation of apartheid.

And of course at the heart of the issue were white South Africans. In the face of growing oppression, drawing together African, Indian and coloured activists and organisations in an anti-apartheid alliance was an obvious step. But what about whites? What to do about whites generally, since they were not colonial servants who would flee back to the metropole come independence, as was happening across the African continent,[9] but were rooted permanently in the country? And what to do about those whites who wanted to join the anti-apartheid struggle? Liberalism, socialism, the internal colonialism thesis of the South African Communist Party, the nationalisms of the ANC and Pan Africanist Congress (PAC) – all had to recognise and accommodate whites, both as permanent residents of the country and as participants in an African-led liberation struggle. All had to consider, debate, wrestle with and take a position on non-racialism, and on what to do about white participation.

Some did so more easily than others. Few, if any, managed to move beyond the general notion of equality under African leadership – exactly the approach of all post-1994 governments. That remains a partial, under-developed and ham-fisted interpretation of what non-racialism could, and should, mean.

Whites were members of the Communist and Liberal parties and SACOD; well-known anti-apartheid whites also tried to join the ANC (Ronald Segal) and PAC (Patrick Duncan, who had previously tried to join the ANC), while others (particularly those on the far left) maintained an ongoing critical commentary on the follies of nationalism and of racially discrete congresses.

This latter group were proponents of an immediate class struggle, rather than a class struggle to be initiated after the national liberation struggle had been executed successfully. They are arguably as marginal in the post-apartheid political discourse as they were during the struggle years – even as their predictions seem to be coming true, and ANC leaders defend instant wealth because 'we did not struggle to remain poor'.[10]

The ANC's dominance within the tripartite alliance (which includes the SACP and the Congress of South African Trade Unions – COSATU – alongside the ANC) has become increasingly pronounced in the post-apartheid era, during which it has formed successive governments, and, while there is contestation over the number and depth of redistributive measures and the growth path chosen by the ANC, the adherents of class struggle seem as few and as disparate as they were sixty years ago. The warnings issued then – that class struggle would be postponed indefinitely by a national bourgeoisie anxious to max-imise personal wealth and advancement at the expense of the urban and rural poor – are repeated, though with less 'we told you so' than might have been expected, suggesting that history does indeed need to be revisited and its lessons relearned.

During the 2009 general election campaign, some media attention was given to arguments – some from within or close to the ruling party, others from more pre-dictable economic sectors and their think-tanks – that affirmative action and black economic empowerment – the two premier vehicles for acheiving either redistribu-tion or an instant national bourgeoisie, depending on your viewpoint – should be done away with, since they were harming the economy. But the lesson has been learned the hard way: race classification linked to economic advancement has utilitar-ian, political and vote-catching value. It would be a harsh historical irony if arguments about the economic irrationality of race classification linked to job reservation and redistribution were to find purchase in the ANC, the party that (with the SACP) so strongly argued that capitalism and apartheid were mutually functional and rejected all arguments to the contrary as gutless liberalism.

The ANC conference in Polokwane in December 2007, which saw the demise of the Thabo Mbeki era, heralded much change. At the time of writing, it is impossible to know if this will translate into substance. Post-Polokwane, the ANC and government speak more forcefully about redistribution and pro-poor growth. The tetchy impatience with (real or perceived) colonial stereotyping that marked the Mbeki era seems to be declining, and hopefully this decline will be accompanied by more open-mindedness to debate and discussion about race, identity, and non-racialism. That such a discussion is urgently needed was made clear by the murderous xenophobic violence of May 2008 and the ethnic undertones of the ANC–Congress of the People (COPE) election battle in 2009.

The current generation of political leaders – and many of their voters – were all affected by apartheid, and may have a race-bred consciousness that will never entirely fade away. But the next generation – those born long after apartheid's demise – deserve so much better. Our challenge is to find the courage to break decisively with the past, the mindsets and the identities it created for and ascribed to us all, and enter a new discursive space where it is, indeed, enough merely to be.

A note on methodology

This book began life as a doctoral thesis, written in the 1980s. The research focused heavily on secondary materials, including existing collections belonging to individuals and organisations, as well as private papers made available to me by many activists of the time (most of which I managed to archive in various university libraries in South Africa and the United Kingdom). I also conducted a series of interviews (listed in the references) with activists from the period.

In the 1990s, however, everything changed: the ANC was unbanned, Mandela released, apartheid crumbled with a whimper, democracy was ushered in and a new South Africa was born. Of course, a great deal did not change – precisely the reason for returning to this topic, where non-racialism remains undefined and racial classification and race-based thinking remain pervasive after fifteen years of ANC rule.

Rewriting the thesis as a book has allowed me the opportunity to introduce new material, primarily from the biographies of many key actors from the period (see the Reference section). But it should be clearly stated that I did not embark on a second round of qualitative research; that the respondents who were interviewed were overwhelmingly white activists from the 1950s, and more black respondents might have provided differing perspectives; and that the book does not attempt to engage with current discourses around race, identity and related topics. How damaging these factors are to the overall thrust of the book is left to the reader to decide.

This is a history book. It tries to tell the story of a remarkably talented, courageous and visionary generation of activists, of all races, and the ways in which they dreamed up a possible future for South Africa. It is the task of those of us fortunate enough to live in 'the new South Africa' to see whether or not we measure up to the standards they set and change accordingly – in areas such as self-sacrifice, service, bravery, camaraderie – in essence, full and active citizenship. Above all, South Africa carries global expectations, as the 'miracle' of the 1990s, that we can and will give meaning to non-racialism, and create a society that truly belongs to all who live in it, black and white.

Chapter 1

Whites and the ANC, 1945–1950

The 1940s saw the rise of nationalist and anti-colonial movements across what we now know as the developing world, including South Africa. In the same decade the African National Congress (ANC) was transformed from a small elite body using courteous and constitutional forms of protest into an extra-parliamentary organisation attempting mass-based mobilisation of all unenfranchised groups in South Africa, and working alongside whites and others committed to non-racialism. In 1947 the ANC entered into an alliance with the South African Indian Congress (SAIC), which was joined in September 1953 by the South African Coloured People's Organisation (SACPO), followed a month later by the white South African Congress of Democrats (SACOD).

In 1956 the Congress Alliance endorsed the Freedom Charter (drawn up the year before), a statement of principle that envisaged a future South Africa based on full equality for all people of all races. The principle that came to guide the ANC – remarkably, given the exigencies of white rule in the guises of both segregation and (after 1948) apartheid – was its commitment to a non-racial future. How did this come about? Why, in the midst of a race-based society, did the ANC espouse a racially inclusive vision rather than an exclusive African nationalism?

The integration of all races in a struggle against the race-based ideology of apartheid, and behind a national liberation struggle led by the ANC, was difficult. The incorporation of whites in the struggle against white supremacy was particularly difficult. This chapter analyses the roots of non-racialism in the post-war years by reviewing the rise of the Congress movement after the Second World War and the responses of whites who supported a non-racial future but differed over its exact form and how (and when) it could be achieved.

The impact of the war years

The years of the Second World War were a remarkable period in twentieth-century South African history, marked by the partial relaxation of discriminatory legislation, a 50% increase in real average earnings for black industrial workers, and rising hopes for a more liberal government policy.[1] During the war, industrial manufacturing became the largest single sector of the economy, since uninterrupted industrial production was essential for the war effort, and the labour requirements of heavy and manufacturing industry began to compete with those of the formerly unchallenged mining and agricultural sectors. Representatives of organised industry opposed the migrant labour system and called for a permanent urban black labour force to meet their demand for semi-skilled and skilled labour. The privately owned commercial and manufacturing sectors joined the call for an urbanised labour force and saw a potential black consumer market 'going to waste'.

Black workers, restricted by law to tribal reserves in rural areas, poured into the urban areas, driven by economic necessity and attracted by the growing demand for labour. Deneys Reitz, Minister of Native Affairs, relaxed influx control in the industrial centres of the Transvaal and Natal in 1942, increasing the number of urban Africans, while the 1943 Landsdown Mine Wages Commission reported that the reproductive capacity of the reserves, on which the migrant labour system was premised, was 'a myth'.[2] By 1948 the Native Laws (Fagan) Commission noted that women comprised a third of urban Africans and concluded that black urbanisation was permanent.[3]

Black urbanisation led to an acute housing shortage and informal settlements increased as thousands of homeless Africans built shacks on deserted land and provided their own services and infrastructure.[4] Their direct action was matched in other urban struggles such as bus boycotts,[5] while black unionisation and industrial action also increased. Although the fact was officially unrecognised, by 1945 more than 40% of commerce and privately owned industry was unionised. According to O'Meara, 145 522 African workers went on strike between 1940 and 1948, accounting for a loss of 409 299 workdays, and prompting organised manufacturing industry to call for the recognition of black trade unions. The Transvaal Chamber of Industries argued that '... if Natives are to enter industry in ever-increasing numbers, it is clear that their being organised and disciplined in proper unions is an indispensable prerequisite to their development as stable and productive workers.'[6]

During the war years liberal discourse moved beyond its former domain in educational or research bodies and was taken up by a series of government commissions whose reports supported the central demands of organised industry. For example, in 1942 the Smit Report called for the recognition of black trade unions and the Van Eck Commission proposed the abolition of pass laws, while the following year the Landsdown Commission called for the payment of a full living wage to urban African workers.[7]

Liberal values were popularised by the war itself, fought as it was against fascism and in defence of individualism, the rule of law and self-determination. These ideals were set out in Churchill and Roosevelt's Atlantic Charter and it was necessary to promote them in South Africa in order to ensure support for the war effort. No wonder the South African Institute of Race Relations (SAIRR) – more a slow-burner than a hotbed of liberalism – in its 1948 *Handbook on Race Relations in South Africa*, offered its own brand of (entirely misplaced) optimism, concluding that 'in South Africa more ill is wrought through lack of understanding than through ill will.'[8]

The United Party (UP) government of Jan Smuts faced a number of problems in the early 1940s – the Allied powers were suffering setbacks in the war, the threat of an invasion grew as the Japanese fleet entered the Indian Ocean and government had to fight a general election in 1943. In a tactical response, government sought to accommodate rather than alienate. In an attempt to win black working-class loyalty and avoid fighting challenges on too many fronts simultaneously, as the Axis powers were doing, the pass laws were partially relaxed and a pragmatic approach adopted to labour unrest. African unions were allowed to develop unofficially and, in 1942, Walter Madeley, then Minister of Labour, promised black union recognition in return for worker loyalty.[9]

Black strikes in areas of industry important to the war appear to have been settled in a manner favourable to workers. Smuts talked of replacing segregation with undefined (but nicer-sounding) 'trusteeship'.[10]

Government also flirted with organisations sympathetic to the Allied cause and which had the potential to cause political or economic disruption. Following the entry of the USSR into the war in 1941, the Communist Party of South Africa (CPSA) threw itself into supporting the war effort – having previously opposed the war and supported the Hitler–Stalin pact – with a 'Defend South Africa!' campaign and soon gained a degree of political respectability. The Smuts government permitted the existence of the CPSA, the Friends of the Soviet Union (FSU), non-racial trade unions and other organisations. Not until 1994 would South Africa again see Cabinet ministers join communists on public platforms.

Smuts opened a 1943 'Soviet Friendship' conference in Johannesburg, while his wife was a patron of the FSU. After 1941 the CPSA placed support for the war above purely domestic issues and discouraged strikes, a remarkable position for a party committed to working-class rights, and another in a lengthy and tortuous history of juggling domestic demands with the 'party line' coming out of Moscow. The Communist Party programme was vague about black political rights while supporting the principle that the government should provide food, shelter and medical services as required.[11]

The particular conditions of the war years allowed organisations such as the CPSA and the FSU to penetrate the white community in a way that was unknown before or after the war. In 1942 more than 6 000 people gathered to welcome the first Soviet consul to Johannesburg, and Medical Aid for Russia received more than £80 000 in the first two months of its existence.[12] The Red Army offensive led the Minister of Justice,

Colin Steyn, to conclude that a '... Russian victory will mean a victory for democracy'.[13] The CPSA won seats in city council elections in Johannesburg, East London and Cape Town. The party also fielded nine candidates in the 1943 general election and, although all lost, they polled an average 11% of the vote.[14]

The war boosted industrialisation, which challenged the migrant labour system. Government commissions argued that African urbanisation and 'economic integration' – of blacks into the 'white' economy – were irreversible processes. A degree of consensus emerged about the direction of future government policy. The ANC and CPSA, as well as liberals in the UP, the SAIRR and among the Native Representatives (who were indirectly elected to Parliament by African voters) claimed that 'nothing could be the same after the war' – that government policy would have to acknowledge that segregation had failed to maintain racial separatism. In 1942 Julius Lewin, a liberal academic involved in the Army Education Service (AES) run by one of the most impressive South Africans of the twentieth century, Leo Marquard, stated:

> We have a definite sense of taking a new direction. The van Eck Report ... expresses this and the war itself means that no new disabilities will descend. On the contrary, old ones are being shaken – the hated pass laws have been relaxed and Native trade unions are to be recognised ... We [can] get along faster now that the principle of this and that is conceded ...[15]

High hopes for a change in direction by government were boosted by a speech made by Smuts in the 'dark days' of the war, even though the words seem more a lamentation than excitement about a possible new future:

> The whole trend both in this country and throughout Africa has been in the opposite direction [to segregation]. The whole movement of development here on this continent has been for closer contacts to be established between the various races and the various sectors of this community ... Isolation has gone and segregation has fallen on evil days too ... A revolutionary change is taking place among the Native peoples of Africa through the movement from the country to the towns – the movement from old Reserves in the Native areas to the big European centres of population. Segregation tried to stop it. It has, however, not stopped it in the least. The process has been accelerated. You might as well try to sweep the ocean back with a broom.[16]

Smuts's commitment to the Atlantic Charter, combined with the relaxation of discriminatory legislation and the findings of various government commissions, seemed to suggest that progressive (if incremental) change was in the air. But what was happening outside the coterie of liberals in and near Smuts, and among the newly respectable (mainly white) communists? How would black organisations respond to the times and to the signals of possible change?

Africans' Claims

The main response of the ANC – still a small, elitist body yet to undergo its own radicalising transformation brought about by wartime conditions – was the 1943 publication of *Africans' Claims in South Africa*, drawn up by a committee dominated by doctors, lawyers, teachers and ministers of religion, and intended to attract 'distinguished University graduates' to the ANC.[17]

The organisation sought to capitalise on the liberal ethos of the period by placing squarely before government the vision of non-racial citizenship. *Africans' Claims* articulated Western liberal-democratic demands in a non-racial South African context and attempted to formulate an ideological path that government, apparently backing away from segregation, should follow. But segregation and trusteeship, tragically, were aeons away from equality.

Africans' Claims was divided into two main parts following a preface written by Dr Alfred Bitini Xuma, President-General of the ANC. The first placed the Atlantic Charter in a South African context and analysed the nature of oppression in the country; the second comprised a Bill of Rights. It tried to achieve two goals simultaneously: to generate black support for the ANC while appealing for wider acceptance of the principle of non-racial equality. Addressing the white audience, Xuma appealed for the anti-fascist values of the war and the Atlantic Charter to 'apply to the whole of the British Empire, the United States of America and to all the nations of the world and their subject peoples'; talking to the domestic black audience he noted that 'we are not so foolish as to believe that because we have made these declarations our government will grant us our claims for the mere asking' and warned that 'this is only the beginning of a long struggle …'.[18]

The Bill of Rights called for equal political participation and universal suffrage, breaking with previous ANC demands for a qualified franchise. One decade's radicalism was the next decade's old hat: when the overwhelmingly white Liberal Party was launched in 1953 its call for a qualified franchise would be scorned by the ANC as garishly out-of-date, rejected by UP members, and savaged by Afrikaner nationalists as a fundamental threat to 'preserving South Africa as a White man's country and a bastion of Western Christian civilisation'.[19]

The Bill of Rights also demanded 'a fair redistribution of the land as a prerequisite for a just settlement of the land problem', 'freedom of movement, residence and equality before the law, as well as equal pay for equal work, employment insurance and unemployment benefits'.[20] The economic sections of the Bill demanded equality with whites and the removal of laws that hampered African economic mobility.

Africans' Claims was 'radical' to the extent that it signalled a shift to the left by the ANC. It was 'radical' in demanding non-racial equality; its other demands were little more than the contemporary liberal canon. It was a moderate restatement of democratic goals and aspirations in a South African context and in tune with international opinion as set out in the Atlantic Charter, flowing from and trying to nudge ahead the apparent liberalisation of government thinking.

In 1943 the ANC also adopted a new constitution which abolished the 'House of Chiefs' set out in its original 1912 constitution, centralised authority with a working committee of members living within a fifty-mile radius of the President-General and attempted to create an effective branch structure. The ANC in 1943 was a small organisation dominated by professionals but, under the influence of the pragmatic Dr Xuma, it began to show signs of 'a more vigorous reaction to the new pressures and challenges created by a rapidly industrialising society'.[21] The initiation of a branch structure was an important (if tentative) first step along a long road towards the mass mobilisation that would be an ANC hallmark by the end of the twentieth century. But it was a long journey. In Xuma's prophetic words, *Africans' Claims* and restructuring the ANC were '… only the beginning of a long struggle entailing great sacrifices of time, means and even life itself'.[22]

But the door was slammed shut. The UP won a landslide victory in the 1943 general election at home while the balance of forces in the war changed overseas, and with the changed circumstances came a changed Smuts government.

Through his secretary, Smuts rejected *Africans' Claims* as 'propagandist' and stated that he was 'not prepared to discuss proposals which are wildly impracticable'.[23] Influx control measures had been relaxed in 1942 but were restored in 1943. Madeley reneged on his promise to recognise African trade unions, and went further and enacted War Measure 145, which made strikes illegal.

In 1946, Acting Prime Minister J H Hofmeyr, a prodigy accepted by Oxford when barely into his teens, able to manage four or five wartime ministries simultaneously, still the doyen of many older (white) South African liberals (and never without his mother),[24] presided over the violent suppression of a strike by some 70 000 African miners, following which the CPSA executive committee was tried for sedition. For the United Party government liberalism was a matter of global justice but had little to do with the 'native question' at home, where it was a tactic not a principle.

Despite this, the Atlantic Charter, to which the South African government was a signatory, continued to inspire black political activity. The 1945 United Nations Charter, of which Smuts was an author, increased black demands for the domestic application of liberal principles. Smuts himself noted:

> The fully publicised discussions at UNO are having a great effect in all directions. We even hear about them from our domestic farm Natives who really have nothing to complain of, but are deeply stirred by all this talk of equality and non-discrimination.[25]

Africans' Claims did not fill the growing ideological vacuum created by an increasingly strident nationalist movement on the one hand and a government unable to please the competing sectors of a rapidly industrialising economy on the other. Nor did it generate a legitimating ideology to replace segregation (which it had assisted in undermining). But it did commit the ANC to a more radical programme than it had previously endorsed, and pressure continued to grow within the organisation for the use of more militant extra-parliamentary methods of protest.

Black unity

During the war, ideological changes, economic necessity and governmental pragmatism combined to generate widespread black militancy. African urbanisation and unionisation increased dramatically. In 1945 the Council of Non-European Trade Unions claimed an affiliation of 119 unions, representing more than 40% of Africans in industry.[26]

In August 1946, 70 000 African miners went on strike; within three days, eighteen had been killed and the strike bloodily broken. As migrant miners fled police brutality in the compounds, they crossed paths – on Germiston Station – with their indirectly elected representative councillors, who were on their way to a meeting in Pretoria.

The Native Representative Council (NRC), an indirectly elected African body set up in 1936 to assess legislation affecting 'native affairs', and presided over by Hofmeyr while Smuts attended the United Nations, adjourned indefinitely after requests to discuss the miners' strike were turned down and in protest over government's handling of the strike. NRC member James Moroka, a wealthy doctor and later ANC President-General, accused the government of a '… post-war continuation of a policy of Fascism which is the antithesis and negation of the letter and the spirit of the Atlantic Charter and the United Nations Charter'.[27]

Meanwhile, Smuts was joined at the UN by a delegation from the ANC and SAIC, as well as by former CPSA member and native representative Hymie Basner. The vexed 'native question' ensured that world attention focused on racial oppression in South Africa, robbing Smuts (some believe) of his moment of international acclaim at the UN, but signalling the shape of the future.

The war years saw the radicalisation of Indian politics and, with the formation of the SAIC, a growing unity between the Transvaal and Natal Indian congresses. The tabling of the Asiatic Land Tenure and Indian Representation Bill, which offered partial political representation for Indians in Parliament in return for accepting restrictions on Indian ownership and occupation of land in Natal, helped foster Indian unity – and militancy. Under the new leadership of medical doctors Yusuf Dadoo and 'Monty' Naicker the SAIC organised a passive resistance campaign against what it described as a 'diabolical attempt to strangulate Indians economically and degrade them socially'.[28]

The campaign, as its organisers stressed, was multiracial; organisations were beginning to work together for common goals while remaining racially discrete. More than 2 000 volunteers of all races, but predominantly Indian, were imprisoned, and the Joint Passive Resistance Council stated:

> The non-white population of South Africa is on the march, in tune with the forward surge of peoples of Asia and Africa and the democratic forces through-out the world ... we feel confident that the decision of the N.R.C. will hasten the day when the alignment and unification of all Non-European forces against racial oppression will become a reality ... We believe that the struggle of the non-whites in South Africa against colour oppression is one and indivisible.[29]

The need for a common front to oppose black oppression was a recurring theme of post-war Congress and CPSA propaganda. Informal co-operation between the ANC, the SAIC and the coloured African People's Organisation (APO) began in 1946, and a year later they jointly organised what Xuma described as a 'historic unity rally'.[30] But as we shall see, a 'common front' was a lot easier to attain than a common organisational form that would give expression to all races but retain African leadership, the essence of the multi-racial Congress Alliance structure that lasted while the congresses remained legal.

In 1947 Dadoo, Naicker and Xuma signed the 'Doctors' Pact', which formally united the African and Indian congresses, not merging them but joining them in an alliance, each remaining distinctly race-based. Though equality was a shared goal, racial separatism was the organisational form for attaining that equality. Race was accepted, along with race-based organisations, in pursuit of racial equality. Unity moves among the black congresses were supported by the CPSA. The pro-Congress newspaper *The Guardian*, edited by CPSA members Betty Radford and Brian Bunting, gave prominence to speeches and articles calling for a black united front. CPSA con-ference resolutions called for the creation of a 'broad fighting alliance' to struggle for equal rights for all – though, as we see later, the Communist Party was less convinced of the need for racial separateness than for the need for unity among all forces opposed to segregation.[31]

Attaining unity at the grassroots level, however, was not a smooth process. In early 1949 violence flared between the African and Indian populations in Durban, leaving 123 dead, 1 300 injured and some 40 000 homeless. Not only were the Durban riots the most violent demonstration of the difficulties of achieving racial unity, they also provided the context for a reaffirmation of the 1947 Pact; the ANC and SAIC issued a statement which traced the roots of racial oppression and strife not to 'racism' but to 'the political, economic and social structure of this country, based on differential and discriminatory treatment of the various groups'.[32]

Both the ANC and the SAIC had a series of internal issues to contend with, which had an impact on their approach to how to give organisational expression to racial co-operation in the fight for equality. That race was accepted as a given is clear, however awkward it may seem seen through a twenty-first-century lens. Various factors worked against the emergence of a single congress for all races, particularly within the ANC.

The ANC Youth League (ANCYL), formed in 1944, led moves to radicalise Congress. The League comprised outstanding young men of their generation, including law students Anton Lembede, Ashby Mda, Nelson Mandela and Oliver Tambo. If the universal franchise had raised the bar for whites sympathetic to black demands for equality, the increasingly radical ANC, contemplating extra-parliamentary protest and pushed by a Youth League committed to 'rousing popular political consciousness and fighting oppression and reaction',[33] would raise it yet further.

During the late 1940s, while many ANCYL members were drawn into mainstream ANC politics, some continued to espouse a racially exclusive form of African nationalism, as well as opposition to the CPSA, which was seen as white-dominated and an avenue for undue white (and communist) influence on Congress. This was a continuum in ANC thinking and was in tune with African nationalism on the rest of the continent at the time. It would bedevil the Congress Alliance throughout the 1950s and result in the Pan Africanist Congress (PAC) splitting from the ANC in 1959, claiming (in the words of one-time PAC Secretary General Potlako Leballo) that the ANC:

> … has made a catastrophic blunder by accepting foreign leadership by the whites. How can we have leaders who are also led? If this white leadership is denied, why was one Joe Slovo of the Congress of Democrats allowed to become Chairman of the ANC Commission of Enquiry in 1954, into disputes involving ANC policies?[34]

At the same time, both the ANC and the SAIC were concerned with internal struggles, particularly over more radical policies and strategies. The transformation of the ANC from a small petit bourgeois organisation using petition and constitutional action into a mass-based extra-parliamentary organisation demanding full and immediate equality was a long process.

White responses to African nationalism

The growth of African nationalism, the emergence of the ANC as the leading domestic African political organisation with an increasingly radical programme, and its alliance with the SAIC, confronted whites who supported a democratic future with a set of ideological and strategic questions.

Prime among these was African nationalism. Both white liberals and socialists warned of its dangers; liberals believed that it threatened to submerge individualism within the fervour of mass action, while the Communist Party maintained that it would obscure class alignments which cut across racial barriers. Both warned that nationalism could degenerate into racial exclusivity and race war. Both (initially, in the case of the Communist Party) supported a single, non-racial organisation.

There is no doubt that in the late 1940s and the 1950s progressive whites exerted undue influence (in relation to their numeric base and certainly in the context of segregation and apartheid) over the nature and course of African nationalism in South Africa.

This is not automatically 'a bad thing'.[35] There was considerable symbolic value to whites joining other progressives in developing the vision of a future where all races would live in complete equality – a non-racial future, where race was not the starting point of analysis or organisation and where they rejected exclusive African nationalism in the face of exclusive Afrikaner nationalism and broader white supremacy. The foundations laid by this small band of progressives shored up the 'miracle' of negotiating the end of apartheid and introducing democracy despite the blood-letting of the 1980s and 1990s.

According to the 1946 census, whites comprised 21% of the population (this halved to 11% by 1996), though barely a couple of thousand, at most, participated in non-racial politics, whether via the Liberal Party (1 500 at its peak), the congress movement (COD had a couple of hundred members at most), the CPSA–SACP (which was even smaller), or the trade union movement. Much of this book details the sacrifice, commitment and sheer bloody-mindedness of white liberals, radicals and communists in their struggle to ensure that non-racial principles shaped nationalism.

An argument can and has been made that more whites opposed apartheid than this book credits, evidenced by the dramatic marches of the Torch Commando, UP voters, early Black Sash members, later Progressive Party members and the like. The point is not to question the motives of the individuals involved but to accept that a very large gap existed between opposing apartheid and supporting full equality for all citizens.

The Torch Commando and Black Sash, for example, had their roots in opposing National Party moves to remove coloured voters from the common voters' roll – a far cry from supporting universal suffrage. Their activities were acknowledged by the Congress movement and other black anti-apartheid groups but they made little or no substantive impact (whether ideological, organisational or intellectual) on those groups, other than, possibly, an emotional one. The focus is on the points of interaction between whites and blacks opposing apartheid together, where practice and ideology mixed and clashed and changed. And this narrows down the field considerably.

The small band of whites who actively supported the dismantling of segregation and then apartheid and wanted to replace it with equality was a motley collection. It included liberals, who, themselves, covered a remarkably wide canvas. They were more or less radical and more or less wedded to parliamentary/constitutional forms of protest or direct action; some were committed to free-market economics, others to varying degrees of socialism. Many of the latter had started out believing in a qualified franchise but were radicalised by their involvement in black political and organisational work either through collaboration or competition with the Congress movement and the SACP.

There were other non-communist radicals, many of them graduates or teachers from the Army Education Service, who felt constrained in the Liberal Party, while sharing its wariness of communists (Helen Joseph is perhaps the best-known example). There were also white socialists, communists and Trotskyists, who reserved their most vituperative language for each other, and who fought out venomous ideological-cum-personal battles decade after decade.[36]

There were activist and beneficent Christians, Jews and atheists; pacifists and militants; and other variations in world view. They had two common values: they hated apartheid, and they hated each other – though not always in that order. They differed over relations with the ANC and the SAIC, the parliamentary or extra-parliamentary nature of their struggle for equal rights, the social and economic goals for which they struggled and the prominence of communists within the congresses and supporting organisations. Definitions of radical and liberal, and even of communist, centred not so much on ideological or economic questions but on participation in, and attitudes towards, the liberation struggle.

Liberals based their vision of future equality on the development of an African middle class through the extension of educational and social welfare services, and gradual incorporation into state structures, which the government was called on to create, in tandem with equally gradual incorporation into the body politic for 'civilised' and later 'suitably qualified natives'. While, initially, no liberal party-political organisation existed, liberals were found in welfare organisations, churches, universities, the SAIRR, among the Native Representatives, and elsewhere.

Radical whites called for the immediate application of universal suffrage and supported mass-based extra-parliamentary campaigns, strikes and similar forms of protest. Some were to join the Liberal Party after 1953, more because of shared anti-communism than shared ideology (at least initially); others joined the Congress of Democrats, formed at about the same time. Radical whites, who included communists, Trotskyists, socialists, social democrats and others, were found in the CPSA, the trade union movement and the Springbok Legion, an organisation which operated as a soldiers' trade union.

Before 1950 (when it was banned), the main political home for radical whites was the non-racial Communist Party, which supported equal rights for all. According to Hymie Basner, who left the CPSA in 1943:

> There was no possible party to which a progressive young South African, whether Marxist or … of moderately liberal views, if he wanted to work in an organised group … against racialism, if he wanted to work even for common social decency, never mind about world revolution or South African revolution … there was no room for him to work in any organisation at that

> time except the communist movement. And during that period hundreds of middle-class youth who normally, in other countries would be joining the Labour Party or the Liberal Party, say in England or in France ... would join the Communist Party.[37]

The support of socialists for the ANC, in contrast with that of liberals, was premised precisely on the absence of a significant African bourgeoisie and the resultant belief that the movement would not, therefore, become a home for black capitalists. As will become evident below, this view changed over time, and had to change as the ANC grew to become a powerful force in apartheid South Africa. Liberals called on the congresses to restrict themselves to constitutional methods of protest as the only means of 'rational' and 'evolutionary' societal development; radical whites, on the other hand, joined the ANCYL in criticising the ANC for failing to develop a branch structure and to deploy mass-based extra-parliamentary pressure.

White opposition to apartheid in the 1950s – where it mattered: in the cauldron of African nationalism, not sitting in the anterooms of white racist politics hoping to be invited into the main chamber – was divided between the South African Congress of Democrats and the Liberal Party; between radicals (including communists) and liberals.

Both Marxist and liberal theoreticians argued that segregation and apartheid restricted economic development. Government, they believed, would have to adopt a 'commonsense' policy and acknowledge the fact of black urbanisation and economic integration by awarding concomitant political representation. Rather than being overtly economic or ideological, as might have been expected, differences between the two were dominated by approaches to the methods and aims of the ANC-led struggle.

In 1947 Edgar Brookes, a Native Representative and leading liberal, stated: 'If Liberalism be interpreted as an economic doctrine in opposition to socialism, not all of us would be very enthusiastic to defend it.'[38] This was not merely the last blush of wartime pro-socialist sympathies: by the late 1950s the Liberal Party programme was considerably more radical in many respects than the Freedom Charter of the Congress Alliance. And both Marxists and liberals shared a viewpoint – later codified by the Communist Party as internal colonialism or 'colonialism of a special type' – from which oppression and resistance were understood in relation to the existence of colonists who lived cheek by jowl with their subject colony and had no metropole to which they could or would flee after decolonisation. For communists this was a theoretical construct to explain and accommodate the contradictions of national and class struggle; for liberals it emphasised the 'logic' of accepting a meritocratic, colour-blind future for South Africa.

Ideologically, liberals and radicals operated within a remarkably similar framework, dominated by the shared demand for the abolition of racial discrimination and the introduction of a policy based on individual merit rather than race. Communists and radicals may have agreed from the outset that this meant equality under African leadership; by the end of the 1950s (though not before) most Liberal Party members would probably have agreed.

The influence of African nationalism is pervasive. Where white opponents of apartheid differed was over the speed at which a non-racial solution could be reached and the best means of reaching it. Liberals sought the separation of middle-class groups from the mass of the African population and their incorporation in state and economy – the classic black buffer class, as it later came to be known. The liberal vision was evolutionary, steady and gradualist. It relied on a quiescent working class; extra-parliamentary action was seen as both potentially revolutionary and anathema to managed societal evolution.

Liberals called for the extension of social services as a necessary precondition for black advancement to a 'civilised' status and incorporation in a modern Western state. In contrast, radical whites supported and worked for the organisation of the working class through mass-based extra-parliamentary campaigns, and called for immediate universal suffrage. White radicals assisted with the formation of black trade unions and offered support for strikes, bus boycotts and other campaigns.

Although relations between liberals and radicals were marked by hostile rhetoric the white liberal/left comprised a relatively cohesive social grouping. Largely drawn from the professional, English-speaking upper middle class, dominated by academics, lawyers and journalists, the liberal/left was interwoven with friendships and professional and personal relationships that criss-crossed ideological and organisational divisions.[39] Through the 1940s the ANC slowly radicalised its programme, adopted extra-parliamentary methods and demanded unqualified white identification with both, a demand that was to sharpen divisions among white liberals and radicals.

The Communist Party 1945–1950

The Communist Party of South Africa, formed in 1921, was, for decades, the only non-racial political party in South Africa. It was a predominantly African organisation with a small white membership. Communists were the only organised body of opinion among whites to offer full support for the goals of the ANC and were also among those few whites who were aware of the deeper political changes afoot in South Africa. As Lionel 'Rusty' Bernstein noted:

> The growth of radicalism in the African National Congress, and especially its Youth League, seemed to be passing unnoticed. There was no attention to its new Charter of African Rights [Africans' Claims] … And no recognition of the calibre of a new black generation with leaders like Nelson Mandela, Oliver Tambo and Walter Sisulu. Only the stock-market speculators seemed aware of the rash of wild-cat strikes spreading across the Rand amongst the black mine-workers.[40]

But, as we see below, communists (black and white) were themselves lulled by wartime pro-Soviet sentiments into seriously underestimating both the strength of anti-communism within the nationalist movement it worked with and within South African society more broadly, and the forces of reaction and the lengths to which they would go in seeking to stop communists, real and imagined.

During the war years the CPSA had scored some minor successes in municipal elections in Johannesburg and Cape Town, but the onset of the Cold War marked the end of white voter support. Black membership increased significantly during the war, as party organisers such as David Bopape and J B Marks concentrated on African mobilisation over civic and trade union issues.[41] The combination of increased African urbanisation and militancy created conditions conducive to the organisational work of CPSA members and, in 1944, the CPSA Central Committee noted both the growth of African industrial and economic action and the lack of political organisation: 'Our members working in the various national organisations have done much in an individual way. A central and active leadership in this direction has been lacking for a time.'[42]

The CPSA was a heterogenous organisation, with both black and white party members playing important, though different, roles. White members had a high profile in supporting the war and fighting (white) elections. Black party members were involved in the 1944 Anti-Pass Campaign and in trade union and civic work. Their combined successes led some sections of the CPSA 'to think in terms of mass membership'.[43] A significant portion of the CPSA regarded legal parliamentary activity as the main field of party work, suffering what would later be termed 'legalistic illusions':

> ... the Party revealed certain weaknesses which had developed in its ranks, as well as its indestructible virtues. A certain tendency towards legalistic illusions had penetrated the Party and sections of its leadership. Despite the open threats of the Nationalist party to ban the C.P., no effective steps had been taken to prepare for underground existence and illegal work.[44]

In 1928 the CPSA had accepted a Comintern thesis that placed South Africa in the ambit of 'colonial and semi-colonial countries' and endorsed 'an independent native South African republic as a stage towards a workers' and peasants' republic, with full equal rights for all races, black, coloured and white'.[45]

In what became popularly known (outside of the Communist Party, at any rate) as the 'two-stage revolution', the CPSA developed a national democratic programme that called for the immediate transfer of power to the majority population and effectively left socialist reconstruction to a later, secondary stage. In the late 1940s, as the ANC grew (in part through the active role played by black communists) and seemed to be taking up a position where it could provide the leadership necessary for the first stage of the revolution, CPSA–ANC co-operation evolved, despite opposition from the ANCYL and some older ANC members.

The post-war CPSA programme was explained in a 1945 pamphlet entitled *What Next? A Policy for South Africa*, which called for democratic rights for all, the nationalisation of the land and banks, a national health service and free and compulsory education, and supported increased industrialisation.[46] Given the heterogenous nature of the party, the call for a national democratic programme met with some internal opposition. Academic Jack Simons, a leading Central Committee member and CPSA theoretician, defending *What Next?* at the party's 1945 Conference, noted (in language that continues to echo in the Communist Party today): 'Some of our comrades describe this pamphlet as "wishy-washy" … they do not consider it revolutionary in content.' He continued:

> Comrades, there are times when to be extreme ultra-revolutionary is to betray the cause for which we are working. Which is the more revolutionary today – to say you want the vote and equality of rights for the non-Europeans? Isn't it more revolutionary to take up the struggle for housing for the people, for fair distribution of supplies and a Ministry of Food? We must find a policy which gives expression to the innermost needs of people of our country. What we lack too much is the spirit of sacrifice, the determination to get among the people and to take up the issues which most nearly affect them.[47]

The CPSA programme was clearly more radical than *Africans' Claims* in its talk of nationalisation, which found increasing sympathy within the ANC and later expression in the 1955 Freedom Charter. The relationship between communists and African nationalists was never straightforward; according to leading CPSA–SACP member Michael Harmel, ANCYL leaders denounced communism as a 'foreign ideology' but '… found common ground with Communists in demanding a more positive and revolutionary ANC leadership and a turn from stereotyped and ineffective methods of struggle to radical mass action'.[48]

Harmel's description is factually accurate, but smoothes over long-standing and deeply felt anti-communism. While many ANCYL and ANC members remained hostile to the CPSA and the high profile of white communists, the role of those white communists in visibly providing unqualified support for the black liberation struggle, including trade union and political work, was of substantial importance.[49] By fully endorsing (the newly radicalised) Congress's aims and activities, whites in the CPSA adopted a position that set the standard for radical whites in the 1950s and against which white anti-apartheid activists of all political hues would be judged.

The Communist Party's decision to participate in alliances with non-socialist, nationalist organisations in pursuit of the 'first stage' of the revolution, rather than going it alone as a class-based party, had considerable effects on opposition politics, positive and negative. The CPSA encouraged the creation of a 'broad fighting alliance' against racial discrimination. Of particular significance for our story was its role in working with the Congress movement to develop grassroots mobilisation in producing statements of principle, starting with *Africans' Claims* and finding its fullest expression in the Congress of the People campaign of 1954/55, which produced the Freedom Charter.[50]

In 1944 the CPSA proposed that '[t]he idea of a People's Charter of Rights should be taken up jointly by three sections [the three national groups]'.[51] This should emphasise a point that will become evident in this book: race was a given in the period under study. Parties and individuals fought for a future based on equality regardless of race, but it was not based on a denial of what they saw as the 'fact' of race. 'National groups' is, of course, a euphemism for race; the ANC's talk of 'the national question' – which lasted beyond apartheid and into democracy – has exactly the same connotation.

Both the CPSA and the ANC expressed the desire to 'get among the people' and reunite formal organisations with the widespread black militancy of the period. With this in mind, in 1945 the CPSA called for the summoning of 'a People's Convention', with the aim of producing a coherent, popular statement of national democratic goals, and to symbolise and give concrete form to the emerging black organisational unity.[52] This became a common goal of the CPSA and the Congress movement in the post-war period.

The production of such a charter could not and did not precede the emergence of a unified alliance of forces opposed to racial discrimination, which took place a decade later. However, the method of drafting what became the Freedom Charter (in 1955) was envisaged in the late 1940s. In 1947 Yusuf Dadoo, president of the SAIC and a leading CPSA member, began implementing a joint resolution of the Transvaal ANC, the SAIC and the APO to convene a countrywide conference of all progressive organisations and to draw up a charter for democracy for all in South Africa.[53]

In early 1948 delegates were invited 'from factories and workshops, townships, hostels, advisory boards and vigilance committees, farm settlements and country towns in all corners of the provinces' to assist in the drawing up and endorsement of a charter for 'Votes For All'. The goal was 'to launch a campaign for the democratic principles of the United Nations Charter', concentrating on universal suffrage and equal political participation for all.[54]

In the end, the conference, which became known as the People's Assembly for Votes for All, was considerably less ambitious in scope, affected by the disputes that marked ANC–ANCYL as well as ANC–CPSA relations, and was restricted to the Transvaal and Orange Free State. The ANCYL and 'old guard' ANC leadership jointly attacked what was seen as Communist Party dominance of the Transvaal ANC and its activities. In particular, organisers of the Assembly were accused of attempting to bypass the existing multiracial alliance of congresses and create a new, non-racial competitor – a single organisation of all races, rather than an alliance of organisations representing different races, led by Africans in the ANC.[55] The organisers attempted to clarify relations with the congresses:

It is not our aim to compete in any way with, or take over the functions of the great national organisations of the African, Coloured or Indian people. It is our aim to secure friendly co-operation and mutual assistance of South African people in championing the great democratic cause of the franchise.[56]

These tensions, and their impact on organisational form, recur throughout the period under study. Despite opposition from the Youth League, the Assembly met in Johannesburg and was opened by Michael Scott, a radical churchman and a leading figure in the 1946 passive resistance campaign. The 322 delegates present endorsed the 'People's Charter for Votes for All' and the Assembly was significant for the interracial rank and file co-operation it produced, compounding that of the 1946 passive resistance campaign. The Assembly ended by calling for a further Assembly where delegates from the whole country could endorse a 'People's Charter'. Popular mobilisation around and participation in drawing up the People's Charter and the penetration of rural as well as urban areas set precedents that informed leading ANC member Z K Matthews's call five years later for a 'Congress of the People'.

The People's Assembly marked a shift away from the cautious style of earlier ANC activity and a step on the way from deputation to confrontation. Propaganda issued by the organisers stressed the illegitimacy of the 1948 general election and called for the election of delegates 'who will represent more citizens than those voting in the General Elections'.[57] Where *Africans' Claims* had tentatively proposed an alternative legitimating ideology for the state based on equal citizenship, the Assembly directly challenged 'the election of the new Parliament by a minority of the people'.[58] The People's Charter, anticipating the Freedom Charter, concluded:

Where there is no freedom the people perish. Raising high the banner of freedom, the banner of the liberation of our people,

WE PLEDGE that we shall not rest until all adult men and women have the right to stand for, vote for and be elected to all the representative bodies which rule over our people;

WE CHALLENGE the existence of a Parliament from whose election the majority of its citizens are excluded, in a country which upholds in words the principles and practices of democracy.[59]

The People's Assembly has been criticised for not producing a programme of action by which to achieve the aims it set out.[60] This may have been a result of the conflicts which surrounded it. Moreover, the ANC at the time was debating what emerged in 1949 as the Programme of Action, largely inspired by the ANCYL. The programme endorsed the 1943 Bill of Rights, repeating demands for universal suffrage and equal political participation, but it was more concerned with methods than aims. The changing nature of the struggle, suggested by the People's Assembly, was made clear in the programme, which resolved to work for 'the abolition of all differential political institutions the boycotting of which we accept and to undertake a campaign to educate our people on this issue and, in addition, to employ the following weapons: immediate and active boycott, strike, civil disobedience, non-co-operation and such other means as may bring about the accomplishments and realisation of our aspirations'.[61]

Liberals and liberalism 1946–1949

During the war '[l]iberalism acquired its greatest influence, both in describing and in shaping South Africa …'.[62]

Lewsen saw the Cape liberals as 'the cultural and intellectual elite of the Cape, its leading parliamentarians and … its most brilliant men',[63] which, of course, would extend in the 1950s to include a woman, leading Native Representative and Liberal Party member Margaret Ballinger. Lewsen's description obtained more generally in the war years and the immediate post-war period.

During those years liberals were well thought of by the then ANC leadership, with whom they shared a class position and broader socio-political views, and were generally regarded as important in South African society. They were well known, enjoyed a high media profile, and were (sometimes self-consciously) part of the white South African elite.

The fact that they were roundly attacked for decades after the war by white radicals, many in the Congress movement, communists, black consciousness movement supporters and others should not allow an ahistorical view. The war years were a period of enormous promise for liberals. Government commissions reported that segregation, under pressure from industrialisation, was breaking down and Smuts acknowledged the irreversibility of black urbanisation. Liberals in the SAIRR and among the native representatives, who emerged at the forefront of liberal public thinking in the late 1940s, adopted a pragmatic stance in response to these apparent shifts in government thinking, believing that capitalist development would inevitably favour their approach to 'race relations'.

Industrialisation was seen to challenge the economic and political stranglehold of agricultural and mining capital and, as such, was regarded as an inherently progressive modernising process. Its apparently objective economic inevitability appealed to liberals (seeking a 'rational' – and apolitical – solution) and socialists alike. Native Representative Donald Molteno argued that the struggle in South Africa lay between vested economic interests that benefited from the status quo and industry, which challenged it (and strengthened liberals in the political arena).

Putting forward a view that would be repeated for the next four decades by businesspeople and others in South Africa (though in language more commonly associated with the left), Molteno argued that industry speeded up both economic and political change; from the 1940s it seemed that 'the objective forces that make for progress are on [our] side'.[64] Liberals felt themselves to be on the side of 'common sense' (the title of one of their journals[65]), both economically and politically.

The liberal position, insofar as a single set of views can be ascribed to an informal group, was set out by Leo Marquard as early as 1943. Marquard, head of AES, Afrikaner 'royalty', mentor of Bram Fischer, author of *Black Man's Burden* (which radicalised a generation of young white conscripts), and probably the most thoughtful of a clutch of highly intellectual wartime and post-war white liberals, remained open to new ideas and directions throughout the life of the Liberal Party, with his own position changing quite radically. He noted that '[t]here is ample evidence that a Bantu bourgeoisie has come into being in the urban areas … their economic position, as they see it, is associated with the European rather than with the depressed Bantu worker'.[66]

Marquard argued that white liberals and the emergent black middle class were natural class and political allies, participating in the joint councils set up by the SAIRR to generate consensus over municipal affairs. Such co-operation, he maintained, together with the 'relatively good economic position' of the black bourgeoisie, 'makes them feel that they have more to lose than their chains'.[67] For liberals, a black middle or buffer class was the best safeguard against revolution; communists had decided to ally themselves with the ANC, home of the emergent black bourgeoisie, and feared precisely what the liberals embraced. Both argued that post-war economic development would drive political change, but differed over the 'how' and 'what' of that change. Liberals argued that the emergence of an urban African bourgeoisie would flow inevitably from industrialisation, and called for representative structures with greater powers than the NRC. As Edgar Brookes noted: 'The liberal-minded South African who takes the line of going all out for a policy which will conform immediately to world liberal opinion has virtually made his decision for rebellion and direct action.'[68]

He went on to note, in words that exemplified the strengths and weaknesses of South African liberalism at the time, 'Our cause is logically so strong that we are tempted to put our whole faith in logic.'[69]

Espousing, as they did, a gradualist reformist vision and opposed to extra-parliamentary strategies that jeopardised the slow evolution of a race-blind meritocracy, the natural course for liberals in their support of incremental change and black socio-economic advancement was to put pressure on the United Party to adopt a more liberal 'native policy'. They opposed demands for significant political reform as premature until 'the basic social and material conditions for an advance towards them have been achieved'.[70] With economic developments appearing to nudge government towards a policy change, liberals called for restraint on the part of the Congresses.

Encouraged by the apparent congruity between the process of industrialisation and political goals, the Native Representatives saw the main task of liberals as being 'to assist, at every point, the forces making for the evolution of the Bantu people into a modern community'.[71]

As Martin Legassick put it, '... their argument that progress could only come by the evolutionary acceptance of "civilised" Africans into the community, became transformed into the belief that because progress had come (as measured in terms of economic indices), acceptance of "civilised" Africans would follow'.[72]

In 1943 the UP was supported by industrial, mining and agricultural capital but by 1946, unity in support of the war had given way before the competition for black labour. As a result, according to O'Meara, 'the UP government fell between at least three stools' in attempting to appease the competing demands of these three main sectors of the economy.[73] Politically, the UP faced an attack on its 'liberal' policies from the right by the Nationalist Party (NP) and for its illiberal policies from the left by the organised black opposition, which expressed itself by means such as industrial action and passive resistance.

The UP's response was mixed as it tried to hold together its own internal factions while appeasing those outside it. Smuts made some cynical moves in the direction of the gradual black inclusion in state structures called for by liberals, among them his offer of white parliamentary representation to Indians. In response to the adjournment of the NRC Smuts offered to enlarge the council to fifty elected members.

Hofmeyr shared the liberal desire to separate perceived black moderates from radicalising influences and warned Smuts of 'the disturbing fact that the moderate intellectuals of the Professor Matthews type have committed themselves to a policy of non-co-operation'.[74] This was confirmed when both Smuts's proposals were rejected by the African and Indian congresses. Liberals outside the UP appealed for black restraint, arguing that South Africa was less like colonial India (where mass-based passive resistance campaigns were effective) and more like nineteenth-century Britain, where gradual extension of the qualified franchise had brought parliamentary democracy into being.

Edgar Brookes argued: 'Most of us believe that given time and opportunity we can do in South Africa in the twentieth century what was done with signal success in England in the nineteenth century; namely, step by step obtain majorities in the privileged groups for the extension of rights to the unprivileged'.[75]

Facing opposition from both white and black the UP lurched to the right in an attempt to appease current (white) rather than possible (and distant) future (black) voters. In 1946 the miners' strike was crushed, the NRC adjourned, and the offices of the CPSA, *The Guardian*, the Springbok Legion, various trade unions, and the homes of prominent left-wing individuals were raided by the police.

Gone were the days of shared platforms; communists (real and imagined) were again the enemy. Finally, in attempting to rationalise its 'native policy' and provide labour, as demanded by the different sectors of the economy, the UP convened the Fagan Commission to investigate influx control with regard to the growth of urban industry and its effects on migrant labour.

The Fagan Commission had an obvious ideological function, namely to repair the growing crisis of legitimacy faced by the Smuts government as segregation was undermined by industrialisation, urbanisation, and the liberal discourse that attended them. Of course the commission could not fulfil this task. Its 1948 report was internally contradictory, favouring both a permanent black urban presence and continued migrant labour.[76] Rather than provide a legitimating discourse the report operated within a framework of economic necessity and expediency. As Ashforth argued, the racist assumptions of the report were in common with the 'grand tradition' of South African 'Native commissions', but the Fagan Report was unique in that it:

> ... does not provide a scheme for the legitimate division of rights and obligations within the state on racial grounds. Fagan accepts the racial division of the state as it stands and rationalises it in purely 'racist' terms ... For Fagan the divided State can be accepted as legitimate merely on the basis of administrative expedience; there is no need for any of the rhetorical paraphernalia of 'civilising mission' or 'development'.[77]

By 1946 liberals were caught between a radicalising Congress movement and a United Party government that resorted to repression rather than concession. Leo Marquard warned Hofmeyr that 'the United Party is frightening off its possible friends by vainly trying to attract its known enemies', noting that liberals were 'profoundly disturbed and bewildered by what we feel to be a drift away from liberalism and an appeasing of reaction'.[78]

Liberals sought to keep in place a moderate ANC leadership with whom dialogue was possible, which forced them (assuming force were required) to oppose an election boycott called for by the ANCYL. They also proposed political reforms that they regarded as pragmatic, implementable responses to the Fagan Report. Both tactics would fail, leaving liberals isolated, ostracised and facing the twin extremes of white racism and black militancy.

Liberals in a corner

Liberals aimed to establish in South Africa what Margaret Ballinger later described as 'a Western state, maintaining Western standards and based on Western values'.[79] The evolutionary attainment of such a society was premised on parliamentary gradualism; this, in turn, required governmental concessions to 'reasonable' black demands. The alternative, as they saw it, was anarchy:

> [Black] resistance, whether by armed rebellion or by general strike or by non-co-operation movement on a national scale would arouse fierce passions and produce results which none could foresee. The whole structure of parliamentary

government through ordered democratic channels would be destroyed, and that before the non-European himself is ready to accept the responsibilities which would be thrust upon him.[80]

No liberal organisation operating in the political arena was established and no liberal programme of action was developed; rather, the Native Representatives and leading SAIRR members attempted to influence the policies and programmes of the UP and the ANC and play a mediating role between the two. The events of 1946 confronted liberals with their inability to influence either side.

The NRC adjournment, argued Margaret Ballinger, amounted to a 'repudiation of the whole representation embodied in the 1936 Act under which we hold our seats'.[81] While the UP seemed intent on kicking away one leg of the stool on which Ballinger and fellow liberals perched awkwardly, another was being kicked out from under them by the ANCYL call for a boycott of all native representation elections.

Apparently lacking an alternative strategy, Margaret Ballinger and her husband, William, jointly advised Z K Matthews in September 1946 that 'the African people are not yet ready for a complete repudiation of the Council' and that '… probably the best next move would be for the Councillors simply to accept the next summons to meet, to turn up at Pretoria as if nothing had happened, and then to begin to argue about the future of the Council when you reassemble'.[82]

But liberals didn't just wring their hands in consternation, they took the battle to the ANC. The ANCYL's proposed boycott in response to the NRC adjournment was supported by ANC–CPSA members such as Moses Kotane and by councillors such as James Moroka. Other councillors, however, opposed the boycott, and these the Native Representatives regarded as their allies.

The Ballingers and Communist Party member Hymie Basner attended an emergency conference of the Transvaal ANC in June 1947, called to discuss implementation of the boycott.[83] Supported by councillors Paul Mosaka and Selope Thema, the Ballingers called on the conference to reject the boycott and to encourage the ANC nationally to do the same.

Indicating the growing gulf between themselves and the ANC, the Representatives described the boycott as a 'silly' idea and warned the conference that 'before you carry it out you will have the fight of your lives'.[84]

While some Representatives took on the ANC, others were trying to squeeze a semblance of liberalism from the post-war UP. Edgar Brookes pleaded with Hofmeyr to grant concessions to the NRC, claiming that 'the more I think about it, the more I am convinced that there is a real case to meet from the Native point of view'.[85] By making concessions, Brookes argued, the government would assist liberals in 'strengthening … the moderate section in the Representative Council so that they might find it possible to carry out the policy of co-operation which in their heart of hearts they would prefer'.[86]

Brookes argued that 'the most important thing' was the development of personal friendship between Hofmeyr and 'a handful of key men among the non-Europeans'.

> If a few men … could be encouraged to visit you from time to time, to open their hearts to you, to feel your friendship, to know your difficulties, political and otherwise, to feel free to write confidentially to you, their influence, spread far and wide among other people, would counteract all the negative propaganda, and help the people, through having confidence in your intentions, to wait for the right moment for drastic reforms.[87]

Hofmeyr warned Smuts that NRC moderates supported the adjournment.[88] But, according to Marks, '… far from responding to their [the NRC's] justifiable anger in conciliatory mode, Smuts … instructed Hofmeyr to stiffen what he saw as the apologetic tone of the statement the latter intended making to the adjourned NRC'.[89]

In January 1948 the electoral boycott, a strategy that had never been popular with the cautious ANC leadership of the time, was openly rejected by Xuma and others.[90] Sustaining the boycott became impossible in the confused situation and the ANC and CPSA (somewhat tortuously) proposed the election of 'boycott candidates', who would call for the 1936 legislation to be repealed.[91]

In justifying the change of tactics the ANC argued that there had been insufficient organisation to sustain a boycott and that NRC candidates should use their positions to undertake such organisation.[91] But by then liberals were seen to be actively opposed to the boycott. A year later, faced with a choice between Margaret Ballinger and a National Party candidate, the secretary of the Port Elizabeth African Organisations advised his members: 'DO NOT VOTE FOR EITHER OF THEM!'[93]

By the late 1940s the Congress movement evinced widespread hostility towards white liberals. Black liberals were, of course, to be found at all levels of the ANC itself, and liberals were not criticised on ideological grounds but rather for their failure to support the methods of the ANC and SAIC. This would be a recurrent theme of the late 1940s and the 1950s. Leading Transvaal Indian Congress member Ahmed 'Kathy' Kathrada, later imprisoned with Nelson Mandela and others, defined liberals precisely as those who refused to support the strategies and campaigns of the congresses. Accusing 'the men and women of the liberal creed' of cowardice, Kathrada stated: 'Our experiences have been that these individuals, who are usually vociferous in their claims for justice and fair play for the black man, have on every occasion when their assistance was required, sadly failed us.'[94]

At a meeting in Durban, liberals were characterised by their use of 'humble petitions and respectable deputations' which failed to 'deliver the goods'.[95] Criticism was also evident among black liberals. Jordan Ngubane, a founder member of the ANCYL and later prominent in the Liberal Party, stressed that white liberals had failed to intervene constructively in black political life:[96] '… the collapse of African Moderation has been largely occasioned by the failure of European Liberals as a group to take an unequivocal and unfaltering stand on the vital colour question'.[97]

By 1948 liberal attempts to mediate between the UP and the ANC had failed. The ANC increasingly favoured extra-parliamentary protest (formally endorsed a year later) in pursuit of unqualified equality, and youth leaguers became increasingly hostile to the perceived cautious obstructionism of liberals. In May 1948 the National Party won power and the UP went into opposition. Seven months later Hofmeyr died. Edgar Brookes, surveying the landscape, saw little but gloom: 'The lot of the European who claims to be, in any sense of that much abused word, a "liberal" is hard. He stands, as it were, on a shrinking isthmus, with the oceans of European passion and non-European passion encroaching on it from day to day.'[98]

By the late 1940s white (and black) communists felt themselves to be on the side of a rising, increasingly radical nationalist movement that was replacing its older bourgeois leadership with a younger – but still essentially bourgeois – leadership (young lawyers, teachers, chiefs and the like replacing old lawyers, teachers, chiefs and the like) willing to utilise fully extra-parliamentary and direct methods of protest.

The Congress movement now demanded full equality rather than politely requesting partial inclusion. But all was not plain sailing: the Youth League leadership was more radical than that of the ANC but it was also strongly anti-communist, though only feebly so compared with the newly elected National Party and those who subscribed to the growing global Cold War hysteria.

White (and black) liberals found themselves opposing ANCYL radicals and their use of extra-parliamentary methods, trying to stop the influence of communists, while seeking to nudge Hofmeyr and shove Smuts into replacing their reactionary platform with some elements of liberalism. They suffered a failure of the colonial (and, arguably, post-colonial) imagination: the notion of full equality for all remained beyond their grasp, and their focus was on securing the franchise for 'suitably qualified' or 'civilised' natives – in essence, trying to keep alive their own version of the Cape liberal tradition, and export it northwards.

But while they were doing so the socio-economic changes triggered by the Second World War led to a significant increase in black, particularly African, political activity and a steadily more radical ANC platform. It also led to African–Indian *political* unity (not necessarily characterised by easy socio-economic relations, as later events would show), as seen in the People's Assembly for Votes for All. This unity was reflected in the ANC and SAIC's pursuit of ideological and racial accord and popular support through the mobilisation of people around the production and endorsement of a statement of principle, while remaining in a multiracial alliance of separate congresses for different races, as they would do with greater success in the 1950s.

Chapter 2

The emergence of white opposition to apartheid, 1950–1953

In the years between 1950 and 1953 the differences between liberal and radical whites took organisational shape. White opposition to the Nationalist Party (NP) rose to a level that would never be seen again, with tens of thousands of whites joining night-time marches organised by the Torch Commando. Bearing torches and symbolic coffins and using anti-fascist/anti-Nazi slogans they opposed the removal of coloured (and some Indian) voters from the electoral roll. A scattering of whites also joined the Defiance Campaign, a passive resistance campaign organised by the Congress Alliance to highlight the increasingly repressive apartheid laws and bolster the profile and membership of Congress.

In November 1952 the African National Congress (ANC) and the South African Indian Congress (SAIC) attempted to capitalise on white anti-NP sentiment and called for the creation of a 'parallel white organisation' to work with them.[1] But divisions among whites opposing the NP ran deep – deeper, certainly, than ANC leaders expected. Liberal and radical whites differed over universal suffrage, relations with ex-communists, participation in a multiracially structured Alliance as opposed to a single organisation for people regardless of race, and the efficacy of extra-parliamentary opposition – a clutch of issues that would separate them throughout the 1950s. White radicals, including a number of former members of the Communist Party of South Africa (CPSA), formed the South African Congress of Democrats (SACOD), while liberals remained within the United Party (UP) fold until after the 1953 election, when one strand of liberal opinion broke away to form the Liberal Party (LP).

For the black population the period after 1948 was one of unremitting repression, falling real wages, and personal and employment insecurity. But for whites, South Africa was a different country. The legislative bedrock of apartheid was laid between 1949 and 1953, with the Group Areas Act, which enforced residential and business segregation; the Population Registration Act, which embedded race classification; the Separate

Representation of Voters Act, which ultimately disenfranchised coloured voters; the Separate Amenities Act, which entrenched the principle of unequal amenities for different races and the Suppression of Communism Act, which gave the government an armoury of repressive powers. The 1948 election was followed by a reduction in capital inflows and a balance of payments crisis that peaked in 1949. But by 1950 the economy was showing real growth, which the opening of new gold and uranium mines promised to sustain.[2] With the strengthening economy came a 'strong' government promising to end black protest, political and industrial.

The rise of the NP was paralleled by the decay of the UP and its continued inability to offer nothing more than tonal differences from the NP. When NP backbenchers proposed concentration camps for participants in the 1952 Defiance Campaign – terrifying in itself – Julius Lewin, organiser of the liberal Hofmeyr Society (within the UP) reported: 'It is already possible to visualise certain United Party members of Parliament solemnly declaring that the principle of concentration camps for Non-European resistance leaders is sound, but that the diet proposed is inadequate and there should be more latrines.'[3]

Internationally, anti-communist legislation was tabled in Canada, Australia and elsewhere in response to the Cold War. In South Africa the NP brought out Sir Percy Sillitoe, head of MI5, to advise them on the best means of combating communism. Through both innuendo and in-your-face smears the NP successfully generated suspicion of any message of racial equality as crypto-communist. Liberal academic Leo Kuper described this tactic as, 'the progressive redefinition of communism as synonymous with non-discrimination on the basis of race or colour'.[4] NP vitriol was so powerful and white racism such a receptive organism that it was easy to extend the stain of communism to cover liberalism as well.

Listen, for example, to the words of George Heaton Nicholls, later leader of the Natal-based Union-Federal Party: 'If Liberalism manifests itself in a humanitarian impulse to assist the downtrodden, if it is a matter of the heart, then I am a Liberal: but if it is a system of government, or aims at a system of government which considers a Hottentot equal in political stature to the astronomer Royal, then I am not a Liberal.'[5]

After Native Representative Hymie Basner took segregation to the United Nations in 1946 all the Representatives were accused by the NP of destroying white racial purity. When CPSA Central Committee member Sam Kahn was elected to Parliament as Western Cape Native Representative, a NP MP '… with his eyes glued on Mr Sam Kahn … said that if he had his way, all agitators would be put against a wall and shot'.[6]

The constitutional crisis and opposition

The early 1950s were dominated by the NP government's battle to disenfranchise coloured (and some Indian) voters (a significant electoral factor in some seven Cape constituencies).[7] The battle began in 1948 with a warning from the government of impending legislation and lasted through to the packing of the Senate in 1956 to force through the changes. It provided a clear indication of how far the NP would go to implement apartheid successfully.[8]

The extended constitutional crisis, which fuelled black and white political mobilisation, saw the Appellate Division set aside both the Separate Representation of Voters Act, passed with only a simple majority in 1951, and an attempt by the government to constitute the legislature as the High Court of Parliament.

The crisis gave rise to the most widespread anti-NP demonstrations by whites in the history of apartheid. Running parallel to white protest was the Defiance Campaign, which marked a new militancy among Congress members. On the occasions that the two movements intersected, white opposition fractured through wariness of black militancy, particularly when harnessed in extra-parliamentary protest, and in a context of widespread anti-communism.

In 1952 the War Veterans' Torch Commando mobilised a paid-up membership of more than 250 000 (overwhelmingly white) ex-servicepeople, while the ANC and SAIC passive resistance campaign saw more than 8 000 volunteers arrested and paid-up membership of the ANC rise to more than 100 000.[9] This 'mass' politics was new to South Africa; even more marked was the fact that all races participated in large numbers – albeit in separate organisations, exemplifying again the apparent contradiction of pursuing racial equality through racially separate organisations.

The Springbok Legion, which was a prime mover in using ex-servicepeople as a basis for opposition and in the formation of the Torch Commando, gave the Commando a militancy and, thanks in part to theatre director Cecil Williams, a Springbok Legion and CPSA member, a flair for dramatic protest action, until an internal purge of Legionnaires by its more conservative leadership. Thereafter, the Commando became a mass-based electoral adjunct to the UP, its creative energy spent and its political purpose lost, and it soon passed away.

The Defiance Campaign, marked by the discipline of the volunteers who deliberately broke apartheid laws and regulations in order to get arrested, grew throughout 1952 until repressed by draconian legislation – supported by the UP and the Torch Commando. It gave the congresses a renewed vigour and profile they would battle to match again during the 1950s as political space closed down, security police clamped down, and membership numbers declined steadily.

The Defiance Campaign breathed life into the ANC and SAIC, led to the formation of the Congress Alliance, and wedded Congress to militant, extra-parliamentary opposition. The Torch Commando, before it fizzled out, represented the first and last large-scale protest by whites against apartheid. Faced with a choice between defending principle and suppressing black militancy, the overwhelming preponderance of whites, even those who began by upholding the former, chose the latter.

Both more and less conservative forms of resistance to the NP contributed to and capitalised on the political ferment that accompanied attempts to force disenfranchisement legislation into the statute book. The political mobilisation of the period between1951 and 1953, in particular the organisation of previously politically quiescent sectors of the population such as coloured voters and anti-NP whites, boosted hopes for the emergence of large white and coloured organisations to work alongside the African and Indian congresses.

In November 1952 the ANC and the SAIC called for the formation of a white congress, expecting an initial membership of 5 000 – one-fiftieth of the membership of the Torch Commando.[10] Even that modest figure wildly over-estimated white opposition. And, instead of a single white political ally of the congresses there emerged a series of competing organisations beset by competition and sniping and pursuing different goals and strategies, some marked by deep antipathy to the goals and methods of the congresses.

White liberal responses to the constitutional crisis

Opposition to NP attempts to disenfranchise coloured voters was initially led by the Civil Rights League (CRL) and the Franchise Action Committee (FRAC). The CRL, which grew out of the Cape South African Institute of Race Relations (SAIRR) and was launched at a 'Citizens Rally' attended by 10 000 people, aimed to rally white opinion against the unconstitutional manoeuvres of the government.[11] It soon gained a popular following and attracted large audiences to its meetings. The left-wing *Guardian* newspaper welcomed it and its ability to rally white support, stating: 'Now, resistance to these attacks is taking shape'.[12]

The League, overwhelmingly white, was led by senior SAIRR figures and recruited whites radicalised by the war but with little previous political involvement.[13] Regarding the parliamentary arena and strengthening the UP as its main area of activity, it stressed the need for constitutional action and saw its role as 'building up a strong body of enlightened opinion throughout South Africa'.[14] Whether this patronising tone and approach could have sustained the political mobilisation of whites, galvanised by opposition to the NP government's constitutional manoeuvring, is questionable.

FRAC, on the other hand, was a non-racial amalgam – black and white ex-communists rubbed shoulders with conservative members of the Coloured People's National Union (which organised voters threatened with disenfranchisement), coloured workers threatened by the white protectionism of apartheid legislation and others.[15] Communists Fred Carneson and Sam Kahn were among the leaders of FRAC, which included among its members a number of former CPSA activists. While the CRL organised petitions and meetings, FRAC concentrated on organising workers and staged a successful one-day strike in the Cape Province in May 1951. Where the CRL insisted on parliamentary methods, FRAC was represented on the planning council of the Defiance Campaign, alongside the ANC and SAIC.

Notions of 'constitutionality' were not restricted to more or less conservative white liberals in the CRL, SAIRR and elsewhere. FRAC stressed the 'constitutionality' of its actions, by which it meant the legality of extra-parliamentary activity for an unrepresented population. The ANC shared the same view, as stated by its President-General, James Moroka: '… a general strike in any civilised country at all is constitutional. Today in South Africa, America, everywhere the white people settle issues by strikes. It is only when a man is oppressed that he is not allowed to strike when the occasion warrants it.'[16]

In part, this was a defensive discourse, emphasising the legality of protest in advance of a predictably suppressive NP backlash. But it was also a discourse common to white and black liberals, radicals, nationalists and communists.

The effect of the constitutional crisis was to focus white anti-Nationalist attention on the black franchise, albeit via the defence of an inequitable and limited coloured vote. The apartheid onslaught on black rights also obliged liberals to confront political issues they had previously avoided. This was most clearly true of the black franchise, ignored by the liberals in the 1940s but suddenly under threat.

For some liberals, such as Leo Marquard, who had long called for a qualified black franchise, this change of direction was a 'relief':

> It is a good thing that we have at last been forced by recent events to face this issue squarely. For far too long we have evaded it, gone around it, behind it, and over it. We have pushed it into the background, as an uncomfortable thing, an embarrassing thing, with which we hoped we would not have to deal. Our children and grandchildren perhaps, but not we …[17]

Marquard was, in most respects, exceptional: it is unlikely his sense of relief at having to confront uncomfortable political realities was widely shared. But liberals also had to change strategy in the new circumstances: appeals to reason had to be supplemented with organisation and mobilisation, traditionally the terrain of the Communist Party and trade unions.

The CRL reflected this change in strategy, with liberals moving from attempting to mediate between political players to appealing directly for public support themselves (albeit while working closely with the UP). The leadership of the CRL comprised senior SAIRR members and its appeal was to English middle-class voters alienated by the NP. The league was an inherently cautious and defensive organisation, committed to retaining the status quo and resisting 'the inordinate curtailment of the liberties of the individual'.[18] This was a long way from demanding full equality. It organised public meetings, and its main activity was a petition signed by 100 000 people opposing the Separate Representation of Voters Bill. As Leo Marquard put it: 'That was all in public. Behind the scenes we continued to work on the U.P. …'.[19]

CRL leaders and senior UP members worked closely together and the CRL failed to offer any political vision or strategy other than to vote UP. The league was soon over-taken by the Torch Commando in leading opposition to coloured disenfranchisement, but both suffered from the same problem – their links with the UP and their failure to offer any options beyond voting UP. The league's leaders maintained a staunchly 'apo-litical' stance, claiming '[o]ur Constitution is in danger … This threat must be resisted on the grounds that it is immoral'.[20]

In place of a political platform the League relied on the 'practical' approach of the SAIRR and others, which seemed scarcely to welcome any form of racial integration but accepted it as inevitable. The CRL stated: 'With the economic integration of the Non-European proceeding apace – and this process cannot be stopped – the internal peace of South Africa depends upon amicable relations between the different groups.'[21]

Within the League there were different tendencies. The CRL attracted a younger generation, politicised by the Second World War, who welcomed the opportunity to articulate clearly a 'liberal' racial policy.[22] The League's leaders strove to maintain a 'moderate' image in contrast with that of the more strident younger liberals in its own ranks and the 'radical' activities of FRAC and other extra-parliamentary organisations. Lewis claimed that the CRL provided 'impressive support' for a strike organised by FRAC in Cape Town[23] but pressure from younger CRL members for active participation was quashed by the movement's leaders.[24]

The Torch Commando

The Torch Commando was formed after a Springbok Legion demonstration at the Johannesburg cenotaph in March 1951, where a symbolic constitution was laid to rest,[25] and soon gained a significant following. Legionnaires in the Commando organised the Steel Commando – a convoy of Jeeps which converged on Cape Town from across the country[26] for a massive protest meeting – with an estimated attendance of some 75 000.[27] The demonstration degenerated into violence, with police baton-charging crowds of coloured sympathisers.

The commando flared brightly but briefly on the political scene, highlighting many of the tensions between radical and liberal whites at the time and subsequently.[28] Ex-service organisations began to form protest committees after the early release from prison of Robey Leibbrandt, a Nazi-trained saboteur, and the premature removal of senior English-speaking defence force officers.

Protests organised by the Combined Ex-Servicemen's Associations drew crowds of 10 000 in Johannesburg and Cape Town.[29] Characterising the NP as Nazis, ex-service organisations drew large crowds around the country by playing on the language and solidarity of the war. The Torch Commando, emphasising wartime comradeship, mobilised whites through a clever combination of deliberately vague goals and virulent opposition to the 'fascists' in power. As a spokesperson put it, 'the men who fought did so for principles they can only vaguely express. But we know that legislation like this is a direct negation of what we fought for.'[30]

Displaying a degree of militancy that was entirely lacking in the CRL, the Legion called for the immediate resignation of the government and threatened to 'bring the country to a standstill'.[31]

The Legion's flair for dramatic street protests invigorated the CRL, giving it an appeal beyond existing party-political affiliations; an appeal later killed off by positioning the Commando too closely to the UP. Joel Mervis noted at the time that the Commando's 'great attraction to the ordinary man was the very fact that it was not a political party, for it thus became a haven for people of all political faiths'.[32]

It is apparent even from this attenuated rendering that similar tensions affected both the CRL and the Torch Commando. On the specific issue of the franchise they blurred their message, concentrating on defending the status quo. The two issues that most directly confronted the Commando, however, were those of open membership and the use of extra-parliamentary means of opposition. The Cape Commando was non-racial, with a large coloured membership,[33] but elsewhere it was a white organisation with racial exclusivity the norm, as one of its branches stated: 'We are South Africans and as such the colour bar is an accepted part of our lives.'[34]

Alex Hepple, a senior figure in the 1953 electoral pact between the UP, the Torch Commando and the Labour Party he then led, later wrote: 'The Government kept attention focused on the race issue and the Torch Commando eventually faltered at this hurdle … it fought on one flank against the curtailment of the political rights of the coloureds and on the other lined up with the forces of discrimination.'[35]

Both the CRL and the Commando also had to confront the issue of extra-parliamentary action, which emerged as a dividing line between radical and liberal opponents of the government. Following the Cape Town violence, according to Hepple, the UP exerted 'political influence and intrigue' to bring the Commando within its ambit.[36] The removal of Legion members from the Commando was a key element in this process; following their departure, the Commando confined itself to purely electoral work. In doing so, of course, the essence of its appeal – its massive extra-parliamentary presence, the drama of its protests, the robust rhetoric – was destroyed.

The UP successfully defused any possible challenge from the Commando and swallowed it whole, pausing only to spit out those few whites who would later populate the Liberal Party, the Union Federal Party and the Congress of Democrats. By mid-1952 radical whites had declared the Torch Commando dead, with liberals not too far behind.[37]

The Defiance Campaign

As the Torch Commando faded from the political scene its place was taken by the Defiance Campaign, a direct intrusion by the Congress movement into the political calculations of white South Africans, including those who opposed apartheid. The campaign generated a flurry of ideological and strategic debate among radical and liberal whites and served to crystallise divisions between the two as support for the campaign deepened, numbers of resisters increased, and Congress leaders called for full white identification with their aims *and* their methods.

Full equality and extra-parliamentary methods became the overt dividing line between the South African Congress of Democrats, the white wing of the Congress Alliance, and the non-racial Liberal Party. Under the surface anti-communism remained an important factor dividing the two.

The Defiance Campaign was launched on 6 April 1952, the tercentenary of Van Riebeeck's landing at the Cape. Rather than demanding the immediate destruction of the entire racist/apartheid state, the organisers highlighted six specific laws – the Group Areas Act, the Bantu Authorities Act, the Suppression of Communism Act, the Stock Limitation Act, the pass laws and the Separate Representation of Voters Act – in order to facilitate their easier repeal.

Initial responses from white liberals – still hoping to influence the UP – were not encouraging. The SAIRR reacted by 'deploring' the 'insensitivity' of the date chosen by the organisers, and criticised the ANC for 'unrealistically demand[ing] the immediate abolition' of the six statutes, concluding that it '… shares with the Prime Minister his concern that public order must be maintained and appreciates the reasons that prompt him to declare that any outbreak of violence must be firmly met',[38] a statement that is unlikely to have done much for hopes for full white identification with the struggle.

Others, however, were less reactionary. Some liberals saw the gradualist approach as evidence of common ground with the ANC. Leading liberal theoretician Leo Kuper sought to persuade his more conservative colleagues that supporting incremental change was preferable to confronting the reality of full, immediate equality for all:

> No immediate claim is made for direct political representation and for full democratic rights, which are held out as goals for the future. The time element is thus conceived in the spirit of liberalism. It is evolutionary.[39]

The Defiance Campaign unfolded in tandem with legal setbacks suffered by the NP government in its disenfranchisement battle as well as with a new optimism on the part of the UP after it had ingested the Torch Commando. After a slow start the campaign grew in size and popular appeal (among blacks) until, by the end of 1952, more than 8 000 volunteers had been imprisoned. The government responded with increased repression, including the introduction of whipping for defiers.

As the campaign continued anti-white sentiment grew. The sentences passed on resisters became harsher, and campaign organiser Joe Matthews, then president of the ANC Youth League (ANCYL), warned of the dangers of black racism, noting, in October 1952, that 'the attitude of those who have been to jail is uncompromisingly opposed to any talks with the whites unless all our demands are going to be met'.[40]

At the same time, whites supportive of the Defiance Campaign began agitating for a greater role than fund-raising or writing letters of support to the press.

This pressure increased markedly when Patrick Duncan, son of a former Governor-General, offered his services to the campaign organisers.[41] Duncan's offer guaranteed massive publicity for the campaign but, probably more importantly, it promised to help counter its increasingly racial nature. As Planning Council member Yusuf Cachalia put it, 'Pat's offer to defy came as a gift from heaven: it stopped the campaign becoming racial'.[42]

Duncan's offer was replicated by other (less high-profile) whites in Cape Town, where Lucas Phillips, chairperson of the ANC in the Western Cape, stated: 'Our reason for accepting Europeans into the movement is to dispel the idea among many Africans that all Whites are oppressors.'[43]

In early December a large crowd, which included Duncan and six other whites, entered Germiston location without a permit and, after making speeches and singing freedom songs, were duly arrested.[44] At the same time, four young white resisters – Albie Sachs, Mary Butcher, Arnold Harrison and Hymie Rochman – broke post office apartheid laws in Cape Town by using the counter set aside for blacks. A week later Arnold Selby of the Textile Workers' Union did the same.

The effects of the Defiance Campaign

The Defiance Campaign triggered important political developments among anti-apartheid whites, among whom its influence grew in proportion to the campaign itself. In response to ANC–SAIC calls for white support, the white liberal/left began to reveal ideological fractures in its commitment to the Congress-led struggle. Leading FRAC members participated in planning the campaign while the Springbok Legion endorsed it and called on the Torch Commando to join the ANC and SAIC in organising a national strike.[45] The hostility evinced by the SAIRR is noted above.

Meanwhile, liberals were trying to plot their own path between the contending forces. In a statement written by Margaret Ballinger and published in October 1952, twenty-two leading liberals – including author Alan Paton, Bishop Trevor Huddleston and others – called for a positive white response to the Defiance Campaign, which they described as 'clearly no sudden impulse … [led] by men who are acknowledged leaders among Africans and Indians'.[46]

The statement, around which the initial organisation of the Liberal Party took place in 1952/3, continued:

> We believe that it is imperative that South Africa should now adopt a policy that will attract the support of educated, politically conscious non-Europeans by offering them a reasonable status in our society. This can be done by a revival of the liberal tradition which prevailed for so many years with such successful results in the Cape Colony.[47]

The statement called for a policy of 'equal rights for all civilised men, and equal opportunity for all to become civilised'. At the same time, it called on Congress leaders 'to recognise that it will take time and patience substantially to improve the present position'. Finally, with an eye on the UP, the twenty-two offered their proposal 'in the hope that it will make negotiations possible and their success probable'.[48]

Go slow, make modest demands, be realistic, don't rock the boat – the Ballinger statement was a perfect distillation of the somewhat effete liberalism of the early 1950s, itself 'the fag end of nineteenth-century' Cape liberalism. E M Forster (from whom the phrase is borrowed), writing at the same time (1951), had said:

> [I am] an individualist and a liberal who has found liberalism crumbling beneath him and at first felt ashamed. Then, looking around, he decided there was no reason for shame, since other people, whatever they felt, were equally insecure … I am actually what my age and my upbringing have made me – a bourgeois who adheres to the British constitution …[49]

South African liberalism – and many liberals, black and white, though by no means all – had no such constitution to cling to. But many would be reinvigorated by their engagement with African nationalism and black resistance politics. Their party and policies would be radicalised and a far more muscular liberalism would emerge, briefly, as a result.

By late 1952, with more than 3 000 defiers already arrested, it looked as though liberals could score an important victory through their self-appointed role as go-between. In November of that year informal discussions began between the congresses and the UP. ANC Secretary-General Walter Sisulu was approached by leading UP and Torch Commando members, directors of the Oppenheimer Trust and others.[50] Influenced by growing white concern about the Defiance Campaign and the announcement of the 1953 general election, and according to John Cope, UP MP and editor of the liberal magazine *Forum*, the UP approached Congress leaders:

> … to discover what their terms would be for calling off the passive resistance campaign on the eve of the parliamentary general election. Such a move, it was considered, would have a reassuring effect on the white electorate which was becoming anxious about the defiance campaign. It would be to the advantage of the United Party to demonstrate that it could influence non-white opinion.[51]

According to Cope, the ANC offered to end the Defiance Campaign in exchange for a public statement from the UP that it would repeal the six laws:

> … the A.N.C. leaders did not ask for these things as a condition for calling off the passive resistance campaign. All they demanded was that the United Party,

if it came to power, should undertake publicly to halt the tide of apartheid and set the flow in the opposite direction.[52]

By the end of November, according to Joe Matthews, Ernest Oppenheimer – 'the highest official in the Millionaire organisation that is behind a great deal of U.P. activity' – had joined 'the wooing of Congress'.[53] Youth League leaders were involved on multiple fronts – organising the Defiance Campaign, talking to the UP about conditions for possibly calling it off – and very possibly giving out mixed signals in so doing. In the end, this counted for little, as a growing right-wing revolt within the UP scuppered any possible deal with the ANC. In order to pacify the party, UP leader J G N Strauss reaffirmed his commitment to 'white leadership with justice' and a programme scarcely distinguishable from that of the National Party, with the exception that the UP accepted that the constitution was sacrosanct. The tentative UP–ANC discussions came to an abrupt end.

The parting of the ways

Calls for white support for the liberation struggle had been a strong theme of ANC and SAIC propaganda in the late 1940s. In 1947 the SAIC's Monty Naicker called for the creation of a new party to carry the struggle to white voters. At the same time he insisted that 'a progressive party can only be forged by unity among all progressive European Organisations'.[54] At a superficial level, white support for the Defiance Campaign, including the participation of whites with no past communist links, and the growing distance between liberals and the UP (especially after talks with the ANC ended abruptly), suggested that such unity was possible.

Despite a common class background, white liberals and radicals were deeply divided by ideology and belonged to a series of small, separate and often hostile organisations and discussion groups. Relations between and among white liberals and radicals (themselves split into Marxist, Communist, Trotskyist and other splinter groups) were increasingly antagonistic, exacerbated by the NP coming to power and the growing importance of African nationalism.

Through an ideological attack and legislative onslaught on all opposition as traitorous, the government fuelled liberal anti-communism. The Suppression of Communism Act – described by Walker as providing 'almost dictatorial powers to deal decisively with anyone who was even faintly tinctured Red'[55] – placed liberals in an awkward position – they supported the aim but not the method of the legislation. Edgar Brookes claimed: 'the terms "Liberal" and "Communist" are as separate as fire and water … You could not slander a Liberal more than by calling him a Communist'. He warned that liberals were being placed in danger since ex-communists would henceforth attempt to act 'under the wings' of liberal organisations.[56]

The *Cape Argus* reported the breakdown of a CRL meeting attended by some 2 000 people, called to oppose the Suppression of Communism Bill, in May 1950. One of the speakers stated that the struggle against communism would go on with or without the Bill, and that the CPSA was 'Cominform-controlled'. Guest speaker and CPSA MP Sam Kahn objected, and the meeting descended into 'uproar' and some physical exchanges.[57]

The dissolution of the CPSA in June 1950 increased liberal suspicion of communist infiltration of their organisations, and liberal groups formed between 1951 and 1953 adopted an anti-communist 'screening' clause. Hostility grew in the 1950s towards the brand of 'existing socialism' and the close links between the disbanded CPSA and the USSR. Winifred Hoernlé, SAIRR president in 1950, stated: 'In our own day we have seen Russia develop first into a communist state ... From that time it has developed into a police state ... Man in all the areas controlled by the Russian Communists is subservient to the state in all the phases of his life.'[58]

The notion of a Soviet-controlled South African communist party was commonly accepted among South African liberals and confirmed for them by such works as Eddie Roux's biography of CPSA founder S P Bunting and by Roux's history of the liberation struggle, *Time Longer Than Rope*, in which he claimed the CPSA repeatedly subordinated 'the South African struggle to the needs of the world situation'.[59] Coupled with the internal vicissitudes of the CPSA in the 1930s and early 1940s, the policy changes, the shift from opposing to supporting the Second World War following Soviet foreign policy dictates, and the purges and loss of membership, clearly projected the image of a party following Comintern directives rather than domestic demands. Of course this should have been balanced against the history of the party in organising among the poor, working alongside nationalist organisations supporting political demands and pushing the frontiers of racial integration, but often it was not.

Negative perceptions of the Communist Party were pervasive within South Africa, as they were beyond its borders. Such views were exacerbated by the anti-CPSA activities of former party members such as Hymie Basner.[60] In the 1950s, suspicion and hostility of the CPSA would continue to be fuelled by former CPSA members who joined the Liberal Party, notably Jock Isacowitz and Eddie Roux.

Roux is said to have told stories of an attempt by KGB agents to assassinate him after the 1928 Comintern meeting (not mentioned in any of his published works), while Isacowitz warned liberals that they would be outmanoeuvred by former CPSA members if they attempted to co-operate with SACOD.[61]

As late as 1997, Liberal Party member Randolph Vigne would still write breathlessly of 'Isacowitz's experienced eye' being able to 'instantly identif[y] ... a front for the banned Communist Party of South Africa' and 'warn ... his liberal colleagues accordingly'.[62] The dissolution of the CPSA is discussed in the next chapter and, as we shall see, it was more the result of cock-up than conspiracy. The fear of communist infiltration was, nonetheless, a reality, and an odd backhand compliment to the importance of the party in working with and for Africans in South Africa.

The ANC and the SAIC – perhaps somewhat naïve about the infighting among potential white allies – expected a significant response to their appeal for a white congress.[63] The precise role that whites would play within the Congress movement was unclear; Joe Matthews stated simply: 'The Whites will have to form a party that is prepared to make definite changes or join Congress' – although prior to SACOD there was no way whites could 'join Congress'.[64]

The Defiance Campaign Planning Council discussed the issue of white participation and, in November 1952, called a meeting at Darragh Hall in Johannesburg to capitalise on white support for the campaign. Some 300 whites attended the meeting, which was chaired by former CPSA member Bram Fischer. Although well-known liberals such as the Ballingers, Marion Friedman and others attended, many of those present were former CPSA members.

The Darragh Hall meeting proved to be a turning point in the development of white opposition to apartheid. But there are many memories, and thus many versions, of why this was so. Many liberals, as is clear from the Vigne quotation above, suspected a communist plot as they entered the room and left convinced of it. Senior liberals had no intention of being too closely identified with the Congress movement.

But if liberals were wary of being duped by communists, a lot of former CPSA members had no desire to work with liberals, whom they scorned for being unable to embrace equality and freedom for all. Former communists such as Rusty Bernstein came to the meeting determined to respond to the ANC call for whites to 'take up their share of the burden' and poured scorn on liberal suggestions from the floor for bridge-building afternoons in 'a park where black nannies and domestic servants could get together in their afternoons off'.[65] But they too had come to the meeting determined to do the opposite to the liberals – to respond positively to the Congress call for white support. Both entered the room with an *idée fixe* about the other, and both left with it confirmed.

ANCYL Africanists such as Tambo and Sisulu finally saw the divisions between liberal and radical whites in a very immediate fashion. Callinicos quotes Walter Sisulu on Tambo's speech at the meeting:

> This speech of OR [Tambo] created a terrific impression on me. I have no way of describing it. You take a thing by the tail. And you expose it. OR, in his artistic way of speaking, created a tremendous impression. Not only to me, but to the people who were there. Because he has a way – you take a snake by the tail and you are exposing its head.[66]

The meeting was also addressed by Yusuf Cachalia, who called for a progressive white grouping 'to co-operate with us, to be supportive … to assist us in bringing justice to this country'.[67] The precise form of the organisation was left to the meeting, the only condition being that it should be fully committed to the Congress ideal of equal rights for all. By implication, it would also have to support the methods used by the Congress movement. It seems clear that Sisulu and Tambo felt they had seen the head of the liberal snake: but liberals saw a communist one. At the meeting, divisions and hostilities between white liberals and radicals became clear, and the gap between them was organisationally fixed; it would remain so for decades.

White responses to the Defiance Campaign had revealed differences previously obscured by common anti-fascist and later anti-Nationalist sentiment. Anti-apartheid whites faced a hostile NP government and an ANC and SAIC increasingly determined to use widespread extra-parliamentary mobilisation to achieve full and immediate equality.

The ANC–SAIC demand for universal suffrage, previously only endorsed by the CPSA, proved an immediate and intractable stumbling block. Margaret Ballinger, acting as liberal spokesperson, rejected the universal franchise out of hand.[68] As a secondary issue, liberals rejected the idea of a white congress working in a multiracial Alliance, calling rather for an 'all-in' congress. This was the first time non-racial/multiracial organisational forms were cited as an issue; as the decade unfolded the issue would reflect deep ideological differences. Finally, with considerable liberal support, Margaret Ballinger refused to co-operate with the large number of former CPSA members present. This was later explained by liberal claims that white communists 'packed' the Darragh Hall meeting and controlled proceedings.[69] Equal rights and extra-parliamentary methods divided radical from liberal whites; anti-communism supplied the fixative that cemented the distance between them.

The Darragh Hall meeting was followed by three further meetings at which attempts were made to find a compromise solution which would allow the creation of a combined liberal/left organisation.[70] The failure of these discussions was followed by the formation of SACOD, which was committed to standing 'for equal political rights and economic opportunities for all South Africans, irrespective of race, colour or sex: and win for all South Africans the freedom of speech, assembly, movement and organisation'.[71]

By the end of 1952 radical and liberal whites had irrevocably split. The SAIC's Yusuf Dadoo had called for an alliance between the ANC and the SAIC on the one hand and the UP–Torch Commando–Labour Party election partners on the other, stating: 'Intra-parliamentary struggle is played out. It is now for the masses of the people to act.'[72]

For many liberals, however, this was unthinkable; the closeness of extra-parliamentary to revolutionary strategies, coupled with the prominent role of former communists, closed the matter. Liberals who attended the Darragh Hall meeting rejected the call to operate outside Parliament as an ally of the ANC and SAIC and returned to the UP fold in time for the 1953 general election – and another routing at the polls.

Radical whites in Johannesburg joined SACOD, where a Founding Committee was elected to draw up a constitution and programme of action.[73] In 1953 SACOD became a full and equal partner of the Congress Alliance. As Bernstein noted more than forty years later: 'Personalities contributed to the COD-Liberal split, but its essence was political and thus unavoidable.'

In 1953 the Liberal Party was launched, initially committed to a qualified franchise and insisting on the use of parliamentary and/or constitutional methods – though, by the time of its demise in 1968, its policies would be indistinguishable from those of the white 'radicals' of 1953. From its inception, white opposition to apartheid was fragmented and internally riven by suspicion, hostility and contestation; personality differences added spice to this already potent brew.

The split divided the already small white opposition to apartheid and diminished its impact on the course of political events, then and also into the post-apartheid era.[74]

Chapter 3

Multiracialism: Communist plot or anti-Communist ploy?

Resistance politics in the 1950s was dominated by the Congress Alliance, which sought to mobilise people of all races against apartheid. However, attempts to foster racial co-operation – especially including whites – in an increasingly racist state came with costs. The internal politics of the resistance movement – including both the Congress movement and the South African Communist Party (SACP)(in its pre-1950 and post-1953 incarnations)[1] – was dominated by wide-ranging and bitter disputes over the form racial co-operation should take. The dispute centred on the *multiracial* nature of the Congress Alliance – that is, an alliance of separate congresses comprising members of a single race,[2] co-ordinated at regional and national levels. This *multiracialism* stood in marked contrast to the *non-racialism* of organisations such as the disbanded Communist Party of South Africa, the reconstituted SACP and the Liberal Party.

It is important to recall what was said in the introduction: that sensitivity about the language of race was not evident in the 1950s – multiracial, non-racial, interracial and similar terms were, initially, used interchangeably. Over time, as the race-based structure of the Congress Alliance became a politicised issue – with liberals and Africanists seeing it as a vehicle for overweening white communist influence over the African National Congress (ANC) – people became more sensitive to the true meaning of the terms they used.[3]

The issue of racial co-operation was being debated as the African National Congress Youth League (ANCYL) came to exert greater influence over Congress, bringing to the ANC a new militancy; a strident and at times exclusive African nationalism; and marked anti-communism. As senior ANC official Dan Tloome put it, the ANCYL's attitude:

> was that our fight is against the white people. 'We are nationalist here, and these white people took away our land' – that was the type of approach ... They were very, very hostile against the CP[SA]. Their cardinal point was that

communism is a foreign ideology and that we shouldn't follow it because it's not applicable to South Africa.[4]

The ANCYL strongly resisted what it saw as an attempt by the CPSA to bypass existing national organisations and create a permanent 'unity movement'[5] – an organisation of all races that emphasised class above national consciousness via a Marxist rather than a nationalist approach.[6] The Youth League, by contrast, insisted on racially separate or multiracial structures, viewing non-racialism not as an organisational expression of anti-racism that allowed whites to participate (as liberals saw it) but rather as a stalking horse for communist dominance.

Debates over multiracialism and non-racialism first centred on the CPSA and, after it disbanded in 1950, on the South African Congress of Democrats (SACOD), which had become the organisational home for many white former Communist Party members. The fact that multiracialism afforded each congress equal representation on all co-ordinating structures meant that SACOD, with an average membership of 250, had equal representation with the ANC, which had an average paid-up membership of between 30 000 and 50 000.[7] Since liberals, Trotskyists and African nationalists viewed SACOD as a communist front, multiracialism generated hostility and suspicion, with SACOD – 'the white wing of the Congress Alliance'[8] – at its epicentre.

SACOD was a small white organisation that supported extra-parliamentary campaigns in pursuit of equal rights. It did include a number of former CPSA members, many with a high profile, but it also provided a home for the tiny number of whites wanting to work in support of and as part of the Congress movement. SACOD's place in the Congress Alliance provided a hostile focus for a wide range of organisations that regarded it as a communist front and multiracialism as the means by which communist influence was being entrenched in the Alliance.

Africanists saw the alliance of congresses as a 'somersault on principles' set out in the 1949 Programme of Action.[9] The Liberal Party (LP) attacked SACOD as a communist front and criticised the ANC for co-operating with it, while some LP members attacked the ANC for being dominated by white communists.[10] Anti-communism made for strange ménages. For example, in a pamphlet issued in Cape Town in 1956, liberals and Trotskyists on the Bus Apartheid Resistance Committee stated: 'COD is a boss organisation in an alliance of racial organisations and is a great believer in the big stick. The organisations allied to it are boy organisations. COD dictates its instructions to them. They never meet as equals: theirs is simply to obey …'.[11]

In an ironic twist the multiracial structure of the Congress Alliance, which was created largely at the insistence of ANCYL nationalists, came to be seen as the product of white communists who engineered it so as to control the ANC they were unable to join.

Explanations for the emergence of multiracialism tend to follow the conventional ANC argument, emphasising that it was a strategy which acknowledged the differing material conditions affecting races politically and geographically divided under both segregation and apartheid. But such explanations ignore the ideological content of multiracialism, whose roots lie in large part in the hostility that characterised relations between the Communist Party and the ANCYL. Both organisations called for the radicalisation of the ANC and the development of a mass base as the only means to achieve successful national liberation. But after that they differed: where the ANCYL pursued a nationalist path the CPSA warned that nationalism could serve to obscure class oppression and called for the transformation of existing organisations 'into a revolutionary party of workers, peasants, intellectuals and petty bourgeois'.[12] Non-racialism in organisational form was clearly allied to a particular argument set forth by one strand of thinking within the Communist Party. Its ideological content made it anathema to African nationalists, despite its obvious symbolic value.

Brian Bunting, a CPSA Central Committee member, discussing the distinction between the CPSA's non-racialism and the ANCYL's multiracialism, attempted to downplay the differences, pleading: 'let us not be confused by semantics'.[13] The distinction was more than semantic; the hostility between the Youth League and the CPSA resulted in the strategic debate over non-racialism or multiracialism being influenced by heavily ideological overtones which fed into the emerging Communist Party theory of 'colonialism of a special type' (discussed further in Chapter 4). This chapter analyses the disputes between the CPSA and the ANCYL in order to locate the ideological roots of multiracialism and, in doing so, it highlights the tensions within the CPSA over the relationship between class struggle and national struggle, which increased in the late 1940s as a result (in part) of CPSA–ANCYL hostility.

The post-war Communist Party: 'a tendency towards legalistic illusions'[14]

In the 1940s and early 1950s the ANC was transformed from a small organisation wishing to enrol 'distinguished university graduates'[15] into a mass-based nationalist organisation pursuing national liberation by extra-parliamentary means, including stayaways and passive resistance campaigns. Those changes were largely brought about by the ANCYL, which dominated Congress politics in the late 1940s. The league set itself the twin tasks of 'impart[ing] to Congress a truly national character' and opposing those who sought to provide 'foreign leadership of Africa'.[16] Youth leaguers stressed 'the need for vigilance against Communists and other groups which foster non-African interests'.[17] In practice the ANCYL's programme entailed gaining control of the direction of Congress, while isolating organisations and individuals who either exerted influence over the ANC or sought to develop their own African support base.

The transformation of the ANC took place largely in the post-war years. During the war the organisation had concentrated on drawing up and popularising *Africans' Claims in South Africa* and in the immediate post-war period it left grassroots organisation around civic issues to other organisations. Black trade unions grew, while squatter movements and bus boycotts represented a spontaneous popular response to the hardships faced by the black population.

In contrast, the Communist Party was directly involved in grassroots organisation in some townships, notably on the East Rand. Sapire describes the case of Brakpan location, where the CPSA mobilised residents around immediate local concerns such as wages, employment practices, the extension of passes to women, the shortage of housing, and pass law raids – precisely the kind of civic organising that would be so effective a few decades later.

The CPSA contested advisory board elections, winning all six seats in East London in 1942. It also won local council seats in Cape Town, East London and Johannesburg.[18] It used the boards and vigilance associations as a means of establishing 'footholds in location communities'.[19] According to Sapire, CPSA members such as David Bopape and Gideon Ngake used their elected positions as platforms from which to defend local interests and instituted the CPSA as 'the undisputed political force in the region'.[20] The CPSA also ran night schools in the major centres, which, according to the Johannesburg District CPSA secretary, were 'a very big factor in the development of the membership of the party'.[21]

The CPSA believed the national organisations would spearhead a national revolution aimed at abolishing racial discrimination and attaining equal rights for all. Thereafter, the struggle for socialism could follow, with the obfuscations of race removed. In 1940, however, the ANC was a small, weak organisation of the black elite, and, as the CPSA complained,

> [t]he year 1940 has arrived with hardship and misery for the oppressed and poor peoples of the Union of South Africa ... Unfortunately the year finds the forces of freedom as scattered as sheep in the presence of wolves. When talking of the forces of freedom, one cannot lose sight of the fact that the African people are potentially the most important of these forces. Therefore, if the Africans do not pull themselves together to face the enemies of freedom vigorously, not only will they let themselves down, but they will let their allies down also.[22]

Together with organisations such as the Springbok Legion and Friends of the Soviet Union, the CPSA successfully mobilised large sectors of the white population – Hilda Watts, for instance, won a seat on the Johannesburg City Council in the whites-only Hillbrow ward. CPSA members were also active in the black trade union movement. As a result of its high political profile and success in various spheres of operation, some in the party began to think of it as a potential mass movement in its own right, ignoring the unique conditions of the war; such thoughts came to a juddering halt when hostilities ended.[23]

In 1929 the party had accepted a Comintern directive which stressed the need to work within 'the embryonic organisations among the natives, such as the African National Congress' in order to transform the latter into a 'fighting nationalist revolutionary organisation against the white bourgeoisie and British imperialists …'.[24] By the end of the war the Communist Party had emerged as a significant force, but it remained party policy to work with the ANC and build it up.

Black CPSA members, however, were reluctant to join the ANC. Elias Motsoaledi, a leading ANC–SACP member jailed for life in 1964, explained:

> [the] Party taught me the struggle. I attended ANC meetings but was not happy with it at the time [the late 1940s]. To me, the ANC did not interpret the aspirations of the masses. But the Party taught me that it was my responsibility to tell the ANC about our aspirations … at the time, the ANC was dominated by sophisticated intellectuals who only spoke in English.[25]

Rusty Bernstein, CPSA Johannesburg District Secretary at the time, also noted that black members resisted joining the ANC: 'They thought the ANC was rather reformist bourgeois nonsense – "that's not for us, we're revolutionaries!" '[26]

The CPSA extended its township work during the war years, but remained concerned with the state of the ANC. CPSA members such as David Bopape, J B Marks, Edwin Mofutsanyana and Moses Kotane were also senior ANC members, in part because the party insisted that national liberation struggles 'fought in the colonial and semi-colonial territories' were 'no mere side issue' but an integral part of the global anti-imperialist struggle.[27]

But, as stated above, the ANC (unlike the Communist Party) failed to capitalise on the changed conditions resulting from the war, and rival organisations aimed at mobilising black support were either established or revitalised. The African Democratic Party (ADP) was formed, while the All-African Convention (AAC) agitated for a 'non-collaborationist' strategy. Within the ANC the restless young urban intellectuals of the ANCYL, who favoured direct, extra-parliamentary action, began to criticise the ANC's moderation and its failure to establish a branch structure and win a mass following.

The CPSA accepted that the ANC remained 'the premier political organisation', both because of historical ties and presumably because both the ADP and the AAC were influenced, to differing degrees, by Trotskyist thinking. CPSA statements between 1942 and 1948 stressed that it was '… the duty of all Communists belonging to oppressed nationalities to join their respective national movements, so as to work for the strengthening of such movements …'.[28]

CPSA literature and internal reports during the war shared three related themes with regard to the ANC and national liberation. In the first place the party acknowledged the progress made by Xuma in reorganising the ANC, but criticised Congress for failing to provide political leadership in a period of considerable black industrial and civic action. In a 1943 report on 'National Movements of the Non-Europeans' the CPSA Executive Committee noted that 'the lack of a strong and influential organisation among the Non-Europeans has been felt time and time again' and criticised the ANC for failing 'in its main task – that of uniting its membership and carrying out the formation of branches in a systematic manner'.[29]

In 1945 the CPSA Johannesburg District stressed the 'unity and solidarity ... militancy and readiness for action' evident in the Alexandra bus boycotts, protests over train fare increases and the squatter movements, but criticised both itself and the ANC for failing to provide leadership.[30] Given its own failure to appreciate what was going on, the party took a gratuitous swipe at Mpanza, the squatter leader, who 'may seem a figure hardly worth taking seriously', as well as at the ADP, which 'suffers from all the faults of sectarianism, political inexperience and stupidity'.[31] But it also acknowledged that they '... gave the people what they demanded ... they were advocating something positive ...'.[32] The analysis concluded that 'the people demand leadership' and called for a 'practical plan of campaign and action' to channel popular militancy.[33]

Flowing from this was a second theme of CPSA commentary on national movements – a repeated call for the elaboration of a minimum shared programme between national organisations, the CPSA and the trade union movement. Such a programme, it was argued, would allow both ideological and organisational unity.

The third theme comprised repeated calls for the development of a united front of organisations opposing racial discrimination. The CPSA argued that '[a]ll genuine movements towards national liberation are progressive', but warned against the tendency to racial exclusiveness, which would obscure the underlying reality of the class-based oppression of all workers.[34] The party supported the emergence of a 'broad fighting Alliance'[35] or 'wide democratic front'[36] which would oppose segregation while underplaying exclusive nationalism.

The CPSA's post-war programme was internally contested, with some members calling on the party to capitalise on its wartime successes and concentrate on furthering class struggle in place of the 'two-stage' revolution, which saw national liberation as a necessary precondition for socialist revolution. This also flowed in part from the changing nature of the ANC, as the ANCYL became more prominent and focused its hostility on the CPSA and its 'foreign' ideology. The CPSA expressed concern that '[t]he realities of the class divisions are being obscured ... Nationalism need not be synonymous with racialism, but it can avoid being so only if it recognises the class alignments that cut across the racial divisions.'[37]

The criticisms levelled by the Youth League against the ANC echoed those of the CPSA, calling for the development of a branch structure and mass membership, and the utilisation of extra-parliamentary means of opposition. The two organisations seemed to be competing over who would direct the future of the ANC, fuelling the

Youth League's twin hostilities – to the CPSA, and to anything other than 'occasional co-operation'[38] with other racial groups.

The ANC Youth League

The ANCYL's 'Manifesto', issued in March 1944, noted criticism of the ANC as an organisation 'of gentlemen with clean hands' which had failed to organise the mass of the African population.[39] The League, it stated, was formed as 'a protest against the lack of discipline and the absence of a clearly-defined goal in the movement as a whole' and was committed to 'rousing popular political consciousness and fighting oppression and reaction'.[40] More significantly, it stressed that 'the national liberation of the Africans will be achieved by Africans themselves. We reject foreign leadership of Africa.'[41]

The programme was based on an African nationalism that rejected non-African leadership and 'the wholesale importation of foreign ideologies'[42] while emphasising African pride and self-sufficiency. The League was influenced, in part, by the growth of anti-colonial movements in the post-war period. Anton Lembede, a lawyer and the League's first president and leading ideologue, stated:

> The history of modern times is the history of nationalism … All over the world nationalism is rising in revolt against foreign domination, conquest and oppression in India, in Indonesia, in Egypt, in Persia and several other countries. Among Africans also clear signs of national awakening, national renaissance, or rebirth are noticeable … [43]

The League saw as its 'immediate task' the need 'to overhaul the machinery of the ANC from within', moulding it into a mass-based organisation pursuing national liberation and mobilising support by means of a militant African nationalism.[44] It stressed *'the divine destiny of the African people'*[45] and the need for 'high ethical standards' to 'combat moral disintegration among Africans'.[46]

Both the ANCYL and the CPSA wanted a more radical ANC, but they also wanted an ANC in their own image. While the CPSA tried to work with Congress, the Youth League saw as part of its task the need to stop non-African nationalists from influencing Congress. Lembede argued:

> No foreigner can ever be a true and genuine leader of the African people because no foreigner can ever truly and genuinely interpret the African spirit which is unique and peculiar to Africans only. Some foreigners Asiatic or European who pose as African leaders must be categorically denounced and rejected.[47]

The first task that faced Ashby Mda when he was elected ANCYL president in 1948 was to clarify the League's position with regard to both communism and liberalism.[48]

In calling for the development of African nationalism as a mobilising force sufficient to challenge the status quo, the League came to see both liberalism and communism as competing ideologies.

The ANCYL and the CPSA

The conflict between the ANCYL and the CPSA in the late 1940s, and its resolution in the early 1950s, has been widely discussed.[49] But that discussion has remained within the parameters set by youth leaguers themselves, who are seen to have started out as ardent nationalists opposing 'Vendors of Foreign Method' who 'seek to impose on our struggle cut-and-dried formulae, which so far from clarifying the issues of our struggle, only serve to obscure the fact that we are oppressed not as a class, but as a people, as a Nation'.[50]

These fervent young nationalists, the literature tells us, later mellowed into inclusive non-racialists and learned that non-racialism 'was not very easy to accept at the beginning, because of immaturity, because of youthfulness', according to ANCYL (and later ANC NEC) member Stanley Mabizela.[51] While this seems true at the level of individuals, it is an inadequate analysis of the processes that took place. It also skips over the fact that it took youth leaguers nearly four decades to embrace the ANC's non-racialism, in the sense that it is used here – a rather lengthy maturation.

The conflict operated on two main levels. Firstly, the Youth League reacted strongly to the CPSA's repeated calls for a broad – non-racial – front of organisations opposed to segregation and apartheid. The broad front envisaged by the CPSA would 'conduct mass struggles against race discrimination' while underplaying exclusive nationalism by 'develop[ing] class consciousness in the people' and 'forg[ing] unity in action between the oppressed peoples and between them and the European working class'.[52]

Non-racialism and class struggle became almost synonymous, which did the former few favours, since it took on the ideological, racial and other baggage of class analysis, guaranteed to raise nationalist hackles. The Youth League rejected the class content of non-racialism as proposed by the CPSA, insisting that in its place 'the national liberation of Africans will be achieved by Africans themselves';[53] co-operation between the oppressed groups was acceptable only when the racial groups were organised multi-racially – in 'separate units'.[54]

Secondly, as we have seen, the two organisations were competing for first prize – managing the changing ANC at a time of growing black political mobilisation. And as such, they had very similar programmes in key areas. The Youth League argued that black South Africans 'suffer national oppression in common with thousands and millions of oppressed Colonial peoples in other parts of the world'.[55] But nationalism did not exclude socialism: it was a matter of priorities, according to Lembede, who argued 'After national freedom, then socialism'.[56] In this he was joined by Ashby Mda, who argued that the interests of the mass of Africans could be protected only by 'the establishment of a true democracy and a just social order'.[57]

Mda defined 'a just social order' to include 'full political control by the workers, peasants and intellectuals' combined with 'the liquidation of capitalism' and 'equal distribution of wealth'.[58] The Youth League did not officially endorse socialism, but Lembede argued that 'Africans are naturally socialistic as illustrated in their social practices and customs' and concluded that 'the achievement of national freedom will therefore herald or usher in a new era, the era of African socialism'.[59]

Nothing in this programme conflicted substantially with the CPSA analysis of the South African situation. Strategically, both organisations called for the radicalisation of the ANC leadership and a branch structure and mass base. Ideologically, the CPSA had accepted the primacy of the national question, following its adoption of the 1928 Comintern thesis, which endorsed '… an independent native South African republic as a stage towards a workers' and peasants' republic, with full equal rights for all races, black, coloured and white'.[60]

The concept of a socialist revolution happening in phases meant that the CPSA programme tallied with Lembede's vision of national revolution followed by (African) socialism. Needless to say, in the heat of the battle neither side acknowledged (or even saw) these similarities.

The ANCYL, with a belief 'in the unity of all Africans from the Mediterranean Sea in the North to the Indian and Atlantic Oceans in the South', saw the struggle for equal rights as part of a pan-African anti-colonial movement.[61] For the CPSA, the notion that black South Africans were colonially oppressed was at least implicit in the 1928 thesis. The idea of internal colonialism – to be the cornerstone of post-1953 SACP ideology – had been hinted at but not developed by the then CPSA member Eddie Roux in 1928:

> [In South Africa] we have a white bourgeoisie and a white aristocracy of labour living in the same country together with an exploited colonial peasantry. Here the participation of the workers of the ruling class in the exploitation of the colonial workers is very apparent … the exploitation occurs within the confines of a single country.[62]

Caught up as it was in the factionalism of the period between 1928 and 1935, and thereafter in the Popular Front politics of the anti-fascist period, the CPSA did not assess internal colonialism and its implications until the late 1940s and early 1950s. At that point it became intimately commingled with debates over non-racial/multiracial organisational forms.

This should not be taken to imply that there were no differences between the ANCYL and the CPSA; the point is to try to focus on the precise location and nature of their conflict, which appears to have been a mixture of ideological disputes and a power struggle. That conflict came to work itself out over a particular issue – the form that racial co-operation should take.

The politics of non-racialism

The CPSA's switch from initial opposition to active participation in the Second World War, following the invasion of the Soviet Union, generated widespread suspicion (while confirming the suspicions of many) of the extent to which it was Moscow's lapdog. The party expended much energy during the war popularising the Soviet Union, and was seen by the Youth League as having an agenda which stretched beyond national liberation, was informed by a 'foreign ideology' and used 'methods and tactics which might have succeeded in other countries, like Europe'.[63]

The issue on which the Youth League's suspicion of the CPSA came to focus most directly was the form racial co-operation should take in organisational terms. The CPSA was concerned to avoid the emergence of a racially exclusive African nationalism of the type espoused by leading youth leaguers, which would obscure and retard the class struggle. In the 1940s the party stressed the need for the liberation struggle to be waged by a broad front of organisations led, not by the black bourgeoisie (which included most ANC and ANCYL leaders), but by 'the class-conscious workers and peasants of the national group concerned' so as to foster class-conscious racial unity.[64]

While both organisations called for the development of the ANC, the CPSA supported the emergence of a broad front of organisations (including the ANC) representing Africans, Indians, coloureds and trade unions[65] in co-operation with which it could '… carry out its task exploring the class purposes of race oppression, creating a working class consciousness, breaking down national prejudices and providing leadership in the struggle for socialism'.[66]

Ironically, those who were members of both the CPSA and the ANC enjoyed the support of more conservative and established members of the ANC national executive.[67] Both rejected the Youth League's call for a complete boycott of elections, while more pragmatic ANC leaders supported CPSA calls for broad unity in opposition to racial discrimination. In 1947 this took shape as doctors Xuma, Naicker and Dadoo, representing the ANC, the Natal Indian Congress (NIC) and the Transvaal Indian Congress (TIC) respectively, signed the 'Doctors' Pact', which accepted '… the urgency of co-operation between the non-European peoples and other democratic forces for the attainment of basic human rights …'.[68]

In 1946 the NIC began to mobilise support for a passive resistance campaign against the 'Ghetto Act'. The campaign lasted for two years and resulted in the imprisonment of more than 2 000 resisters of all races (though predominantly Indian). Rallies and public meetings began to be held under the joint auspices of the African and Indian congresses, as well as the (coloured) African People's Organisation (APO).

The Youth League's position on racial co-operation was complicated by the presence of both an exclusive approach, which rejected any such co-operation, and a more inclusive approach.[69] The leadership of the League was drawn increasingly from the latter category, comprising men who accepted greater racial co-operation while stressing the centrality of a strong African nationalist organisation.

In 1946 Lembede stated that co-operation among Africans, Indians and coloureds 'can only take place between Africans as a single unit and other Non-European groups as separate units'[70] – multiracialism, in other words. The League endorsed the 1947 Pact, stating in its 'Basic Policy' that '… the National Organisations of the Africans, Indians and Coloureds may co-operate on common issues'.[71]

The Communist Party had endorsed a similar position in 1943, calling for separate organisations representing Africans, Indians and coloureds, co-ordinated at regional and national levels.[72] With the rise of the Youth League and the growing influence of its nationalist programme, however, the CPSA came to support the idea of one mass organisation with which it would co-operate and, at the end of the decade, in its 1950 Central Committee Report, it called for the transformation of the existing separate national organisations:

> … into a revolutionary party of workers, peasants, intellectuals and petty bourgeoisie, linked together in a firm organisation … guided by a definite programme of struggle against all forms of racial discrimination in alliance with the class-conscious European workers and intellectuals.[73]

Organisational non-racialism, in other words; and with special room for white left-wing intellectuals.

The language of the report was imprecise and unclear. For the Youth League, however, it implied the creation of a non-racial organisation, pursuing class struggle, with, in effect, strong influence exerted by white communists – and this immediately cemented the League's rejection of the CPSA approach to the integration of structures. This mix of issues meant that the question of racial co-operation – that is, the form racial co-operation should take – was a key issue of contention between the two organisations.

The conflict spilled into the open in relation to participation in the 1948 People's Assembly for Votes for All, when the Transvaal branches of the ANC, CPSA, APO and TIC proposed calling a non-racial assembly to highlight the franchise issue on the eve of the (white) general election. The assembly soon became caught up in the ANCYL–CPSA conflict, with youth leaguers on the ANC's Transvaal Executive declaring themselves willing to participate in the assembly only if the organising committee was restricted to representatives of the ANC, TIC and APO – in other words, accepting co-operation between national organisations, but not with the CPSA.

Youth League agitation ensured that the ANC refused to participate officially in the assembly. Transvaal ANC President C S Ramohanoe later faced a motion of no confidence for issuing a statement in support of the assembly.[74] The point at issue was not mere anti-communism, argued law student Nelson Mandela of the Transvaal ANC Executive (and a leading Youth League member) in *The Guardian*, but that

> ... the working committee of the People's Assembly had invited the African National Congress to send delegates to the Assembly. The A. N. C. Executive was not in opposition to the general aims of the People's Assembly, but felt that it was being summoned in an incorrect manner, in that the established national organisations were being by-passed ... The organisers of the People's Assembly had departed from ... agreed methods and there were suspicions that a permanent 'unity movement' was being formed.[75]

The clash in 1948 between the ANCYL and the CPSA is illustrative in two respects. The dispute over the assembly highlighted the way in which ideological differences were being fought out over the issue of non-racialism – not simply on the basis of Youth League racism or exclusivity, as conventional wisdom has it, but because moves towards non-racialism were seen to be part of an ideology which stressed class above race, and would retard the emergence of a strong African National(ist) Congress. (It is not disputed that the League included anti-white and anti-communist elements.)

Secondly, the dispute reflected the growing influence of the ANCYL within the ANC. The League had initially set itself a three- to five-year programme to change Congress,[76] but in the next four years it made few moves towards developing a mass base or radicalising its methods of opposition. The political space was occupied by others – the squatter movement was being organised by Mpanza into the Sofasonke Party, which contested Advisory Board elections; the ADP gained representation on the Native Representative Council with the election of Paul Mosaka; and the CPSA extended its township base. Sensing the need for action and the competition it faced, the League adopted a more assertive tone in 1948:

> From the very outset, the Congress Youth League set itself, inter alia, the historic task of imparting dynamic substance and matter to the organisational form of the A.N.C. This took the form of a forthright exposition of the National Liberatory outlook – African Nationalism – which the Youth League seeks to impose on the Mother Body.[77]

In a private letter written in 1948 Mda acknowledged that a clash between the ANC and the Youth League was 'inevitable' because '... the Congress Senior leadership reflects the dying order of pseudo-liberalism and conservatism, of appeasement and compromises'.[78]

The rise of the Youth League

In order to implement its programme successfully the League had to transform the ANC, and to do so it had to be in a position from which it could determine Congress policy. It also had to squeeze out any other organisation or group seeking to do the same thing. In the first instance this entailed building up its own ranks, and branches were established in Durban, Cape Town and at Fort Hare, although the majority of youth leaguers remained in the Transvaal. League members also began to move into ANC provincial structures.

It was also necessary to counter competing ideologies that sought to influence the development of the ANC – including those of (white) liberals and (white) communists. As stated above the League turned on white liberals such as the Ballingers, Edgar Brookes and members of the Institute of Race Relations who had influence over some leading Congress personalities. Hostility towards the liberals was exacerbated by disputes in 1946 over the adjournment of the Native Representative Council (NRC) and the League's call for the boycott of all 'Native Representation' elections. The process of weaning Congress from the influence of white liberals was largely completed by 1947.

Finally, if the Youth League were to direct a militant movement for national liberation under the aegis of the ANC, competing organisations (as well as ideologies) had to be isolated. The AAC remained a small organisation, primarily based in the Eastern Cape and increasingly dominated by the Non-European Unity Movement (NEUM) to which it had affiliated, while the ADP had begun to collapse by 1947. Both were accused of causing 'rift[s] in the national unity front at this critical moment' with the effect of 'invit[ing] more oppression for Africans'.[79] Put simply, anyone who sought to mobilise Africans was attacked, including the CPSA, which had largely set the pace in township organisation in the 1940s, and which proposed to 'draw in thousands of members of each racial and national group, provide them with a Socialist education, and organise them for work among their own people …'.[80]

Paradoxically, however, as the power and influence of the ANCYL grew within the ANC in the late 1940s, older ANC leaders revealed a willingness to work with communists. The League failed in its attempts in 1945 and 1947 to have all CPSA members removed from Congress, with communists and the older ANC leaders jointly outvoting its call for a boycott of all elections.[81] Nonetheless, youth leaguers occupied increasingly important positions within the provincial structures of the ANC and, by 1948, were sufficiently entrenched to prevent the organisation from participating in the People's Assembly.

By 1949 the League was powerful enough to insist that any candidate for the post of President-General of the ANC must endorse the Programme of Action. At the annual conference of the ANC in 1949 the League succeeded in ousting Xuma from the post and securing the election of Dr James Moroka, while ANCYL members including Ashby Mda, V V T Mbobo, Dr J L Z Njongwe, Godfrey Pitje, Oliver Tambo and Walter Sisulu were elected to the National Executive Committee (with Sisulu in the important post of

Secretary-General). Two years later youth leaguers were able to remove A W G Champion as President of the ANC in Natal, securing in his place the election of Albert Luthuli, later to be elected ANC President-General and to become Africa's first Nobel Peace Prize laureate.

While the influence of the Youth League within the ANC grew, the fortunes of the CPSA were in decline. After the 1946 African miners' strike the CPSA Executive Committee was tried for sedition by the once liberal-seeming Smuts government, in a process that dragged on from 1946 to 1948. White wartime support for the CPSA disappeared as the Cold War gathered force, and organisations such as the Springbok Legion, Friends of the Soviet Union and the Left Book Club either withered or closed, along with their wartime ability to reach a large white audience.

The Trades and Labour Council was divided as the Nationalist Party (NP) made a serious bid for white working-class support. Attacks on the CPSA by both the United Party and NP governments culminated in the Suppression of Communism Act of 1950, which outlawed the CPSA and also any doctrine 'which aims at bringing about any political, industrial, social or economic change within the Union'.[82]

The Communist Party and national liberation

The CPSA in the late 1940s revealed differing approaches to the 'national question' and the national liberation movements in South Africa. Reduced to their simplest form these differences revolved around the emphasis given to class struggle in relation to the national struggle waged by the ANC and SAIC. To a perhaps surprising degree the differences took a regional form, with the party's Cape region differing from those in Natal and the Transvaal.[83] Finally, race complicated all these differences. As Ben Turok has noted, the Communist Party in Cape Town was 'probably the only fully non-racial organisation in the country at the time' – but 'it was apparent that, in Cape Town, whites played a disproportionately dominant role in the movement, to a degree not seen elsewhere, causing some resentment …'.[84]

After the internal ructions of the 1930s the headquarters of the CPSA had been moved from the Transvaal to Cape Town and, as a result, both the executive and central committees were dominated by communists from the Western Cape. Throughout the late 1940s the Transvaal tried unsuccessfully to have the headquarters returned to Johannesburg, arguing that it was the political centre of South Africa.[85] But differences within the party went beyond race or region. CPSA members in the Transvaal and Natal (and some in the Cape) argued that the Cape leaders' approach to the national organisations was grounded in 'traditional concepts of Communist Party activity' and that they did not 'adequately understand the national movement'.[86]

A number of factors were responsible for the Cape party's emphasis on class struggle. Firstly, the Cape Town branch of the ANC was small and weak in comparison with those in similar centres elsewhere. This was in part the result of demographic factors, Cape Town being the only centre where Africans were in a minority and where much of the African population consisted of migrant labourers. As Cape CPSA secretary Fred Carneson put it,

> the majority of the population were coloureds, down in Cape Town. And they were articulate, they had been well organised for years, they were used to participating in trade unions and the whole atmosphere was different down in the Cape. So certainly, Johannesburg and Durban and Port Elizabeth, we were each operating in a different political ambience.[87]

The leading Congress and Youth League personalities were concentrated in the Transvaal and, to a lesser extent, Natal, so the CPSA in Cape Town worked with a small ANC, led by Thomas Ngwenya, who would later work closely with the Liberal Party, and an even smaller Youth League. In addition, the coloured population was partially enfranchised and had a long tradition of trade unionism, and the Cape CPSA faced competition from organisations such as the NEUM and the Coloured People's National Union.

The major political battles of the late 1940s were largely fought in the Transvaal ANC, where youth leaguers clashed with ANC–CPSA members over a series of initiatives, including the People's Assembly.[88] Leading Transvaal CPSA members such as J B Marks, David Bopape, Edwin Mofutsanyana, Dan Tloome, Yusuf Dadoo and others worked within the Congress movement and supported moves to radicalise the ANC and SAIC. Communist Party politics in the Transvaal was, to a large extent, bound up with Congress politics, as CPSA members resisted the strand of exclusive nationalism within the ANCYL while supporting the militancy it injected into the ANC. Leading black CPSA members were also heavily involved in Congress politics in the Transvaal and Natal.

In the Cape, however, the dominant personalities were white, adding fuel to Youth League attacks on 'foreign' bearers of non-African ideologies.[89] Johannesburg, says Ben Turok,

> … was a different world. In Cape Town the whites were the strongest personalities, around *The Guardian* – you could on two hands pick out a good number of intellectuals, very experienced political cadres – Jack Simons, Brian Bunting, Carneson, Ray Alexander, a whole group of them. Whereas the African group was small, inexperienced, and much less senior.[90]

To some extent, the dominance of whites in the Cape arose from the political activities undertaken by the party there, which differed from those of communists elsewhere. As Fred Carneson put it, 'we had to tailor our approach, it had to be completely different in the different areas, and so it was'.[91]

Cape Town was the headquarters of *The Guardian* (later published as *The Clarion, People's World, Advance* and *New Age*),[92] a left-wing newspaper which focused on the struggle against racial discrimination and carried news of the African and Indian congresses and other organisations ignored by mainstream newspapers. Its foreign news was consistently pro-Soviet and anti-American. In the late 1940s *The Guardian* was edited by Brian Bunting, its editorial board comprised many leading Cape CPSA members and a large number of CPSA members worked for it as journalists and newspaper sellers. As Turok put it, 'when you joined the movement … you joined *The Guardian* and its circle'.[93]

The Cape had a different centre of gravity, primarily because it lacked a strong Congress presence, allowing the focus of CPSA activity to be divided between *The Guardian* and trade union work, in which Ray Alexander, James Phillips and others had been involved for many years. A third distinguishing feature in the Cape was the continued and successful participation in parliamentary and provincial council elections. In the rest of the country the CPSA failed to maintain the electoral successes of the war years but in the Cape it continued to win seats on the city council and, in 1948, it won the Cape Western Native Representative and Provincial Council seats.

The political milieu in which Cape Communist Party members moved was also, in many ways, different from that elsewhere. Debates in the non-racial Forum Club, the Africa Club and in organisations such as the Modern Youth Society centred on class struggle and were dominated by hostilities between communists and Trotskyists.[94] The major ideological conflict facing the CPSA in Cape Town was not with nationalist youth leaguers but with the Marxist-cum-Trotskyist NEUM, the major political influence among coloured intellectuals such as Benny Kies and Kenny Jordaan, who constantly criticised national liberation struggles and their supporters (including the CPSA) for having 'as [their] objective the triumph of capitalist democracy'.[95]

Many Communist Party members in the Cape – and elsewhere – shared these views. Fred Carneson noted that 'it was not only the communists that did not see things, at that stage, as a struggle for national liberation. Africans themselves did not see it as clearly as they see it now.'[96]

Jack Simons argued that 'the history of nationalism, whether of the progressive or imperialistic kind, is intimately bound up with the history of capitalism … and the rise of bourgeois democracy'.[97] He continued: 'Communism is not *necessarily* the antithesis to Nationalism. It is the antithesis to Capitalism. But it must be remembered that the rise of Capitalism is closely associated with Nationalism.'[98]

Simons went on to argue that 'nationalism is progressive in so far as it is aimed at the removal of discrimination and the achievement of democracy'. However, nationalism 'can be exploited by an aggressive movement directed towards the suppression of another group or nation'.[99] Such views were not restricted to intellectuals like Simons, brave enough to air them in public. The 1950 Central Committee Report expressed a similar viewpoint, emphasising that 'South Africa is entering a period of bitter national conflict ... On all sides the national and racial divisions are being emphasised and the realities of the class divisions are being obscured'.[100]

In such a situation, the report argued, 'nationalism need not be synonymous with racialism, but it can avoid being so only if it recognises the class alignments that cut across the racial divisions'.[101] The need to emphasise class struggle was heightened by the accession to power of the Youth League and the anti-communist agitation of influential journalist Selope Thema and others within the ANC.[102] In response, the CPSA called on its members to 'make a practice of issuing immediate and critical comment on the statements of the bourgeois leaders' and to prevent 'the bourgeois elements in the national movements' from attacking 'the working class movement, ... the party, or ... adopt[ing] a negative or hostile attitude to the international working class forces'.[103] This was not a strategy geared to calming the fears of the ANCYL and generating close working relations.

The Communist Party in the Transvaal was a very different animal, with activists primarily engaged in nationalist rather than class politics. Many leading members of the party were simultaneously ANC or SAIC members, and CPSA members in the Transvaal and Natal Congress movements fought to prove the party's commitment to national not class struggle.

The squatter movements, bus boycotts and the 1946 African miners strike had all been located in the Transvaal, which also had the largest and most radical ANC membership in the country. The Johannesburg District of the CPSA urged black CPSA members to join the Congress movement. Central Committee member Yusuf Dadoo was a leading figure in the TIC, which, with the NIC, had shed its conservative leadership during the war years and moved into an alliance with the ANC; and the ANC in the Transvaal was led by joint CPSA/ANC men such as J B Marks and David Bopape.

Bopape, who was both Transvaal ANC Secretary and a member of the Youth League, had succeeded in making Brakpan location the political centre of the East Rand and establishing the CPSA as a dominant force. The successful stayaway on May Day 1950 was seen as largely a result of Marks's organisational skills, which resulted in his election as Transvaal ANC president.[104] ANC–CPSA members worked closely with the ANC president, C S Ramohanoe, who expressed little support for the ideological battle waged by the ANCYL against the CPSA, characterising leaguers as 'armchair politicians who keep on going from place to place preaching Congress and doing nothing'.[105]

But the Transvaal ANC was also the political home of leading Youth League members who opposed the Communist Party and, in consequence, became the site of the ANCYL–CPSA struggle. The period was one of political ferment in which, according to Rusty Bernstein, Transvaal communists sensitive to the Congress movement '... began to adjust the Party's view of the significance of the national liberation movement. It placed the national liberation movement much more in the forefront than it had done.'[106]

This was made easier at the end of the decade as leading members of the Youth League began to show signs of modifying their former hostility to both racial co-operation and the CPSA.

Resolving the ANCYL–CPSA conflict

In the early 1950s the Youth League began to split into two camps, one remaining strictly Africanist, the other supporting racial co-operation via the (multiracial) Congress Alliance. In the same period the conceptual approach of leading youth leaguers came to resemble that of the CPSA, particularly its language of anti-imperialism. By 1953 Nelson Mandela spoke freely of the ANC 'uncompromisingly resist[ing] the efforts of imperialist America and her satellites to draw the world into the rule of violence and brute force' and condemned 'the criminal attacks of the imperialists against the people of Malaya, Vietnam, Indonesia and Tunisia'.[107]

As Mandela, Tambo, Sisulu and others moved into leadership positions within the ANC (Mandela was co-opted to the ANC NEC in 1950) leadership of the Youth League passed to a younger generation of Fort Hare intellectuals, of whom Z K Matthews's son, Joe, was the most prominent.

As Walshe has shown, by 1951 Joe Matthews was clearly linking the South African struggle to a broader international struggle against the 'indirect enemy', the United States.[108] According to Matthews, Africans were exploited under capitalism in 'the final stage of monopoly capital gone mad, namely fascism'.[109] Support for communist countries grew among some youth leaguers because of the clear opposition to racism and support for decolonisation which distinguished them from the Western countries. Joe Matthews wrote in 1952: 'I must say I am pretty fed up with the U.S.A., their stand is rotten and the Eastern nations have beaten the West on the colour issue ... I ... think America has lost African friendship. As far as I am concerned I will henceforth look East where race discrimination is so taboo that it is made a crime by the state.'[110]

Leading youth leaguers also came out in support of extra-parliamentary action, with Matthews, along with Mda, Bopape and others, arguing that the 'labour power of the African people' was the key to success in the struggle.[111] By the end of the 1940s, the relationship between the CPSA and the ANCYL was clearly more dynamic than earlier, as both underwent significant changes.

Some Communist Party members continued to maintain that the ANC was an anti-communist petit-bourgeois nationalist organisation aiming to maintain capitalist relations, albeit in a non-racial society.[112] This (it was argued) created the possibility of a rapprochement between the ANC and some sections of capital, lubricated by the 'progressive industrialisation' that had emerged during the Second World War. Joe Matthews rejected the argument: 'the possibility of a liberal capitalist democracy in South Africa is exactly nil' because the 'political immorality, cowardice and vacillation of the so-called progressives … render them utterly useless as a force against fascism'.[113] Mda, however, conceded the point. The removal of legal statutes that enshrined discrimination:

> … might under certain circumstances very well mean that the African middle class joined hands with the European, Indian and Coloured middle class in order to impose further chains and to exploit the black peasants and toiling millions. It has happened before in many Colonial territories even in Africa. It must not happen here.[114]

Significantly, Youth League members who had taken up positions within the ANC began to accept the strategic need for allies. This acceptance was informed by increasingly vicious laws such as the Population Registration Act (1950) and the Group Areas Act (1950), which discriminated against the entire black population, and the threat to all resistance movements posed by the Suppression of Communism Act (1950).

Among those who looked to such alliances were some of the most virulently anti-communist league members, such as Jordan Ngubane, editor of *Inkundla ya Bantu* and later a prominent Liberal Party member. In 1950 Ngubane castigated the CPSA for 'stampeding our people into the May Day demonstrations' in which eighteen Africans were shot by the police.[115] Nonetheless, Ngubane argued, although 'Communism and apartheid are two similarly vicious evils',

> … the most dangerous of those at the moment is apartheid. The African Nationalists will do well to exercise a little more statesmanship and realise that they can carry their fight against the Communists only up to a certain point if they are not going to play right into the hands of [Prime Minister] Malan … it is more important to exercise statesmanship in our dealings with the Communists than to help the Malanites by weakening their political enemies.[116]

Attempts to extend the ANC–SAIC alliance to include trade unions and coloureds threatened with disenfranchisement failed. Following the May Day deaths and facing the imminent enactment of the Suppression of Communism Bill, 27 June was declared a Day of Protest and, after consultations between the ANC, the SAIC, the CPSA and the APO, a stayaway was called. ANC leaders hoped to create a co-ordinating committee of the Congress and trade unions but, in the event, the CPSA disbanded while the APO and trade unions sent only moral support.[117] By June 1950 the Alliance remained limited to the ANC and the SAIC.

By the end of 1950 youth leaguers controlled the ANC, which was now wholly committed to a programme of extra-parliamentary action. In 1951 plans were made for the

Defiance Campaign, which transformed the ANC into a popular extra-parliamentary movement. With the CPSA having disbanded, individual black communists increasingly worked within the ANC and, by 1952, debates among former CPSA members across the country highlighted the growing emphasis on the national liberation struggle. The power struggle that had largely characterised ANCYL–CPSA relations in the 1940s had been settled – in the Youth League's favour.

Existing explanations for the resolution of the CPSA–ANCYL conflict stress the reduction in hostility following the election of youth leaguers to the ANC National Executive Committee, where 'their personal experiences of close co-operation'[118] with communists resulted in their 'anti-communist tendencies … [being] modified'; implicit is the assumption that the same happened with regard to whites and contributed to the diminution of exclusive African nationalism.[119] These are only partial explanations; the context in which CPSA–ANCYL hostility diminished was one of ideological shifts on both sides, the dissolution of the Communist Party, and the accession of Youth League leaders to power in the ANC.

Class and race in South Africa: the CPSA in 1950

As a more dynamic relationship developed at the end of the 1940s between the ANCYL and the CPSA, sections of opinion within the latter began to adjust the party's understanding of, and approach to, national struggle. But this simultaneously highlighted regional differences within the party.

The Communist Party in the Cape maintained what one (Cape) member described as 'a long tradition of suspicion of the ANC' as a bourgeois, anti-communist organisation,[120] a perception that was by no means restricted to the Cape or shared by all members of the Cape CPSA. The Johannesburg CPSA chairperson, Building Workers Union official Danie du Plessis, argued that the ANC should be assessed not in terms of its constituent membership, but of its leadership. He characterised the latter as an 'incipient' black bourgeoisie that aimed 'to integrate themselves into the existing local capitalism rather than to oust the oppressors'.[121] The ANC leaders, du Plessis argued, were 'bourgeois agents' who, at a point of crisis, 'would join forces with the government against the workers, and would first protect their own interests'.[122]

The party in the Cape placed less emphasis on the national liberation struggle than those elsewhere. According to Bernstein:

In Cape Town, where the national movement was really not significant in that way [i.e. as in the Transvaal], the same emphasis did not exist and there began to be an emphasis on the Party as the leading element in the whole struggle and the national liberation movement to be somewhat insignificant. So this political difference began to show itself.[123]

Facing a strong African nationalist movement, sections of the Communist Party in the Transvaal began a theoretical debate that sought to reconcile class and race, arguing that blacks suffered both capitalist and colonial oppression and that the growing national movement was a natural response to colonialism. Appropriately it was Eddie Roux, who had hinted at this in 1928, and who picked up the argument again in 1952:

> I do not agree that South Africa is a capitalist country. I think one may say that here we have an imperial and colonial relationship co-existing in the same country. The African people cannot only be considered to be the subjects of proletarian exploitation as in other countries; they are subjected to an extra exploitation because of their colour, something which is not usually found in other countries with laissez-faire.[124]

In the next two years leading members of the new South African Communist Party (SACP) elaborated on Roux's statement and developed the theory of 'Colonialism of a Special Type'. At the same time they also debated and finalised the form that racial co-operation should take in opposition to apartheid.

For the purposes of the present discussion the significance of internal colonialism lies in the approach to national struggle implicit in the theory. Those who emphasised class struggle argued that the 'businessmen, financiers, landlords' and others in the ANC leadership would always 'place their vested interests first', making them a 'traitor class'.[125] In contrast, Bernstein, Transvaal central committee member Michael Harmel, and others argued that segregation and apartheid, in oppressing all blacks equally, had successfully stunted the growth of an indigenous black bourgeoisie. As a result, the 'traitor class' was not to be found among blacks – rather, 'the traitor class in South Africa is the European bourgeoisie'.[126]

It was argued that the Congress Alliance, and the ANC itself, represented 'an alliance of the working class and the petit-bourgeois strata of the colonially oppressed peoples of South Africa ...'.[127] Within that alliance the working class represented 'the most energetic, whole-hearted and thoroughgoing section of the fighters for bourgeois democracy, for national liberation'.[128] Moreover, it was argued, precisely because of the colonial oppression of blacks and the absence of a significant black bourgeoisie, Congress members and leaders were predominantly working class in character. Pointing to the adoption by the ANC and SAIC of extra-parliamentary strategies, Harmel argued that 'in recent years, the militant working class tendency has wielded increasing influence in our national movements'. As a result, 'the policy of genuine workers' leaders' should not be 'to drive out the allied classes, but rather to broaden out the movements ...'.[129]

In the post-war years black Communist Party members began to emphasise demands such as abolition of the pass laws above the traditional CPSA concern with the white working class.[130] The latter, according to Fred Carneson, sounding like the good Cape Town communist he was, stemmed from 'the fact that your most active section amongst the working class was either your white workers or your coloured workers'.[131] The change in direction was also the result of a leadership struggle within the party, supported by Harmel, Bernstein and others, who castigated:

> … the pedantic arm-chair socialist types of 'theoreticians' who are apparently unable to see that on practically every main issue of home and foreign policy, the outlook and aims of such bourgeois elements as, for example, Dr. Moroka, are far more progressive in content than such working class elements as the Mineworkers Union, the S.A.R. Staff Association or the S.A.T.L.C (Trades and Labour Council).[132]

Transvaal communists argued that while colonial oppression blurred class oppression it also ensured that the national organisations were overwhelmingly working class in composition.

According to Harmel, changes in ANC policy and strategy (brought about, to a large degree, by tensions with the ANCYL) were evidence of growing working-class influence. As the struggle intensified and the influence of the working class became stronger, Harmel argued, the national movements would move away from formulating political demands and concentrate on economic issues. Moreover, internal colonialism would ensure that the content of such demands would not represent the interests of the bourgeoisie; rather, it would highlight the economic content of national liberation. For Harmel this entailed land redistribution and 'nationalisation of the principal means of production (for the power of imperialism in this country can only be broken by divorcing the imperialists from the means of production)'.[133]

The Transvaal communists who put forward the notion of internal colonialism concluded that the role of communists was to work with the national movements for the attainment of national liberation. This would lead to 'the clearing away of the race versus class issue', highlighting class oppression and leaving it 'exposed for all to see'.[134]

In the event, the tension between race and class was not resolved before the CPSA dissolved in June 1950. The elaboration of internal colonialism by members of the South African Communist Party, which replaced it, represented an attempt to strike a new balance for a reconstituted party working with a newly invigorated Congress movement.

The 1950 Report of the CPSA Central Committee – the last it issued – revealed the tensions within the party. The report tentatively put forward the notion of internal colonialism, arguing that South Africa exhibited 'the characteristics of both an imperialist state and colony within a single indivisible, geographical, political and economic entity'.[135] The black bourgeoisie, which should be leading the national struggle, was '… small, fragmentary, pinned down in the poorest areas, forced to use subterfuge and illegalities to evade discriminating laws, starved of capital, and exposed to constant insecurity. It is not a class that could provide effective, militant leadership.'[136]

Transvaal communists argued that this meant that the ANC 'is not dominated by the unstable and potentially treacherous elements which have led similar movements elsewhere', and that communists should therefore work in and with the national organisations.[137] The 1950 Central Committee Report, by contrast, argued that the black congresses were vague and contradictory and revealed a 'tremendous capacity for evasiveness and ambiguity'.[138]

The 1950 report revealed a party in crisis – not just externally, where the Suppression of Communism Act threatened to behead it, but internally as well. Attempting to weld the colonial analysis of the Transvaal to the class bias of the Cape the report argued that while nationalism need not be racist it could avoid being so only through the transformation of existing national organisations into a single party of 'workers, peasants, intellectuals and petty bourgeois ... in alliance with the class-conscious European workers and intellectuals'. The aim of such a party, which would work in co-operation with the CPSA, would be to strive for national liberation. However, it would have to be led by 'the class-conscious workers and peasants of the national group concerned' in order to 'develop class consciousness in the people, and to forge unity in action between the oppressed peoples and between them and the European working class'.[139]

By contrast, Transvaal communists acknowledged the class content attached to non-racialism – that is, the sublimation of national in favour of class revolution – against which the Youth League reacted. Rusty Bernstein claimed that while '[t]here is no doubt scope for an organisation representing all races', this was 'only possible under a philosophy of socialism'. In the present circumstances, he argued, '... it is difficult to believe that the national liberatory struggle can be waged by any organisation other than that representing the people who are nationally oppressed'.[140]

The CPSA, far from being, as popular belief would have it, a collection of single-minded Stalinists never deviating from the party line, or (its own image) a dedicated and disciplined cadre, was heterogeneous, incorporating various strands of thought and members who were involved in a variety of forms of struggle including parliamentary elections, trade unionism and Congress politics.

Throughout the 1940s the CPSA called for the emergence of a militant mass-based national organisation to prosecute the first stage of the 'two-stage' revolution. But when it got the organisation it wanted, and the ANC began to grow in size and militancy, it was largely at the instigation of the Youth League, which endorsed an aggressive African nationalism and hostility to the Communist Party.

The CPSA was divided in its response, with one section, strongly associated with the Cape-based party leadership, calling for a greater emphasis on class struggle and arguing that the rise of African and Afrikaner nationalism was, in the words of Jack Simons, 'camouflag[ing] the Universal Exploitation of All Workers, whatever their race'.[141] In response to the Youth League's insistence on multiracialism, supporters of class struggle called for one Congress for all, claiming: 'Real and absolute unity between all races can only be achieved in a workers' struggle'.[142] The form racial co-operation should take – in particular the participation of whites – was, from the outset, linked to the importation of 'foreign' ideologies compounding suspicion of the bona fides of white activists.

A second strand of thinking within the CPSA, and which was prominent among those who assumed leadership positions in the SACP after 1953, stressed the working-class content of national liberation in South Africa, and called on communists to work in close co-operation with the Congress Alliance.

The 1950 Central Committee Report was an attempt to reach a compromise between the two, using an analysis of oppression in South Africa developed in the Transvaal, but reaching conclusions associated with the Cape, which stressed the primacy of class struggle and the need to underplay nationalism. Until its demise the CPSA's attempts to balance the requirements of national and class struggle remained unsuccessful.

Multiracialism was commonly perceived by many outside the Congress movement (and quite a few within it) to be a mechanism of control engineered by communists after the CPSA disbanded in 1950, giving white communists undue (and certainly unrepresentative) influence in the Alliance. In fact, multiracialism was engineered by youth leaguers and represented a clear setback for those CPSA members who argued that class struggle was obscured by nationalism. The dissolution of the CPSA and the emergence of the Congress Alliance generated a wide-ranging debate among former CPSA members over the relationship between class and national struggle in the country. In the middle of the debate the South African Communist Party, the South African Congress of Democrats and the Liberal Party were formed. These are discussed in turn.

Chapter 4

From CPSA to SACP via CST
Socialist responses to African nationalism, 1952–1954

By 1953 the African National Congress (ANC) had emerged as the major extra-parliamentary organisation in the struggle against apartheid. The belief of some cynical observers that the Defiance Campaign 'totally failed to achieve its objective: the revocation of unjust laws. In its way it failed gloriously in that it became the prologue to the great legend of Congress's role in the freedom struggle'[1] rather misses the point: the Defiance Campaign succeeded, politically, in making the ANC something akin to what the youth leaguers wanted – popular, militant, and the driving (and leading) force in opposition to apartheid.

As a result the ANC's political philosophy and strategic thinking were a matter of concern to communists, liberals and others who hoped to influence events. To do so now required creating a relationship with the ANC and this, in turn, required a strategic framework within which to engage. Thus it was that, in the early 1950s, anti-apartheid organisations and groups were forced to review the political situation. Whites were particularly affected. They were unable to join the ANC, were alienated by the anti-white sentiments which marked the final stages of the Defiance Campaign and were wary of the militant nationalism of the ANC Youth League (ANCYL) and of the (real or imagined) influence of communists. The debates of the early 1950s among anti-apartheid whites of all political hues set the parameters within which white opposition to apartheid operated throughout the 1950s and beyond.

White opposition: the wider context
The post-war years saw an increasingly militant ANC as well as growing co-operation between African and Indian congresses and other organisations. The African and Indian congresses moved into an alliance and, with representatives of the largely coloured Franchise Action Committee (FRAC), co-ordinated the 1952 Defiance Campaign. Although

the attainment of unity was not a simple or linear process the general thrust was clear. With the formation of the South African Coloured People's Organisation (SACPO) in September 1953, representatives of the coloured population formally joined the Congress Alliance. The 1952 Darragh Hall meeting called by the ANC and SAIC was an attempt to capitalise on white opposition to apartheid and find an organisational home for whites.

ANC President-General Albert Luthuli saw the growth of white opposition to apartheid as a direct response to the increasing resistance of blacks, saying that 'as soon as the African people started to be militant ... more whites have begun to think more of our needs'.[2] In a speech in Port Elizabeth ANC Secretary-General Walter Sisulu similarly argued that:

> ... no matter what anyone feels or thinks about the Defiance Campaign, the fact is that it changed the political life of South Africa. The vacillating elements, both in our camp and in that of the ruling class, have been exposed; they have been forced to make their clear choice. Whilst we have gained considerable strength, the ruling class has been confused and divided. The coming into being of different parties is very significant.[3]

As Luthuli saw it the South African Congress of Democrats (SACOD) and the Liberal Party (LP) were 'the children of the Defiance Campaign'.[4] But the twin processes of black unity and radicalisation symbolised by the Defiance Campaign were precisely the factors that exacerbated ideological differences among whites and led to organisational fragmentation.

For whites opposed to apartheid, the early 1950s was a time to adjust themselves to a new political situation, including an increasingly vicious Nationalist Party (NP) government, a disbanded Communist Party and a more militant Congress movement. White radicals – who demanded full and immediate racial equality, to be achieved by extra-parliamentary means, including a restructuring of the economy in a more or less socialist direction – debated the best means of pursuing class struggle with or without national liberation. Liberals, meanwhile, sought a reasonable middle course that would restrain the excesses of African and Afrikaner nationalism and allow the gradualist inevitability of economic development to restructure South Africa's political economy. As a result, mutually suspicious radical and liberal whites participated in two parallel streams of activity, with each group keeping a watchful – and often scornful – eye on the other.

The cause of this separation is commonly (and erroneously) traced back to the Darragh Hall meeting of November 1952. The failure of that meeting to produce a single, unified white anti-apartheid organisation has been ascribed to the prominent role played by 'former Communists and other left-wing whites' in forming the South African People's Congress (later the Congress of Democrats).[5] Most commentators saw COD (the 1952 Johannesburg organisation),[6] and later SACOD (the national white Congress), as either 'Communist-controlled'[7] or operating as a 'front' for white communists.[8] Working backwards from this assumption the Darragh Hall meeting has been presented as a lost opportunity where white unity was squandered by the wilful actions of communists intent on creating a 'front' through which they could control the ANC, and who thereby alienated white liberals.[9]

Such claims, however, assume that the broader white left was a monolithic entity which acted in concert on agreed goals. They show little understanding of the differences among former CPSA members or between them and the broader left, which included former communists such as Eddie Roux, Trotskyists such as Baruch Hirson, and non-Marxists such as Helen Joseph.[10]

Disagreements about how to approach African nationalism at some times united and at others cut across these labels. Moreover, simplistic claims about communist fronts are a-historical: they ignore the long history of white liberals, communists and others in South Africa, stretching back decades, and the fundamental differences in ideology, strategy and tactics, between these different anti-apartheid whites.

Although these differences became clear at the Darragh Hall meeting, they were pre-existing and were not Johannesburg-specific. In Durban, Cape Town, Port Elizabeth and elsewhere, radicals and liberals disagreed over the way the anti-apartheid struggle should be waged and the nature of post-apartheid society, with the result that most major centres in South Africa hosted parallel and separate discussion forums incorporated into either the Liberal Party or SACOD.

The dissolution of the CPSA

The Communist Party of South Africa disbanded itself on 20 June 1950, shortly before the Suppression of Communism Act was passed at the end of that month. Announcing the dissolution in Parliament, CPSA MP Sam Kahn stated that 'Communism will outlive the Nationalist Party. Democracy will be triumphant when members of this Government will be manuring the fields of history. Millions in South Africa will echo my final words: "Long Live Communism"'.[11]

Kahn's bold statement – much of which, in the 1990s, was to prove to have been prophetic – belied the confusion that existed within the ranks of the CPSA about its demise, the future role of communists and the regional and ideological differences that divided them.

The dissolution of the CPSA generally receives a cursory mention in most works covering the period,[12] with most of the analysis of the decision produced by protagonists, with the attendant analytic problems.[13] Only in the post-apartheid era have some memoirs (and even then only very few) strayed from the party line – and on this issue a 'party line' has indeed been maintained for decades – and amplified slightly what we know.

We still do not know very much about the debates in the Central Committee which led to the decision to disband, and virtually nothing about the attitude of party members to the dissolution.[14] The disbanding of the CPSA has been presented as a largely consensual act necessitated by the provisions of the Suppression of Communism Act, and the formation of the SACP three years later has been portrayed as a smoothly planned reconstitution of the party with a new name and new operational imperatives resulting from conditions of illegality. These interpretations tell only part of the story.

The decision to disband the CPSA was taken hastily by a weak and divided Central Committee and it left the general party membership confused and without direction at precisely the time that the ANC and SAIC were mobilising support for the Defiance Campaign. In an attempt to gain theoretical and analytic clarity on the swiftly unfolding events of 1951–1952, former CPSA members and others vigorously debated the nature and goals of the ANC. Discussion was soon dominated by the theory of internal colonialism, developed by Transvaal communists in the late 1940s. In 1953 the same Transvaal communists founded the SACP, which, under their leadership, tailored its policy and strategy towards an intimate working relationship with the Congress movement. The roots of both the SACP and SACOD lie in the debates and disputes of 1950–1954.

The passage through Parliament of the Unlawful Organisations Bill (renamed the Suppression of Communism Bill) gave rise to a major campaign of opposition by extra-parliamentary organisations. The campaign was significant in that, despite disputes between the CPSA and the ANCYL in the late 1940s, the congresses and the CPSA acted jointly against the Bill. The ANC national working committee convened a conference in Johannesburg in May 1950 to which representatives from the SAIC, the ANCYL, the CPSA, the African People's Organisation (APO) and the Council for Non-European Trade Unions (CNETU) were invited, and focused on the need for united resistance to the Unlawful Organisations Bill, which, the conference organisers stated, would convert South Africa into 'a fully fledged fascist state'.[15] The conference concluded: 'The NATIONAL ORGANISATIONS present here jointly pledge themselves to take immediate steps to mobilise all sections of the South African people and offer concrete mass opposition to this vicious Bill with the aim of defeating it.'[16]

It was a bitter irony for the CPSA that the point at which it became an accepted and equal partner, campaigning in concert with all existing national organisations, coincided with the point at which it was about to disband itself. The party threw its energy into campaigning against the Bill, issuing thousands of fliers and stickers and holding public meetings. But little thought was given to its future. As Rusty Bernstein put it, 'We'd concentrated so much on a campaign to oppose the Bill and to try and frustrate the Bill, we didn't really concentrate our attention on what was going to happen after [it] became law! We almost talked ourselves into thinking we could stop it. So to some extent when it happened … we weren't prepared for it.'[17]

Significantly, Bernstein concluded: 'And that goes for the Central Committee like anybody else'.[18]

Bernstein's dry, self-deprecating wit hid a steely commitment. In his fascinating memoir, *Memory Against Forgetting,* he writes of the near-unanimous decision to disband the party, which was taken on the basis of a legal opinion. Members were in shock, trusting their leaders to have a secret plan for a secret party – but there was none. Bernstein describes the feeling:

> Had we, even now, been told the truth? Was [Moses] Kotane not covering the illegal successor to the Party which was already being developed? We all had questions, but not ones that could be answered in public. What we wanted to hear, what we hoped to hear could not be spoken. We knew that. There was nothing left to say. Finis. We sang the Internationale without enthusiasm for the last time, and went out into the night as though from a funeral. All our years of work and dedication had disappeared in dust – without warning. Only uncertainty and doubt about the future remained.[19]

Bernstein notes that his colleagues, who, with him, remained silent at the meeting, all later admitted that they too were expecting 'that an underground was being built up somewhere in secret', but goes on to note that such hopes were 'Sleep-walking. Delusion'.[20]

In Parliament only the Native Representatives and Labour Party MPs opposed the passage of the Suppression of Communism Act. Sam Kahn announced the party's response to the enactment:

> Recognising that the day the Suppression of Communism Bill becomes law every one of our members, merely by virtue of their membership, may be liable to be imprisoned without the option of a fine for a maximum period of ten years, the Central Committee of the Communist Party has decided to dissolve the Party as from today.[21]

As Michael Harmel (writing under the name Lerumo), Transvaal journalist, official historian of the party, chairperson throughout the 1950s and then-emerging ideologue noted, when the CPSA dissolved itself it did so 'by majority vote and without consulting the membership'.[22] The decision was taken at 'a hastily convened' Central Committee meeting in early May 1950,[23] where the Bill was considered. No formal discussions had been held within the ranks of the party, and Central Committee members 'hadn't had time to really think through a position before they got there'.[24] When the motion was put to the vote fifteen of the seventeen Central Committee members supported it.

The two who opposed it were Harmel and 1930s veteran Bill Andrews. Twelve years later the SACP publicly criticised the dissolution, stating:

> Despite its great achievements and struggles, the Communist Party of South Africa proved incapable of surviving under illegal conditions. Legalistic illusions had penetrated into the ranks of the Party, including its leading personnel. The

party was unprepared and unable to work underground. These errors culminated in the dissolution ...[25]

Bernstein's description of what happened is less anodyne, although his analysis is basically the same as that offered by Harmel in his *Fifty Fighting Years*.

> For years, the Party had had to fight for its legal rights. It had done too well. Its very success had corroded its political sensitivities and given rise to the illusion that its legal rights had been won forever. Safeguards against possible future illegality could have and should have been in place, but were not. Attention had been focused solely on open and legal activity, so that in the moment of crisis, past sins of omission caught up with the CC. Forty years of legality had coated its revolutionary edge with fat, and principle had been overtaken by pragmatism. By the time the CC met to see its defences they had already fallen into disuse. It had clutched at the 'legal opinion' like a drowning man at a straw.[26]

The legal opinion sought by the central committee argued that if the party agreed unanimously to dissolve itself (there being insufficient time to call a national conference to do so), it would safeguard against the persecution of party members.[27] The fear of persecution was a real concern, particularly in light of the tone used by Minister of Justice C R 'Blackie' Swart, when he introduced the Bill in Parliament, speaking of communist plans for armed insurrection and the poisoning of water supplies.[28] Typically, the United Party's position on any Nationalist Party proposal surged from supine to asinine, and it proposed an amendment to the Bill that would make communism a treasonable offence punishable by death.[29] Given the anti-communist hysteria of the time, as CPSA member Rowley Arenstein noted, '... when the Party was declared illegal, none of us knew what it meant – whether we were going to be picked up and put into concentration camps, we had visions of Nazi Germany ...'.[30]

The 'legalistic illusions' referred to by the SACP, coupled with the rigours of underground activity, have been taken by most commentators to be adequate comment on the dissolution of the CPSA, the three-year gap before the SACP was founded, and the non-appearance in the ranks of the new party of such leading (and very different) communists as Sam Kahn, former CPSA Johannesburg District Secretary Danie du Plessis, Cape lawyer Harry Snitcher, Edwin Mofutsanyana and others.

While influenced by considerations of safety – or, in Bernstein's more caustic view, having left itself completely unprepared and with no 'alternative to this whimpering finale'[31] – Central Committee members who voted in favour of dissolution seem to have done so from two mutually antagonistic positions. Some had 'convinced themselves that there was no future for the party in the new conditions',[32] while others saw the dissolution as a means of sidestepping the legal sanctions of the Suppression of

Communism Act. Harmel stated: 'Subsequent events made clear the distinction between those among the former leadership who regarded the dissolution as a temporary and tactical expedient and those who had come to doubt the need for the very existence of the independent Marxist-Leninist Party of the working class.'[33]

Once the decision was taken Moses Kotane toured the country to explain it to party members and to get the required endorsement. CPSA members Jack and Ray Simons have stated that the dissolution was 'accepted without dissent'.[34] This is, however, at best, dissembling. Rowley Arenstein explains:

> Most of us got the impression that this was a legal ploy. And the next thing was that Moses Kotane arrived in Durban, called everybody together and said 'Look, I'm just telling you something, whatever motion I'm going to put I want a unanimous decision, it has to be a unanimous decision.' Now, the ploy was that we didn't have enough time to disband the Party in terms of the Constitution, so the advice we got was that every district must unanimously agree that the Party must be disbanded. In other words, we were given instructions that we must unanimously decide to disband the Party. So, after he told us to do it unanimously, we did it unanimously![35]

Just as Central Committee members had a variety of reasons for voting for dissolution, the unanimity of the rank and file vote for dissolution similarly obscures their different attitudes to the move.

The overwhelming feeling within the ranks was that dissolution was a 'ploy'.[36] As Transvaal member Hilda Bernstein (née Watts) put it, 'we thought that what they intended was officially above-ground to say the Party had been dissolved, whereas actually it would continue'.[37]

It was widely expected that the CPSA would reappear underground almost immediately[38] but such hopes were soon dashed: 'legalistic illusions' had taken a firm hold on the party leadership. Earlier calls for the CPSA to move into underground work had been rejected by the Central Committee, which argued that it was not possible to convert the legal CPSA into an illegal party.[39]

Central Committee members argued that the CPSA had operated 'in the full glare of publicity'[40] and that its members were known to the police, who had seized membership lists in 1946. In addition, many members had joined the party during its period of wartime 'respectability' and could not be expected to operate illegally.[41] Central Committee member Fred Carneson, speaking 'from my point of view and from the organisation's point of view, being [Cape] Party secretary', stressed that 'you couldn't take the apparatus that we had at that stage and take it underground'. Furthermore, the Party wanted to control its own disbanding 'rather than wait until the bloody Special Branch struck at us with all that that meant'.[42]

This analysis of the situation was not universally shared. For Michael Harmel the 'legal-istic illusions' of the CPSA leadership were represented precisely by the lack of prepared-ness of the party, which, '[d]espite the open threats of the Nationalist Party to ban the C.P.' had taken 'no effective steps … to prepare for underground existence and illegal work' and by their unwillingness to at least try it.[43] Harmel did not write simply with the benefit of hindsight. The Transvaal division of the CPSA had unsuccessfully attempted to institute a second-string leadership that could operate in the event of mass arrest,[44] and a number of Transvaal members had agitated for full preparation for underground work.[45]

These proposals had been rejected by the Central Committee, whose members argued that 'if your Party is threatened, you concentrate your attention on beating off that threat'.[46] Differences over the issue were significant, for they fed into existing regional disharmony between the Cape and the Transvaal.[47] The decision to dissolve the Party came to be seen (in part) in the light of such regional differences; as Bernstein explained, 'more than half of the Central Committee were Capetonians … and the Cape Central Committee dissolved the Party'.[48] When the SACP was launched, in 1953, it was very firmly based in the Transvaal.

Central Committee members had supported dissolution, believing there to be 'little alternative at that stage'.[49] But they had different understandings of their future role, which only became clear once the CPSA had been disbanded. Where some members had seen dissolution as a tactical manoeuvre, for others it was final. Carneson noted that 'all sorts of arguments were put forward but basically they didn't want to get mixed up in anything illegal, didn't want to stick their necks out'.[50] Similar scorn is evident among others who later joined the South African Communist Party.

The formation of the SACP

Disquiet grew when dissolution was not followed by the reconstitution of the party, and it slowly dawned on the general membership that the decision was, indeed, final.

Hilda Bernstein recalled that 'the ones who took the decision on the Central Committee intended that it should be disbanded. We waited to be contacted, to be told "you're appointed to such-and-such a group", and "you're going to work with so-and-so" – we were sort of innocent or naïve or stupid members of the Party'.[51] In the event '… we waited, and we waited, and we waited, and it didn't happen!'[52] The 1950/51 period was 'a very strange time'[53] during which 'a lot of people [were] running around saying, "what's happening to the re-formation?" Nothing was happening'.[54]

Many former members, waiting for news of the underground reconstitution of the Party, maintained contact and formed small, informal socialist groups and ad hoc com-mittees; in some cases these groups included left-wing whites who had not been CPSA members.[55] But without some central guidance the situation was confused, as Hilda Bernstein explained:

After a while when we weren't approached and nothing happened, people ten-tatively began to speak to others and little groups began forming. It was at that time that … some people in Johannesburg decided, well, it's going to be dangerous. Everybody's going to be forming little Communist Party groups, we'd better get together and establish a proper party.[56]

While at local level small socialist groups were forming, nationally the former CPSA lead-ership met irregularly to review political developments and discuss their future strategy.

In Cape Town former Central Committee members held informal meetings 'to dis-cuss current political issues and always, invariably, what about restarting the party'.[57] It was during these discussions that differences between them over the future of the Party became clear. A national meeting of the Party's leaders was called in 1951 to discuss the question of restarting the party; as Fred Carneson explained:

It became clear at this last meeting we had where we were all together, the old leadership, that there was an unthinkable gap there between those who were determined to reform the party on an illegal basis and those who weren't pre-pared to come in. So it was at that stage that we parted company as far as the Communist Party organisation was concerned.[58]

The lengthy reassessment taking place within the national leadership did not include rank-and-file party members. As a result, and in the absence of any national initiative, communists began at a local level 'a slow process of feeling each other's attitudes out'.[59]

The Central Committee members' different understanding of dissolution was also reflected among ordinary party members. This was the moment when those who sup-ported the permanent disbanding of the CPSA ceased their active political involvement.[60] Those who had regarded the decision to disband as a ploy became disillusioned with former colleagues and leaders. According to SACP members, dissatisfaction grew among rank-and-file former CPSA members who were excluded from moves to reconstitute the Communist Party. Turok noted that former CPSA members in the Western Cape confronted Congress organisers in the 1950s about the issue:

I came across a coloured village in the Western Cape where the members buried their cards in a tin box with plastic around it. When I came there for the Congress of the People in 1954, they spoke to us in very angry terms. They said before we talk to you about the Congress of the People you must please explain to us what happened to the party because we were told to dis-solve, we buried our cards – they sent somebody out and brought the cards in – and as far as they were concerned they were totally opposed to dissolu-tion. I'm told this story could be repeated up and down the country. It's quite clear that the membership was neither consulted nor accepted the decision. I can't put a figure on it but I think that a substantial number of members were in that position.[61]

The roots of the SACP lie in the initiative taken by the Transvaal group, which was headed by Michael Harmel and included (among others) Rusty and Hilda Bernstein, Moses Kotane (who had moved to Johannesburg), Yusuf Dadoo, J B Marks, Jack Hodgson, Bram Fischer, and a number of Young Communist League members such as Joe Slovo and Ruth First. The Transvaal initiative appears to have cut across discussions taking place among former CPSA leaders, although the precise relationship between the two processes remains unclear. The founders of the new party were, however, former CPSA Transvaal District Committee members: 'it started with them, and later it was canvassed around the country'.[62] The Cape's leadership of the party had had its time.

The Transvaal group began a process of national consultation prior to forming the SACP.[63] With new rules about recruitment and observing strict security, the SACP was formed between 1951 and 1952; its first national conference was held in 1953, and by the time its second national conference took place, in 1954, 'a pretty solid skeleton', with some 100 members, was in place.[64] Having decided to combine legal work within existing organisations with 'persistent planned illegal work to rebuild and strengthen the party as the vanguard of the most advanced class, the working class', the SACP did not make its existence public until 1960.[65]

While Peter Delius[66] cites as part of the story of the emerging SACP its organisational work in the old Northern Transvaal, and Raymond Suttner has described the activities of various communists and small left-wing groups which slowly came together in the new Party, the fact that the Party grew from many organisational roots (albeit thinly populated) does not detract from the point being made here – that the Johannesburg debates created the *ideological* basis for the SACP and its alliance with the congresses. As Suttner notes, 'Insofar as there may be some truth in the argument that advancing of "Colonialism of a Special Type" was crucial to the SACP's reconstitution, it would certainly have been a factor that facilitated the development of an alliance between the SACP and the national liberation movement, led by the ANC.'[67]

The SACP is commonly presented as the *reconstitution* of the CPSA,[68] implying that the ideology of the CPSA and those members prepared to work underground was taken over intact by the SACP. Because the SACP operated illegally, the non-appearance within its ranks of some senior CPSA members has been ascribed to an aversion to the stringencies of illegal work. Discussing CPSA members who did not join the SACP, however, Bunting couldn't resist a dig:

While not disavowing any of their former ideals, they felt either that they as individuals could not meet the requirements of underground work, or that the Communist Party itself could not survive in the face of the expected Government attack. Later, inevitably, some of them were to rationalise their own weakness and develop 'ideological differences' with the party and its leadership.[69]

The SACP, according to Bernstein, 'came out of the old Party'.[70] It did so, however, with its headquarters in the Transvaal and with a new leadership dominated by Transvaal members. It was influenced in particular by Michael Harmel, described by a former SACP member as 'the theoretical giant of the movement' and a leading proponent of internal colonialism.[71] The last two years of the CPSA's existence were marked by tension over the question which, according to one commentator, had 'almost obsessed' the CPSA since its inception – the relationship between class and the national struggle, and that of a class party to a national liberation movement.[72]

As the centre of power within the new party shifted from the Cape to the Transvaal it came under the control of communists who believed in a closer relationship with the Congress movement and greater support for the national struggle. While the basis for the SACP was being laid between 1951 and 1953, former CPSA members freely debated this relationship, a debate dominated by the theoretical perspectives of leading SACP members and given fresh urgency by the concurrent Defiance Campaign. In this context ideological differences emerged which represented more than the rationalisations of timorous former CPSA members.

Race or class – the debates of 1952–1954

The debates of 1952–1954 were crucial in creating the ideological and strategic context within which white radicals – communist and non-communist – operated throughout the 1950s, although these remain under-researched. Lambert's work was an early exception, but he analysed the implications for trade unionism of internal colonialism and ignored the wider context of CPSA politics in the late 1940s, of which the debates of the 1950s were an extension. Lambert also restricted his analysis to the journal *Viewpoints and Perspectives*, issued by the Johannesburg Discussion Club, and thereby missed an essential point: that the debates took place nationally and involved the South African left as a whole, not just former CPSA members.[73]

The debates of the early 1950s were, in many ways, an extension of the internal discussions of the CPSA in the late 1940s. As Jack Simons explained in 1954,

> The problem has become even more complicated than it used to be by reason of the attacks which the Nationalist Government has carried on against the working class organisations. The old balance, arrived at by constant interaction between the two sections, has been seriously upset, and the working class point of view tends to be overlooked.[74]

Communists and Marxists were searching for an adequate response to the rapidly changing political terrain of post-war South Africa, which was dominated by the rise of African and Afrikaner nationalism. According to Fred Carneson:

> Until the African National Congress, or the Congress movement, emerged as a real political force in South Africa, I think there was a tendency among the activists inside and outside the party to see things in class terms more than in national liberatory terms. Particularly so, I think, amongst some of the white communists, though it was not confined to the white communists by any manner of means.[75]

The central point at issue for the white left as a whole was the place of class struggle in a period dominated by nationalism and nationalist organisations. And, at a more immediate and personal level, the place of whites in an African nationalist struggle was also at stake. This was exacerbated by the confused interlude between the dissolution of the CPSA and the formation of the SACP, and the fact that while black former CPSA members worked in the Congress movement, white communists were without a political home.

The problem was given added urgency as the Defiance Campaign grew in size and significance. The increasingly anti-white nature of the late stages of the campaign generated fears that extreme nationalist sentiment was spreading in the country, and in the ANC. Such fears were not restricted to former communists, nor to whites generally. Defiance Campaign volunteer-in-chief Nelson Mandela appealed for whites to identify themselves with the campaign and not unite in opposition to it; if they did so, they would be 'digging their own grave' by 'turn[ing] the whole movement into a racial front with disastrous consequences for all'.[76]

The white response to Mandela's appeal was twofold: on the one hand, organisations such as the Congress of Democrats and the Democratic League were formed, while on the other, socialists and former CPSA members debated the best means of highlighting underlying class alignments, which, they argued, were being obscured by rising nationalism.

Discussion groups were set up with the aim of 'furnishing an opportunity for frank theoretical discussion'.[77] Participants in the debates stood 'solidly behind the broad aims of the Liberatory struggle' but were not committed 'to the policies of any particular group, tendency or movement within the democratic camp'.[78] The debates were marked by free and open discussion as former CPSA members, freed of party discipline, joined socialists, Trotskyists and others (also freed by the absence of a communist party) in debating the place of class struggle in a period dominated by nationalism. It is worth noting that most of the debaters were white leftists; South Africa's 'uniqueness' was seen to derive from the permanent presence of a sizeable white population and much of the debate focused on the place and role of white activists in the anti-apartheid struggle.

Leading members of the new party called for closer relations with the Congress movement and for all progressive whites to work in and for the Congress Alliance. In so doing, however, they alienated a number of former CPSA members and others, who warned that nationalist movements would stop well short of the complete social transformation desired by the working class. As a result, some members of the white left called for the building of a 'cohesive organisation ... [of] the major protagonist, the industrial working class' and an alliance with its 'natural' allies, 'the rural workers and the migrant labourers'.[79] The same positions would be bitterly fought out in the 1980s.

Initially the debates were not polarised between two coherent opposing positions but by the time the last edition of *Viewpoints and Perspectives* came out in 1954 it was clear that there were two different positions: 'The two most frequently heard formulations of the liberation struggle depend on this assessment of "a capitalist or imperialist exploited South Africa".'[80]

These differing analyses of South Africa society generated different understandings of the best means of pursuing class struggle – through an intimate working alliance with the congresses or by building an independent working-class organisation which would enjoy limited co-operation with the Congress Alliance but would be organisationally (and ideologically) separate. Communists could be found supporting both positions.

Lambert has suggested that the two positions represented 'subtle' differences of 'emphasis';[81] those who called for the independent organisation of the working class are described as marking 'a shift of emphasis *within* the dominant position'.[82] This attempt to finesse fundamental rifts was no more true of the debates in the 1950s than it would be of those between 'workerists' and 'charterists' in the 1980s.

Perspectives on oppression

The expression 'internal colonialism' was first used by Lenin, and later by Gramsci, to describe a situation where, in a given society, there are political and economic inequalities between regions; it has also been used to describe the uneven effects of state development across regions and by race relations theorists:

> to describe the underprivileged status and exploitation of minority groups within the wider society ... The members of [an internal colony] may be differentiated by ethnicity, religion, language or some other cultural variable; they are then overtly or covertly excluded from prestigious social and political positions ...[83]

In the 1960s it was used by Malcolm X and Martin Luther King and, since then, has appeared in the work of a number of theorists and activists in different parts of the world.[84] Despite its robust pedigree, the concept of internal colonialism, as it emerged in the early 1950s, was premised on a broad left consensus that South Africa was unique and required an amended theory of struggle.

This uniqueness was seen to derive from a number of factors, of which the most important was the presence of a white community, which, while permanently settled in the country, nonetheless controlled a system of exploitation whose main features (discrimination against the entire indigenous population, migrant labour, a racially divided working class) were found in colonial situations elsewhere.

Secondly, under this system the growth and development of an indigenous black bourgeoisie had not been encouraged; in fact, all agreed, it had been deliberately frustrated. Moreover, the 'industrial revolution' triggered by the Second World War promised to increase the size and significance of the industrial proletariat, although black South Africans were seen to exhibit little class consciousness.[85]

These factors had considerable implications for the resistance movement in South Africa. As in colonial situations elsewhere, racial discrimination had given rise to a national liberation movement. In South Africa, however, the lack of a significant indigenous bourgeoisie affected both the nature and goals of the national movement. Some argued these were overwhelmingly working class in composition and, increasingly, in leadership; others saw the opposite – a proletarian membership but bourgeois leadership and goals. Some argued that while the working class grew in size, its ability to organise was restricted by the lack of basic citizenship rights for blacks. As a result, according to trade unionist and CPSA/SACP member Eli Weinberg, '[i]t is natural that in these conditions the African workers have developed a class consciousness tinged with nationalism'.[86]

The possible permutations of these different factors led participants in the debates of the early 1950s to conclude that orthodox models of resistance in colonial and semi-colonial countries did not apply to South Africa. The debates were significant because it was argued that the South African resistance movement could not be understood in terms of models developed elsewhere. Jack Simons argued in 1954 that 'the solution to our problems here will call for a great deal of Original, Independent, Creative thinking'.[87] He continued: 'In order to be true Marxists … we must be truly Africanist (this is a term of convenience to describe Marxists today).'[88]

Without a Communist Party in place, former CPSA members questioned the usefulness to South Africa of both Stalin's contribution to thinking on the national question and the various positions adopted by the Communist Information Bureau (Cominform). The relationship between national liberation and socialist struggle had been the subject of intense debate among Marxists (and others) throughout the twentieth century. Early meetings of the Communist International (Comintern) were dominated by debates between Lenin and the Indian Communist, Roy, over the correct approach to colonial movements which were simultaneously bourgeois and anti-imperialist.

Roy argued for the complete separation of working class from national movements while Lenin supported temporary alliances between the two in the broader anti-imperial struggle. The Second Comintern Congress resolved to support what Lenin termed 'national revolutionary movements' where they did not hinder working-class mobilisation, but stressed the need for separate working-class and national organisations; a strategically useful fudge.[89]

Hudson has shown how positions on these issues fluctuated in subsequent congresses, largely in response to the needs of the Soviet Union's foreign policy. The Cominform, created in 1947, initially accepted Zhdanov's analysis of a post-war world divided into two hostile camps – the 'anti-imperialist democratic' and the 'imperialist anti-democratic'.[90] Bourgeois-led nationalist movements were seen to be part of the latter category.

Two years later the Cominform changed its view, arguing that the national bourgeoisie in colonial situations could best attain its goals through an anti-imperial alliance with the working class and peasantry. Such national movements would bring about 'national democracy', a state neither capitalist nor socialist in which the bourgeoisie could flourish, and increase the productive forces and size of the working class.[91]

Shifts in Cominform thinking came as conditions in South Africa were changing rapidly and forcing Marxists to undertake a domestic review of the relationship between socialist struggle and national liberation. They consciously strove to develop indigenous theories of change, with some arguing that 'the South African liberatory movement has no exact precedent' and that, as a result, South African conditions required 'an amended theory of struggle'.[92]

Initially, debates within the white left were dominated by speakers hostile to nationalism and supportive of class struggle. The broader context within which the debates took place, however, was that of the underground regrouping of communists and the formation of the SACP in 1953. After 1953, leading SACP members made highly significant interventions in which they outlined 'colonialism of a special type' (CST) (i.e. internal colonialism). In so doing, they appealed for what they saw as a middle course between the poles of class and national struggle. This could be attained, they argued, by merging the two. The new line was clear by the time the debates ended and organisational work again became important in SACOD, the SACP, for some the Liberal Party, and for others a clutch of tiny Trotskyist groups.

The minority view: the primacy of class struggle

Two perspectives on the liberation movement in South Africa became clear during the debates of the early 1950s. Summarising the two, former CPSA member Myrtle Berman stressed South Africa's 'unique' position in having 'neither a well-developed Non-European bourgeoisie nor a class-conscious Non-European proletariat'.[93] Because of this, two conflicting interpretations of the course the resistance movement would follow had arisen. The first argued that:

> In the course and realisation of the National Liberatory Struggle an African bourgeoisie will develop, and the classic pattern will follow from then onwards. The proletariat will have gained certain political freedoms but not its economic freedom … Only when this political freedom has been achieved, will the proletariat become truly aware of the nature of their still present economic disabilities and develope [sic] class consciousness.[94]

The second position argued that the specific conditions in South Africa would directly affect the nature and course of the national liberation struggle.

> Just because there is no well-developed bourgeoisie it is just as likely that the class conscious elements will assume leadership and that the interests of the bourgeoisie will be pushed aside. In this case, the nature of the struggle will broaden to include economic demands, ie. the demands will be not only for the extension of existing freedoms and privileges to all, but a fundamental change in economic relations.[95]

In the 1940s the Communist Party had stressed the primacy of class struggle and the dangers of nationalism obscuring class oppression. In the changed conditions of the early 1950s, however, class struggle and the development of separate working-class structures lacked the support (and thus legitimacy) of leading black communists, and emerged as the minority viewpoint within the white left. This perspective also lacked the coherence provided by a single leading theoretician (as Michael Harmel was to provide for CST). Rather, a number of counter arguments were proffered in response to calls for close working links with the Congress movement. Some argued that South Africa was a capitalist country in which national struggle served to obscure class oppression, while others focused critical attention on the dangers of nationalism generally and the weaknesses of the ANC in particular. All, however, reached the same conclusion – that the interests of the working class could not be safeguarded within a nationalist movement.

Those who contended that nationalist movements were a home for bourgeois emancipation but not working-class freedom argued that the focus of activity for the white left should be the organisation of the working class in separate structures. As the size of the working class grew, it was argued, its independent organisation was feasible. With rapid industrialisation and the creation of modern factories with large concentrations of workers, 'the possibility and likelihood of powerful, stable, mass social and political working class organisations coming into being is created'.[96] Echoing the CPSA position, it was argued that because the working class was growing rapidly, conditions existed that allowed for non-racial class unity where 'the immediate value of the colour bar has become much less by comparison with the long-term value to the white workers of working class unity'.[97]

Industrialisation, it was argued, had transformed South Africa into a capitalist country. The massive growth of secondary industry, with its need for a stable, urban labour force, its stated opposition to migrant labour and the higher wages it paid to black workers, was seen as a critical turning point in the country's economic development. Summarising the 'industrial revolution' of the war years, CPSA member and economist Guy Routh (later to be the young Thabo Mbeki's tutor at Sussex when both were in exile) stressed the challenge that had emerged to the migrant labour system and the colour bar: 'Whole new industries have come into being, staffed almost entirely by non-whites, whilst others have been converted from a white to a non-white working force.'[98]

Routh's assessment of these economic changes was taken by some to mean that colonial forms of exploitation – migrant labour, the racial division of the working class, the industrial colour bar – were no longer determining factors in the economy. While debaters agreed that secondary industry was too closely tied to mining capital to amount to a serious challenge to existing relations, some saw its effect as being to expose colonial forms of exploitation as mere *'forms or external appearances'*.[99] According to one commentator: 'The fact that the ruling class was overwhelmingly white and the working class overwhelmingly black should not affect the conclusion that this is a class society and that it is a class struggle that is being waged.'[100]

For supporters of class struggle, colonial forms of exploitation served merely to obscure the underlying reality of capitalist exploitation. The resistance movement, they argued, should act accordingly. As one participant explained:

> To my mind, the absence of a *conscious* class struggle should not obscure the fact that a class struggle actually exists. If one accepts as I do that South Africa is a capitalist country it should be clear that however the struggle manifests itself, it nevertheless remains a class struggle ... it is only lack of experience and technique that holds back the development of the class struggle.[101]

Capitalist relations, it was argued, were not restricted to mining and industry but were spreading to the rural areas. The result was the capitalisation of agriculture and the replacement of labour; in the process, a rural proletariat was coming into being. The techniques of class struggle could be exported to the rural areas precisely by means of migrant labour, through which the rural population experienced 'growing contact with the towns and with the concepts of the industrial worker and miner'.[102]

Finally, because South Africa had 'no [black] bourgeoisie worth speaking of', the needs of blacks were said to be 'largely in accord [with each other]'.[103] Taken with the claim that white workers had a diminishing interest in the maintenance of the colour bar this led some to conclude that national struggle was obfuscatory. 'The problems are those of a capitalist country with remnants of colonialism still existing and the chief opposing forces are the capitalists and the industrial workers.'[104]

Thus, the first task of the liberation movement should be to concentrate on organising 'the major protagonist' in the struggle, the industrial proletariat.[105]

While some argued in favour of class struggle because of prevailing conditions, others focused on the dangers to working-class struggle of nationalism and nationalist movements. Critics, ranging from the NEUM to former Communist Party members, argued

that 'Every national movement has as its objective the triumph of capitalist democracy.'[106]
The weakness and slow growth of the ANC before 1952 was ascribed to 'its failure',
laid at the door of its bourgeois leadership, 'to bring the economic (or class) issues
before the people'.[107] According to former CPSA Johannesburg District Chairperson
Danie du Plessis, ANC leadership was overwhelmingly bourgeois.

> In South Africa, where a strong local capitalism has developed, the aim of the
> incipient bourgeoisie among the oppressed people is to integrate themselves
> into the existing local capitalism rather than to oust the oppressors. The
> demand is for equal rights and not 'quit South Africa'.[108]

Du Plessis went further, arguing that because of its bourgeois leadership the ANC
would by no means be immune from the crises that would afflict capitalism as
decolonisation speeded up. For Du Plessis, capitalism had reached its highest stage,
imperialism, and, as access to colonial markets contracted, so opposing classes would
coalesce into two hostile blocs. Such a situation, he argued, provided 'the necessary
conditions for working class unity'.[109] It also allowed for an alliance between working-
class organisations and the national liberation movement, but with an important
caveat: the (bourgeois) leaders of the national movement would not be unaffected by
the polarisation of society.

> ... [It] must be remembered that businessmen, financiers, landlords, etc., place
> their vested interests first ... The Liberatory Movement is to be assessed by its
> leadership and policy, irrespective of its constituent membership. The leaders
> are bourgeois or bourgeois-agents. The class composition of its leadership,
> the slogans adopted by them, the passive methods of struggle, are proof of
> the weaknesses of the movement ... In a depression [the leaders] would join
> forces with the government against the workers and would first protect their
> own interests.[110]

Du Plessis's comments highlight a number of key assumptions that informed the discussion of national movements in the early 1950s, many of which had been raised in
the earlier Lenin–Roy debates. The first was that national liberation movements were
launched by the oppressed national bourgeoisie, who maintained control of the movements even if they gained a mass following. The second assumption, flowing from this,
was that the aims of the movement reflected the aspirations of the oppressed bourgeoisie – that is, the desire for integration in existing capitalist structures where they
could operate freely.[111] Consequently, national liberation movements were seen as
characterised by political demands rather than the economic demands of working-
class organisations. As Kenny Jordaan of NEUM explained:

… a national liberatory movement must not be confused with the movement for the social ownership of the instruments of labour. The one involves a political revolution, nothing more, nothing less; the other argues a social revolution to change the very economic basis of society.[112]

Du Plessis argued that in South Africa the realisation of national liberation would result in a situation where '[s]egregation between the races may disappear but social segregation between classes will remain'.[113]

As a result, a number of participants in the debates called for working-class structures to be built separately from the bourgeois-launched and -led national movements. While limited co-operation over specific campaigns was possible, it was stressed that:

[t]he two classes can and should retain their separate identities. Also, it is clear that the two classes can only co-operate when, and in so far as, their interests are the same. This situation has never lasted for long. The bourgeoisie only wishes to carry the democratic struggle far enough to remove the restrictions on their business interests.[114]

Those who called for greater stress to be laid on class than on national struggle did so for a variety of reasons. Some saw South Africa as a capitalist society in which remnants of a colonial past still existed, so African nationalism was a response to the external forms adopted by capitalism and had misread the nature of oppression in the country. Others argued that the aims of the working class simply could not be realised through national struggle and called for the development of independent working-class structures. After 1953, with the birth of the SACP, the debate came to be dominated by the ideological perspectives of leading SACP theoreticians … and the theory of colonialism of a special type.

The majority view: colonialism of a special type

As the ANC grew in the late 1940s the Communist Party had to reassess its approach to nationalism and nationalist organisations. This move was led by the Transvaal and Natal districts, where party members worked closely with the growing Congress movement. In 1950 the CPSA Central Committee could argue that South Africa represented 'colonialism of a special type', that is, it exhibited:

… the characteristics of both an imperialist state and colony within a single, indivisible, geographical, political and economic entity … The Non-European population, while reduced to the status of a colonial people, has no territory of its own, no Independent existence, but is almost wholly integrated in the political and economic institutions of the ruling class.[115]

The new SACP, led by former CPSA members from the Transvaal, adopted CST as its policy[116] and Michael Harmel and Rusty Bernstein spelt out its implications at the Johannesburg Discussion Club. Equally significant contributions, however, came from outside Johannesburg. In 1954, Jack Simons – who did not join the party for another two decades, believing no independent party was needed given the rise of the nationalist liberation movement[117] – gave an important series of lectures outlining the implications of the theory,[118] which, in the same year, also featured in a Cape Town Forum Club symposium on the national question.[119]

Finally, it is argued here that the theory of internal colonialism also drew on the colonial analysis of South African oppression proposed by the ANC Youth League, reflected, inter alia, in a 1954 speech by former Youth League president Joe Matthews, one of the first public speeches outlining CST.[120] CST was a very South African admixture of domestic theorising and strategising emerging from resistance, grafted onto and morphing imported theory.

The proponents of CST started from what they saw as a pragmatic position. South Africa, as the 1950 Central Committee Report had argued, had entered a period of heightened national conflict. The situation imposed its own constraints on the actions of socialists generally, and whites in particular, as Rusty Bernstein explained:

> We could, in other times … have blueprinted ideal schemes, and formulated ideal organisational arrangements. To do so today would be to isolate ourselves from the forces that are already in action for democratic advance … We have to work with what we have.[121]

Bernstein, Harmel and others began by analysing the relationship between class and national struggle as they saw it. Secondly, founding members of the SACP recognised that the debates of the white left were, in large part, a product of the confusion generated by the disbanding of the CPSA. The elaboration of CST should thus be seen in context, as an ideological intervention specifically aimed at resolving the confusion engendered by the sudden disbanding of the CPSA, the delayed formation of the SACP and the growing importance of nationalism.

Transvaal communists, having taken the initiative in establishing the organisational basis of the SACP, had also to make an ideological intervention in the debates that were marked by support for class struggle and hostility to national struggle. Both Bernstein and Harmel roundly attacked those '… who stand outside the struggle; who stand on a lofty peak of class purity, and condemn the struggle for the alliance and the co-operation of classes within it'.[122]

Stressing the need to tailor strategies to existing conditions, CST supporters also attacked those '… even amongst former Communists who reject the movement because it does not conform to their ideas of a pure exclusive working class movement, struggling alone and unaided against all other classes'.[123]

Those hostile to national struggle were seen 'to disrupt the movement, confuse the active people in it, and if unchecked and uncountered in the field of ideology will destroy it'.[124]

CST had as its starting point the assertion that South Africa was unique, marked by a singular social and political arrangement which flowed from the permanence of a large white community: 'The whole character and aims of the national question is complicated by this white element which is not a feature of any other colonial or dependent country'.[125]

According to Michael Harmel, although whites had settled permanently in South Africa, there was:

> ... no qualitative difference between the status of the Africans (and, in the main, the other non-white population groups) in the Union and those else-where in Africa – or the people of any other colonial territory. 'Colonial' living standards, deprivation of political rights and constitutional liberties, the delib-erate efforts to prevent their economic and cultural developments – all these are characteristics of colonialism. Similarly, the relationship between the white rulers of South Africa and the non-white masses is essentially imperialistic. In a word: there are two nations in South Africa, occupying the same state, side by side in the same area. White South Africa is a semi-independent impe-rialistic state: Black South Africa is its colony. This almost unique dualism has its roots in our history.[126]

The historical roots of internal colonialism were traced back to the discovery of gold in the 1880s: thereafter, the main drive of the South African state had been the main-tenance of 'a mass, stable, cheap labour force', which was crucial 'if they were to derive maximum profits from gold-mining'.[127]

Supporters of CST accepted (though their critics strongly disputed that they followed through on this) that 'of course, every question is at its roots "a class question"...'.[128] They also agreed that the organisation of race relations in a capitalist society facilitated racial exploitation that 'serves the same purpose as the usual type of class exploita-tion'.[129] But Jack Simons argued that South Africa did not fit such a pattern: 'the special features of race exploitation are often so numerous and marked, as is the case in South Africa, that it is almost qualitatively different from class exploitation'.[130]

Because of these special features, which were seen to stem from the essentially colonial relationship between black and white, 'the class struggle is greatly affected by divisions based on racial features'.[131] The major factor that affected the class struggle was the fact that, in response to colonial forms of oppression, black South Africans had launched an increasingly popular national liberation struggle. As a result, the ANC lay at the centre of the debate over CST.

The ANC: bourgeois nationalism or peoples' movement?

A central argument used by those hostile to, or suspicious of, national struggle was that colonial movements comprised an alliance of classes, which were dominated by the oppressed national bourgeoisie which sought inclusion in capitalist structures, rather than their overthrow. Harmel accepted that in South Africa the national movement was an alliance of classes, 'a familiar characteristic of such movements among oppressed colonial peoples everywhere'.[132] He further noted that colonial movements were commonly 'marked by the dominance of the bourgeoisie', which, at times of crisis, 'betrayed the movement in order to reach a compromise with imperialism at the expense of the masses'.[133] But Harmel, Bernstein, Simons and others all argued that it was entirely wrong '… to generalise mechanistically from overseas experience and assume that the Congresses are mere "bourgeois affairs" from which "pure working class elements" should stand aloof or which they should attempt to disrupt'.[134]

In the first place, it was argued, international comparisons did not take account of the fact that a particular function of racial oppression in South Africa had been deliberately to restrict the development of a black bourgeoisie.

> The special feature of imperialism in South Africa is the existence of the large population of the dominant imperialist nationality, side by side in the same territory as the oppressed colonial people. This has resulted in the virtual exclusion of the non-white peoples, especially the Africans, from the commercial and other opportunities which the development of imperialism afforded to a small minority in other colonies …[135]

As a result, Bernstein explained, black South Africa had no bourgeoisie of note: 'The South African bourgeoisie of the oppressed consists of petty traders, money lenders and landlords.'[136] Because of this the ANC could not be compared with colonial movements elsewhere.

The difference between the ANC and other colonial movements was further apparent in its demand for equality rather than self-determination. According to Jack Simons, 'that demand is not the same as the programme of "cultural autonomy" or "secession" … it contemplates a common society with the Europeans on a completely equal basis'.[137]

Legal equality, however, as Du Plessis and others had predicted, could be realised within a capitalist state. Moreover, the ANC's concentration on formulating political rather than economic demands signalled a bourgeois dominance. Up to this point differences within the white left could still be seen as issues of emphasis, as noted earlier; subsequent analyses, however, diverged sharply.

The central argument used by Simons, Bernstein, Harmel and others in favour of working closely with national movements was that the Congress movement was in a transitional phase with regard to its leadership, the strategies it adopted and the demands it made. All argued that the influence of the working class was increasingly evident within the ANC in particular; the endorsement of extra-parliamentary action in the 1949 Programme of Action was offered as an example.

In a neat reversal, the opponents of national struggle argued that the central question was the place (and power) of the bourgeoisie in the national movement; those who favoured CST, on the other hand, argued that the central point was the place of the working class within a rapidly changing ANC.

None of those arguing for CST went so far as to claim a working-class leadership for the ANC. For Bernstein, '[t]he question of which class leads is still in the melting pot and may stay there for a long time'.[138] Jack Simons argued that the national organisations as constituted at the time 'must … be described as a form of inter-class nationalism which embraces both an exploiting and an exploited class'.[139]

All argued that what was significant in the Congress movement was not the position it had reached but the future trends evident within it. All called for a close working relationship between communists and nationalists because '… conditions … are conceivable, where the working class is dominant and therefore tends to assume the leadership of the struggle for national liberation'.[140]

Journalist and SACP member Lionel Forman believed the transformation of the Congress movement was already well under way. Control of the congresses, he argued, had '… to a great extent [been] wrested from the hands of the bourgeois and more conservative elements, and leaders who understand the need for struggle against both national oppression and its imperialist economic roots have come to the fore'.[141]

Harmel was somewhat more restrained, but similarly definite, arguing that, in recent years 'the militant working class tendency has wielded increasing influence in our national movements'.[142] The new leaders of both the ANC and the SAIC were cited as evidence; the results of their 'progressive working class policy'[143] was the use of the Defiance Campaign as a tool for mobilisation rather than the 'consent by submission' of Gandhian satyagraha.[144] Walter Sisulu repeated the point decades later, noting: 'We didn't really accept the "passive" aspect … Ours was defying the laws of the country – actively, not passively. We wanted to show the big difference between the two. That is why we called it a "defiance", deliberately.'[145]

The growing influence of the working class, according to Simons and Harmel, would come to be reflected in the methods and demands of the national movement. As the working class took control of the national struggle, according to Simons, so 'this struggle will develop characteristics of the class struggle'.[146] The political demands of previous years would give way to a growing emphasis on economic demands. For all supporters of CST this was central.

Harmel described the ANC as representing 'the advanced progressive anti-imperialist tendency in our country'[147] that would increasingly highlight the economic aspects of national liberation.

The liberation movement has concentrated on formulating political demands. But the economic content of national liberation in South Africa must centre in the redivision of the land and the nationalisation of the principal means of production (for the power of imperialism in this country can only be broken by divorcing the imperialists from the means of production). As the movement grows in strength, confidence and political clarity it is bound to give expression and emphasis to such demands.[148]

The white left as a whole clearly shared a similar set of general assumptions about national movements in South Africa, but, as a result of the way they analysed them, reached very different conclusions. The lack of a significant black bourgeoisie was seen by some to clear the way for working-class unity in a socialist struggle, but, for SACP leaders and others, it provided conditions in which national liberation and class struggles could be merged. Those who remained hostile to nationalist movements because of their perceived incompatibility with working-class demands were accused of an 'undigested and misunderstood reading of a formulation by Stalin that "the slogans of nationalism arise in the market place"'.[149]

The central point at issue was the place of the working class and working-class demands in a national liberation struggle – in South African conditions. To the white left the working class represented 'the most energetic, whole-hearted and thoroughgoing section of the fighters for bourgeois democracy, for national liberation' precisely because it had 'nothing to fear from a revolutionary solution to the crisis of liberation'.[150] But SACP theorists argued that the working class would make specific gains with the realisation of national liberation; these would include political experience, the most conducive conditions under which to organise along class lines, the abolition of the colour bar 'and the clearing away of the race versus class issue, which will leave the class issue clear and exposed for all to see'.[151] Their opponents demurred, believing black bourgeois leaders would sell out their working-class countrymen and women. The contemporaneousness of the debate is striking.

SACP theorists argued that it was incorrect to call for separate working-class structures. The national movement was growing in appeal and militancy, it was argued, because of the influence of the working class within it: 'It is such an alliance – an alliance of the working class and the petty-bourgeois strata of the colonially oppressed peoples of South Africa that is now gaining ground and conducting the Defiance Campaign.'[152]

Because of this, they argued, 'it is precisely the working class that should lead the struggle and that must lead if the struggle is to be completely victorious'.[153] From this essentially pragmatic perspective the supporters of CST called for the broadening of the Congress Alliance rather than a narrow concentration on working-class politics. Speaking directly to the white left, the leading SACP theorists concluded: 'at present it is correct for all democrats to struggle in the national liberation movement of the masses'.[154]

It is ironic – but perhaps more appropriate – that it was Liberal Party leader Leo Marquard who provided the most complete early statement of internal colonialism, in a lecture given at the SAIRR.[155] Despite his leadership position in the (fractious) Liberal Party (discussed in Chapter 6), Marquard's lecture and subsequent pamphlet remain the clearest statement of CST, lacking the jargon and intra-left jabs other versions would carry and reminding us that the roots of the notion of internal colonialism went back into history and had attracted a range of intellectuals as the best conceptual tool for understanding white supremacy and black resistance in South Africa.

The ANCYL and CST

The theory of internal colonialism was a self-consciously pragmatic analysis of South African oppression and the form the resistance movement should take, which took forward an analytical framework implicit in the programme of the CPSA following its endorsement in 1928 of a 'two-stage' revolution. Under pressure from a growing national movement, the CPSA, in the late 1940s, had been unable to balance the requirements of national and class struggle. One section of opinion within the party stressed the primacy of class and the dangers of bourgeois nationalism, another was 'much more sensitive to colour issues and the national question';[156] there was a view that 'these two things had to be resolved and clearly they were slowly resolved through the internal colonialism theory'.[157] But the resolution left many former Communist Party members deeply disaffected, and deeply hostile.

It was clear that CST was a contemporaneous political project, developed by Transvaal communists who had previously called for a closer relationship between the CPSA and the national movements, and who constituted the leadership of the new SACP. The first aim of CST was to resolve differences over race and class. The second was to establish a rapport with the former youth leaguers, now in senior ANC positions. The SACP sought to ally itself in particular with African nationalists and, according to Ben Turok, this was given 'very high priority … [it] was the first issue on the agenda'.[158]

The ANCYL saw itself as part of a pan-African anti-colonial movement and, by the end of the 1940s, was increasingly anti-imperialist and anti-American. As youth leaguers moved into senior ANC positions and began to look for allies among coloureds and whites, they did so explicitly in terms of an internal colonial analysis. The search for non-African allies was explained in the Youth League journal *Afrika!*.

> The path of liberation for the colonial people in the twentieth century lies in the building of powerful national movements which, united with progressive forces in the metropolitan countries, will defeat the imperialists. South Africa is both colonial and imperial at the same time, the liberation movement having to be built in close proximity with advanced elements in the oppressor group.[159]

The SACP saw CST as a means of marrying class struggle with national liberation struggle. For the Youth League, internal colonialism performed a similar function in reverse, incorporating both a nationalist analysis and the growing class analysis used by youth leaguers in the late 1940s. Joe Matthews outlined CST from a nationalist perspective, his starting point closely approximating that of Bernstein, Harmel, Simons and others who stressed South Africa's 'unique' conditions.

Matthews argued: 'South Africa is a colonial country. But it is not a typical colonial country'.[160] South Africa's atypicality derived from its white population, which, because it had settled permanently in the country, was able to exert 'a more complete control of political and economic power than is possible in a typical colonial country ...'.[161] White South Africa did not have to win the support of 'a middle or capitalist class from among the oppressed' and, as a result, 'no middle class (or capitalist class) worth talking about among the Africans has emerged, nor is there ever likely to be one'.[162]

For Matthews, an analysis based on internal colonialism served to emphasise the Youth League's central assertion that Africans suffered dual oppression – 'economic exploitation as workers and labourers and oppression and humiliation as a Nation'. To remove both necessitated an anti-imperialist struggle, in alliance with 'all oppressed and colonial peoples', against 'the major Western powers who are supported in their plans by the U.S.A'. The aims of the national liberation struggle in South Africa, in Matthews's words, were 'Political Power and Independence; Complete Equality, Land, Economic Progress and Culture for all peoples in Afrika'.[163]

Colonialism of a special type was a distinctly pragmatic theoretical tool evolved by a variety of activists between 1950 and 1954 to resolve what Jack Simons described as 'the major problem confronting the Non-Europeans', that is, 'the relationship between the national liberatory struggle and the struggle of socialism'.[164] The same problem, of course, faced white left and liberal activists, and more acutely, as African nationalism was clearly on the rise. The major problem facing the 'Europeans' was whether they fitted into the struggle? And if they did, where? CST sought to answer both questions simultaneously. Drawing on the differing analytical frameworks of the SACP and, to a lesser degree, those of former ANCYL members, CST was taken to mark a major turning point in the South African liberation struggle, the point where 'the class struggle had merged with the struggle for national liberation'.[165]

The adoption of CST brought about 'a very perceptible difference' in the SACP's approach to the ANC from that which had prevailed in the CPSA.[166] CST provided an ideological midpoint at which both nationalists and communists could meet and this, in turn, was the result of a move by ANC members away from extreme nationalism, and the support by SACP members of national struggle. For the white left, the calls from Harmel, Bernstein, Simons and others for whites to work within the Congress Alliance gave added weight to the call from the ANC and SAIC for whites to participate directly in the national liberation struggle. As will be discussed in Chapter 5, it was from this context that the South African Congress of Democrats emerged.

Chapter 5

The South African Congress of Democrats

In November 1952 the African National Congress (ANC) and South African Indian Congress (SAIC) intruded directly into white liberal/left politics, calling for 'a parallel white organisation' which could join the Congress Alliance.[1] The Congress initiative cut across a lengthy process of debate and reassessment taking place among liberal and radical whites, triggered by the growth of African nationalism and reflected in the rise of the Congress movement. The Congress of Democrats (COD) was formed in Johannesburg in response to the call and, a year later, was launched nationally as the South African Congress of Democrats (SACOD).

SACOD emerged as a small, highly vocal and visible white partner of the Congress Alliance, with two main aims: to educate whites about their 'real interests' – a non-racial future with equal rights for all – and to ensure that political conflict took place between 'the progressive forces and the forces of reaction' and did not degenerate into 'a clash on colour or racial lines'.[2] It provided a political home for whites who supported the aims and methods of the ANC, and ensured that white concerns were aired within the Congress Alliance.

Its formation, however, highlighted and exacerbated differences within the white left over the relationship between national and class struggle, and triggered hostility among Africanist elements in the ANC. It is important to locate the launch of SACOD in the wider context of ideological and strategic debate which marked the early 1950s.

White opposition to apartheid 1951–1953: 'Moving into the zone of perpetual crisis'

SACOD was only one of a number of new organisations formed in 1953 to oppose the Nationalist Party (NP) government and its policy of apartheid. Others were the Liberal Party (LP), the Union-Federal Party, the South African Communist Party (SACP) and the South African Coloured People's Organisation (SACPO).

The legislative bedrock of apartheid was laid between 1950 and 1953, when a series of laws, among them the Group Areas Act, the Suppression of Communism Act and the Mixed Marriages Act, entered the statute book. The NP's attempt to disenfranchise coloured voters led to abrogation of the Constitution and an extended constitutional crisis. In response, blacks and whites were mobilised in unprecedented numbers.

The ex-service movement emerged as the leading white opponent of the government and, by 1952, the Torch Commando had approximately 250 000 paid-up members. In the same year the ANC, SAIC and the Franchise Action Committee (FRAC) launched the Defiance Campaign. By the end of 1952 more than 8 000 resisters had been imprisoned for breaking apartheid regulations, and the stature and membership of Congress had changed dramatically. In September 1952 an editorial in the liberal journal *The Forum* summed up political developments thus:

> Let us be frank and confess that things are not going very well in South Africa at present. The Africans are openly flouting the law; the Prime Minister is more or less openly flouting the courts; and racial tensions, between white and white as well as between white and black, are mounting. Why have our affairs been brought to this stage? Why are we moving into the zone of perpetual crisis?[3]

The political upsurge of the early 1950s had two related effects for both liberal and radical whites. Firstly, both were left largely as observers of events whose direction they were unable to control or influence; secondly, as a result of their relative political isolation, both initiated lengthy internal debates to help them accommodate themselves to the new political conditions. Organisational responses, in the shape of the Liberal Association and the Congress of Democrats, were forced on anti-apartheid whites by the need to respond to a rapidly changing political situation and, in particular, to the rise of African nationalism, a force neither liked nor wanted, but which neither could (any longer) avoid.

The disbanding of the Communist Party of South Africa created a political void for whites who supported full equality. While black communists were able to work in the Congress movement whites had no political home. Radical whites in the early 1950s were ideologically divided and disorganised, belonging to a host of often tiny, campaign-oriented organisations as well as small discussion groups scattered across the country. Although lacking a national structure whites remained active in organisations such as FRAC and the Springbok Legion (SL). The Legion, although only a few hundred strong, provided a home for many white activists; it also maintained channels of communication with the ANC and SAIC through which it later played a decisive role in bringing about the formation of COD.

Among the small organisations of the time was the Personal Liberties Defence Committee, a Johannesburg-based body which protested against inroads into civil liberties made by the Suppression of Communism Act; the Western Areas Protest Committee, formed by Father Trevor Huddleston to protest against the forced removal of black residents from the racially mixed suburbs of Sophiatown and Newclare; the Modern Youth Society, a non-racial Cape-based organisation which organised lectures and social events; anti-ban committees, which protested against the prohibitions on political and trade union activists; an anti-Group Areas Act committee in Durban and other ad hoc bodies in different centres.

A number of former Communist Party members became increasingly active in the Springbok Legion, and Legion members were fully involved in the creation and early campaigning of the Torch Commando, to which they brought their flair for dramatic extra-parliamentary action. Responding to anti-communist sentiment, however, the Torch Commando purged legionnaires from its ranks. Organisations such as the Civil Rights League and liberal discussion groups were markedly anti-communist.

In 1952 the Torch Commando formed an electoral alliance with the United Party and Labour Party and moved from extra-parliamentary action to house meetings and voter registration. The political prominence enjoyed by the Commando was rapidly taken over by the Defiance Campaign. In the words of Len Lee-Warden, later SACOD vice-chairperson and a Native Representative, 'while the fever of the Torch Commando cooled off, the temperature in the Congress Alliance increased'.[4] The white left was rendered inactive in the Torch Commando, their lack of an organisational base leaving them impotent if supportive spectators for most of the Defiance Campaign.

The Defiance Campaign, which was primarily intended to mobilise blacks and get them to join Congress, highlighted both the long process of radicalising the ANC, which had begun in the mid-1940s, and the assertiveness of its new leaders, drawn, in large part, from the ranks of the ANC Youth League (ANCYL). Like much Congress activity in the 1950s, however, it was also aimed at white South Africa. By submitting to arrest for breaking apartheid regulations defiers hoped to highlight their lack of status in the country; as ANCYL president Joe Matthews noted: 'We have the white man flat in the moral battle'.[5] A difficult lesson to learn – it would take all of the 1950s – was that victory in the moral battle made no dent in the white power structure. In addition, campaign organisers hoped to influence the white Parliament and white voters to repeal the six 'unjust laws' singled out for protest, and Nelson Mandela argued (sounding uncannily like white liberals with their appeals to reason and common sense):

> If the government refused to [repeal the Acts], we would expect the voters, because of this situation, to say we can't go on with a government like this, we think that this government should make way for a government that is more sensible, more responsible, a government which will change its policy and come to terms with these people, and then they would vote it out of power.[6]

The Defiance Campaign aimed to generate a political cleavage along lines of principle rather than race, but, by the end of 1952, political divisions closely followed racial lines.

This was, in large part, a result of the absence of an unequivocal white rejection of racial discrimination, as previously expressed by white Communist Party members. The Torch Commando approached the 1953 general election by appealing somewhat fatuously for race to be 'taken out of politics', while the United and Labour parties campaigned for 'white leadership with justice'. The differences between these positions were invisible to most observers. White liberals were alienated by the congresses' increasingly forthright assertion of demands for universal suffrage and returned to the UP fold in time for the 1953 election.

Some Congress leaders expected the campaign to have an impact on whites who had expressed sympathy or support for the Congress movement. Joe Matthews noted: 'At the beginning of the campaign I predicted that the country would gradually divide up into reactionaries behind the Nats and progressives of all shades behind the A.N.C. The whites will have to form a party that is prepared to make definite changes or join Congress.'

To highlight principle above race, however, the Defiance Campaign required public white support. In the event, it met only with the liberal 'manifesto' of October 1952, which counselled moderation and called for the resuscitation of the old Cape liberal tradition.

The Defiance Campaign presented the white left with two particular problems. Firstly, the emergence of a militant and popular national liberation movement highlighted ideological and strategic differences over nationalism within it. Secondly, radical whites had no national or regional structures which could be incorporated into the campaign. By late 1952 anti-white sentiment in the final stages of the campaign led to fears of racial polarisation and, as a result, a number of whites called for direct participation in both the Defiance Campaign and the broader Congress movement in order to ensure that 'the pending clash [does] not ... take place on racial lines'.[7]

For whites who supported the Defiance Campaign and wished to participate in it the situation was complicated by the reluctance of campaign organisers to endorse white defiance before the campaign had achieved its objective of mobilising blacks. Albie Sachs, the youngest white defier in 1952 and later a SACOD member, attended an early Defiance Campaign meeting in the Western Cape.

> People were rushing forward saying, 'Take my name, take my name!' and everybody was given great cheers, and I was saying to the comrade next to me, 'You say it is a freedom struggle – why can't whites participate? It is for everybody. We believe in a non-racial South Africa, why can't I join?' They responded with, 'Wait, wait, it not time yet – we are just starting ... we will take up the question'.[8]

The sanctioning of white defiance came through 'from the leadership in Jo'burg'[9] only towards the end of 1952, following outbreaks of violence in Kimberley, Port Elizabeth and East London. Writing from Port Elizabeth's New Brighton township, Joe Matthews noted that angry crowds of protestors 'started the anti whiteman cry'.[10] Faced with the possible spread of extreme nationalism, Cape ANC President James Njongwe reasserted the ANC's rejection of black racism, noting that '[e]ven if it is popular it is dangerous'.[11] In November 1952 Lucas Phillips, Chairperson of the ANC in the Western Cape, introduced Sachs and three other white volunteers to a Defiance Campaign meeting, noting that their participation was intended 'to dispel the idea among Africans that all Whites are oppressors'.[12] In early December the four white Cape defiers were arrested for breaking apartheid regulations in the post office a week after Patrick Duncan – later a prominent Liberal Party member – and six other whites had been arrested in Germiston.[13]

White involvement in the last few weeks of the Defiance Campaign was intended to combat the spread of racist nationalism and the anti-white sentiment that had begun to mark the campaign. The Springbok Legion endorsed the campaign; there were calls for direct participation from individual whites supportive of extra-parliamentary action; and more muted support in the form of the liberal 'manifesto' and statements of qualified support from the South African Institute of Race Relations (SAIRR).

In an attempt to capitalise on this support and turn it into white support for the Congress movement, the ANC and SAIC intruded directly in white liberal/left politics by staging the Darragh Hall meeting in November 1952 and challenging whites to join the (Congress-led) anti-apartheid struggle.

The immediate concern of all those calling for a white role in Congress was the need 'to prevent the African liberatory movement from assuming an exclusively anti-white complexion'.[14] The urgency of this concern was stressed by both Oliver Tambo and Yusuf Cachalia when they addressed the Darragh Hall meeting.[15]

The formation of a white organisation committed to the goals of Congress would, it was believed, highlight both the colour-blind principles that had precipitated the Defiance Campaign and Congress's commitment to a non-racial and equal future.

Both liberal and radical whites were disorganised and involved in an ideological and strategic reassessment occasioned by the rise of the ANC. The Darragh Hall meeting – the first white meeting to be addressed by Congress leaders – cut across those internal debates and aimed to give organisational form to white support for the congresses. As Luthuli later explained, 'Being a national movement we really couldn't deal with individuals, and that's what gave rise to the need for having a body on a national level, to make it possible for us to co-operate with whites.'[16]

The meeting did not lead to the creation of a single, unified white organisation but rather marked the point at which liberal and radical whites finally separated. It also led to the birth of the Johannesburg Congress of Democrats and marked a turning point in the history of opposition to apartheid – Congress's first-ever sanctioning of white participation in the movement.

First steps: the Johannesburg Congress of Democrats

The formation of the Congress of Democrats, initially called the South African People's Congress, has received scant mention in most works covering the 1950s. In most cases it is analysed coterminously with the national launch, nine months later, of SACOD; or it is assumed to be the same organisation.[17] This approach disregards the different conditions under which COD and SACOD were launched; the purpose appears to be to allow easy comparisons between SACOD, on the one hand, and the Liberal Party, on the other.

According to Karis and Gerhart, in calling for a white Congress, ANC and SAIC leaders envisaged '… the creation of a body that would generally support the ANC's aims and appeal to a wide spectrum of whites rather than a tiny activist group that would be identified with the ANC'.[18]

It must be said from the outset that COD and SACOD failed resoundingly in this respect, despite some remarkable achievements in other areas.

The founders of COD and SACOD, described as 'former Communists and other left-wing whites', are seen by Karis and Gerhart to have subverted the Congress proposal by taking the initiative at the Darragh Hall meeting and alienating white liberals through an unnecessary insistence on universal suffrage and extra-parliamentary action.[19] The result was the creation of an organisation described as so closely identified with the ANC 'that it proved unable to win the wide sympathy from whites that had been hoped for'.[20]

As a result, they write, Congress leaders were 'disappointed' with the Congress of Democrats (and SACOD).[21] This was probably true as far as the failure to mobilise whites is concerned, but the notion that Congress leaders would have warmly embraced liberals calling for Congress to support a qualified franchise, the use of constitutional and parliamentary means, caution and gradualism, rather stretches the notion of what was possible.

In fact, neither the ANC and SAIC leaders who called the Darragh Hall meeting nor the provisional committee it elected had a clear concept of the nature or role of what became the Congress of Democrats.[22] Yusuf Cachalia, who addressed the meeting on behalf of the SAIC, stated later that 'we wanted the progressive element among the whites to co-operate with us', but that 'we left the matter to the people who had gathered there to, if possible, bring about an organisation'.[23] The only qualification was that the new organisation should endorse basic Congress principles. As described by senior ANC member Dan Tloome, who clearly also remembers Tambo pulling a snake by the tail:

> Congress … took the bold and unprecedented step of calling a meeting of Europeans who had expressed their sympathy [for the Defiance Campaign], and there called upon them to form an organisation which would work for Congress principles of freedom and equality among their own people. One section present at the meeting asked whether Congress insisted on a policy of full equality, or whether it would not be satisfied with, for example, a qualified

franchise. They were told by Mr Tambo, on behalf of the ANC, that nothing less than full equality would be acceptable, and they thereupon went their own way.[24]

The Darragh Hall meeting was followed by talks between radical and liberal whites in search of a formula which would enable both to belong to a single organisation. Liberals refused to endorse universal suffrage, extra-parliamentary action, or close working links with former Communist Party members. The breakdown of talks was inevitable and was followed, in January 1953, by the launch of both COD and the South African Liberal Association. By the beginning of 1953 the division between radical and liberal whites was organisationally fixed.

By running together the formation of COD and SACOD, Karis and Gerhart allow themselves to contrast both organisations with the Liberal Party, which they describe as fulfilling the aims of Congress leaders in that it 'did serve as a link between black and white and generally supported the ANC's aims'.[25] The hostile criticism with which the ANC and SAIC greeted the formation of the LP is ascribed to (and thus disregarded as stemming from) 'the more radical nonwhites' in Congress, which, of course, included communists.[26] Its causes are seen to be the result of competition between the ANC and LP for African members, and the loyal defence of COD and SACOD by the black congresses.

But the underlying problem is that Karis and Gerhart, like South African liberals of the time, took as their starting point a direct and determining link between the dissolution of the Communist Party of South Africa (CPSA) and the formation of COD and SACOD. They then present the split between liberals and radicals as the result of communist manipulation of a Congress initiative (the call for whites to join their struggle).

The formation of COD is presented as the wilful squandering by former CPSA members of the possibility of a unified white congress that would have brought senior liberals into the fold, in order to entrench themselves in positions of influence within the Congress Alliance. There is a degree of truth in this – communists certainly wanted to work in and with Congress – but it ignores principled differences, most notably over universal suffrage, between white liberals and radicals, and between liberals and the congresses. It ignores the fact that communists were, in fact, engaged in their own process of debate, member selection and formation of the SACP. Moreover, it is premised on a perception of the white left as a monolithic entity acting in concert on agreed goals, and ignores the deep differences which emerged in the white left of the early 1950s. Such analysis is both chronologically confused and factually inaccurate.

The roots of radicalism

Calls for white participation in the Congress movement came from a variety of sources – from individuals such as Patrick Duncan, one of the most significant whites to attempt to find a permanent home in the Congress movement and the most prominent white defier in 1952; from former CPSA members acting in their individual capacity; from white liberals and from representatives of the Springbok Legion. In each case the role envisaged for whites differed significantly.

When Patrick Duncan resigned from the colonial service in Basutoland and participated in the Defiance Campaign he was already clear about his support for universal suffrage and Gandhian extra-parliamentary methods and about his deep-seated hostility to communism and the broader white left, a hostility that grew throughout the 1950s.[27] Duncan's support was sought by members of the Springbok Legion, who were negotiating with the ANC and SAIC for a separate white congress, but, while accepting that their ideas were 'fundamentally on the right lines', he felt their left-wing credentials were a problem. He argued that there were '… difficulties which make it difficult for many South Africans particularly if they are (in overseas language) right-wing or centre, to join …'.[28]

As a result, Duncan spent much of 1953 attempting to join the ANC and SAIC as an individual. According to his biographer he applied for membership of both organisations 'several times'.[29] His local ANC branch, in Ladybrand (in the Orange Free State), appears to have accepted his membership application, but neither the ANC nor the SAIC national leadership concurred.[30]

Their objections were based on a number of factors, one of which was the announcement of Duncan's decision to stand for election as a Native Representative, earning the hostility of ANC leaders who, as youth leaguers in the 1940s, had led the movement for a complete electoral boycott. Moreover, Duncan's call for individual white membership of Congress was made at the same time as SL members were negotiating the creation of a separate white congress. Had Duncan's application been less contentious he might have succeeded in bringing about non-racialism far earlier than was, in fact, the case.

As it was, ANC leaders rejected the call for individual white membership of Congress, particularly at the end of the Defiance Campaign, in favour of a multiracial alliance where whites could join their own structure and collaborate with the black congresses. While endorsing the ideal of a single, non-racial Congress, ANC leaders argued that the time for such a move had not yet arrived; according to Albert Luthuli, multiracialism was '… purely a matter of present policy, representing as we do, a large section of people who think tribally. We have to carry our people with us.'[31] It was to remain policy until all the congresses had been banned and their leaders were in prison or in exile.

While Duncan sought individual membership of Congress, former CPSA member Guy Routh, General Secretary of the Industrial Council and editor of the Labour Party newspaper *Forward*, proposed the formation of a broad white group in support of the general aims of the Congress movement. In 1952 Routh held discussions with leading Congress and trade union members 'of all political complexions', with the intention of creating an organisation that would continue to articulate white's sympathy for black aspirations that the Defiance Campaign had generated.[32]

The organisation was to express support for black emancipation while providing legal, financial and other assistance to the congresses and trade unions – in more modern terms, it was more of a non-governmental organisation than a political one. Routh wanted to create an organisational home for all whites who had expressed support for the Congress movement, with a political standpoint based on the qualified franchise. As he explained, by insisting on adult suffrage '[y]ou immediately cut off a whole lot of well-intentioned, wealthy many of them, and well-disposed people. It seemed to me needless since there was absolutely no hope of getting universal suffrage … why cut off those people who might otherwise be led to join it, and possibly change their views?'[33]

Routh's proposed organisation lay somewhere between SACOD and what became the Liberal Party. The middle ground he sought to occupy proved untenable, mainly because of anti-communism.

The most important negotiations over the future role of more radical anti-apartheid whites were undertaken by Cecil Williams and Jack Hodgson, wartime 'desert rat' and former miner respectively, both of whom were prominent Springbok Legion members. Hodgson and Williams were the only two among those who proposed a new white organisation who were mandated representatives of an organisation and, as such, their position carried more weight than the individual efforts of Duncan or Routh.

Moreover, the Legion's proposal was premised on an acceptance of multiracialism and of the leading role of the ANC. As Hodgson explained:

> The form and content of the activity of the new organisation are determined by factors beyond its control. The organisation exists as *part of a Movement* which has to meet a *particular and immediate historical need*, it exists in a *particular situation* and has *to work in an existing set of conditions to achieve certain relevant immediate and long term objectives.*[34]

Clearly sensitive to past disputes between the Communist Party and the ANCYL over non-racialism, Hodgson emphasised the 'sectional' nature of the proposed organisation, which, he argued, stemmed from the fact that black South Africans bore the brunt of apartheid and would bear 'the main burden of the struggle'.

The task of the white congress was 'organising and leading the whites and all other unorganised progressives scattered throughout South Africa who could be contacted and recruited'.[35] Such optimism stemmed from the Springbok Legion's understanding of apartheid as a form of domestic fascism.

According to Hodgson, blacks had a 'compelling and urgent motivation' to resist, which whites did not, but he argued that the spread of fascism would result in the diminution of civil rights for all South Africans.[36] As COD Executive Committee member Eddie Roux put it in 1953: 'Those freedoms hitherto denied in large measure to the

Non-Europeans, are now being taken away bit by bit from Europeans also. This development, long prophesied ... is the outcome of the traditional indifference of the white minority to the injustice suffered by their fellow South Africans. We must either go forward to full democracy or witness the rapid growth of a fascist dictatorship.'[37]

The Congress of Democrats, launched in Johannesburg in January 1953, was to highlight white support for a non-racial democracy. According to Hodgson, 'unless some political relationship was formed between Black and White' South Africa would enter 'a Black/White struggle ... This the Congress [of Democrats] was determined to prevent'.[38] The nature of the black–white political relationship, however, was disputed. For Legionnaires and others the only way to defuse black racism was through an unequivocal endorsement by whites of Congress principles. As stated by COD Chairperson Bram Fischer, and Vice-chairperson Cecil Williams:

> What is urgently needed today is a body of Europeans who will ally themselves with these organisations – a body which will not seek to bargain with or buy off the non-Europeans, but will march with them to the attainment of their legitimate democratic demands. Only in such a body can Europeans make a real contribution to democracy and racial peace in South Africa.[39]

This was by no means universally accepted. Guy Routh and his supporters called for a postponement of the COD's launch until liberals had organised themselves, in order to see what common ground existed, and opposed universal suffrage for the same reason.[40] Routh was heavily outvoted, the majority opinion stressing the urgent need for a white organisation that had the support of the Congress movement. As one participant at the meeting noted, 'It was felt that a "liberal" party would not, with its restricted franchise, obtain non-European support. The crux of the matter was whether one should alienate the 8 million non-Europeans for the sake of possibly winning some additional support from Europeans.'[41]

The COD programme merged the proposals of Routh and the Legion. COD was to rally white support for the Congress movement; to educate whites by means of propaganda, lectures, conferences and petitions; and to provide practical support to Congress in the form of speakers, witnesses to police actions, legal advice, assistance with transport, and so on.[42] The quasi-NGO element remained strongly evident. In the short term, the COD was 'to harass, hamper and retard the programme of the Nationalists' by challenging each repressive piece of legislation through unambiguous support for equal rights for all, and the 'active and militant assertion of the legality of these concepts and aspirations' – much more the activist side of the organisation.[43]

The long-term objective was 'the mobilisation and preparation of the people for decisive action to bring about the defeat of fascism'.[44] The roots of white participation in the Congress movement lay in the approaches made to the congresses in the early

1950s; the nature of SACOD itself was affected by differences in membership and operation between the various organisations that constituted its component parts.

Radical white organisations, 1952–1953

The Johannesburg COD initially worked in isolation from similar radical white bodies formed in other centres. In October 1953 it merged with these bodies – the Democratic League (DL) of Cape Town, the Durban Congress of Democrats, and small white groups in Port Elizabeth and elsewhere, to form SACOD. The three main organisations – COD, the SL and the DL – all brought distinctive characteristics to the organisation. SACOD took over the offices and equipment of the Springbok Legion as well as its active membership and, soon after its launch, the Legion disappeared.

The Democratic League was launched in 1953 after a meeting held to protest against the Public Safety and Criminal Law Amendment Acts, at which Labour Party MP Leo Lovell suggested that those present form a 'watch-dog organisation' to protest against similar measures being passed.[45]

It was one of two non-racial organisations in Cape Town to enrol African and coloured members in considerable numbers – more than half its members were coloured. The other organisation was the Modern Youth Society (MYS),[46] an organisation of young socialists, which held interracial functions.[47]

The League, which adopted the Universal Declaration of Human Rights, was formed by Harry Wright, chairperson of the Western Cape Trades and Labour Council, and Len Lee-Warden, then local Torch Commando secretary and printer of *The Guardian*. Initially a small ad hoc body organising public meetings in protest against various apartheid measures, within three months it had more than 150 members, at which point, according to Lee-Warden, 'we began to take it more seriously and organise more efficiently'.[48]

Unlike the liberal Civil Rights League, which was formed to fulfil a similar role, the Democratic League was non-racial and favoured extra-parliamentary action and an overtly political public profile. It mobilised coloureds threatened with disenfranchisement and sought to rally liberal-minded whites by stressing the threat posed by the NP to the rights of all South Africans. One of its pamphlets urged:

> Don't believe the Nationalists when they say that the [Public Safety] Act is to be used only against the African and Indian people … The punishments are not for Africans, Indians and Coloureds alone. They may be applied to any person who commits an offence by way of protest or in support of a campaign against any law.[49]

By passing the Public Safety and Criminal Law Amendment Acts, the League maintained, Parliament had 'committed suicide, just as surely as did the German Reichstag … this is Fascism!'[50]

One reason for the rapid growth of the League was the fact that, unlike COD, it was non-racial, a response, perhaps, to persistent calls for non-racial organisations emanating largely from the Western Cape. In 1951 S M Rahim, a leading FRAC member, called for multiracialism to be abandoned, arguing:

> We are all in the same boat … We do not want sectional groups any more. The South African Indian Congress and the African National Congress must prepare the ground amongst their followers so that we can all be in one organisation, where we will also have the Europeans who want to see equal rights for all South Africans.

Non-racialism, said Rahim, was not a new idea; it had 'been debated in progressive circles in South Africa for years'.[51] Rahim's call met with considerable support in the Western Cape, where leading ANC member Dora Tamana spoke out against the transformation of FRAC into a purely coloured congress,[52] while Johnson Ngwevela, former CPSA member and a senior ANC figure, directly endorsed Rahim's proposal.[53] Support came also from Joe Nkatlo, another former CPSA and ANC member, who joined the Democratic League and soon became its Vice-chairperson.[54] Opposition to multiracialism also came from members of the Non-European Unity Movement (NEUM). Kenny Jordaan, a leading NEUM intellectual, noted: 'It is unfortunately an indication of our political primitiveness that certain groups and individuals can conceive of our struggle, our organisational forms and the future of South African society only in terms of those racial categories foisted on us by Herrenvolkism.'[55]

The absorption of the Democratic League into SACOD brought disputes over non- and multiracialism to the fore. Both the DL and the MYS attracted white former CPSA members (among others) and, because of the weak local ANC branch in the Western Cape, black former CPSA members also joined the two organisations.

Anti-communism affected almost all anti-apartheid organisations during this period, and the appearance of communists in the League 'caused some concern to some committee members who felt that the organisation would fall into the hands of the radicals if they were allowed to occupy executive posts'.[56]

Liberal organisations responded to anti-communist pressure by removing or barring the white left from membership *en bloc*. The leadership of the DL, however, comprised people who had close working links with former CPSA members, most obviously Len Lee-Warden, who pointed out that 'I would not allow myself or the organisation to be used as a front for any political party. But also … I would not be a party to any witch-huntings. So it was left at that.'[57]

The founding of SACOD resulted in the Springbok Legion and the Congress of Democrats working together, sharing both offices and activists, circumstances that arose in part from the longstanding political involvement of the Legion, which had steadily increased in the late 1940s, as noted in a Legion circular.

The aims and objects of the Legion, our aspirations for ex-soldiers, economic, political and social, are now inextricably tied up with the fate of democracy in South Africa. Increasingly over the last few years the emphasis of our efforts have had to be directed towards the struggle for democracy.[58]

The COD and the Legion jointly submitted a lengthy memorandum on racial discrimination to the United Nations, hosted public meetings protesting against the Public Safety Act, assisted in forming the Western Areas Protest Committee, and submitted evidence to the Group Areas Advisory Board and the Select Committee studying the possible removal from Parliament of former CPSA member and Native Representative Brian Bunting.[59]

The Legion also played a significant role in negotiating the formation of COD with the Congress movement. Legionnaires called for a new organisation '... not restricted by our ex-service exclusiveness, and not tarred with our past record as it has been presented in distorted and contorted form to the public'.[60]

While the motivation for the establishment of SACOD flowed from the need for an adequate white response to the Defiance Campaign which would highlight principles above race and help defuse tendencies towards extreme nationalism with the announcement of a (white) general election for April 1953, its activities, like those of the COD and the Legion, focused on the white parliamentary arena.

The 1953 general election and anti-fascism

Radical white organisations in the 1950s occupied an awkward position, attempting to straddle both black and white political arenas. COD, and later SACOD, rejected parliamentary politics as unrepresentative and undemocratic and regarded the United Party (UP) and NP as committed to maintaining white supremacy. Attempts to liberalise the UP from within, it was (correctly) argued, had produced nothing. The COD leadership concluded that: 'South African democrats must, then, seek a solution outside the Parliamentary parties' – and outside the parliamentary system, from which blacks were, anyway, excluded.[61] This would prove to be a key point of difference with the Liberal Party.

COD's approach to white politics, however, was heavily influenced by the internal colonialism theory evolving in the discussion clubs of the time. The notion that South African oppression represented 'colonialism of a special type' (CST) had considerable implications for both COD and SACOD. The task of the Congress movement was seen to be to build the broadest possible alliance of forces in opposition to colonial oppression. According to Moses Kotane, former CPSA general-secretary and ANC NEC member, that alliance should include the United and Labour parties,

... the churches, business and professional organisations, women's associations, the multifarious local vigilance, tenants, civic, educational, patriotic and sectional bodies. All must be drawn into the broad alliance of the people of South Africa against the Malanazi menace …[62]

Proponents of CST argued that there were 'two nations in South Africa, occupying the same state, side by side in the same area'.[63] For whites, South Africa was an independent and democratic state; COD had been set the task of organising whites, which required participation in the white political process. COD had, moreover, to make the link between the two 'states', to win over what were seen as the 'considerable' white forces opposing apartheid (including sections of the UP, Labour Party, Torch Commando and others) and educate them: 'Their natural allies in defence of democracy are the ten million Non-Europeans. In union with the Non-Europeans, democrats and democracy will survive in South Africa. There is no other way.'[64]

COD's position was clearly potentially awkward. In outlining CST, leading SACP theoreticians (some of whom, such as Rusty Bernstein, were also leading COD and SACOD members) argued that all capitalist sectors were committed to the maintenance of the status quo. But their ANC leaders wanted them to win over 'considerable' progressive segments of these groups. These apparently included secondary industry, a vocal critic of migrant labour and influx control championed by the liberal wing of the UP. Michael Harmel differed, criticising those 'who chatter about "progressive capitalism"' for making analogies with countries fundamentally different from South Africa. As he put it, '[t]he secondary industrialists of this country are basically the junior partners of imperialism; the last thing they would advocate would be the abolition of the imperial system on which they depend.'[65]

While they slated capital they saw the liberal wing of the UP as a potential anti-Nationalist ally. In January 1953 the SL and COD jointly hosted a meeting of all anti-Nationalist organisations in Johannesburg to develop a common electoral platform. According to SL chairperson Piet Beyleveld, 'The spirit of fear and election compromise had eaten deep into the majority of the organisations, and no agreed basis for co-operation and unity to oust the Government could be found.'[66]

COD continued to put out election propaganda that reflected its contradictory position, arguing in a leaflet issued in March 1953 that South Africa had been brought 'to the edge of fascist dictatorship!' but not quite able to endorse voting for the UP as a progressive act.[67] The only thing that could save the country was 'the power of the people to call a halt to martial law fascism!' The immediate task of all 'supporters and upholders of democracy' was to call on the UP to retract its support for the Public Safety Act and to oppose the NP with greater vigour. COD did not explicitly call on whites to vote for the UP; rather, 'supporters … of democracy' should:

… encourage the United Party to come down firmly, with both feet, in the democratic camp … They must force the United Party to fight without

appeasement against the threat of home-grown fascism. This is the way forward for all South Africa's democrats, to the defeat of the Martial Law Acts,
to the ousting of the Nationalists.[68]

COD and the Legion tap-danced awkwardly, their sympathies clearly with Congress
and completely opposed to racist white election politics, their political role, however,
forcing them to try to engage with it. They tried to overcome the contradictions inher-
ent in their effort to bridge the gap between black extra-parliamentary politics and
white parliamentary politics by campaigning under an anti-fascist banner.

The NP government had long been described as 'fascist' by various organisations,
most notably the Springbok Legion and the Torch Commando. For such ex-service
organisations, fighting fascism was a means of rekindling the unity of purpose of
the war years, and the NP was accused of fascist tendencies because of its leaders' wartime
Nazi sympathies, the early release of convicted fascist saboteur Robey Leibrandt, and
the simultaneous removal of a number of senior, English-speaking military personnel.
Anti-fascism was a means of harking back to the liberal ethos of the war years and thus
hoping to win broader white support for progressive change in South Africa, without
having to raise awkward issues such as equal rights or the franchise. It failed lamentably.

In analysing the use by radical whites of the terminology of anti-fascism in the early
1950s Lambert concluded that the acts of the NP (such as Leibrandt's release) were
being confused with the nature of the South African state.[69] But this, perhaps, under-
states the extent to which anti-fascism was consciously deployed as a political tactic; it
was the only way white radicals (and liberals) knew to reach other whites less open to
messages about racial equality.

Anti-fascism had a wider set of associations and uses than Lambert acknowledged,
having been at the centre of the Springbok Legion's programme for ten years, and in
the political lexicon of the DL, COD, and the broader Congress movement. But critically,
it had a specific political function.

Through the language of anti-fascism, radical whites sought to use conceptual terminology similar to that used by the Congress movement, while attempting to mobilise
whites in terms they could recognise and respond to. In effect, anti-fascist slogans
focused attention on the diminution of the civil rights of all South Africans rather than
specifically on the lack of rights for blacks, which would not win white support. As a
result, fascism and apartheid became largely interchangeable terms. The NP was the
source of both, and the solution to South Africa's political crisis was equated with the
removal of the Nationalist Party from power. As Jack Hodgson put it, 'We are presented
with the need to withstand and defeat fascism ... fascism can be defeated only by the
defeat of [the] Nationalist Government.'[70]

Within the white left and away from the public arena, however, fascism was widely
and variously defined. The white left saw the capitalist world as rapidly approaching a

point of crisis as markets and sources of raw materials shrank under the impact of decolonisation and the spread of socialism. Participants in the discussion clubs of the early 1950s agreed that '[i]t is against [the] background of growing economic crisis and the consequent regrouping of forces that the future must be considered.'[71] In this context, fascism was a term used (optimistically) to describe the final stage of colonialism; Jack Simons argued: 'Today we live in a fascist country … Fascism is imperialism gone mad. Imperialism is the final stage of capitalism.'[72]

The drive for profits, it was argued, would lead to more ruthless exploitation of the country's resources, in the interests of big capital and carried out by '[t]his Government, which is a bossboy for monopoly capitalism …'.[73] In extending and strengthening its control over South African society in order to extract profits, COD leaders argued, the NP would increasingly resort to 'totalitarian' methods.[74] The result was that '… all anti-Nationalist South Africans must be affected, both white and non-white … since – like Hitler and Goering – the Nationalists' ultimate aim is to control the economic wealth of South Africa.'[75]

Importantly, anti-fascism also resonated with the Congress movement, with some ANC members equating fascism with extreme racism[76] while others, as is clear from the 1954 report of the ANC National Executive Committee, used fascism, apartheid and capitalist exploitation interchangeably: 'After six years of Nationalist rule, fascism has arrived in South Africa … Fascism does not arise until conditions call for it. It arises when the ruling class can no longer look forward to unlimited profits and to acquiescent people willing to be exploited.'[77]

Anti-fascism was a tool used by COD and the Springbok Legion to try to link the black and white political arenas. The victory of the NP in the 1953 general election, however, widened the gap between the two. A month after the election Albert Luthuli noted that 'The African peoples have lost faith in the good intentions of the Whites to improve their conditions, and the Congress movement has become more and more a liberatory one. It is no longer possible for an African leader to appeal for better conditions only: what the people demand is political rights.'[78]

Such expressions served to refocus the attention of white radicals on the black, extra-parliamentary arena.

The Congress Alliance and white politics in 1953

In a joint statement after the general election the ANC, SAIC and FRAC argued that the NP victory highlighted electoral support for white supremacy, reinforced by UP commitment to a similar policy.[79] For Dilitanzaba Mji, ANC acting Secretary-General, the difference between the NP and UP was 'as a thief from a pick-pocket'.[80] Z K Matthews, president of the Cape ANC, noted that the government had been returned to power 'with a majority which in the view of some of its supporters entitles it to put into effect a policy of "white South Africa" first, second and last…'; the policies of the opposition parties, he continued, were 'pale reflections' of apartheid.[81]

ANC leaders argued that the Defiance Campaign and the election results had 'so sharpened the political issues in the country as to leave no room for middle-of-the-road individuals or groups'.[82] As Luthuli saw it, whites opposed to apartheid had:

> … to accept the justice of the claim of the Non-whites for freedom and work
> unreservedly and openly for its realisation or be guilty of directly or indirectly
> assisting the Nationalist Party in its relentless and unmitigated oppression and
> suppression of the Non-white peoples in their claim for free democratic rights.[83]

The ANC, SAIC and FRAC called on 'all those sections of white South Africans who still treasure freedom, liberty and democratic traditions to join the non-white peoples of this country'.[84] In response, COD and the SL began to focus on the need to bring into being a single national organisation of whites which could join the Congress Alliance. The time for fudged liberal/radical solutions, if there had ever been such a time, had ended.

This was true for all whites opposed to apartheid, and was the context in which, three weeks after the election, the Liberal Party was launched. The party's programme was based on a qualified franchise for all 'civilised' people and a commitment to use 'only democratic and constitutional means' of opposition.[85]

The LP bore the brunt of post-election anger from the black congresses. Karis and Gerhart claimed that anti-Liberal hostility emanated from 'radical' blacks in defence of SACOD (stoked by white communists) but in fact the LP was attacked even by moderate leaders such as Z K Matthews and Luthuli; their criticism began from the moment the Liberal Party was formed. Their anger can be partly ascribed to the fact that, as a non-racial party, the LP would be competing for black support, rather than complementing the Congress movement. For Matthews, all political parties '… from the extreme right wing of the Nationalists to the Liberals are anxious to preserve a portion of privilege for one section of the population; whether they describe it as "white" or "civilised" makes no difference'. [86]

Luthuli warned Congress to be 'on guard against members of the ANC becoming members of political Parties whose objectives are different from our own'; any African 'desiring an unqualified emancipation', he continued, should join not the LP but 'the Liberatory movement through the African National Congress'.[87] Transvaal ANC president Nelson Mandela believed that 'talk of "democratic and constitutional means" can only have a basis in reality for those people who enjoy democratic and constitutional rights'.[88] The LP, he concluded, feared the liberation movement and sought 'to divert it with fine words and promises and to divide it by giving concessions and bribes to a privileged minority'.[89]

Congress leaders called for whites to join the Congress movement, but insisted that co-operation could only take place 'ON THE BASIS OF EQUALITY AND MUTUAL

RESPECT'.[90] Natal Indian Congress President 'Monty' Naicker summed up the feelings of Congress:

> Let me say most categorically that only those Europeans belong to the democratic camp, who without reservation accept the inherent fundamental right of all the oppressed people in South Africa to exercise equal franchise with those who enjoy it at present. Any person who denies the right of the non-Europeans to have equal franchise and speaks of a qualified franchise for them, by his very stand places himself outside the democratic camp, whether such a person happens to be White or non-White.[91]

In contrast to the claims of Gerhart and Karis that the LP effectively fulfilled the requirements of the white organisation proposed at the Darragh Hall meeting, Congress leaders unanimously spoke out against the policies and programme of the party, going further to call on whites to join the Alliance.

Mji contrasted the LP with those whites 'who had come out courageously and associated themselves with the defiance campaign'.[92] Such whites should join the Alliance and thereby 'challenge directly the contention of the racialist from the Nats to the Liberals that the liberation of all Africans is an express or implied threat to the Europeans in this country'.[93] In the context of the 1953 election result, the hostile criticism directed at the LP and its programme, and the call for a non-racial endorsement of democratic ideals, SACOD was formed.

'More radical, more progressive, more democratic'

The 1953 general election was a watershed for liberal and radical whites. After the election the pro-Congress newspaper, *Advance*, counselled radical whites against 'losing heart at the election result', calling on them to turn to 'the task of forging that democratic alliance of all races which will be the only protection of the people against the Nationalist tyranny'.[94] Rusty Bernstein argued (with breathtaking overstatement) that 'the long-standing United Party monopoly of allegiance of progressive and democratic Europeans has been shattered'[95] and, as a result, a white congress should make '… a bid for the allegiance and support of the sincere European democrat who had been finally disillusioned with the United Party and the Torch Commando and was seeking a new way out'.[96]

As the Congress movement distanced itself from white parliamentary politics, the need for a nationally constituted white congress was increasingly felt. In a reversal of COD's support for the UP during the election, executive committee member Eddie Roux argued that both the UP and the NP were committed to white supremacy and the suppression of legal black protest. In such circumstances, Roux asked, what could stop black political organisations from becoming anti-white?

> In this situation Europeans of democratic and liberal views would be failing in their duty … if they did not take immediate steps, firstly to demonstrate that there still exist many white people who are not hostile to the legitimate human aspirations of the Non-Europeans and who sympathise with them in their struggles; secondly, to work for the overthrow of the present unjust and dangerous system which will ultimately bring disaster to the country.[97]

Arguing for the formation of a single white congress after the election, COD members maintained that the NP victory and the decline of the Torch Commando had led to 'the development of new, more radical, more progressive and more democratic concepts … than have existed for many years'.[98] White society was seen to be witnessing 'a ferment' of debate, 'all of which inevitably comes to revolve around the basic question of the rights … of non-white South Africans'.[99]

The two-day conference called by COD, the SL and the DL out of which grew SACOD, was attended by eighty-eight delegates from the three convening bodies, as well as from white organisations in Durban and Port Elizabeth, individual whites from other areas, and the black congresses.

Rusty Bernstein and Jack Hodgson presented papers outlining the nature and programme of the proposed organisation, both stressing its broad nature and the need for a white congress to take its place in the existing multiracial alliance. Neither put forward a detailed programme of action; rather, they argued, the first task of the new organisation was symbolic, to show that '… the struggle is one between white and non-white democrats on the one hand and white and non-white reactionaries on the other'.[100]

SACOD's aims were set out in general terms. In the short term the organisation was to 'react rapidly to every single issue that arises in South Africa' and assert a democratic programme in opposition to apartheid.[101] The longer-term objective was the mobilising 'of the people … to bring about the defeat of fascism'.[102]

SACOD's founders were deliberately vague about the organisation's programme, although it adopted the United Nations Declaration of Human Rights as its statement of principle. As an activist body, not a political party, SACOD did not require policies covering all aspects of national life. Moreover, it was a political home for a white left that was deeply divided over a host of issues, none of which had yet been resolved. It was supposed to absorb the white left as well as the (hoped for) growing number of whites who, it was argued, would be driven to understand 'that ours is the only alternative future to the grim and primitive future of full-fledged Nationalist fascism'.[103]

The hostile reception of the LP's programme had highlighted the need for a white organisation based on complete equality; 'a body', as Bram Fischer and Cecil Williams put it, 'which will not seek to bargain with or buy off the non-Europeans, but which will march with them'.[104] Moreover, if SACOD's programme was limited it might succeed in including within its ranks:

Life in wartime Alexandra

The 'dompas'

Prime Minister Smuts. The liberal who never was . . .

Hofmeyr, the great liberal hope

Eddie Roux, early Communist Party and later Liberal Party member

Brian Bunting, Communist Party stalwart

CPSA meeting. From left to right: Ruth First, Bram Fischer, Joe Slovo and Rusty Bernstein

Harry Snitcher of the CPSA

Bill Andrews, who voted against dissolution of the CPSA in 1950

The Springbok Legion

A Springbok Legion Conference

The Torch Commando in action

The Defiance Campaign

Patrick Duncan and Manilal Gandhi join the Defiance Campaign in Germiston

Mary Turok, one of the young, white defiers from Cape Town

Margaret and William Ballinger:
Native Representatives and early Liberal
Party leaders

Alan Paton

Leo Marquard – liberal polymath

Walter Stanford

Oscar Wollheim

J.T.R. Gibson

Randolph Vigne

Z.K. Matthews and students

A young Dr A.B. Xuma

Yusuf Dadoo and O.R. Tambo

Left to right: Joe Matthews, unknown, unknown, Nelson Mandela, Robert Resha, Oliver Tambo, Duma Nokwe

Congress of the People

Congress of the People

Chief Albert Luthuli

Policing the pass laws

Jack Hodgson under house arrest

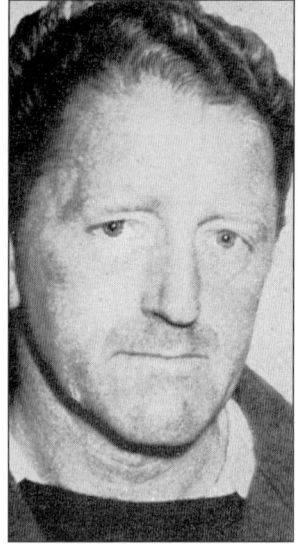

Rusty Bernstein

Helen Joseph under house arrest

Fred Carneson

The Black Sash and the white right clash

FSAW meeting

Mary Turok and Ruth Mompati, 1958 meeting

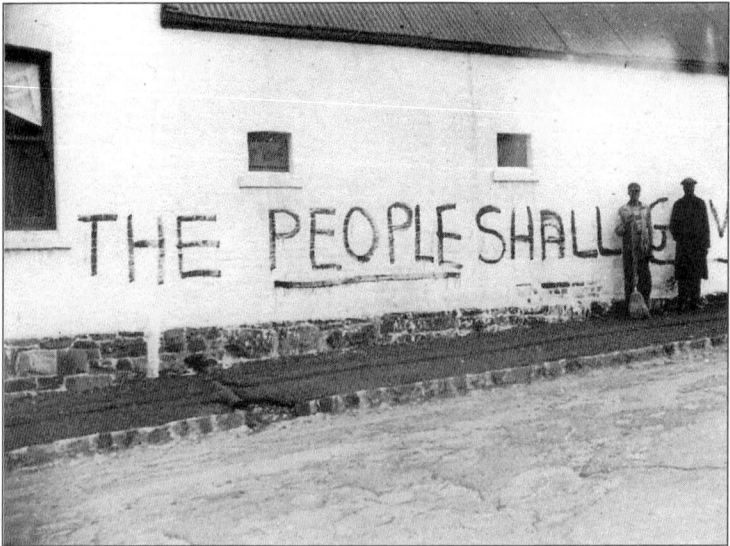

Congress of Democrats graffiti, 1958

1958 ANC Congress

Anton Lembede and A.P. Mda

Potlako Leballo

Philip Kgosana leads the march that shook Cape Town

Sharpeville – the end of the decade

... people who agree upon our limited aims, but who differ on the legislative programme to be adopted by a truly democratic South African government, and who
accordingly belong to different political parties and hold differing political ideologies even while being loyal and effective members of our new organisation.[105]

In other words, the programme should be sufficiently blurry to hold together the fractious
white left. In more formal terms Bernstein noted that SACOD's aims were limited to
'cover in reality only one great subject, the subject of fundamental human rights'.[106]

Perceptions of SACOD

Most analysis of SACOD takes as its starting point the assumption of a direct link
between the dissolution of the CPSA and the formation of COD and SACOD. In 1958
Anthony Sampson, a former editor of *Drum* magazine, characterised SACOD members
as 'the familiar band of white communists and fellow-travellers who had for years been
associated with Congress'.[107] Edward Feit claimed that the leadership of SACOD was
'virtually the same' as that of the disbanded CPSA.[108] Janet Robertson saw SACOD as
'Communist-controlled';[109] Douglas Irvine described it as 'Communist-influenced'.[110]
Gail Gerhart, commenting on Africanist claims that SACOD was formed to allow white
communists to subvert African nationalism, stated that this was '*probably* not a primary
factor behind the participation of most members of COD' but she nonetheless
described SACOD as an organisation of 'white Marxists'.[111]

As these quotations make abundantly clear, SACOD has commonly been seen as a
'front' for communists, an assertion premised on the prominence of former CPSA members in the organisation's ranks rather than its programme and activities, or even its wider
membership. Commentators have, on occasion, preferred inaccuracy to truth, using circular arguments to 'prove' that SACOD was the Communist Party in mufti. Feit accepted
that 'some members were not communists' but nonetheless concluded: 'that is, of course,
the aim of a front'.[112] Karis and Gerhart asked why SACOD adopted the Universal
Declaration of Human Rights 'rather than ... any Marxist program'.[113] In answering their
own question, they fell back on Gwendolen Carter's 1958 assertion that regardless of its
programme SACOD's 'emotive language' was 'characteristically Communist'.[114]

White communists – ex-CPSA as well as SACP – certainly needed an organisational
home, but so did white radicals with no communist history. SACOD undoubtedly gave
some SACP members formal access to the senior end of the Congress Alliance but its
value lay in *not* being or acting a like a communist front, given government and
Africanist hostility towards communists. There is as little value in arguing that SACOD
had nothing of value to offer (white) communists as there is in arguing the reverse –
that it was a puppet of communist inveigling.

SACOD has been characterised in most existing literature as having considerable
power within Congress. Support for 'left-wing' ideas such as nationalisation and anti-

imperialism (and anti-Americanism) within the black congresses are traced back (in more or less patronising ways) to its influence and thus to the influence of communists.

Some commentators attempted to distance the ANC from SACOD in order to sanitise the former from the contagion of the latter. Gerhart argued that the ANC–SAIC decision to create a white congress did not represent what Luthuli referred to as a 'step along our road towards a broader South Africanism'.[115] Rather, and without any evidence to support her claim, she writes it off as 'simply a "realistic" effort to tap every readily available resource in the African's favour'.[116] Gerhart concludes, in the face of a wealth of evidence to the contrary, that for ANC leaders the decision to bring SACOD into being was 'primarily a tactical, not an ideological one'.[117]

SACOD and multiracialism: the white 'freak group'

The historiography of the white left – at least until 1990, after which biographies and autobiographies began to change the picture somewhat – was almost entirely informed by anti-communism, and included the notion that the white left was a single, cohesive entity that could act in concert in pursuit of clear and accepted goals – a singularly inaccurate assumption, but one that suited the anti-communist sympathies of authors.

In reality, the formation of SACOD occasioned a serious dispute within the white left over the 'racial' structure of the organisation, a dispute which, moreover, saw former CPSA members ranged against each other, and ultimately led to a number of senior members of the disbanded CPSA refusing to join SACOD. That some (former and current) communists helped form and lead SACOD is not in question; that they did so in order to pursue a communist agenda certainly is.

At the time of SACOD's formation ANC membership was at its highest for the 1950s, and the Congress movement as a whole was infused with the healthy belligerence engendered by the Defiance Campaign. As a result, the founding documents of Hodgson and Bernstein, both Communist Party members, concentrated not on the details of SACOD's programme but on its subordinate position within the Alliance.

The black congresses still insisted on multiracialism for a variety of reasons. ANC leaders argued that the black population was not yet ready for a non-racial organisation, however desirable that might be. Congress leaders also argued that multiracial structures 'had their roots in the realities of the situation' – that is, of geographically, racially, culturally and politically separated communities.[118] In addition, they continued to unearth positive nuggets from the deeply depressing political landscape, pointing to the flurry of new white political parties as evidence that 'the ruling class has been confused and divided', and called on radical whites to further the process by working among whites.[119] Albie Sachs recently described Congress's feelings on the issues. Moses Kotane, according to Sachs, gave him a little lecture:

'You whites, [he said] you all love running to the location. You get big cheers from the people.' He says, 'Water always follows the path of least resistance. We don't have access to the whites, we can't organize amongst them. That is really where you people have to be, but you always run away from that. Because it is more difficult'.[120]

Hodgson and Bernstein revealed extreme sensitivity to the possibility of new disputes breaking out over the question of non-racialism. Hodgson argued that the 'social, economic and political structure of South Africa' had imposed on the entire Congress movement 'this sectional form of organisation'.[121] Each congress was given responsibility for 'that group to which it alone has the most ready access, and of whose problems it alone has the clearest understanding'. With regard to SACOD Hodgson stressed: 'We should recognise at the outset that the new organisation is but a section of the Movement … As a consequence in general therefore the character and tempo of the struggle can only be determined together with the mass organisations of the Non-White people.'[122]

Of course, multiracialism ignored the fact that whites breaking out of apartheid's shackles wanted to meet and work with their black countrymen and women – not with white leftists. And that white anti-apartheid activists did indeed want to follow 'the path of least resistance' by working in the townships, not doing the depressing door-to-door work in hostile white suburbs. These challenges would face radical white organisations until democracy dawned in the 1990s.

SACOD, Bernstein and Hodgson argued, would have no colour bar and would 'welcome into its ranks all those South Africans, irrespective of their race or colour, whose understanding of democracy is the same as ours'.[123] At the same time, however, the new organisation had the 'responsibility for organising and leading the Militant democrats not catered for by the Congress movement'.[124] Somehow SACOD was going to be simultaneously non-racial and white-only. Aware of how tortuous their proposal was, Bernstein continued:

I do not want to be misunderstood – and on issues like this in our race-conscious country it is too easy to be misunderstood. I am proposing the formation of an organisation which will have no colour bar … But I am simultaneously proposing the formation of an organisation which will, from the outset, understand that the democratic cause in South Africa is today predominantly represented by the Congress movement. I am proposing the formation of an organisation which will not attempt to supersede the Congress as it is presently constituted, which will not attempt to take [on] itself the status of a super, all-in, non-national Congress … [125]

SACOD's founding conference endorsed a policy statement that stressed the deep scars left on all South Africans by decades of racial discrimination, reinforced by differing educational, cultural and social patterns that divided communities. The statement accepted the ideal of 'a single, united democratic organisation of people of all races'; it warned, however, that it '… would be visionary and impractical to imagine that the acceptance of a policy of full and equal rights for all racial groups automatically sweeps these factors aside'.[126]

The conference also endorsed, as a maxim to guide SACOD's work, 'what is good for one Congress is good for all'.[127]

Opposition to multiracial forms of organisation had come most strongly from the Western Cape, and this was equally true in relation to the formation of SACOD. The non-racial Democratic League, a convenor of the founding conference, was deeply divided over the question of merging into a white Congress. Len Lee-Warden noted that 'I, for one, was against joining up with an organisation that was for whites only, even if the ANC had wanted it that way'.[128] When the merger was put to the vote, the majority of the League's members supported it, although the League's delegates to the founding conference 'argued all the way to Johannesburg'.[129] The DL's main concern was the fate of its coloured members (SACPO being not yet a month old) in an all-white organisation. DL delegates 'argued our case for two days' and won acceptance of continued coloured membership until SACPO was operational.[130]

The DL's objections to multiracialism were essentially practical, relating to the future of existing members. However, the objections triggered off a far more widespread dispute over the nature and future direction of SACOD. The formation of a white congress, whose members would work to break 'the hidebound prejudices of Europeans',[131] exacerbated differences within the white left. CST had partially reconciled supporters of class struggle to working for national liberation by stressing the need to concentrate on building existing national organisations. Working among whites, however, was a step further away from black politics.

Supporters of CST pointed to the existence of large and active national organisations which were 'not artificial but based on strong national feeling among the people'.[132] Senior CPSA members such as Jack Simons argued that internal colonialism had divided the working class along racial lines, and concluded that while the white working class should not be ignored, 'it might also be better strategy to concentrate for some time on the largely unorganised but reliable elements of the working class (mainly African)'.[133] In this version of events, former CPSA members would continue their previous work but would do so for the benefit of the ANC and SAIC.

The formation of SACOD, however, further divided the white left. Working within the organisation, white former CPSA members would have to switch their focal point from organising blacks to working among whites. For some CPSA members who had endorsed CST this further shift marked a final concession to racial division above class unity and was unacceptable. In 1954, Jack Simons, who never joined SACOD, stated: 'As far as the National Democratic Movement is concerned in South Africa, it is true that the immediate task is to secure freedom from National Oppression. But there is no such thing in social movements as freedom by the instalment plan ... There can be no liberation apart from class liberation.'[134]

The most vocal critics of SACOD, and of multiracialism more generally, were former CPSA members and others from the white left who rejected CST. For Danie du Plessis, former CPSA Johannesburg District Chairperson, multiracial structures were the final capitulation to nationalism, starting from his stated premise that nationalist organisations were 'school[s] for herrenvolk ideology, narrow-mindedness and race prejudice'.[135] A number of separate national organisations combined in a multiracial alliance, he argued, simply multiplied the problems:

> Nationalist organisations and federalism can in the end only lead to disintegration and their own destruction. A national liberation movement either assumes a mass character and grows, which it can do only when all the forces of liberation are organised and actively fight for its aims under a common leadership, or it is converted and degenerates into a series of petty squabbles over whose right it is to sit on which bench, or who enters which door.[136]

Du Plessis argued that whites who 'desert the camp of the oppressor' should be incorporated within a single national organisation, and not be treated 'as a freak group'.[137] He opposed the formation of SACOD and called for a single, non-racial congress. With support from within the Johannesburg Discussion Club he proposed 'one organisation with its ranks open to all South Africans who are prepared to fight for its programme and aims and under one leadership elected by all'.[138] The easiest way to attain such unity, he argued, was for the ANC 'to open its ranks to all who want to fight for freedom'.[139]

Congress leaders, as we have seen, opposed the call for a single congress for a variety of reasons, including the ideological connotations that had become attached to non-racialism as a result of the disputes of the late 1940s. Du Plessis and his supporters argued for a single non-racial Congress for the same reasons Congress rejected it: the primacy of class above national struggle. '[T]here is no room for numerous small organisations functioning separately and shouting unity, but in practice remaining in separate camps', he maintained.[140] '[R]eal and absolute unity between all races can only be achieved in a workers' struggle', he contended.[141] In complete contrast with the call for SACOD members to bring more whites into the struggle, or with Jack Simons's call for work within the black nationalist organisations, Du Plessis argued that the primary task was to build 'a strong and powerful trade union movement ... and a peasant's [sic] organisation' as the backbone of black emancipation.[142]

Disputes over the need to work among whites took place within SACOD throughout the 1950s. Nonetheless, as SACOD Executive Committee member Helen Joseph observed, those former CPSA members who joined the white congress were 'only too happy to find a political home where they could really renew their contacts with the political world'.[143]

The dispute had two effects. Firstly, a number of senior communists, including Simons, Du Plessis and a considerable number of rank and file CPSA members, refused to join the white congress. Secondly, it led to the founders of SACOD blurring the precise demarcation of the organisation's sphere of operation.

The policy statement adopted at SACOD's founding conference stated that the organisation had no colour bar; in evidence of this, Maulvi Cachalia, of the SAIC, was elected to the Executive Committee.[144] The statement stressed that SACOD did 'not seek to compete with the existing Congress organisations for membership or for first place in the struggle', and committed the organisation to 'winning the support of Europeans for the fight against all aspects of race discrimination and hostility'.[145]

Its members were to work among 'groups not eligible for membership of existing organisations, or catered for by them'.[146] At one level this blurred phrasing referred to the coloured members of the Democratic League. At another, however, it was an attempt to compromise with those who objected to working with whites. The document stated that SACOD members should work to improve 'the membership and prestige of whichever organisation is most appropriate and readily accepted by the local population'.[147] Aware of white resistance to working among whites, the statement concluded:

> There can be no rigid pattern for C.O.D. branches, their composition and their activity. Local conditions vary considerably. Each branch and region must adapt the general policy of co-operation and mutual assistance of the three Congresses to the real situation existing in the area. Where there is no local A.N.C. branch, the S.A.C.O.D. may well work mainly amongst Africans to recruit [them] to the S.A.C.O.D. and to urge the most enlightened to form an A.N.C. branch.[148]

SACOD was launched at a time when many of the advances made during the Defiance Campaign were being rolled back in the face of a renewed legislative onslaught on black rights. Its members, noting the lack of a clear strategy, which was forcing Congress campaigns to adopt a defensive tone,[149] believed the organisation must develop a strategy for work in white areas while forging links with the broader Congress Alliance. As a result, it immediately endorsed the proposed Congress of the People, which was intended to further the mobilisation of the Defiance Campaign and produce a coherent and popular statement of principle which would unite the whole Congress movement.

By October 1953, thanks to the creation of SACOD, whites were full partners in the Congress Alliance, but the dispute within the white liberal/left meant that the organisation lacked the support of both liberals and a significant number of former CPSA members and other white Marxists. The black congresses, however, saw it as standing in stark contrast with the UP, 'the liberals and reformist trade unions'. 'Our policy of co-operation with other racial groups through their national organisations has made great strides and constitutes a very real threat to the present regime which is anchored on the idea of racial exclusiveness and domination', noted the ANC NEC.[150]

Chapter 6

The Liberal Party of South Africa

The Liberal Party of South Africa (LP) was launched on 9 May 1953. Led by Margaret Ballinger, with Donald Molteno, Leo Marquard and Alan Paton in senior positions, and guaranteed to generate media coverage, the LP seemed to mark the culmination of the liberal activism of the 1940s and early 1950s, while speeches and party literature harked back to the Cape liberal tradition. For its founders, the launch of a party which freely expressed a 'liberal' race policy was a liberation from the constraints of working within the United Party (UP). Margaret Ballinger rather overstated the case, describing the new party as '*the* significant product of the history of the last forty years'.[1]

The LP endorsed a qualified franchise, bound members to use 'only democratic and constitutional means' of opposition and, in its constitution, proclaimed its opposition to 'all forms of totalitarianism such as communism and fascism'.[2] With the formation of the LP liberals were, for the first time, forced to compete for popular support. Many in the South African Liberal Association (SALA), from which the LP emerged, and in the South African Institute of Race Relations (SAIRR), were unhappy with the idea of a new political party competing with the UP and refused to join the LP. Given its tentative political programme, the LP was attacked by the Congress movement, hampering its attempts to recruit black members.

The LP was an umbrella organisation, its members drawn from different political traditions and with varied political outlooks but united in opposition to the Nationalist Party government and in their belief in the need to 'bridge the racial gap' and to 'win out against Communism'.[3] Although non-racial the LP initially concentrated on parliamentary politics, and saw white voters as its main constituency – just what the African National Congress (ANC) had asked for, in some ways, though from a starting point too conservative for Congress to stomach.

Younger party members, however, believing the key function of the party to be to win black support, began pushing almost immediately for the founding policies to be changed. The LP became a vehicle through which liberalism was challenged, amended and developed throughout the 1950s.

Liberals and liberalism

Janet Robertson, in *Liberalism in South Africa*, sketched the early history of the SALA and the LP, but did not offer a detailed contextual analysis of liberalism as it developed in the late 1940s and early 1950s, under pressure from both a growing Congress movement and the Nationalist Party apartheid programme. Rather, she roughly equated liberals and liberalism with common-sense moderation and anti-communism – mimicking the way liberals liked to see themselves – and presented the LP as the South African representative of an internationally recognised liberal creed which found fullest expression in the United Nations Charter. For good measure, she contrasted the LP with 'the communist-controlled C.O.D'.[4]

Paul Rich, in *White Power and the Liberal Conscience*, rejects what he describes as Robertson's 'pluralist party politics model', sketching a wider political and intellectual context within which white liberals operated.[5] He portrays post-war liberals as the tail-end drabs of nineteenth-century Cape liberalism – and indeed, while many would have accepted the pedigree, others would have rejected it out of hand. The wider context Rich provides is concerned with delineating the containment of 'paternalism' and 'the more general state of political despair to which liberals had been driven' attendant upon the decline of 'paternalistic Cape liberalism'.[6] Leading liberals are presented as the last heirs of the (paternalistic) Cape liberal tradition.

Neither Rich nor Robertson recognises the emergence of new liberal thinking or of a new generation of strident and assertive young liberals. The specific attributes of South African liberalism in the 1940s and 1950s, and the wider ideological functions of the political activities of the Native Representatives and others, are not recorded, or their significance is missed.

Martin Legassick similarly drew a determining line from the Hoernlé-Hofmeyr era to the LP in the 1950s, concluding that 'liberals found themselves united not by any positive vision, nor, uniquely, in standing for any principles … but by negative factors, dislikes of nationalism or communism or populism, and by *guilt*'.[7]

The kernels of truth in these different analyses are covered by a politically correct layer of negative commentary which simplistically wrote off liberals as little more than a sad, historical relic, ignored the energy and vigour liberals were to bring to their work in the 1950s and also failed to take into account the massive political and ideological distance liberals would travel as a result of their contact (and competition) with African nationalism, or the interplay between the LP and Congress, which had an impact on both. Neither pays heed to the effect of the war years in creating a potential white constituency, which the Torch Commando later successfully approached, or the way in which large numbers of highly capable young South Africans were exposed to new, liberal ideas and, having been reached by Leo Marquard's Army Education Service (AES), left the war with an understanding of liberalism influenced by the Atlantic and United Nations charters – not the nineteenth-century Cape tradition.

Rich, Robertson, Legassick and others draw an understandable but overly simplistic genealogy through the formation of the SAIRR in the 1920s, the anti-Hertzog white activism of the 1930s, the work of the Native Representatives and supporters of the Hofmeyr Society and the SAIRR in the 1940s, and the Liberal Party as the culmination of such activity in the 1950s, all saturated with the Cape's 'liberal' tradition. The development of South African liberalism was a more complex process than this suggests and (in the 1950s) not very linear.

The formation of the LP marked a split between the Native Representatives and the SAIRR leadership as the latter rejected the call for a more activist political role. Throughout the 1950s the LP suffered internal strife as the broader party membership challenged central tenets of the 1953 policy settlement achieved by the early leaders, many of whom better fit the Rich/Legassick version of liberalism. Margaret Ballinger, her husband William and their coterie wanted the LP to be the contemporary expression of a century of South African (largely unchanged) liberalism; to a growing majority of LP members this was anathema – liberalism, they believed, needed to be dragged into the realities of the post-war world.

The end of the war saw the ANC and its allies endorsing a liberal-democratic programme based on universal suffrage, the rule of law, a mixed economy, and an emphasis on the provision of social welfare. White liberals, on the other hand, developed a programme that did not demand an end to segregation but rather its gradual modification, aimed at separating a black urban bourgeoisie from the bulk of the black population. As Alan Paton later wrote (privately), he 'could not honestly support the opening of the doors of our society to tribal Africans, Indian labourers, and the large depressed portion of the Cape Coloureds'.[8] Liberals proposed a non-racial but qualified franchise, while supporting social and residential segregation which included even the separated 'cream', the black middle class. Liberalism in the 1940s was an incremental administrative creed that opposed the Congress movement's calls for full equality. Within a decade, however, it was to change fundamentally.

Within the LP people of different political outlooks came to work alongside the Native Representatives and their conservative supporters (located largely in the Cape), as well as well-known former ANC member Selby Msimang, former Communist Party members Jock Isacowitz and Eddie Roux, and others. The LP attracted a small number of socialists who rejected the perceived closeness of South African Congress of Democrats (SACOD) and the Communist Party, and who would not join the Labour Party despite its adoption of a more liberal programme in the early 1950s.[9] It also enrolled a large number of social-democratic members such as Leo and Hilda Kuper, Christopher Gell and others, who maintained a steady critical commentary on the party from within it. Leo Marquard,

Julius Lewin and others joined the discourse. As the party's black membership grew, the attitudes of white party members began to change. Social democrats found increasing support for their calls for closer relations with the congresses and acceptance of universal suffrage. Their influence on the LP was considerable, maintained through newspaper articles, letters and private discussion, and grew as the decade progressed.

The development (and radicalisation) of liberalism in the 1950s resulted in part from the younger generation of liberal activists enrolled by the LP, from the influence of older more radical figures such as Eddie Roux, and from attempts to win black support for liberal principles. The gradualist and cautionary liberal creed of the Native Representatives and others in the late 1940s was successively challenged from within the LP (as well as attacked externally by critics to left and right).

The party had little opportunity to be a static monolith of nineteenth-century ideas. As calls increased for its programme to move away from restrictive participation and avoidance of extra-parliamentary activity it became apparent that the early leaders had to be removed from office, and many members left for the Progressive Party when it was launched in 1959. Julius Lewin later commented: 'Under the new dispensation, the older liberals lost heart. The elderly ones were due to disappear from the scene, anyway. After an interval of some years – an unfortunate break in continuity – new and younger men, who had served no apprenticeship in public life, brought a more indignant tone and new style to the situation.'[10]

Lewin – himself one of 'the elderly ones' – failed to acknowledge that the LP was in fact a clear break from the values of the Cape liberal tradition and from the political creed of liberals in the 1930s and 1940s, even if this fact was obscured by the presence of the Ballingers and a few others. The LP was a vehicle that subjected earlier liberal creeds to a series of challenges which focused on the franchise and extra-parliamentary activities.

The LP was not the culmination of a single strand of nineteenth- or twentieth-century liberal thinking, but the melting pot for a number of political traditions. The party itself became the vehicle that challenged and amended liberalism in South Africa. Many core elements of its political programme in the late 1950s were far more radical than those adopted by the ANC in the 1994 Reconstruction and Development Programme (RDP).[11]

The cumulative effect of launching the party was to draw together a wide spectrum of white political opinion (not to be confused with a large membership base!) through interaction with the congresses and participation in grassroots black opposition politics. Because of the growing black party membership an initially elitist party was democratised and a cautious programme was radicalised. Possibly because 'liberal' became a dirty word as the struggle against apartheid intensified and positions polarised, there has been little detailed analysis of post-war South African liberalism. Much of the existing commentary either adopts the hostile line of Congress or Black Consciousness adherents or indulges in liberal platitudes.[12] Neither of these positions does justice to a dynamic party and its ideology.

South African liberalism

The post-war years saw growing co-operation between the ANC and the South African Indian Congress (SAIC) and the Communist Party of South Africa (CPSA) in support of a liberal-democratic programme, pursued by extra-parliamentary means. South African liberals, on the other hand, developed an incrementalist strategy that aimed to influence the implementation of 'Native policy'. In these circumstances, the terms 'liberal', 'radical' and 'communist' came to be defined and understood not simply by reference to an internationally accepted lexicon, but predominantly in the light of domestic circumstances. This redefinition was compounded by the NP government's self-serving redefinition of communism to include any opposition to Afrikaner nationalism. Liberalism in South Africa – according to liberals – was concerned, above all, with the post-war deterioration in race relations.

Julius Lewin remarked in 1952 that 'Liberals have always held that race relations are the vital problem';[13] similarly, Alan Paton later stated that 'Liberalism in South Africa, though it has common roots with liberalism in other countries, and though its roots are the roots of liberalism everywhere, has nevertheless one characteristic which is especially its own, and that is its particular concern with racial justice.'[14]

After the 1948 election the United Party became the main focus of liberal activity as the Native Representatives and the SAIRR sought to rekindle its progressive embers (despite their ashen appearance). Liberal thinking was strongly influenced by the Fagan Commission report.[15] The SAIRR and the Native Representatives had presented evidence to the commission and, although they were disappointed that the final report did not espouse an explicitly liberal programme, it did give liberals enough to work with, especially passages that spoke of the inevitability of economic integration and the permanence of black urbanisation.[16]

The Fagan Report relied on economic necessity in place of ideological legitimation in support of a permanent black urban presence. Liberals, in turn, attempted to create a broad area of non-ideological concurrence on 'practical' issues, arguing, in essence, that urbanisation and the 'economic integration' of blacks into the 'white' economy were necessary side effects of an industrialising economy. From this basic premise liberals argued firstly that a stable urban black labour force required access to health, education and other services, and secondly that black urbanisation necessitated some form of political dispensation, if only as a safety valve. Without it, the economy would stagnate or be disrupted.

In 1948 both the UP and the NP were finalising their policies in the light of the Fagan and Sauer reports, the two major proposals for sustaining white supremacy in the post-war years.[17] The Ballingers argued that the time was ripe for a 'reasonable and sensible' liberal intervention[18] and, in 1948/9, leading liberals presented a series of programmes. These shared two main thrusts: the first was to outline a non-ideological space for 'practical politics', the second to develop an incrementalist programme by which liberals could help, if not hurry, change.

Liberals deprecated demands for a major political rupture such as universal suffrage. The reasons for this attitude were partly anti-communism and wariness of sudden change, but many leading liberals at the time simply did not believe that the majority of Africans, Indians or coloureds were yet sufficiently 'civilised' to vote. J D Rheinallt Jones, president of the SAIRR, argued in 1948 that blacks 'must be brought within the influence of our civilisation', because '… before a people of another and lower civilisation can claim citizen rights, it is just that they should prove that they have been imbued with the principles of our civilisation. It will be necessary to demand proof of participation in and an understanding of our culture.'[19]

This and many other statements like it were motivated by the desire to do good and effect positive change but it is easy to see how liberal thinking could appear to be indistinguishable from the dominant white racist creed of the time.

Margaret and William Ballinger based their 'Programme for Progress' on the Fagan Report and submitted it to the ANC, fully expecting it to be adopted at the 1948 ANC conference. Margaret Ballinger described her main role after the 1948 general election as 'helping Africans to build up their own policy'.[20] Privately she stated that Africans had to do 'some fresher thinking … instead of drifting on a sea of old thoughts and emotions'.[21] The Ballinger 'Programme' avoided political demands and concentrated on influx control and urbanisation, seeing the latter as 'practical' issues on which pressure could successfully be brought to bear, and their 'Programme' outlined a policy of separating 'civilised' from 'uncivilised' blacks: 'Let us have locations for the new and untrained people but for all others there should be freedom to live as Europeans do (although we shall probably have to accept separate areas).'[22]

The 'Programme', written in carefully seductive language, attempted to translate the need for a permanent urban black labour force into the vision of a fully integrated black middle class, to which influx control and social (if not residential) segregation need not apply.

The Ballingers were by no means alone among liberals in trying to find a 'reasonable' way out of the ideologically riven and polarised society in which they found themselves after the war. In January 1948 Donald Molteno, scion of a famous (liberal) Cape family, presented a 'Democratic Programme' at a public lecture.[23] Like the Ballingers he rejected demands for the black franchise and delineated a 'practical' area of political activity. Liberals shared in the search for 'practical' solutions that operated in a zone where intellect applied, not ideology or nationalism. Molteno described their shared goals as follows:

> The main features of a democratic programme … would be the elevation of practical achievements above doctrinaire considerations, the fostering of inter-racial goodwill and the avoidance of all rigidities in legislation and administration, thus leaving the door open to adjustments in accordance with changing conditions.[24]

Black rights in the areas of trade unions, urban freehold tenure and the abolition of the pass laws were seen to be necessary concessions if economic growth were to be maintained (not for political or ideological reasons). The adjournment of the Native Representative Council revealed the urgency of providing adequate means of political expression for 'civilised' or middle-class Africans. Liberals also called for improvements in black housing, sanitation, medical facilities, education and other areas of social policy.[25] These calls stemmed from humanitarian concerns and the perception that the Communist Party, in mobilising Africans around civic issues, was making political capital from their socio-economic position. According to Edgar Brookes:

> The only real way to deal with Communism in the Union of South Africa, par-
> ticularly among the depressed classes, is to remove the grievances from which
> they suffer ... They have grievances and they have aspirations. You must remove
> those grievances and satisfy those aspirations. Communism will never take
> root among a satisfied people.[26]

Confronted with ideological developments to the left and right as African and Afrikaner nationalism came to dominate the political arena, liberals attempted to withdraw into a non-ideological area of consensus politics. The refusal of a group of highly principled people to appeal to principles of universal equality and freedom is striking. Nationalist ideology drove liberals into ever-weaker arguments about what *could* be done rather than what *should* be done. Their political role, outlined in their various programmes, comprised entrenching themselves in the opinion-forming and administrative machinery, where, through a hard-nosed and objective acceptance of economic facts unpalatable to white voters, they would advise where incrementally progressive 'adjustments' could be made.

'Adjustment' was a key liberal notion in the late 1940s. Liberals initially saw them-selves as mediators between government and its extra-parliamentary opposition, but, by 1948, this vision had given way to a more incremental position, with liberals arguing that their sphere of operation lay *between* policies dictated by ideology and the eco-nomic realities of the day. Liberals would not arbitrate between two opposing political forces; rather, with a creed based on a 'sane belief in reasonableness'[27] they would mediate between 'unreasonable' policies and their implementation. Such a role was seen to be urgently necessary after the 1948 election and the threat that the new NP government would legislate according to ideology rather than economic necessity and roll back the advances of the war years. SAIRR director Quintyn Whyte argued that it was inevitable that there would be conflict between economic integration and apartheid, and as a result,

> ... there must be constant adjustment and it will fall to the lot of the liberal
> mind to try to ensure that those adjustments are made with the minimum

friction. This will not be an enviable task; it will please neither the radical no[r] the reactionary: but it is an essential function in our society.[28]

Liberalism was premised on evolutionary, parliamentary gradualism, coupled with slowly developing political participation for the 'civilised' of all races. The driving force of change, for liberals, was economic integration; the beacon of future victory lay in the perceived incompatibility of apartheid and capitalism. Economic integration entailed the enmeshing of all races in the economic infrastructure of the country, and the dependence of industrial production on semi-skilled and skilled urban black labour. In this liberals were not alone. Economic integration was acknowledged by industrialists as an inevitable result of economic development. I G Fleming, president of the Federated Chamber of Industries in 1949, stated: 'The urban Native has been integrated into every level in the economic system, and whether in the producing stage, in the distributing link, or at the consumer end his function is unquestionably permanent.'[29]

For the Native Representatives and the SAIRR the inclusion of blacks in the economy, increasingly at skilled levels, was both a reason for change and a peaceful means of achieving such change.[30] It also allowed liberals to side-step hostile nationalist ideologies and argue the colour-blind logic of economic necessity, maintaining that for economic integration it was necessary to have skilled black labour and would therefore challenge job reservation and require that the migrant labour system be streamlined. In effect, liberals sought to attach a particular political dispensation to the labour requirements of industry and thereby win over capitalists as 'rational' allies and detach a black urban bourgeoisie, which would participate in (undefined) political structures 'in unity but not in equality'.[31]

Economic integration drew on the social-welfare commitments of the UP government, tentatively acknowledged by Hofmeyr during the war years. The SAIRR called for the relaxation of economically 'restraining' measures: 'only by liberating the potential energies of both the European and Non-European peoples', the SAIRR argued, would government be able to pay for 'those social welfare measures which are recognised today as the basic duty of the State to provide for all its people ...'.[32] The defeat of the UP in the 1948 election meant that the Fagan Report was not implemented and liberals switched focus and attempted to influence the implementation of the Sauer Report, the apartheid plan of the NP.

The Sauer Report, as Posel has shown, was an internally contradictory document, with areas of confusion similar to those of the Fagan Report: the precise implications of economic integration, and the status of 'urbanised' blacks.[33] What Posel termed the 'practical' faction within the NP alliance (which did not believe that black urbanisation could be reversed) controlled the Native Affairs Department in the early 1950s. 'Practical' Nationalists accepted economic integration as an established fact; their viewpoint, as expressed in *Volkshandel* in 1948, shared some common assumptions with the liberal position:

It must be acknowledged that the non-white worker already constitutes an integral part of our economic structure, that he is now so enmeshed in the spheres of our economic life that for the first fifty to one hundred years (if not longer), total segregation is pure wishful thinking. Any government which disregards this irrefutable fact will soon discover that it is no longer in a position to govern.[34]

Liberals sought to add a political programme to the integration acknowledged by the Nationalists. They pointed to economic integration as evidence of the failure of segregation, and of apartheid, which Margaret Ballinger characterised as 'segregation writ large',[35] to maintain racial separation alongside economic growth. The second and more important part of liberal strategy lay in the area of black urbanisation.

Both the Sauer and Fagan reports acknowledged the existence of permanently urbanised Africans, as did the 'practical' Nationalists.[36] According to Posel the 'ideological and administrative differentiation' between tribal and 'detribalised' Africans was central to the policy of the Native Affairs Department (NAD). 'The architects of NAD policy went along with the "practical" blueprint [for apartheid] in accepting that "detribalised" city dwellers, who had no "tribal" ties or base in the reserves, had the "residential right" to remain in the urban areas permanently ...'.[37]

The Ballinger 'Programme' attempted to combine the apartheid concept of 'detribalisation' with its own concept of 'civilisation'. The ideological and administrative kernel of both was control of the labour supply, and the Ballingers called for locations and influx control for rural migrants with their 'special problems'; 'civilised' Africans would enjoy freehold rights while subject to social and residential segregation.[38] Their political status was not discussed in the 'Programme'.

The point of difference between the liberal and the NAD positions was the way they proposed to deal with increased black proletarianisation, politicisation and unionisation. Liberals, viewing the political and industrial ferment of the 1940s as the result of a contradiction between the reserve-based cheap labour system and steady industrial development, called for the creation of co-optive structures for labour, as they did in the political arena – to separate 'civilised' or 'urbanised' Africans and absorb them in state structures. As Leo Marquard put it, 'I am not afraid of being swamped by civilised non-Europeans.'[39]

In their attempts to influence apartheid and its implementation, liberals believed economic integration was the pointer to the need for a new, liberal political dispensation that would ultimately overcome ideological distaste because of the imperatives of economic growth. To the government, however, the labour control crisis of the 1940s was evidence of a weak state, which early apartheid legislation aimed to rectify. As a result, liberals were rapidly alienated by the government.

Running parallel to the diminution of liberals' parliamentary influence after 1948 was their growing isolation from the Congress movement. They were also, moreover, increasingly alienated from international opinion.[40] Leading South African liberals considered themselves part of an 'enlightened' international community. The SAIRR had close American ties, and a number of leading liberals, such as Hoernlé and Margaret Ballinger, had attended British universities. Liberals claimed a legitimacy from their links with a body of 'disinterested' opinion that operated above the ideological battleground of South African politics.[41] By the late 1940s, however, the situation had altered significantly.

The formation of the United Nations (UN) and organisations such as the World Council of Churches resulted in the international mobilisation of a human-rights consciousness. This coincided with the onset of post-war decolonisation and the growth of the non-aligned movement. At the UN, India led newly independent countries in a series of attacks on South Africa's race policies, beginning in 1946. The Congress movement was far more successful in gaining international support for its call for equal rights. Liberals lacked an organised support base and were estranged from the ANC, the UP and the NP. Edgar Brookes noted that:

> … unfortunately for the modern South African statesman, South Africa does not live in a vacuum … the catchwords of communism and extreme nationalism form a kind of wine of freedom which has gone to the heads of many … and which renders the sober handling of practical issues on practical lines very difficult.[42]

Liberals and the Defiance Campaign: the search for an 'honourable compromise'

The year 1952 was a watershed one for white opposition politics. The dual mobilisation of anti-Nationalist opposition by the Torch Commando and the Defiance Campaign heightened the political ferment created by the constitutional crisis and growing black militancy. The Defiance Campaign led to a flurry of activity among liberal and radical whites, triggering a range of responses including the disapproval of the SAIRR, calls for a rejuvenation of the old Cape tradition, and the formation of the Congress of Democrats.

The Defiance Campaign put especial pressure on liberals by its assertion of mass-based extra-parliamentary (albeit passive resistance) techniques. During 1952 the campaign grew in size and significance, while the Torch Commando, the potentially liberal organisation that might have fought for some qualified degree of black participation in state structures, declined correspondingly. Commenting on the commando Marquard later noted:

> Liberals threw themselves heart and soul into the movement but never thought it was a liberal movement … The Torch Commando could never be a liberal movement, but it could scare the U. P.; it certainly did scare the

Nationalists, it put new heart into opposition, it gave many non-whites the feeling that all whites were not illiberal; and it might just possibly accustom a few more people to liberal ideas.[43]

And it probably did. Liberals participated in Torch Commando activities and liberal groups emerged in Cape Town, Johannesburg, Durban, Pietermaritzburg, Port Elizabeth and elsewhere during 1952. They were later to form the basis of the Liberal Party.

As the political environment changed, liberals responded in different ways. Before the Defiance Campaign began the SAIRR – then the only formally organised body of liberals in the country – stated: 'The Institute can in no way associate itself with the sweeping and impractical demands made.'[44] The statement was amended by a member of the SAIRR, who objected to an appeal for police restraint, stating: 'This casts a slur on the Police and contains an implied criticism of their actions.'[45] The SAIRR exhibited increasing opposition to the ANC's programme and campaigns in the early 1950s, relying on the old liberal favourite, the inevitability of gradualism, driven by economic integration as the vehicle for effecting change, while rejecting equality for the 'uncivilised': '[The SAIRR] accepts that the lines of certain developments in South Africa are set, for example, economic integration and residential and general social separation, but it demands the transfer of the material and cultural values of civilisation.'[46]

Liberals in the SAIRR and elsewhere banked on alliances with 'civilised' or 'educated' Africans to usher in a new era of colour-blind meritocracy – after all, this had served them well in preceding decades, when petty bourgeois ANC leaders had shared similar aspirations. But the new environment was increasingly threatening to the liberal project. The SAIRR argued that the Defiance Campaign showed that the politicisation of the 'educated and otherwise sophisticated African' had begun to 'permeate' black society, and repeated the call for co-option of 'civilised' urban blacks.[47] As the possibility of a black–white liberal alliance retreated, the SAIRR suffered increased internal pressure as members called on it to play a more overtly political role.[48] Internal divisions grew as some members called for direct negotiations with the ANC.[49]

As the Defiance Campaign grew in size and significance in 1952, the SAIRR stance altered. In August 1952, with more than 3 000 volunteers imprisoned, the SAIRR called on the government to negotiate with the ANC, and accepted black passive resistance as legitimate 'because there is no real avenue of approach and expression'.[50] By October 1952 more than 5 000 volunteers were in prison, and a statement by leading liberals published in *The Forum* in October went further than the SAIRR in calling for the Union-wide implementation of the old Cape franchise.

Both had a single shared message, namely that 'the country [is being] hurried towards a position in which honourable compromise will no longer be possible'.[51] Both centres of liberal opinion – the SAIRR and the Native Representatives – understood that the Defiance Campaign had resulted from the closure of channels of political expression to 'civilised' blacks; and both called for the detachment of 'civilised' Africans from the mass of the migrant and rural black population. The statement in *The Forum* continued:

> We believe that it is imperative that South Africa should now adopt a policy that will attract the support of educated, politically conscious non-Europeans by offering them a reasonable status in our country. This can be done by a revival of the liberal tradition which prevailed for so many years with such successful results in the Cape Colony.[52]

One of the tragedies of liberalism at this critical time in South Africa was its hankering for a glorified past and its concomitant inability to picture the future without hedging it with qualifications, means tests and unequal entry points: a tentative tête-à-tête between whites and civilised blacks and an unspecified future for the 'uncivilised'. In this, leading liberals were as much a post-war relic as Jan Smuts had found himself to be. The LP was a necessary vehicle for overhauling this exhausted creed.

Liberal faith in the progressive nature of secondary industry suffered setbacks in the early 1950s, which, over time, would cumulatively generate an appreciation of the need for liberal agency. In 1952, for example, Margaret Ballinger attempted to secure the support of industrialists for the statement in *The Forum*. The reply of the president of the Federal Chamber of Industries, G E Williamson, indicated the gap between the labour requirements of secondary industry and the political dispensation that self-proclaimed liberals attempted to attach thereto.

Writing at the height of the Defiance Campaign, Williamson stated that his federation was opposed to the abolition of the pass laws and was not unhappy with the Group Areas Act. 'Speaking … primarily for the Cape,' Williamson continued, 'I do not think that social segregation is opposed by any section of the community.'[53] In such a context conservative figures such as Native Representatives Brookes and Molteno were portrayed as extremists.[54] Liberal industrialists may have found it expedient to distance themselves from the activities of liberals in the early 1950s. Alternatively, it could be that capitalism and capitalists were far more comfortable with apartheid than liberal theory said they should be. Williamson's reply to Margaret Ballinger concluded: 'What really worries me is an inability to say who the "we" in the circular may be!'[55]

The Defiance Campaign drew its main strength from the rural areas of the Eastern Cape. With more than 8 000 volunteers imprisoned and ANC membership reaching some 100 000 the campaign extended well beyond liberal descriptions of a clerics' revolt. This was emphasised by Joe Matthews, writing to his father in America about the statement in *The Forum*: 'The Whites do not realise that the educated are just not in this thing to the extent that one would expect. I for one am not prepared to tolerate any suggestion that will give the benefits of the Defiance Campaign to the people who did not actually suffer, or work for its success …'.[56]

Discussing the call for the reintroduction of the Cape franchise Matthews commented that: 'The U.P. group is completely mixed up. The liberals are trying to stage a comeback but I think their campaign died two days after they had issued their statement.' Of the qualified franchise itself, Matthews simply asked: 'Can papa think of anything more unrealistic?'[57]

The Defiance Campaign highlighted the gap between liberal and radical whites in South Africa, as it did the ideological distance between Congress and white liberals. By 1952 white liberals were under attack on all fronts. As Edgar Brookes had gloomily portended in 1948: 'Those who believed in constitutional methods ... found themselves ground between the upper and nether millstones of conservatism and what they felt to be the undesirable elements of direct action and boycott.'[58]

Seen from a different perspective, liberal influence on Congress was ground to dust by the two liberal millstones – insistence on a qualified franchise and rejection of extra-parliamentary action. But the Torch Commando had also indicated that a white anti-Nationalist opposition existed and could be mobilised, albeit around a very basic (and not terribly 'liberal') programme. In this uncertain political context liberal groups were formed in various centres in 1951–1952 with the intention of formulating a distinct liberal policy and launching a political vehicle of some sort as a means of attracting support for liberal ideals. As we have seen, the same was happening among whites of a more radical hue, as it was among communists.

Liberal resurgence

The flutter of liberal activity between 1951 and 1953 was influenced by a number of factors. The exclusion of liberals from political influence was clearly significant. At the same time, there was considerable optimism, engendered by the rise of the Torch Commando, as well as enthusiasm about the prospect of articulating a clearly 'liberal' policy, rather than (in Marquard's words) having 'to choose the lesser of two evils as between the two major parties'.[59]

The first liberal group was the Hofmeyr Society, founded in August 1950 by Julius Lewin 'to maintain in the public life of South Africa the aims and ideals that inspired the late Jan H. Hofmeyr'.[60] It was restricted to UP members and aimed to 'liberalise' the UP from within. As Lewin himself put it, 'we *don't* want another body of liberals *avoiding* party politics'.[61] The Hofmeyr Society did not affiliate to the SALA, and opposed launching the Liberal Party.[62] As if its tiny membership were not enough of a problem, the Hofmeyr Society also enjoyed the disapproval of UP leader J G N Strauss, who, Lewin noted, 'is unfriendly to the idea and even to our name!'[63] Overtaken by the Defiance Campaign, the flurry of liberal-left activity, and Strauss's restatement of traditional segregation beliefs at the 1952 UP Conference, the Hofmeyr Society had faded away by the end of 1952. Its importance lay firstly in its journal, *Agenda*, which was distributed within the UP and among South African liberals. Secondly, and of greater significance, it was the last champion of 'economic liberalism' before the emergence of the Progressive Party in 1959.

Early in 1951 the South African Liberal Group (SALG) was formed in Cape Town. Led by Oscar Wollheim, an energetic schoolteacher and social worker, the SALG also included a Springbok Legion member among its six founders, a departure from the effete membership of other liberal groups.[64] By mid-1952 similar groups – none with a membership of more than twenty – had been formed in Durban, Pietermaritzburg, Port Elizabeth, East London and Johannesburg.[65] By October 1952 Johannesburg boasted three separate liberal groups – the remnants of the Hofmeyr Society; a second group, led by Jock Isacowitz and advocate Jack Unterhalter, which sought contact with the SAIC and ANC, and, finally, a group of prominent academics, church people, SAIRR members and others, led by Margaret Ballinger.

The emergent liberal movement was soon dominated by the Ballinger group, which was a study group set up 'to clarify the specific implications of a liberal programme'.[66] The group was formed in response to the statement in *The Forum* and included most leading white Johannesburg anti-Nationalists (apart from those already in COD).[67] However, the group was alone in its open opposition to forming a new political party or association. Despite its objections, the South African Liberal Association was formed in Cape Town in January 1953, with Oscar Wollheim as the driving force. Margaret Ballinger, as the leading liberal figure in the country, was elected chairperson; her own liberal group, however, refused to affiliate.[68]

According to Wollheim the SALA was formed because 'the time had come for a lead from the intelligent people of the country'.[69] The liberal groups of the early 1950s reflected the Fabian inclinations of earlier decades, and saw themselves as an explicitly elitist grouping. Their function was to channel liberal opinion while developing and popularising a liberal policy. Wollheim insisted that 'any really Liberal group must have the support of the intellectuals',[70] and argued further that it was:

> ... time to bring into the political field that large body of educated, cultured and articulate opinion represented by the professions, universities, teachers etc. We feel that a large proportion of the mass would be prepared to follow the lead of such a group of persons who have never joined a party because existing parties sicken them and who are known for their integrity, common sense and good judgements.[71]

All the liberal groups maintained a degree of secrecy in order not to embarrass the UP, of which most were members. As small educative units working with an eye on the UP they restricted their size, while the Ballinger group, remarkably, maintained a whites-only membership.[72]

A SALG *Newsletter* published at the height of the Defiance Campaign outlined liberal thinking at the time. Black society, the *Newsletter* argued, was stratified along similar lines to those of white society. These included a small 'cultured and highly developed' upper class, a trading middle class 'who have reached a stage of development comparable with similar groups of whites'; and the black working class, 'which stretches from the similar groups of whites down to the most primitive forms of tribal culture'.[73] The danger of apartheid, the *Newsletter* warned, lay in ignoring such stratification and treating all blacks in the same manner. The black 'upper class' individual, it warned, 'cannot be expected eternally to gaze with philosophical calm at "Europeans Only" notices wherever he goes', or disregard maltreatment by those 'much below his own cultural standards'.[74]

In a similar vein Margaret Ballinger, in 1949, asked of apartheid: 'Will it not lead, must it not lead to the emergence of a united anti-European bloc?'[75] The liberal groups of 1951–1953 all echoed this warning and began to develop common strategies to deal with black radicalisation, as their chances of stopping the white slide into racism evaporated and their stomach for the fight went with it. Oscar Wollheim claimed that politicised Africans were 'intransigent and radical' and would only speak with white radicals.

Apartheid was rapidly extending this attitude to Indians and coloureds as well, and Wollheim argued that liberals had to act soon in order to 'hold them', to separate the black elite and to stop the wholesale black political estrangement that apartheid was producing.[76] The chairperson of the Pietermaritzburg liberal group, a young Peter Brown, repeated this sentiment more frankly in a speech in June 1952, stating that liberals had to 'split the Non-Europeans … [they are a] solid block and regard us as [the] same …'.[77] The notion that such an approach may have been regarded by black South Africans as malign rather than benign would have been greeted with shock.

In essence, liberal strategy comprised the cultivation of a support base among 'civilised' blacks, who would be enfranchised under the qualified suffrage endorsed by the SALA and LP. This would stop wholesale black political estrangement and would also allow liberals 'to win out against Communism'.[78] The main focus of the early LP was on parliamentary politics; the qualified franchise was also intended to appease white fears of being swamped at the polls.

The formation of the Liberal Party

Central to the various liberal strategies developed in the early 1950s was the need for an active political organisation of some sort to popularise liberal values and to rally electoral support for them. Liberals in various centres had made calls for a 'liberal party' at regular intervals after 1936, mainly directed at Jan Hofmeyr, but nothing had happened.[79] Following Hofmeyr's death Margaret Ballinger was frequently approached with the same request, but, although she showed more interest, she too refused to launch or lead a new party.[80]

The Ballinger group rejected calls for the transformation of the SALA into a political party; at the centre of their objections lay what Margaret Ballinger argued was '… a fundamental difference between liberal principles and seeking mass support. In sticking to the former we would largely forego the latter.'[81]

The Ballinger group was the most explicitly Fabianite of the 1951–1953 liberal groups and influenced the development of liberal thinking among the various structures most clearly by insisting on the adoption of a clause endorsing 'only democratic and constitutional means' and opposing 'all forms of totalitarianism such as communism and fascism'.[82] Despite its evident intellectual authority, however, the group was isolated in its opposition to calls for a more activist liberal role. The political 'new blood' in the other groups pushed increasingly assertively for the formation of a political party. Margaret Ballinger was looked to as the natural leader of such a party, despite the resistance of her own group. The chairperson of the Pietermaritzburg group stated: 'we have been hoping for a lead from someone in authority ... [but with] no sign of that ... we'll have to do it ourselves'.[83] In the event, Ballinger was out-manoeuvred and ended up – reluctantly – leading a party she thought should not exist.

The fact that political conditions between 1950 and 1952 influenced the development of liberalism and liberal strategies was made evident by the opposition to extra-parliamentary action enshrined in the programmes of the various liberal groups, adopted at the height of the Defiance Campaign and reflecting their primary focus – the United Party, not the Congress movement; white voters, not black mobilisation. The aim of the emerging liberal movement, according to Wollheim (in rather illiberal language), was to act as 'a pistol pointed at the head of the U.P.'.[84] Liberals did all they could to avoid embarrassing the United Party through close public association with it, but the liberal groups focused on influencing it.[85] Groups of liberals were active in UP constituency organisations in Durban, Johannesburg and elsewhere, and succeeded in influencing candidate selection in a number of cases.[86] Helen Suzman, John Cope and other (later prominent) UP liberals were elected to Parliament for the first time in April 1953.

The various formations (the Ballinger group excepted) continued to envisage the formation of a new party at some future date.[87] The failure of the UP to 'liberalise' its policies was compounded by its failure to defeat the NP in 1953. The SALA Federal Council concluded that liberals were 'thinking that they might just as well have been defeated on an honest liberal programme as on the compromise which they had adopted'.[88] After the election SALA's Transvaal Region was reported to be 'almost unanimously' in favour of launching a 'liberal party'.[89] In May 1953 the Transvaal called a national meeting of SALA to debate the issue.

The manner in which the Liberal Party of South Africa was launched, on 9 May 1953, reveals the confusion and contradictions which beset post-war white South African liberals. At the SALA meeting those in favour of a new party pointed to the imminent formation of the Union-Federal Party in Natal, and possible unilateral action by the Transvaal SALA, as reasons for launching a party. It was also argued that, following the launch of the Congress of Democrats, there existed a 'need to provide an alternative to Communist influence on African organisations, especially on the Rand'.[90] Margaret Ballinger, however, urged liberals to refrain from what she saw as precipitate political action, repeating her argument that 'a lot more precise thinking [is] needed on liberalism'.[91] Marquard, ever the strategist, advised that there would have to be consultation with black leaders before such a step was taken. Molteno questioned this, stating, 'The leadership of the Non-Europeans would not have anything to do with Liberalism at present anyway.'[92]

The opposition of the three most prominent liberal figures – Ballinger, Molteno and Marquard – to the (immediate) formation of a new party had to be overcome if the new party were to have any chance of success. Oscar Wollheim and Leslie Rubin, a Cape lawyer prominent in the Torch Commando and the SALA, tipped off the press before the SALA meeting. On 6 May the *Cape Times* carried a story reporting the history of the SALA (which had previously shunned publicity) and associated the names of Molteno, Marquard, Ballinger and author Alan Paton with moves to form a new party.[93] This despite the fact that Ballinger's liberal group had mandated her to oppose the formation of a new party[94] and that Natal delegates had a similar mandate.[95] Voting on the issue on the first day was fifteen to five in favour of a party; not the required majority. On 9 May the Natal delegates switched their votes, and only two voters opposed formation – quite remarkably they were the first Liberal Party chairperson, Margaret Ballinger, and its Vice-chairperson, Donald Molteno.[96] Leo Marquard later explained that Rubin and Wollheim '… to some extent jumped the gun by publishing our names (Molteno, Margaret Ballinger and me) and facing us with a *fait accompli*. Once that was done we had either to dissociate ourselves from the move or help to found a Liberal Party.'[97]

The immediate reaction within the South African Liberal Association was enthusiastic and optimistic. A number of members believed that a large liberal constituency existed and would vote for their progressive racial message.[98] An approach from the Labour Party calling on liberals to join it rather than continue with a separate organisation was rejected, liberals arguing that they would soon be the larger organisation.[99] Alan Paton spoke giddily of the Liberal Party enjoying up to 40% of the popular vote, and believed that 'the Party could be launched in every town and city'.[100] Other party members predicted a UP split and the accession by the LP to parliamentary representation.[101] As it was, the Liberal Party was launched with some 500 members, a number that had risen a year later to 971.[102] Branches were overwhelmingly located in cities or large towns. The only representation the party enjoyed were the Native Representatives, until their position was abolished by the NP government in 1961.

The LP adopted the SALA's constitution and, in 1953, emerged as a non-racial party with constitutionally enshrined anti-communist sentiments and supportive of a qualified franchise. Both the SALA and the LP stated their opposition to extra-parliamentary activity, a stance that bore the clear imprint of the Ballinger group, which, in its statement of principles, used a phrase adopted by other liberal groups and the LP, that they would pursue 'only democratic and constitutional means' of opposition. The Ballinger group's statement ended by reiterating that 'the Liberal group affirms its faith in the Parliamentary system',[103] a clause that was one conservative step too far. The LP did not adopt it.

In endorsing only parliamentary activity an important section of liberal opinion (led by Margaret Ballinger) was concerned to distance itself from the extra-parliamentary activities of the Congress movement and, more particularly, from the newly launched Congress of Democrats. In so doing, however, the leadership of the LP placed itself at odds with much of the party membership. The tensions within the SALA and later the LP created a series of contradictions that played out within the LP throughout the 1950s. The party experienced internal discord on core issues of strategy and party policy as competing factions sought either to maintain its focus on white parliamentary politics or to shift it to the black extra-parliamentary arena. This division was compounded by the wide range of political perspectives included within the SALA and LP and, as a result, a number of important issues were subsumed within a wider-ranging internal dispute.

Economic liberalism?

One such issue was economic policy. Both the SALA and the LP were marked by the almost complete absence of an economic policy or set of economic proposals. Liberalism in South Africa was about a particular approach to race relations and (partial) equality not about economics, so liberals could be found supporting laissez-faire economics, social democratic approaches or variants of socialism. The administrative thrust of liberalism as it had developed in the late 1940s began to give way, between 1951 and 1953, to a growing stress on civil rights and the affirmation of moral values. United Party MP and SALA member Robin Stratford warned – accurately – early in 1951 that '… it is too readily assumed … that policies dictated by goodwill and reason have only to be widely proclaimed to be as widely accepted … [liberals] are content with principles and tend to shy away from practical politics …'.[104]

The liberal movement was held together by opposition to racism (and by extension to the NP government), to communism, and to the mass-based extra-parliamentary campaigns of the Congress movement. Unified in these three areas, the LP formation sought to paper over some very deep ideological cracks.

In the early 1950s the affirmation of principle took almost complete precedence over the development of a liberal economic policy, an attitude personified by the call by Christopher Gell, an influential liberal critic with close ANC and SAIC links, for the LP to avoid committing itself to either a socialist or a laissez-faire programme 'in order to fight the main issue of colour domination'.[105] This should not be taken to mean that liberals did not spend a great deal of time thinking and writing about economics. 'Economic liberalism' was a concept widely debated in *The Forum* and elsewhere in the late 1940s. In a series of articles and editorials *The Forum* called for the creation of a 'black middle class', which, with a stake in society, would not be amenable to 'communistic' influences. Other articles claimed that South Africa's 'salvation' lay in economic progress and a steadily rising standard of living for blacks.[106]

The Forum accepted that political separation was incompatible with 'economic integration' and proposed solving this by a return to the old Cape franchise. Faced with the intractable problem of white fears of *oorstrooming*, *The Forum* explained that this could be overcome 'by heavily loading the franchise of the non-European in comparison with that of the European'.[107] By focusing on the UP and attempting to appease a racist white electorate, liberals inevitably watered down their message and sounded weaker, and their repeated appeals to principle sounded increasingly disingenuous. The LP was meant to allow liberals to throw off these shackles and openly propose liberal solutions rather than attempt, tortuously, to elide its own beliefs with the forces of reaction.

The Hofmeyr Society followed a similar line to that in *The Forum*, attempting to align itself with commercial and industrial capital, which it described as 'the forces of progress'.[108] Eleanor Hawarden, a noted educationalist and Hofmeyr Society founder, stated: 'We should stand for a liberal capitalism.'[109] For the society this meant that within an expanding economy black income and opportunities could be increased without threatening white standards of living. The society called on liberals to concentrate on developing a sound economic policy because (with no apparent hint of irony) the NP was 'weak on such subjects and because we can't compete with them on racialism'.[110] The Hofmeyr Society, however, was unable to convince other liberal groups to concentrate on economic issues.

The SALG was the only liberal group other than the Hofmeyr Society to raise the question of economic liberalism, including economic proposals in its 'Ten Point Programme' circulated for debate among various liberal groups. The draft economic clause called for the development of human and material resources 'for the benefit of all' and for 'the regulation of our economic machine to eliminate the unhealthy exploitation of the many for the few'.[111] This was later amended to call for 'the need to control state or other monopolies', indicating the social-democratic and socialist influences within the group.[112]

The Ballinger group sharply rejected the SALG formulation 'for its Socialist orientation' but offered no alternative.[113] Other liberal groups were unable to reach agreement on the issue and, as a result, largely ignored the economic arena. The SALG concluded: 'it was felt that the necessity existed for some reference ... to an economic policy' but that it 'should not be worded so that it could be interpreted as favouring either Socialism or free enterprise ...'.[114] In the absence of consensus no coherent statement of liberal economics was produced by any of the groups, and the SALA Principles were not specific in dealing with economic issues; the association endorsed 'economic integration' and called for the 'stabilization of labour and sound family life'.[115]

The economic debate was further complicated as it became caught up in an internal power struggle which afflicted the LP after its rushed formation in May 1953. In most of the internal LP disputes there were two clear opposing sides: what was called the 'radical' wing of the party, which supported universal suffrage, extra-parliamentary action and close links with the congresses; and the more conservative wing, which regarded the qualified franchise as a principle and saw the LP as a classic parliamentary political party. Anti-communism was a shared trait. As Christopher Gell pointed out, 'the "Left" and "Right" wing division in the party ... coincide[s] so nearly with provincial boundaries'.[116] The Transvaal was most frequently associated with the more 'radical' grouping, in opposition to the more conservative Cape, whose (early) leaders still hankered after their century-old, much vaunted liberal tradition.

LP economic policy became embroiled in the Transvaal–Cape power struggle, which continued from 1953 to 1957. By the end of 1953, although LP candidates were already contesting provincial elections, the party had still not agreed on an economic policy.[117] The Cape division had the majority of members and could thereby ensure that its influence was translated into policy. The Cape elected economists Sheila van der Horst and Ralph Horwitz to the 1953–1954 Labour and Economic Commission, thereby excluding any Transvaal representatives.[118]

In 1954 Horwitz advised the LP National Committee that to attract financial support from industrial concerns the party would at least have to state clearly its support for free enterprise.[119] Transvaal delegates rejected Horwitz's argument, warning that if forced to they would oppose it with a call for a fully socialist policy. The National Committee, unable to negotiate a way out of the impasse, simply left the issue alone. The party's economic preferences, the committee argued, should be understood 'by implication'.[120] The resultant policy document, like its SALA predecessor, was non-specific and obscure. In 1954 Leo Marquard, ever pithy, described it as 'vague and full of pious sentiments'.[121]

Liberal attempts to rally business support were not successful, and there was a clear gap between the labour requirements of the secondary industry and even the more conservative proposals of the various liberal programmes. The early 1950s witnessed the implementation of apartheid measures alongside a strengthening economy, and wartime liberal faith in the incompatibility of economic expansion and segregation came to be expressed in terms of the inescapability of economic integration: business might not like a degree of racial equality but would have to stomach it to keep profits up. The LP took economic integration as its starting point, concentrating not on winning support for such integration but on outlining the political dispensation which should result from it.

The middle ground liberals hoped to occupy became increasingly untenable. The LP could not develop an economic policy capable of appeasing its own left and right wings, let alone others outside the party (whether to the left or the right). Industrial capital rejected even the conservative proposals of the 1950s, and the gap between organised liberal opinion and industrial capital grew. Liberal faith in the transforming power of economic integration was undermined by the steady economic growth of the 1950s, despite (as they saw it) the increasingly harsh implementation of influx control regulations. This was compounded by the changed political climate of the 1950s, which saw the Liberal Party roundly attacked by both government and opposition as idealists (at best), negrophiles, or extremists. Julius Lewin later noted: 'The businessmen whom one might have expected to rally round a liberal party, did nothing of the kind. They even discouraged their wives from doing so on the grounds that it was bad for business if their own private sympathies were suspected.'[122]

The Liberal Party received no major capitalist support throughout its fifteen-year existence.[123] Attempts to generate financial support from industry in particular were unsuccessful.[124] The party survived on membership dues, donations and fund-raising events such as book and cake sales; its main source of financial income came privately from wealthier members Peter Brown and Alan Paton.[125]

'Not yet liberal enough'[126]

Another fundamental point of disagreement among liberals was whether the prime focus of their activity should be in the parliamentary or extra-parliamentary, the white or black, political arenas. This generated a series of tensions that divided the SALA and the early LP.

One such issue was the question of non-racialism. Recently described as the 'guiding principle' of the LP[127] – much as it has been claimed as the 'unbreakable thread' of the ANC since 1912[128] – non-racialism was not automatically accepted by the liberal movement; certainly not in the early 1950s. The Ballinger group maintained a whites-only membership; most of the other groups accepted non-racial membership. The claim made by the editors of *Democratic Liberalism in South Africa* that the LP 'was formed with many African members and some African leaders'[129] is patently inaccurate, since none of the liberal groups succeeded in enrolling more than one or two black members.[130]

In attempting to change this situation the LP adopted what later party Chairperson Peter Brown described as a 'genuine anomaly' – namely open party membership alongside a qualified franchise.[131] By this means the LP enrolled members regardless of whether they would be enfranchised under the party's franchise proposals.

The Ballinger group, typically, had analysed the political motivation behind non-racialism. In debating the issue, one member pointed out that to reject black members would mean that 'we would be falling behind even the U. P. which had a Coloured branch'.[132] Torch Commando chairperson Louis Kane-Berman, later closely linked to the Union-Federal Party in Natal, stated more bluntly: 'We [have] two instruments, 1. Natal and 2. the Non-European', and noted that having black members '... might be dangerous but bold measures were needed and the Nats would be really alarmed at any overtures made to the Non-European'.[133]

The need to enrol black liberals as a bulwark against the spread of 'communist' influence was also widely expressed.[134]

The opening of party membership to all was opposed by those members who saw the parliamentary arena as the prime focus of liberal activity. One such member warned: 'we are letting the liberal idea run away with us. It is possible to be so liberal that we have no standards at all',[135] while another stated: '… the movement can only achieve results if it gains public support, which will be alienated if the Group is stampeded into flaunting its liberalism by giving office to non-Europeans, particularly if they are not very carefully selected'.[136]

For those who focused on black political work and sought closer relations with the ANC and SAIC the 'civilised' franchise was seen as a major obstacle, and the LP soon split over the franchise issue. Anti-communism, which engendered hostility from Congress, also divided the party, with a section of its 'left wing' campaigning for its deletion from the party programme. Each of these disputed attempts to democratise the party programme was opposed by precisely those leaders the LP had 'hijacked' in May 1953.

The election from the 1940s of prominent liberals as leaders of the LP obscured the nature of the party itself. The Native Representatives were respected, in some cases almost revered, figures; their political creed, however, was deeply conservative. The Liberal Party was a hybrid which fed off a number of political traditions, born, moreover, in the specific conditions of 1952–1953. The socialists, social democrats and others who joined the LP because of its anti-communism, or its non-racialism, were soon drawn into open conflict with the party leaders and their supporters. Within a year of its formation Margaret Ballinger tendered her resignation, complaining that 'I find it quite impossible to carry the burden of responsibility that the leadership requires in this formative period, without the active support of a group of people of my own type in whose judgement and integrity I can have confidence.'[137]

Chapter 7

Overhauling liberalism

By 1956 the Liberal Party (LP) had a new leadership and articulated a vision of change based on mass non-violent pressure in which it would play a part alongside the congresses. This replaced the earlier notion that by offering a living example of racial co-operation and 'by argument, much organisation, and ceaseless constitutional action'[1] the party would emerge as the only rational vehicle for evolutionary change. While changes in the party were influenced to a degree by Congress's criticism they resulted largely from an internal critique and overhaul of liberalism initiated by party progressives and intellectuals in 1953.

The Liberal Party in 1953

When it was formed the LP was hailed in the English press as 'a new party formed to revive and keep alive an old idea'.[2] Margaret Ballinger saw it as a support group for the native representatives and the principles they espoused in Parliament:

> The policy of the Liberal Party is an evolutionary policy aiming at the pro-
> gressive widening of the field of personal liberty for all sections of the popu-
> lation … By general admission, this line has always been taken by those of us
> who have represented Africans over the last seventeen years, and who are now
> identified with the Liberal Party.[3]

The party emerged from its first national conference in July 1953 with a statement of principle almost entirely derived from the South African Liberal Association (SALA). The LP endorsed a qualified non-racial franchise and segregation by consent but not by force,[4] and opposed 'all forms of totalitarianism such as communism and fascism'.[5]

Moreover, it was committed to using 'only democratic and constitutional means' of opposition.[6] Margaret Ballinger claimed that its constitutional approach would ultimately offer blacks 'a full share in the life of this country' and obviate another 'unparliamentary outbreak like the Defiance Campaign'.[7]

Joined by her husband Senator William Ballinger, together with LP members Walter Stanford and Leslie Rubin, elected as Native Representatives in 1954, Margaret Ballinger advised the LP to concentrate on the general principles it had endorsed and to leave 'practical decisions on day to day issues' to the parliamentarians.[8] This was not the role many liberal activists had in mind.

Ballinger called on the 1953 Party Conference to concentrate on strengthening the central machinery of the LP and on raising funds for a newspaper and national organiser. Above all, the party had to avoid 'being stampeded' into 'hasty' policy formulation.[9] Ballinger was supported by a number of leading LP members, who reacted to the hostile reception the African National Congress (ANC) had given the LP by claiming that the 'enemies' of the party 'want ... something to twist'.[10] Leading LP members argued that the acceptance of a 'common society', reflected in the non-racial franchise proposals, was sufficient for a party barely two months old; it would give the parliamentarians 'plenty of time to give the best elaboration of our principles'.[11]

Liberal Party members, with their widely divergent views, were united by opposition to apartheid and the Nationalist Party's abrogation of the constitution in its attempts to disenfranchise black voters. Among the members were those who were opposed to the Congress Alliance, including its multiracial structure, the methods it employed and the presence of former Communist Party members in all four congresses. The rushed formation of the LP had precluded all but the most general discussion of the policies the party should adopt or the strategies it should follow.

Both the Natal and Transvaal divisions had socialist and social-democratic members who saw the party as a vehicle for working with both black and white communities. Jock Isacowitz, a leading personality in the Transvaal LP, envisaged a party 'acceptable to whites but with an entrée to blacks. A party of today but tuned to tomorrow.'[12] Many members were interested primarily in organising blacks, and those in Natal turned immediately to developing a black membership.[13] The confusion over the identity and purpose of the LP meant that the party 'Principles' were themselves contested by the Transvaal and Natal divisions. As a result, the 1953 conference ignored the advice of its leaders and adopted a wide range of policies covering education, health, labour and economics, relations with other organisations, the franchise and other issues.

As noted above, conflicting economic visions saw the Transvaal directly opposed to the Cape, but this was merely one of a slate of divisive issues. All the office bearers elected in 1953, apart from Alan Paton, were members of the Cape division. The Cape also had a numerical preponderance, with 380 members against the Transvaal's 329 and Natal's 201.[14] The challenge from the Transvaal in support of universal suffrage and close co-operation with the Congress Alliance was overridden by the Cape, and the party adopted the SALA 'Principles'.

The locus of disagreement at the 1953 Conference was the role, if any, of the LP in black politics. While many believed that black politics was the main arena in which the party should be working, others considered the LP to be a parliamentary party concerned with winning white voter support. The party's policy on 'Relations With Non-European Organisations' was pushed through by the Cape, whose dominance ensured that it stopped well short of endorsing the struggle waged by the congresses. The policy professed 'profound sympathy' with the struggle and only in 1954 did it name the African National Congress and South African Indian Congress (SAIC) as representative black political organisations.[15] But the Natal and Transvaal divisions did exert sufficient pressure to commit the LP to accepting joint Congress–LP membership.[16]

The most hotly debated issue at the 1953 Conference was the franchise policy. After 'considerable discussion'[17] delegates endorsed a qualified but non-racial franchise, with the Cape representative arguing:

> There is … a justification for withholding political rights from people who are not sufficiently civilised to use them in a responsible manner. It is therefore necessary to lay down a test as a means of distinguishing between civilised and uncivilised South Africans, and to grant political rights to all who can pass the test … It is desirable that the test should be a fairly stiff one in a country where there is a wide range of cultural levels.[18]

The Transvaal delegates called for universal suffrage, or at least its inclusion as the 'ultimate goal' of the party. Pressure from Natal – the only division with influential black members – succeeded in altering the franchise qualification from 'civilised' to 'suitably qualified' and linked to a policy of universal compulsory education. The Cape delegates compromised on their call for high voting qualifications and the party proposed enfranchising those over twenty-one years of age who had a Standard 6 education, or earned £250 a year, or owned property valued at £500 or more; it also proposed a tribunal for those over the age of thirty-five not enfranchised by the above criteria but who were 'adjudged … to deserve the franchise on the grounds that they occupy positions of special responsibility or have rendered meritorious service to the community'.[19] The tortuousness of the proposals indicates how fiercely the battle was fought.

Transvaal delegates also called for deletion of the clause in the party 'Principles' that called for opposition 'to all forms of totalitarianism such as communism and fascism', arguing that the clause should at least include the party's main antagonist, apartheid.[20] This was defeated. Cape dominance of the early LP ensured the development of a party with policies tailored to nurturing gently the fragile emergence of a racially tolerant white electorate; in essence, blacks had to wait until whites were ready for them. The party leadership rejected calls for the LP to become active in the black political arena, insisting that 'the Liberal Party is an ordinary normal Party, pledged to attain its objects by normal methods'.[21]

The LP accordingly turned to contesting the 1953 Johannesburg City Council elections, where, after a vigorous campaign, its candidates received an average of 29% of votes cast.[22] Although the party was soundly defeated by United Party (UP) candidates – no Liberal Party candidate ever won an election[23] – the LP in 1953 functioned as a conventional political party, concentrating on electioneering, fund-raising and membership drives.

In 1953 the party's leaders and most of its members were white and drawn from the professional English-speaking middle classes. The National Committee was entirely white and included one professor, three university lecturers, an author, a publisher, a surveyor, four lawyers, a chemist and a social worker alongside Margaret and William Ballinger and Bishop Parker of Cape Town. In 1954 the composition of an enlarged National Committee was similar, with ten university lecturers and seven lawyers, out of a total of thirty-two Committee members. The Executive Committee, which effectively ran the day-to-day affairs of the party, was restricted to office bearers, all of whom were white.[24] The various provincial committees were overwhelmingly made up of (white) lawyers and academics.

In 1954, however, after black membership increased in Natal, black representatives from the Natal division were elected to the National Committee. Within the LP there were different interpretations of the party's function – should it concentrate on wooing white voter support, enrol black members and instil liberal values in them, co-operate with the congresses, or challenge Congress by transforming the party into a significant black political organisation in its own right? As a result, party divisions (and groups within them) undertook different political activities. These, in turn, both reflected and stemmed from a deeper ideological debate within the party over the nature of liberalism in South Africa and the correct organisational form it should adopt – the same kind of ferment that had engulfed communists, shorn of their party, at roughly the same time.

Liberalism and the Liberal Party

The disputes within the party centred on its role in black politics. Relations between the LP and the Congress movement were soured from the start as the LP was seen to have been formed in competition with the South African Congress of Democrats (SACOD) and because it threatened to compete with the congresses for membership. Joe Matthews advised the 1953 Cape ANC Conference not to trust 'the appeal of those who call themselves "Liberals" or "friends" of the African people'.[25] His father, the redoubtable liberal and ANC leader, Z K Matthews, stated in the same year: 'The question is whether they have enough strength and enough ability to overcome the reluctance of the average liberal white South African to work *with* instead of *for* the African.'[26]

The general antipathy of the Congress movement to the LP – it accused the party of standing 'outside the democratic camp'[27] and offering the Congress movement 'little sops' which were of 'no value'[28] – was replicated in formal meetings between representatives of the LP and the congresses across the country in 1953.

Natal Indian Congress (NIC) representatives criticised the LP's franchise policy and its rejection of extra-parliamentary action; a meeting with Natal ANC leaders produced similar criticism, as did meetings with Thomas Ngwenya and Joe Nkatlo of the Cape ANC, and with ANC Secretary-General Walter Sisulu in Johannesburg.[29] Jock Isacowitz reported that hostility to the LP in Johannesburg – the headquarters of SACOD and the ANC – was such that even informal meetings with representatives of the ANC were all but impossible to arrange.[30] At the ANC's 1953 Annual Conference its President-General, Albert Luthuli, accepted co-operation with the LP on agreed issues but rejected its policy of joint membership: 'We must be on guard against members of the A.N.C. becoming members of political Parties whose objectives are different from our own. Divided allegiance would be difficult for the individual concerned.'[31]

Congress's criticism focused the attention of LP members who sought closer relations with the ANC and SAIC on the franchise and the status of extra-parliamentary activity. These policies also stood in the way of those who sought to penetrate the black community without developing close links with the Congress movement, including young Turks who joined the party in the Cape. As a result, these two issues became the centre of a party-wide dispute that lasted throughout the 1950s, where it was joined as a point of contention by anti-communism.

The anti-communist clause in the LP 'Principles' was reflected in attacks on SACOD as a scarcely veiled communist front intent on manipulating the other congresses. Jimmy Gibson, a young Cape lawyer and one of the more energetic members of the Cape LP, for whom anti-communism was more theism than creed, claimed that in the Cape 'the regional branch [of the ANC] had become the plaything of politically interested persons and had no power whatsoever'.[32] Gibson and his supporters saw the best means of combating communism to be an all-out attack on SACOD via the Cape Western by-elections which followed the ejection from Parliament of (SACOD and former CPSA members) Brian Bunting and Ray Alexander.[33]

Where party progressives saw the main task of the LP as developing a significant black support base, the party's early leaders were primarily concerned with gaining white voter support. Vice-chairperson Leo Marquard stressed that the LP '*must* consult Africans and Coloureds and Asians'; but argued: 'We should *not* place ourselves in the position of negotiating with the A.N.C., except on a purely informal and almost personal basis.'[34]

In the early years of the party many of its leaders were openly hostile to the potentially 'revolutionary' methods used by the Congress movement, which they saw as communist-influenced. Vice-chairperson Oscar Wollheim stated:

> Few people of liberal thought would complain about the basic principles of what ... [the Congresses] eventually aim at but many disapprove heartily of the methods envisage[d], of the tempo at which they wish to attain their ends and many shudder to think of the chaotic consequences likely to ensue if false hopes are raised among large sections of the non-white population and if agitation to form a liberation front is engaged in.[35]

The LP's Cape division exhibited a general antipathy to the ANC, which grew as younger members ousted the initial, older leaders. In June 1953 Nelson Mandela concluded an article hostile to the LP with the question: 'Which side, gentlemen, are you on?'[36] In reply, Professor T W Price of the University of Cape Town, a member of the National and Executive Committees of the LP, attacked Mandela's article as 'the usual critical mumbo-jumbo, a sort of intellectual throwing of the bones'.[37] Price's riposte centred on the Defiance Campaign as a 'hazy, romantic and over-ambitious plan' which ended in 'mob-murder', and continued:

> The present shaky control which African leaders have over their followers is no guarantee that any Campaign of this sort in the future can be carried out peaceably [sic]. No constitutional party, however sympathetic to Africans, can in any way encourage or contemplate a movement which, it seems inevitable, will end in useless tragedy for hundreds of Africans – or, for that matter, for Europeans ... [The LP] believes that by argument, much organisation, and ceaseless constitutional action it can arrive at the objectives of true freedom for all – and that without any storming of [B]astilles ... or waving of tattered banners.[38]

The dispute between conservative and progressive elements within the LP boiled down to a dispute over the party's constituency. Conservatives wanted little or nothing to do with the ANC, its allies, or black politics generally. Progressives wanted policy changes to allow closer working relations with the ANC and to facilitate the enrolment of a significant black membership. Only then, they argued, could the LP wield any influence over future political developments.

The conservative and progressive wings of the LP also disagreed over Margaret Ballinger's claim that the LP should embody the principles of the old Cape liberal tradition. Party leaders were intent on melding the LP into a support group for the native representatives and stressed the nineteenth-century heritage of the party, which was launched on the centenary of the introduction of non-racial voting qualifications in the Cape. Margaret Ballinger, a historian before she entered politics, stated in 1953 that liberalism and the LP had 'the oldest formal political tradition in the country ... with great names in our calendar, and a great practical tradition to guide us'.[39]

For Ballinger, liberalism, as expressed by her nineteenth-century forebears and contemporary native representatives, was the 'acceptance of the right of all to aspire to full citizenship in the land of their birth'.[40] The LP was a vehicle to further this tradition and its focus, therefore, was, she argued, the long-term education of the white electorate 'as to the nature of its true interests' – that is, common citizenship.[41] The non-racial qualified franchise was the cornerstone of the liberal tradition; those who challenged the party leadership over the issue were characterised as 'the newer converts to liberalism' who lacked an understanding of liberal history and its contemporary application.[42]

In contrast with the party's leaders, liberal intellectuals such as Christopher Gell called for the development of a modern South African liberalism, arguing that the principles of the Cape tradition should be reinterpreted 'in the light of today's conditions'.[43] Behind Gell's call lay a different conception of liberalism, with a different understanding of contemporary politics. For Gell, 'the Congresses are fighting for liberal and democratic ends by liberal and democratic methods'. The LP, he argued, should work in alliance with the Congress movement.[44]

Gell was joined by other party members – most of whom were a generation younger than the Ballingers – who questioned the political lineage traced back to Rhodes, Schreiner and others prominent in the liberal canon. They saw themselves as a new and essentially modern political phenomenon born of the rise of twentieth-century socialist movements as well as the Cold War and anti-Soviet opinion.

Some, among them Patrick Duncan, who joined the party in 1955, were also deeply influenced by Gandhian passive resistance and satyagraha.[45] LP progressives were as firmly anti-Soviet as many Communist Party members were slavishly pro-Soviet, and saw themselves modernising liberalism in accordance with the aims and ideals of the United Nations Organisation (as it then was). Peter Hjul, who emerged as a leading Cape liberal in the 1950s, stated in 1964:

> The Liberal Party, wrongly, at that time was linked with the old Cape Liberal tradition … A lot of us joined without any sort of feeling for Cape liberalism. We were pure radicals, probably more radical socialists almost than liberals. We liked this party; we felt that here was something being done at last; that here was a group which was non-racial in character.[46]

Neither the conservative nor the progressive group was cohesive. Jock Isacowitz observed at the 1953 Conference that 'one couldn't generalise about the political "line" of delegates. People who were most uncompromising on one issue, took an entirely different attitude on another.'[47] Those who were labelled 'radicals' (or 'communists') within the LP campaigned for universal suffrage, an economic policy based on redistribution and social-welfare provision for all races, extra-parliamentary activity, and the deletion of the anti-communist clause from the party 'Principles'.

On each issue, however, the composition of the internal pressure group changed. The Cape group supported universal suffrage and extra-parliamentary action but fiercely resisted deletion of the party's anti-communist clause, which had been accepted under pressure from the Cape in 1953.[48] The group also called for a firm rejection of socialism, though many were social democrats. Similarly, some party leaders, Leo Marquard for one, were not unhappy with universal suffrage as the ultimate goal of the LP, following an interim period in which universal compulsory education would be introduced, but rejected calls for its immediate application. Nonetheless, there were clearly defined conservative and progressive positions on the three basic issues that most divided the party immediately after its formation.

The divisions became increasingly apparent as different strategies were evolved for growing the LP. Younger progressives, building both on liberal faith in economic integration as an ineluctable force for change, and their own sense of being in tune with world opinion, argued simply that 'world trends being what they are' blacks would inevitably have to be brought into the structures of government.[49] In this they were encouraged by black commentators such as Jordan Ngubane, a well-known journalist and a prominent LP member, who argued that decolonisation showed that the South African future was black; the issue was whether that future would be attained 'with or without the co-operation of the local European minority'.[50]

The question was not when, but how, such change would come about. Peter Brown argued in 1956: 'Against the background of world opinion and particularly against the background of what is happening in the rest of Africa, perpetual white domination is out of the question in South Africa. It is the manner of its going that is important.'[51]

Progressives did not initially develop a coherent theory of change, but relied on the 'impossibility' of maintaining apartheid in the face of worldwide hostility and condemnation and the 'inevitability' of economic integration. (Reliance on the inevitability of economic progress was by no means restricted to liberals – black or white – as we saw in earlier chapters – communists, socialists and others did the same.) The progressive wing of the LP saw the main role of the party as building a sizeable black membership which would both maintain liberal values in an increasingly polarised political arena and give the LP a voice in black politics. It would also militate against the onslaught of apartheid legislation, which, it was argued, by treating all blacks in the same manner, was ensuring 'that they will vote as a block when they get it [the vote]'.[52]

The more conservative party leaders shared the view of apartheid as anachronistic in the age of decolonisation; however, they saw the LP as formed to fulfil 'the real function of a political party, which was to win over the White electorate'.[53] The aim of the LP, according to Oscar Wollheim, was to replace the United Party as the new 'middle-of-the road' party in South African politics.[54] Wollheim saw the attacks on the LP from both left and right as proving its political health. The party, he noted, quite rightly, 'in any context other than the South African one would be regarded as a "safe" Party with nothing alarming in its proposals'.[55]

These competing visions of the nature and function of the LP were not automatically contradictory. For much of the 1950s the party operated in both spheres, though with growing emphasis on extra-parliamentary black mobilisation. The two nonetheless came to be seen as directly opposed as the dispute became increasingly bitter and spread throughout the party.

Regional differences

The debate about extra-parliamentary activity and the qualified franchise was, at one level, a dispute over strategy and tactics, but it also flowed from a deeper debate about the nature of liberalism. The dominant view within the LP in its first months was that it was a political vehicle for the continuation and development of 'Hofmeyrism', taking up the liberal tradition it accused the UP of discarding, and calling on the government to partially accommodate black political demands before it was too late. The LP, Margaret Ballinger argued, aimed to create 'a Western state, maintaining Western standards and based on Western values'.[56] Its primary task was the education of white voters and the eventual winning of power or, at least, influence. Its aim was incremental change, won through gradualism, nudged along by the inevitability of 'economic integration'.

In contrast, party progressives and intellectuals – who ushered in a new, more muscular, liberalism – argued that 'the resistance movement is conceived in the spirit of liberalism [but] with … the rejection of a passive role'.[57] The Liberal Party's role should be in support of the moderate ANC leadership and aimed at maintaining liberal values in the Congress Alliance. The party, they argued, should develop a black membership to give it political weight and to counteract the influence of SACOD (for which read 'the Communist Party').

The party's internal conflicts centred on the correct balance between the imperatives of black extra-parliamentary political developments and the white parliamentary arena. The dominance of the Cape leadership ensured that the initial focus of liberal activity was not black politics but the white Parliament. By the time the party held its 1954 national congress it was deeply divided.[58] Opposition to the views of the leaders operated at a number of different levels within the party. Activists in all three divisions exerted considerable pressure for policy changes in order to facilitate co-operation with the congresses and to develop black party membership.

Grassroots pressure from activists differed in each region, reflecting both the different political forces confronting them in various areas, and the different strategies they developed for penetrating the black community. Their demands, however, focused on the universal franchise and the centrality of extra-parliamentary action, and coincided with an intellectual critique of the LP by social democratic members that began almost as soon as the party was launched.

The Cape

When the LP was launched the Cape division was overwhelmingly made up of supporters of Margaret Ballinger. It also included a small number of younger, more progressive members, led by Jimmy Gibson, who were active in black politics in the province. Gibson supported universal suffrage and extra-parliamentary action, was fiercely anti-communist, and was the 'radical' voice on the National and Executive committees.[59] He was supported by journalist Peter Hjul, and younger party members such as Benjamin Pogrund, also a journalist. All rejected the 'adulation of leadership' of the early LP and were in continual conflict with the Cape provincial committees.[60]

While they demanded universal suffrage and extra-parliamentary action the Cape progressives also called on the party to endorse explicitly private enterprise and a clearly capitalist economic programme.[61] They advocated co-operation with the ANC and participation in its campaigns because, as they saw it, 'ex-communists' – particularly in SACOD – were trying to 'control' Congress.[62] In order to pursue his battle against SACOD, Gibson was nominated as a candidate in the two Cape Western Native Representative elections of 1954, opposing (and losing to) first Ray Alexander and, following her ejection from Parliament, Len Lee-Warden.

Gibson's election platform was based on anti-communist attacks on the SACOD candidates; attacks, he reported, that 'went down well' with ANC members such as Thomas Ngwenya and Joe Nkatlo.[63] Nkatlo, a former member of the CPSA and the Democratic League, had, together with some Cape-based former CPSA members, rejected the multiracialism of the Congress Alliance and later joined the LP. Gibson and Hjul were aware of arguments within the ANC over co-operation with former communists, and the related dispute over multiracialism, which had been particularly fierce in Cape Town.[64] As a result, Gibson's election propaganda self-consciously echoed the anti-communism of the ANC Youth League, arguing: 'The liberal voice is a free voice. It is not tied to any foreign ideology.'[65]

Gibson and his supporters attempted to woo the Cape Western ANC away from supporting SACOD candidates. At the height of the second election, in late 1954, the government banned Thomas Ngwenya. In response, Gibson wrote a 'highly confidential' letter to Justice Minister C R 'Blackie' Swart requesting that the ban be lifted.[66] Gibson assured Swart that he opposed 'many aspects of your Government's policy. One thing we have in common, however, is a hatred of communism and all the disruption it means in the political scene.'[67]

The LP, Gibson claimed, was 'struggling against a powerful machine' in the Cape, and the ban (which Gibson and his supporters had previously assured Ngwenya would not be imposed if he voiced anti-communist sentiments) had deprived them of an ally. Gibson concluded his appeal – which, of course, was ignored – by stating:

> I have made it number one priority in my life to smash Communist influence amongst the African people and have had a good deal of success.

The one time dominance of Communist ideology in the Cape Western area is a thing of the past and for this we in the Liberal Party have been largely responsible.[68]

It is difficult to know which of Gibson's assertions would have irritated Swart most.

While Gibson found support for his anti-communist views within some sections of the Cape ANC it was insufficient to override opposition to the LP franchise policy or its proscription of extra-parliamentary activity. The Cape progressives called for changes to the party programme and began recruiting black members to give weight to their demands. They attempted to develop a branch structure in black townships, forming an all-African Cape Western branch in 1954.[69] In attempting to win ANC support they successfully put forward a resolution at the 1954 Cape Provincial Congress calling on the LP to take 'all possible steps' to co-operate with the ANC.[70]

The Cape Provincial Committee, however, was overwhelmingly made up of supporters of the 1953 statement of principle and was increasingly antipathetic to the progressives. Wollheim advised Margaret Ballinger that he was 'perturbed' by the increase in black members and feared the progressives were 'doing it with a purpose'.[71] A provincial committee member complained about the lower membership fees paid by African members and noted that 'Gibson can lead his followers anywhere ... [they] could easily outvote us'.[72] Attempts to remove Gibson from the committee failed, however, because he was believed to represent the African viewpoint and to be 'one of the few' committee members in touch with black opinion.[73] Given the hostility of the party's leader to Congress it is not surprising that radical Cape liberals moved closer to the Non-European Unity Movement and other small, splinter Trotskyist groupings, forming distinctly odd alliances that ebbed and flowed as issues came and went, until, in the Pan Africanist Congress (PAC), they finally found a kindred spirit.

The Transvaal

Activists in the Transvaal worked in very different political conditions from those in the Cape. The LP was based almost exclusively in Johannesburg and its surrounding areas, which was also the headquarters of the ANC and of SACOD. The Provincial Committee, in contrast with that in the Cape, unanimously rejected the qualified franchise.[74] A strong body of opinion in the Transvaal called for participation in extra-parliamentary activity, as well as deletion of the anti-communist clause from the party principles. It was the same party, but seemingly in a different political world.

The Transvaal LP was hemmed in by the proliferation of political organisations active in and around Johannesburg. UP candidates consistently defeated their LP opponents in city council elections, while areas such as Rosettenville and Benoni were Labour Party strongholds. In attempting to co-operate with the ANC the LP had first to contend with hostile ANC and SACOD criticism. SACOD focused attention on the LP's qualified franchise and the proscription of extra-parliamentary means of protest and, in 1954, stated, in a lengthy booklet:

> To talk of using only 'parliamentary' methods is to treat the movement for political rights in this country as one for whites alone; for this community alone has parliamentary power … South African Liberals must shed any illusion that the Europeans will bring liberty to the Non-Europeans. The Non-Europeans will emancipate themselves by their own political actions.[75]

The LP was united in mistrust of SACOD and was hostile to co-operation between the two organisations, summarily rejecting approaches from SACOD in 1953 and 1954 for a joint campaign against the emerging 'police state'.[76] The Transvaal party wanted to co-operate with the black congresses but not with SACOD and withdrew from Trevor Huddleston's Western Areas Protest Committee after a dispute with SACOD over whether the ANC and SAIC should be invited to join the committee.[77]

Unable to co-operate with the black congresses or to penetrate black areas while burdened with a conservative programme, the Transvaal committee led moves to change the policy that had been settled in 1953. In doing so it became the focus of continual criticism from party leaders in the Cape. When Jock Isacowitz organised a series of public meetings to promote the newly launched LP in 1953, Margaret Ballinger stated that she was 'doubtful about the wisdom' of such meetings, arguing huffily that 'it is not the normal procedure of parties'.[78]

As a result of political conditions in Johannesburg the Transvaal division almost immediately turned to alliances, seeking to co-operate with the Labour Party, with UP liberals such as city councillor Jack Lewsen (who later joined the LP), and with the Black Sash after it was formed in 1955 as the Women's Defence of the Constitution League, comprising predominantly English-speaking middle-class women, who evolved a dramatic form of protest, standing in silence wearing a black sash (from which they took their later name) in mourning for the Constitution and the abrogation of civil rights.[79]

Having left the Western Areas Protest Committee the Transvaal LP, in 1956, formed the Civic Vigilance Association, which was intended to broaden the base of co-operation on civic issues to include the congresses, the Federation of South African Women and other organisations, in an umbrella body that would monitor the implementation of apartheid policies by the UP-controlled city council. (Disputes between representatives of the different organisations involved soon killed the association.)

Natal

The most important pressure for change came from party activists in Natal. The Natal division, initially concentrated in Pietermaritzburg and Durban, included socialists such as Hans Meidner, and social-democrats such as Leo Kuper and Violaine Junod, all of the University of Natal; also author Alan Paton, initially a supporter of the 1953 policy settlement, and Peter Brown, who held similar political views. Both Brown and Paton moved, as did the party, from conservative to radical, so that under their leadership Natal assumed national leadership (after 1956) over a radicalising and expanding LP.

The Natal division was unable to penetrate the white political arena, where it was crowded out by the UP, the Labour Party, the secessionist Union-Federal Party, which had a policy 'just Liberal enough' to draw off potential white LP support, and later with the Anti-Republican League.[80] As a result, the division consistently produced the worst electoral results in the LP.[81] In contrast, it enjoyed the least conflictual relationship with the Congress movement. Natal members argued that there was room for both the Congress movement and a non-racial political party, fulfilling different tasks but co-operating closely. Leo Kuper led the LP into co-operation with the NIC, and LP speakers addressed NIC rallies in 1954 and 1955.[82]

The Natal division refrained from publicly attacking the congresses and, in contrast with other divisions, soon established a cordial relationship with the Congress movement. This resulted, at one level, from the close personal relationships between some LP members and Albert Luthuli, Monty Naicker and other Congress leaders. The LP also had direct access to senior Congress members through Selby Msimang, a founding member of the ANC and of the LP, who was Natal ANC secretary after 1951. Msimang arranged meetings between the ANC and LP in Natal and advised other LP divisions which 'moderate' ANC leaders they should approach.[83]

In 1953 Hyacinth 'Bill' Bhengu, a Durban lawyer and ANC National Executive Committee member, joined the Liberal Party. The LP was also supported by Durban ANC member Franklin Bhengu, who wrote to Peter Brown: 'I feel I … can serve no purpose as a member of the Liberal Party. I can definitely be of great service to your party and mine, as a liberal member of the A.N.C in terms of your party's policy.'[84]

Jordan Ngubane, who increasingly opposed what he saw as communist domination of the ANC, was sympathetic to the LP in the early 1950s while remaining an ANC member. Ngubane attended a series of meetings in Natal in 1953, between the LP and senior ANC members, among them Albert Luthuli and M B Yengwa.[85]

Co-operation between the LP and the congresses concretised around the dual threat posed by the Group Areas Act to African freeholders in designated 'white' areas and to the Indian community. At the first official meeting between LP and ANC representatives Luthuli criticised the LP's 1953 programme but invited the party to co-operate with the ANC in undertaking a survey of freehold areas in northern Natal. The LP, with Mary Draper of the South African Institute of Race Relations, surveyed the threatened communities and publicised the threat to Charlestown, the first targeted area. Between 1954 and 1956 LP members undertook tours of the area with ANC members.[86] In early 1957 the LP and the ANC jointly formed the Northern Natal African Landowners' Association (NNALA) to channel resistance to the removals.[87]

The LP in Natal also had access to the Indian community. The collapse of the Natal Indian Organisation, a conservative body set up by former NIC leaders in disfavour with (and deposed by) the more militant Naicker and Dadoo, gave the LP an entrée to middle-class Indian areas in Natal. Manilal Gandhi, editor of *Indian Opinion*, supported the LP and invited its members to write leader articles for his journal.[88] The LP also recruited well-known Indian moderates such as E V Mahomed and Pat Poovalingham.[89] Access to the Indian community was further eased by growing co-operation with the NIC, which increased as Indian communities came under threat from the Group Areas Act.

The concrete co-operation between the LP and the congresses led Brown to report that relations had improved since the initially hostile reception of 1953, with 'misunderstand-ings removed'.[90] Natal soon began to recruit black party members, and grew in size by an annual average of 60% between 1954 and 1957 (starting, of course, from a low base). At the end of 1953 the Natal division had eight branches (more than either the Cape or the Transvaal). These included African branches at Edendale and later in Charlestown.

By late 1954 Natal reported a 50% increase in branches, including Indian branches in Stanger and elsewhere.[91] In 1955 the Natal division had a paid-up membership of 424, which comprised 188 whites, 128 Indians, 104 Africans and 4 coloureds.[92] In February 1955 Alan Paton wrote to Margaret Ballinger, querying the predominantly white membership of the LP in other areas, asking 'Do you know that our Party has a *deep* appeal for Indians?' [93]

Despite the relatively good relations between the LP and the congresses in Natal, Congress leaders continued to criticise the LP programme. LP leaders in Natal, although initially supportive of the 1953 settlement, over time revealed a different understanding of the role of the LP from that of the national leadership. Peter Brown had noted early in 1953: 'Anything we do must have the confidence of non-Europeans. Certainly any-thing political. Until we have got something that will inspire their confidence we would probably be better not to start.'[94]

In response to Congress's criticism of the LP's programme Natal advised the National Committee that if the party were to increase its black membership it would 'have to become more militant but not identify ourselves altogether with one side'.[95]

Resolutions passed at the 1953 Natal Provincial Congress called for 'regular consul-tation … and … collaboration' with black organisations, noting: 'The Party has con-stitutional means at its disposal – they do not. To ask them to transfer their allegiance [to the LP] would be merely to add insult to injury.'[96]

By 1954 activists in all three party divisions were focusing on demands for universal suffrage and an endorsement of extra-parliamentary activity. Pressure also grew for closer co-operation with the black congresses. The Cape leaders remained opposed to close relations with the ANC and rejected policy changes aimed at facilitating such co-operation. Above all, they opposed calls for the deletion of the clause committing the LP to constitutional means. Leo Marquard argued that the motivation was emotional, not rational. 'The urge to delete those words from the Constitution springs, I believe, from the desire for identification with those non-Europeans who, deprived of Constitutional power, are forced to think in terms of revolt.'[97]

In the face of hostility from party leaders Jock Isacowitz refused to organise further LP–ANC meetings, and summarised the feelings of both Transvaal and Natal LP members.

> I am reluctant to take this much further personally, because I was not happy with the attitude of many members of the National Committee towards the A.N.C. as expressed at our last … meeting. I recognise the difficulties arising from personality differences within the A. N. C. but I am afraid that some of our members can't divide this from a proper appreciation of the historic role of the A. N. C. I do not feel justified in opening discussions again and carrying them on further, until we have clarified our own basic attitude towards the A.N.C.[98]

A new liberalism?

Pressure from activists for policy changes was linked to an intellectual critique of the 1953 party programme, which had far-reaching effects. The LP had been formed in opposition to racism and repressive apartheid legislation. The party presented itself as the 'obviously practicable and reasonable alternative … It is essentially the child of humanity and common sense.'[99] LP leaders called on the party to establish itself before becoming involved in ideological and political battles. As Paton later noted, 'Liberalism is not an ideology. It allows a freedom of thought and opinion to its members that an ideology does not allow. But some of our members were more ideologically inclined than others.'[100]

Activists and intellectuals together attacked the 1953 policies, arguing for an interpretation of liberalism in tune with the UN Declaration of Human Rights and an acceptance of the legitimacy of non-violent extra-parliamentary tactics. Gell, a leading figure in the debate, supported the creation of a non-communist and non-racial political party but refused to join the LP because of its commitment to parliamentary means, which he neatly described as 'a declaration of inactivity'.[101] Gell also called for co-operation between the LP and SACOD, stating: 'I entirely deprecate your continued battle with the far left … [it is a] luxury, to start a factional struggle within the all-too-weak movement for liberation against those suspected of communism.'[102]

Gell had close contacts with SAIC and ANC members – ANC volunteers carried the coffin at his funeral in 1958 – and wrote a stream of articles for journals and newspapers which urged the LP to recognise the liberal aims and methods of the congresses, and to co-operate with them.

He and other party progressives stressed that the congresses had to be recognised as the representative voice of black political opinion,[103] with Gell arguing: 'Since the declared Congress policies are liberal in principle, this recognition should be without qualification.'[104]

He also argued that the LP should play two roles: 'educating White-supremacists' into changing their voting patterns, and creating a political meeting ground for black and white.[105] This was impossible because of the rushed formation of the LP and the 1953 policy statement, which he characterised as 'vague' and 'unfortunate'.[106]

The criticism of LP policy launched by liberal intellectuals focused on the same issues, which party activists wanted deleted, or at least amended. Gell criticised the 1953 settlement for 'elevating a political step or tactic (the qualified franchise) to the status of a "principle".'[107] The main focus of criticism, however, was the party's commitment to parliamentary means. The party's leaders argued that an existing democratic state was in danger of being dismantled by the Nationalists and should be protected by constitutional means.[108] Liberal critics preferred the point of view expressed in *The Forum* at the height of the constitutional crisis over coloured disenfranchisement, arguing: 'The dictatorship is here already. The revolution is in the process of being completed.'[109] Leo Kuper extended the intellectual critique by arguing:

> The goal of equality is set, but at the same time the means for its realisation are denied. Two of the basic tenets of a democratic creed, respect for the law and respect for constitutional procedures, are the very instruments by which domination is maintained. Domination is rooted in the sanctity of the law.[110]

The critique of liberalism both influenced and advanced the pressure exerted by party activists. The underlying theme of both was a different conception of the role the LP should play and the nature of liberalism. Activists and intellectuals both argued that liberalism had to be non-racial and unqualified in appeal and application. Gell asked Margaret Ballinger in 1953, 'If we cannot show that a genuine White liberalism evokes a Black response, have we any justification for existence as a separate party?'[111]

Going head to head with 'the communist gang': the 1954 National Congress

At the 1954 Congress, progressives and intellectuals within the party, in an attempt to put the LP more in step with the Congress movement and facilitate the growth of black party membership, tabled a series of resolutions calling for universal suffrage, the endorsement of extra-parliamentary activity, the development of a clear economic policy (with different resolutions calling for commitment to socialist and to free enterprise policies), and the deletion of the anti-communist clause from the party 'Principles'.

The congress erupted into a showdown between the party leaders and party activists. The leaders were clearly unprepared for the range of issues on which they would be challenged. The Ballingers, Marquard, Molteno and others did not attend, leaving Leslie Rubin and Oscar Wollheim to represent their views. Despite the intensity of the criticism, calls for party unity and loyalty to Margaret Ballinger resulted in a victory for the leaders.

Progressives from the different regions lacked consensus over economic policy, relations with the Congress movement, the specific extra-parliamentary activities they supported, and the deletion (or not) of anti-communism from the party's constitution. The only issue on which they agreed was the demand for universal suffrage.

As a result, the only change to the 'Principles' related to the franchise policy. After a full day of debate the party endorsed a formula in which the attempted compromise was more evident than the intent, which was to:

> … achieve the responsible participation of all South Africans in government and democratic processes of the country, and to this end to extend the right of franchise on the common roll to all adult persons. As it may be impracticable to introduce universal adult suffrage immediately, some transitional period may be necessary in which it may be brought about in stages.[112]

The formula reflected the balancing act necessary to avoid splitting the party before its first birthday.[113]

On all other issues the party programme remained as it had been. The Cape leaders present carefully chose the concessions they were prepared to make. Rubin explained to Margaret Ballinger that without 'the big guns' present to defend the 1953 settlement 'the franchise decision was the best we could achieve in the circumstances'. Rubin strategically gave way on the franchise for two reasons: 'At one stage it looked very much like being adult suffrage without any reference to an interim period of qualified franchise at all' and, Rubin argued, 'what is more important is that we stopped deletion of "democratic and constitutional" from the objects'.[114]

LP leaders regarded the 1954 congress as a victory and renewed calls to abandon ideological debates in favour of developing the party's bureaucracy. Wollheim demanded 'less waffling about all these matters of doctrine and theory'[115] and threatened to 'get tough if swathed in dialectics' at the next National Committee meeting.[116] Margaret Ballinger rightly described the 1954 franchise policy as 'a collection of nonsense', but recognised privately that it could be stretched to include the principle of qualified suffrage.[117] According to her husband, 'it is all a question of a formula'.[118]

The Cape Provincial Committee, however, regarded the new franchise policy as a 'departure from the principles upon which the Party was founded'[119] and decided that it could 'not accept the policy',[120] which it described as an attempt by 'the left element' to 'push out the moderates'.[121] According to one member, 'by taking this stand we may be able to get rid of the communist gang'.[122]

LP candidate Peter Charles was in the midst of an election campaign for the Cape Town City Council when the National Congress took place; with the support of the majority of the provincial committee, he decided to ignore the new policy and continue campaigning for a qualified franchise. The only Cape members to oppose the decision not to accept the new policy were Peter Hjul and two representatives of the new black Cape Western branch, who welcomed it. The black branch unanimously dissociated itself from the provincial committee decision.[123]

Margaret Ballinger was advised by Ellen Hellman of the SAIRR that the 1954 franchise decision had convinced any liberal 'waverers' to stay with the UP rather than join the LP.[124] The Cape leaders attempted to recruit former Torch Commando leaders to take over the Transvaal division, and thus win over liberals who had remained in the Civil Rights League, the SAIRR and elsewhere.[125] Leslie Rubin and others began discussing with Labour Party representatives a possible merger, which would allow the Transvaal leadership question to 'be fairly easily solved'.[126] Wollheim later commented:

> If the Johannesburg side of the thing had been played properly we would have had Ellen Hellman and Helen Suzman and that crowd coming in. Instead of which Jock Isacowitz who was an ex-communist leapt in and kidnapped the whole thing ... and the more reasonable crowd hived off.[127]

Following their victory at the 1954 congress, party leaders demanded that the franchise question should not be raised again for five or six years. They repeated the call for national congresses to set only broad policy outlines; the details of LP policy should 'crystallise' out of parliamentary speeches.[128] Margaret Ballinger threatened to resign if the disputes continued, and her supporters argued that '... after 15/16 years of taking up a particular point of view ... Mrs Ballinger finds herself in extreme difficulties when she is expected to change the stand which she has always taken so that it may be in conformity with the Congress decision'.[129]

From 'gradualism' to 'mass evolution': moves towards a muscular liberalism

By 1955 the Liberal Party was in stasis. Ideological struggles continued to rack it, and, as Margaret Ballinger noted, '... there is no national party – there are three segments, each doing what seems to it best, without guidance or control in the matter of either principle or practice'.[130]

The Cape division, in particular, was deeply divided and, by the end of 1955, both conservatives and progressives had withdrawn from active participation in party activities. In the Transvaal the LP fought a series of battles with SACOD members over the Western Areas campaign; nationally the LP had withdrawn from participation in the Bantu Education boycott and the Congress of the People, and Congress hostility, which had begun to wane in 1954, was renewed.

Four years later the LP and the ANC jointly organised the first overseas boycott of South African goods and the LP, through the NNALA, was a significant force in resisting removals in Natal. Disputes over the party's programme waned as party activists effectively ignored constitutionally enshrined structures. The party began to develop a policy calling for radical land redistribution and an economic policy which emphasised wealth redistribution and the creation of a welfare state. In 1960 disputes over the franchise were resolved as the LP finally endorsed universal suffrage.

The political impasse was resolved in part by Margaret Ballinger's resignation as party leader in 1955. She complained that she was no more than a 'so-called leader' and that her political position was 'being damaged'.[131] Her conservative supporters became less active in LP politics, and were increasingly outnumbered by younger, more radical members. The Natal division, which had steered a middle course through the disputes which saw the Transvaal and Cape divisions pitted against each other, assumed national leadership of the party and called for 'matters of doctrine' to be placed in 'cold storage'.[132] The radicalisation of the LP, which, in 1960, devised a programme for the party that differed little from the Freedom Charter, resulted at one level from the new party leaders' conscious avoidance of internal strife. More significantly, however, after 1955 the party began to confront the need for a theory of change and to tailor its politics and activities to the attainment of such change.

The starting point . . .

The Liberal Party had been formed hastily in response to political developments in the white parliamentary sphere, most notably the 1953 general election result; the influence of black extra-parliamentary politics was significant but less immediate. Martin Legassick has argued that the LP was unified 'not by any positive vision ... but by *negative* factors': opposition to nationalism and communism.[133] This is a partial reading of events: it is more accurate to note that, while there were unifying negatives, the positive factors (including opposition to racial discrimination and living out non-racialism in the day-to-day affairs of the party) were more important, bringing together people 'whose views may vary from true-blue conservative to outright socialist'.[134]

Nonetheless, the LP was soon deeply divided over the best means of ending racial discrimination and the nature of the system that should replace it. Leading party members argued that the party was an embodiment of the old Cape liberal tradition – 'not an extraneous growth but an essentially South African product'.[135] The party's policies were premised on the notion of evolutionary development, in contrast with the perceived revolutionary goals of communism and the mass fervour of extreme nationalism, both of which were seen to submerge individualism in categories of race or class and subordinate them to the state.

The LP's 1953 programme was presented as the product of reason, in contrast with the emotional nationalism of the Nationalist Party and the ANC: 'emotion and prejudice have too often and for too long been allowed to hold the stage at the expense of reason and fact'.[136] Paton argued (in the face of considerable scepticism) that the party was 'not a set of well-intentioned fools'.[137] In 1953 notions of evolution and gradualism were largely interchangeable. The most marked change in the Liberal Party after 1955 was to replace the inevitability of gradualism with calls for rapid 'massive evolution'.

The LP in 1953 was a white parliamentary party with policies tailored to gently courting a racist white electorate. It was sarcastically described at the time as 'a sort of political Institute of Race Relations'.[138] The party's leaders saw liberalism as essentially a European import; blacks had to be educated into its practices and philosophy.

Alan Paton, while asserting the political gravitas of LP members, noted that '[w]e were, on the whole, a moral set of creatures'.[139] According to Peter Brown, 'many people who started the party were there for, to put it grandly, moral reasons'; their experience in the party forced them, however, to confront questions of ideology and strategy[140] and, as a result, the party had become a battleground for competing concepts of liberalism.

LP leaders argued that South Africa was a democratic society under immediate threat from nationalism, and a longer-term threat from communism. White South Africa had to educate and inculcate 'civilised' standards of political practice and process into the black population, and gradually draw those who reached the required levels into state structures. Margaret Ballinger argued that the Liberal Party:

> … stands again for what the Cape brought into Union – a tried policy and a practice which appealed, and which appeals again, to all those people who believe that it is the destiny of the European in South Africa to establish and maintain the principles of Western civilisation and that he can only do this by sharing them.[141]

Hostile to extra-parliamentary action, party leaders insisted that the only orderly means by which such changes could be brought about were parliamentary, which entailed winning white votes.

The arguments . . .

Progressives and intellectuals within the party rejected the assumed link between liberalism and parliamentary gradualism, particularly in the South African context. Leo Kuper argued that democratic practices regulated white South African society, but their function was to secure and maintain white supremacy; the non-racial realisation of democratic values would subvert the entire structure of apartheid. Whites were under pressure to abandon liberal values, 'while it is among the Non-Whites … that we find the staunchest and most uncompromising upholders of democratic values'.[142] Christopher Gell, deprecating the 'means' clause in the party's constitution, pointed out that 'what is democratic in the western sense is not necessarily constitutional in South Africa'.[143]

Disputes about strategy centred on issues that hampered the growth of black party membership. At a deeper level, however, were competing versions of liberalism. The central tenet of South African liberalism, it was argued, was its approach to race relations, 'because it is in this field that the most serious encroachments are made on individual liberty'. From this perspective, according to Peter Brown, 'Liberals are found in the leading African, Indian and Coloured Congresses, in the Congress of Democrats ... the S.A. Labour Party, in some trade unions, and a few will even be found in General Smuts' old United Party.'[144]

From their non-racial starting point, party progressives argued that the hallmarks of South African liberalism should be non-violent methods and resistance to extreme nationalism and to communism. A black liberal constituency already existed within the Congress movement, they argued:

> There is a great deal of the Liberal spirit in the present non-European leadership in the liberation movements. Many are disciples of the non-violent technique of Mahatma Gandhi, surely the most civilised technique for a liberation movement the world has known? In so far as these men are patriots of their own sections they may be compared with the elder Hofmeyr rather than with Dr Malan.[145]

Gell appealed to the LP to 'sustain the [Congress] leadership in its hitherto heroically patient refusal to yield to purely anti-white nationalism'. The LP, he argued, could offer resources and parliamentary access denied to the black congresses, and should strengthen liberalism within the congresses against both extreme nationalism and communism.[146]

The solution ...

In this context the principal debate in the early LP was about extra-parliamentary activity. Conservative members associated such activity with illegality, while party progressives saw it as the only means of developing a black support base. The conservative element held sway from 1953 to 1955, while the intellectual critique led by Gell, Kuper and others, gathered force within the party and gave weight to calls from activists for the party to focus at least equally on black politics. As Peter Hjul noted:

> In the old school they could sense, I think, that this intellectual ferment was building up and they tended to tolerate it. I think they were very sympathetic in many ways but what really upset them was when it began to transfer into actual action. I think we were very unfair in the sense that we were very contemptuous of them, I think wrongly so in retrospect, but we were very impatient and we worked very actively against them.[147]

Progressives in the party's three divisions established 'an undercover link' with each other and won greater representation on provincial committees.[148] At the same time, they became increasingly involved in black grassroots work in the vigilance associations set up to resist the implementation of the Group Areas Act in the Western Areas campaign in Johannesburg and in other, similar, initiatives.

As the activities of party members changed so did their profile. In 1956 Alan Paton and Leo Kuper were charged with the offence of addressing a black meeting which did not comply with municipal regulations and police took the names of all who attended their trial; Violaine Junod and LP secretary June Somers were arrested for demonstrating against the extension of passes to women, while party organiser Patrick Duncan was charged with entering Queenstown location without a permit.

Within the party, differences over the content and direction of its activities were compounded by differences over political style, as Hjul explained:

> We had this backroom for African members and Arden Winch [an LP member] used to turn up there at lunchtime and play the clarinet, and all the Africans used to turn up and have a big jolly. The Ballingers would be having a meeting next door and get terribly upset. This is when the divisions began to build up between the established people and the newcomers. We then got out to the townships.[149]

The 'path of least resistance', as Kotane had described it, was of course available to white liberals.

Party leaders deprecated attempts to radicalise the LP programme, characterising radicals as political *ingénues*. Oscar Wollheim, now National Chairperson, advised Margaret Ballinger to ignore the radicals, arguing that 'one is sympathetic and understanding, but one goes one's own way which in the end, they will follow since they cannot do without us'.[150] Differences were generational and cultural, not just political.

> We'd have these committee meetings and there would be Jimmy [Gibson], myself and one or two others causing all this ruckus. I'll never forget one evening when Tom Price blew up and said: 'If I wasn't a gentleman Mr Gibson I'd punch you on the nose'. It was quite a hectic period.[151]

The growing focus by the LP's radical members on black politics led Patrick Duncan and Jordan Ngubane to join the party. Increasingly hostile to the communist influence he saw in the ANC and in SACOD, Duncan brought to it an overt Cold War antipathy to all suspected of communism. He openly stated his opposition to both the LP franchise policy and the 'means' clause, and soon emerged as the dominant personality in the Cape division. As a result, the LP enrolled a growing number of younger and more radical white members, while black party membership increased nationally. These differences led to a political separation within the party, its two wings operating in different areas with different interpretations of party policy. What appeared to the pro-Congress newspaper *Advance* as political duplicity was, in fact, a reflection of a fundamental division within the LP – cock-up rather than conspiracy, to put it crudely. *Advance* described the LP as:

> … speak[ing] one language to their European audience and another to Non-Europeans. To the European there is stress on the go-slow, the reservations, provisions, interim qualifications and so forth. To an African audience there is nothing but a bold demand for equal rights, including the right to vote.[152]

The shift …

Legassick, Robertson and Rich have all seen the LP as the culmination of white liberal thinking and activism stretching from the nineteenth to the twentieth centuries. Legassick argued that the party was an expression of a liberal impulse '*primarily* concerned with *saving* what they believed to be existing democratic values', in contrast with white democrats in SACOD, who were 'concerned with the *creation* of democratic values, with the transformation of white or fascist domination *into* democracy'.[153] He described his distinction as 'crude' and, indeed, it ignores the fact that both SACOD and the LP appealed for white support by arguing that the NP was dismantling existing democratic structures; both recognised that blacks lacked any such dispensation. The distinction also ignores the very different currents of thinking within the LP and the importance at the individual level of crossing the colour bars of apartheid and living out the principle of non-racialism. The transformation of the LP and the evolution of a more radical liberalism came precisely with the acceptance by leading LP members that 'we are *not* living in a democratic society'.[154]

Characteristically, LP members such as Alan Paton, rather than being proactive had to be forced, in this case by the 'church clause', to confront the nature of South African society. This clause, an amendment to the Native Laws Amendment Act, imposed a limit on the number of blacks allowed to congregate in white areas. Paton declared himself willing to defy the law, which threatened to prohibit the right of Africans to attend churches in white areas, and called on the LP to follow suit.[155]

By late 1956 the early LP leaders and their replacements were divided by fundamentally different perspectives, reflected in an exchange of letters between Leo Marquard and Alan Paton. The exchange was initiated by concern on Marquard's part about renewed calls for the deletion of the 'means' clause. He argued that all agreed that apartheid was fundamentally unstable and could not last. Divisions arose, he argued, because LP members allowed their concern with questions of when and how the system would go to overly influence an assessment of what the role of a liberal in such a situation should be. Underlying Marquard's letter was the contention that extra-parliamentary action was the path followed by those who 'are forced to think in terms of revolt'.[156]

For Marquard the basic premise of liberalism was acceptance of the evolutionary attainment of a just society:

> It seems to me that the 'policy' of a liberal is clear: to state his belief in the attainment, by evolutionary processes, of a just and common society, and to try to convert others to that belief. The evolutionary process by no means excludes a sudden break-down. In fact, history is full of sudden break-downs. But a liberal cannot, I believe, assume or in any way countenance working towards that end – not because it is unconstitutional, but because it is not a real end; it is only a violent means which destroys where the liberal hopes to construct.[157]

Marquard insisted that the LP's task was to persuade white voters of the need for change. Deletion of the 'means' clause, he argued, was 'dangerous' in that it threatened the sanctity of the law, basic to any liberal programme: extra-parliamentary action meant, 'in plain words, breaking the law'. He also argued that extra-parliamentary action by a white political party was essentially a 'hypothetical test ... I don't have to steal in order to demonstrate my undoubted sympathy with those who steal through force of circumstance.' He ended his letter with a warning to Paton that 'once the Liberal Party commits itself to the possibility of unconstitutional action it has become a façade for something else'.[158]

In his reply Paton noted that all liberals 'desire to be governed constitutionally'; however, 'more and more do I realise that these words have also a hypocritical content': 'The Government would like nothing better than an Opposition which confines itself to constitutional means, because this lends colour to the view that it is really a constitutional game we are playing in South Africa. I find this impossible to accept ...'.[159]

Paton's letter summarised the thinking of those liberals who had emerged as LP leaders by 1956 and who steered the party through to the 1960s. 'My own view is that massive evolutionary changes must come, and to my mind a non-racial body of opinion devoted to the ideals of democracy is the only force which will be able to guide such an evolution without allowing it to fall into the hands of evil men.'[160]

Under the influence of Paton, Peter Brown and others, the Liberal Party in the late 1950s and 1960s reinvigorated liberalism in South Africa. Brown noted in 1959:

> The alternatives which face South Africa are not between the maintenance of the status quo, gradualism and revolution. They are between revolution and what Alan Paton terms 'mass evolution'. And in the nature of political arrangements in South Africa many of the pressures to induce 'massive evolution' are bound to be mounted outside Parliament.[161]

Chapter 8

The Congress of the People

In June 1955 some 3 000 delegates attended the Congress of the People (CoP) in Kliptown, Johannesburg, and endorsed the Freedom Charter, a statement of principle distilled (to a greater or lesser degree) from demands submitted by people across South Africa during a sixteen-month campaign sponsored by the Congress Alliance. According to Albert Luthuli, president-general of the African National Congress (ANC),

> Nothing in the history of the liberatory movement in South Africa quite caught the popular imagination as this did, not even the Defiance Campaign. Even remote rural areas were aware of the significance of what was going on. The noisy opposition in most of the white Press advertised the Congress and the Charter more effectively than our unaided efforts would have done. So the awakening spread further. The participation of all race groups in this effort underlined the scale of awakening resistance.[1]

Perhaps. Others saw the CoP as a high point of malefic white influence over the ANC, reflected in the Freedom Charter's bold assertion that 'South Africa belongs to all who live in it, black and white'; and/or the influence of (particularly white) communists, reflected in the economic clauses of the charter calling for nationalisation of key sectors of the economy.[2]

The campaign was an attempt by Congress to capitalise on a perceived receptivity in white liberal circles to new ideas and to draw whites from the cautious middle ground into co-operation with the Congress movement. Far from being asked merely to rubber stamp a Congress blueprint, liberals were invited to help co-ordinate the campaign, to participate in the creation of local committees, and to canvass black support for their ideals and programme. It was an invitation rejected by all white organisations except the South African Congress of Democrats (SACOD).

White influence in the Congress Alliance grew as post-Defiance Campaign ANC membership and energy dropped. While cause and effect were often a matter of opinion most agree that 1955/56 was a critical time for the Congress movement as it developed (in 1955) and then formally adopted (in 1956) non-racialism as a core principle – despite its multiracial organisational structuring – and never wavered, even when, in the late 1950s, the Africanists, ANC members who accused Congress leaders of betraying the principles of the 'Programme of Action', split off. That said, the ANC only opened up partial membership to 'non-Africans' in 1969, and full membership only in 1985.[3] Hilda Bernstein rightly observed that non-racialism was always a lesson to be learned in the struggle, in contrast to the easy pull of nationalism.[4]

The CoP campaign was the culmination of a particular strategy introduced by the Congress movement in the 1940s, with *Africans' Claims*: that is, using popular participation in the production of documented statements of principle as tools of mobilisation and organisation.

The campaign, which was to be the largest and longest undertaken by the Congress Alliance in the 1950s, was initiated in a context dominated by the renewed zeal of the Nationalist Party, strengthened by the 1953 general election, in implementing apartheid. It was intended to help rally the anti-apartheid forces that had faltered in the face of a savage battery of apartheid laws and heightened oppression.[5] The Congress movement had to reverse 'the alarming decline which began in the Congress during the post-Defiance Campaign period'[6] and grow the ANC, while keeping the (still new) Congress Alliance functioning. In the words of Cape ANC President Z K Matthews, who first proposed the CoP, the campaign was intended to '... galvanise the people of South Africa into action and make them go over to the offensive against the reactionary forces at work within this country, instead of being perpetually on the defensive, fighting rear-guard actions all the time'.[7]

Those involved with the CoP envisaged the creation of local committees across the breadth of South Africa to discuss a simple theme: 'Let us speak together of freedom'.[8] The CoP was to be 'a campaign of national awakening',[9] its main aims being mobilisation, organisation and instilling in the people a 'Freedom Consciousness'.[10] For the congresses the CoP was of singular importance in providing a unifying national campaign to further the mobilisation (and reverse the subsequent decline) of the Defiance Campaign.

Rusty Bernstein, who played a central role in the CoP campaign, observed: 'The Freedom Charter was NOT the aim; it was like the crown cork on the Coca-Cola bottle – a capping to prevent the fizz evaporating.'[11]

Nonetheless, the Freedom Charter became a potent symbol of resistance and a key statement of ANC goals, and guided the movement from the 1950s until the late 1980s. It committed the ANC and its allies to a non-racial future, by stating boldly:

> We, the people of South Africa, declare for all our country and the world to know: That South Africa belongs to all who live in it, black and white, and

that no government can justly claim authority unless it is based on the will of the people.[12]

The charter symbolises a key moment in South Africa's history, when the ANC – despite the political environment in which it operated – turned its back on exclusive nationalism and fully embraced a non-racial future (if not a non-racial organisational structure). It had direct organisational costs for the ANC, as Africanist anger rose and culminated in the formation of the Pan Africanist Congress (PAC).

The wider context

By 1954 the political boundaries in South Africa were delineated by African and Afrikaner nationalism, a polarisation whose effects were felt in both the parliamentary and extra-parliamentary fields. The United Party (UP) polled more votes than the Nationalist Party (NP) in 1953, but returned to Parliament with a smaller number of MPs. New MPs included Helen Suzman, John Cope and others, who joined the liberal wing of the UP, but, unable to influence UP policy in any markedly liberal direction, later left to form the Progressive Party. By 1959, when they left, the Liberal Party was a very different beast from that of 1953, and too radical for this new generation of liberals in the Ballinger mould.

The 1953 election was the last the Labour Party fought in alliance with the UP and it was guaranteed four seats uncontested by UP candidates. Under the leadership of John Christie and Alex Hepple, the Labour Party steadily adopted more liberal policies, including a qualified non-racial franchise, free compulsory education for all and the abolition of the pass laws.[13]

The Union-Federal Party, formed in May 1953, also called for the gradual inclusion of qualified Africans in state structures, although its policies remained blurred.[14] The Liberal Party inherited parliamentary representation through Native Representatives Margaret and William Ballinger and adopted a programme which, while criticised as conservative by the congresses, was nonetheless the clearest parliamentary opposition to apartheid.

In the extra-parliamentary arena the successful mobilisation around the Defiance Campaign saw the ANC win mass support. The NP government, undeterred, ratcheted up the implementation of apartheid. Section 10 of the 1952 Native Laws Amendment Act aimed to curb drastically the rights of Africans to remain in urban areas and the 1952 Natives (Abolition of Passes and Co-ordination of Documents) Act required all Africans (including women and those previously exempt) to carry a reference book (known among those forced to carry it as a 'dompas').

Group Areas evictions and 'blackspot' removals increased, the largest target being the 60 000 people living in Johannesburg's mixed-race Western Areas. The Bantu Education Act placed control of African schooling in the hands of the Native Affairs

Department and introduced a differentiated syllabus. Father Trevor Huddleston, active in the struggle against the Western Areas removals, noted in 1953 that '[t]he thrust and speed of these measures is getting beyond anything and seems to have the effect of mesmerising whatever opposition there may be'.[15]

The ANC recognised that it had to organise itself into a strong enough organisation to withstand the growing number of banning orders imposed on its leading officials, sustain the influx of new members brought into the Congress Alliance by the Defiance Campaign, manage internal dissent and meet the wide-ranging attacks on black rights. Transvaal ANC President Nelson Mandela noted: 'It is our own weakness, the lack of unity and solidarity, the defensive nature of our struggle, that gives the Nationalists the chance to strike us one by one and to cripple our organisation.'[16]

Mandela devised what became known as the 'M-Plan', which envisaged the creation of street, block and area committees across the country to develop grassroots membership as a bulwark against the restriction of leadership figures. The M-Plan, however, was only effectively implemented in parts of the Eastern Cape; its real moment came thirty years later, at the peak of repression and resistance. The ANC–SAIC Joint Co-Ordination Committee, set up during the Defiance Campaign, reported in December 1953 that 'a disquieting lull … has descended over the mass activities of Congress'.[17]

The Congress movement faced a range of problems. While at a formal level the Alliance was meant to represent the major race groups in South Africa, there was no co-ordinating machinery beyond the National Action Council (NAC), which replaced the Co-ordinating Committee. At a local level, branches of different congresses operated largely in isolation from each other.

An editorial in the pro-Congress newspaper *Advance* complained that previously criticised failings within the Congress movement 'still exist today … we do not yet seem to have found an effective way of co-ordinating our campaigns, of uniting all who are fighting the same enemy on different fronts'.[18] In addition, the ANC (and the Alliance) did not have a clearly articulated ideological position. The 1949 'Programme of Action' dealt specifically with African nationalism and, as Lodge has noted, was vague and open to 'differing interpretations so that opposed factions within Congress could each legitimise their position by reference to it'.[19]

The racial exclusiveness that, in the 1940s, had marked a significant section of the ANC Youth League (ANCYL) in the 1950s infused the 'Africanists', who claimed that African nationalism was being diluted by racial co-operation and opposed SACOD in particular, claiming that whites had joined the Congress Alliance in order to dominate it, and convert it to a Marxist programme.[20]

Whites were by no means the only point of racial tension in the Alliance. For example, Luthuli warned that Natal Africans 'are being misled by the Indian bogey' and called for the development of closer relations between the ANC and the Natal Indian Congress (NIC):

I have deliberately referred to the need for a multi-racial democratic front because there is much confusion on the subject ... All people in their struggle seek allies. Africans must get it into their heads that the stumbling blocks to progress are the many discriminatory laws made by a white Parliament and not by Indians. What privileges Indians enjoy which we do not enjoy were given to them by a white Parliament. Why blame the recipient and not blame the giver for not giving Africans those rights and privileges?[21]

Finally, Congress membership began to decline, particularly in the rural areas that had been reached by the Defiance Campaign but were insufficiently organised thereafter. The ANC National Executive Committee (NEC) warned in 1954 that 'there is a danger of the African National Congress becoming an urban-based and urban-oriented organisation'.[22]

The CoP in context

In the mid-1950s activists mainly worked on campaigns against the Western Areas removals and the implementation of Bantu Education.[23] Lodge has demonstrated the local complexities confronting the ANC in these campaigns, where grassroots responses varied widely across the country and the ANC was insufficiently organised to provide effective leadership. Both campaigns showed the congresses to be 'isolated from the people' and, according to a document drawn up by SACOD's National Executive Committee and distributed within the Alliance, not involved in work 'which brings us closely in contact with people'.[24] In SACOD's view, both campaigns highlighted the need for political understanding to go 'hand in hand with organisational work', but

> ... we allow our activities to go on in our branches, amongst our own members, losing our contact with the people outside ... From this has flown, on the one hand, (as in the Western Areas) the issuing of unreal 'calls' for say, strike action; and on the other hand, (as in the schools' boycott) a lagging behind the people and a hesitation to call for action for fear that the people are not ready.[25]

The two campaigns compounded the decline in both enthusiasm and Congress membership that followed the Defiance Campaign. According to NIC President Monty Naicker this was not unusual. 'We ... find that during the previous chapters in our struggle we were able to rouse people by mass propaganda and at the cessation of our activities we lost support and general interest in the struggle waned.'[26]

By the end of 1953 the situation was cause for real concern. Luthuli was blunt: 'At the moment we are only concerned with rescuing ourselves out of the mire and we cannot yet say which direction we shall follow after that.'[27]

Congress needed to initiate a campaign that would both unify the Alliance and 'capture the imagination' of the people.[28] Such a campaign, according to SACOD, had to be 'designed to bring our organisations closer to the ordinary people of South Africa'.[29] In response, Z K Matthews formed a small discussion group which proposed a series of public meetings, culminating in a national convention, which would adopt a manifesto. By the time the Cape ANC Conference took place in August 1953 Matthews had refined his idea, arguing that Congress had to rekindle grassroots mobilisation on a mass scale but in a very traditional ANC manner.

I wonder whether the time has to come for the African National Congress to consider the question of convening a National Convention, A CONGRESS OF THE PEOPLE, representing all the people of this country irrespective of race or colour to draw up a freedom charter for the DEMOCRATIC SOUTH AFRICA OF THE FUTURE. [30]

Described in such cautious language it is difficult to believe that the Freedom Charter the CoP would generate would become the centrepiece of a lengthy treason trial and would later be regarded as a revolutionary document.

At the ANC's annual conference in December 1953 Matthews described a CoP 'to which ordinary people will come, sent there by the people. Their task will be to draw up a blueprint for the free South Africa of the future.'[31] Matthews then took his idea to a joint meeting of Congress executives. His initial proposal was not simply for a mass assembly of people, but rather that the congresses draw up a voters' roll of the entire population, divide South Africa into constituencies, and hold non-racial nationwide elections to a constituent assembly. Rusty Bernstein, who was present at the meeting, later suggested that Matthews's proposal was 'deliberately provocative in order to shape peoples' thinking': 'Coming from a professor of law – if you take it seriously – this constituent assembly, he didn't describe what it would do, but a constituent assembly would presumably draw up a new South African constitution. That really was seditious!'[32]

A sub-committee assessed the idea and concluded that Congress lacked the resources to undertake the task as set out by Matthews. As a result, his original proposal was whittled down to the holding of a Congress of the People, which would produce not a constitution but 'a vision of the future – a Freedom Charter'.[33]

The instigators of the CoP campaign envisaged the creation of a corps of 'freedom volunteers' who would spread the message of the CoP across the country. Urban and rural committees would be set up to discuss the nature of a democratic future for South Africa, draw up demands for inclusion in the Freedom Charter and select delegates to the CoP. The plans initially retained the proposed national election of delegates and, from the start, the emphasis was on popular mobilisation. To Bernstein,

I think what's not understood by most people is that in the forefront of our minds at that time was not the Freedom Charter. That wasn't the big thing, that was the spin-off. The big thing was going out and consulting people and saying to them 'look here, what do you want in the future?' This was the central aim of the campaign.[34]

The focus on mobilisation resulted in part from the need to reinvigorate Congress, and in part from the expectation that the actual CoP might be banned.[35] Matthews stated that the aim of the CoP was 'the instilling of political consciousness into the people and the encouragement of political activity'.[36] The ANC noted that 'the creation of a network of local committees in every corner of South Africa will in itself be a major political achievement'.[37] The CoP presented the congresses with the opportunity to fulfil their two main needs: the politicisation and mobilisation of a wide section of the population, and the production of a unifying ideological statement. The CoP campaign, it was argued, 'opens the way for the rectification of weaknesses'.[38] But for the Liberal Party, which initially agreed to co-sponsor the CoP, it opened the door for 'Communist manipulation of the CoP', while the Freedom Charter was identified for them (by Jordan Ngubane) as 'the new Communist party line'.[39] As ever, Liberal Party members managed to see conspiracies where confusion was more common.

The need for ideological unity

The Congress of the People drew inspiration from a number of different sources, some immediate, others long-term. The Congress movement and the Communist Party's tradition of popular mobilisation around the production of statements of principle had produced, among others,[40] *Africans' Claims*, the Votes for All charter and the Federation of South African Women's charter. The 1948 Votes for All Assembly ended with a call for a future assembly where nationally elected delegates would endorse a 'People's Charter'.

The call for a 'People's Charter' was a recurrent theme of both Congress and the CPSA. The production of such a charter could not precede the emergence of a coherent anti-apartheid alliance but the need for unity among anti-apartheid forces kept the idea high on the agenda of Congress leaders. SAIC President Yusuf Dadoo, in his 1951 'new year message', called on the ANC to issue 'a clarion call' for:

… a mass National Convention in the immediate future to bring together at a central conference representatives of all sections of the South African population both white and non-white, in order to resolve on a programme which would oppose apartheid in every form, and work for the … basic human rights of all groups of people in consonance with the principles and purpose of the United Nations Charter and the Declaration of Human Rights.[41]

In 1952 former CPSA general secretary and ANC NEC member Moses Kotane had maintained that the Congress movement should concentrate on raising black political consciousness: 'a new spirit is needed [if] the great mass of Non Europeans are [to be] brought actively into the struggle against fascism'.[42] Kotane called for campaigns to be grounded in the realities of everyday existence, through which the Congress could develop a 'people's policy', and to avoid 'the academic drafting of paper Utopias'.[43] Similarly, the ANC–SAIC National Action Council argued that to be effective future campaigns had to emerge from 'the concrete conditions under which people live'.[44] Calls for a mass assembly and the development of a 'people's policy' increased in the early 1950s as unity became an imperative in the face of the apartheid onslaught.

The years between the 1948 People's Assembly and the CoP saw the resolution of the most divisive disputes within the Congress movement, most notably between the ANCYL and the CPSA, and acceptance of the need for racial co-operation. At the same time the ANC grew in size and significance, to the point where it could encourage the formation of the South African Coloured People's Organisation (SACPO) and bring SACOD into being.

The ANC remained the senior partner within the Congress Alliance; Luthuli stressed that the CoP campaign was initiated by all the congresses, 'but *at the invitation* of the African National Congress'.[45] Invitations were sent to the Labour Party – which sent a message of support to the CoP – and to the Liberal Party, which, as stated above, was initially keen but later withdrew in fear of communist manipulation.

By 1954 an alliance of anti-apartheid forces necessary to develop a consensual statement of principle had emerged. The CoP campaign looked beyond the formal Congress Alliance, placing ordinary people at the forefront. The collection of demands for inclusion in the charter, Bernstein noted, was 'an exercise in getting the people to tell the leadership and self-regarded elite what THEY ought to work for in the name of the people'.[46]

The CoP was the culmination of a process, the roots of which lay in the 1940s but, in proposing it, Z K Matthews was also responding to immediate circumstances. Matthews described it as a campaign aimed at both black and white, a characteristic of much activity in the 1950s. He noted that 'various groups in the country ... are considering the idea of a national convention at which all groups might be represented'.[47] (As we see below, Matthews had recently participated in one such event.) Through the CoP, he argued, Congress could capitalise on concurrent thinking in white politics and 'the need for a new approach' reflected in the flurry of new political parties formed in 1953.[48]

The ANC and white politics

After the Second World War the ANC had begun to develop strategies aimed at attracting a mass African support base while remaining committed to a non-racial future. Non-racialism, in this context, meant organisational separateness under African leadership; in a free society, the same would occur.

ANC leaders argued that, in contrast with Afrikaner nationalism, 'our nationalism should be progressive and liberal and thus embrace co-operation with other communities on the basis of equality'.[49] For ANC leaders the main danger facing the Congress movement was not the possible subversion by communists, stressed by liberals and other critics outside the ranks of Congress; rather, it was the growth of a black racism equal to white *baasskap*. Luthuli argued:

> What in fact South Africa is hearing from the African National Congress is the voice of African Nationalism, rather than Communism. African Nationalism will become a much more powerful and appealing force than Communism. In fact our task as leaders is to make this Nationalism a broad Nationalism, rather than the narrow nationalism of the Nationalist Party ... Extreme nationalism is a much greater danger than communism, and a more real one.[50]

Congress's commitment to non-racialism was strengthened by the fact that both liberals and Marxists argued (from rather different starting points) that apartheid and economic development were mutually exclusive. Some Congress theoreticians argued that the 'fascist' NP was creating contradictions within the capitalist class itself, resulting from the use of '... the machinery of State not only against the working class and in the interests of the capitalist class but also to increase, to enlarge its own share of the economic spoil. It does this at the expense of other *sections* of its *own class*.'[51]

As a result, it was (very optimistically) argued that the 'less reactionary section' of the white population, 'if they are to survive ... find themselves – howbeit unwillingly – allies of the anti-fascist majority'. To argue that all whites bar 'the enlightened few' would remain in the NP camp, it was concluded, 'is based on racial patterns of thought and not on objective factors'.[52]

The ANC aimed to exert the pressure of mass struggle on the existing economic and political system, rather than working for its complete overthrow. Luthuli stated: 'The African National Congress has consistently, through its presidents and other leaders, indicated that they are interested in democracy *within the present framework of the Union*.'[53]

With this in mind, campaigns such as the Defiance Campaign aimed to persuade through moral example, thereby influencing white opinion and weakening NP hegemony. It would be another thirty years before the ANC called on supporters to make South Africa 'ungovernable'. Congress leaders were sensitive to developments in white politics, which were strengthened by the formation of SACOD and the space given to articles on the subject in pro-Congress journals and newspapers such as *New Age*, *Fighting Talk*, *Liberation* and *Counter Attack* (all edited entirely or in part by SACOD members). They were also aware of an ongoing, if subsiding, white opposition to the NP's disregard for constitutionalism.[54] This, in turn, compounded ANC speculation about the possibility that the NP would lose white support; a proposition based on the belief that there were 'thousands of honest democrats amongst the white population who are prepared to take up a firm and courageous stand for unconditional equality'.[55]

'There may be no necessity for eating together'

The CoP campaign aimed – in part – to influence white opinion and draw white liberals into closer co-operation with the Congress movement. In proposing it, Matthews was influenced by the SAIRR's earlier preparations for a new national convention. UP members such as former justice minister Harry Lawrence had argued for a national convention, because, 'in dealing with our multi-racial relationships, White South Africa should speak as one'.[56]

This was not quite what liberals were looking for – a stronger white hand on the whip handle – and they demanded black participation in any convention. In 1950, following the violence that attended the May Day stay-at-home, Edgar Brookes and Margaret Ballinger called for '... the sinking of party differences in a round-table conference between all parties, including the Africans, to see what can be done to counter the unrest ... and to re-establish confidence among White and Black alike'.[57]

Their call was supported by Labour Party leader John Christie and former SAIRR director J D Rheinhallt Jones, who maintained that racial conflict stemmed from the 'fierce political partizanship' attendant upon debates on racial issues.[58] Two years later Leo Marquard said 'we have failed lamentably in the matter of political integration'. Marquard saw the most serious problem as 'the lack of political contact between the races', the only solution to which had become 'the urgent matter for the leaders of all population groups to meet in a new national convention'.[59] There seemed to be a moment where black and white, liberal and conservatives, were all thinking along largely similar lines – getting together to develop a blueprint for what South Africa *should* look like. The question was, could all sides sink their (often vituperative) differences for long enough to organise, let alone successfully stage, a convention or a CoP?

Calls by liberals outside the UP for a new national convention were marked by appeals for black leaders to be brought into the debating forum as a preliminary to their inclusion in state structures. After the 1953 general election the SAIRR and the Labour Party began preparatory work for a national convention. In the first week of August 1953 a private conference, to which both black and white representatives were invited, was held at Adams College in Natal, paid for by Harry Oppenheimer of the Anglo-American Corporation.[60]

Eight Africans and eight whites were invited to discuss 'the question of how Africans can be more fully associated with the government and development of the country'.[61] The SAIRR approached the undertaking with caution, advising white invitees that 'there may be no necessity for eating together'.[62] The Africans invited included leading ANC members Albert Luthuli (who did not attend) and Z K Matthews, Jordan Ngubane, then still a member of the ANCYL, as well as formerly prominent and more conservative ANC members A B Xuma, James Moroka and Paul Mosaka. Among the whites invited were Leo Marquard, Margaret Ballinger, Winifred Hoernlé of the SAIRR, and the industrialist H J van Eck.

The conference condemned the migrant labour system and agreed on short-term economic reforms such as the extension of the provisions of the Industrial Conciliation Act to Africans – both of which had been UP policies before its electoral defeat in 1948. On more fundamental issues – black political rights and the vote – there was no agreement. The white members of the conference suggested a number of different possible qualifications for the franchise. One such proposal, presumably put forward by Leo Marquard, was the Liberal Party's (qualified) franchise policy. All were rejected:

> The attitudes of Non-European members of the Conference was they would not be able to take part in furthering the attainment of the alteration of the present franchise laws along one or other of the … lines [proposed] by European members. They indicated that, if the European members wished to work for alteration along those lines, this was the concern of the European members.[63]

The growth of the ANC, its successful adoption of mass-based extra-parliamentary strategies, and the political polarisation of the 1950s forced liberals to accommodate themselves to the demands of both the NP and the Congress movement and seek a middle course between right and left. Liberals claimed: 'We are not extremists. We are sitting in the middle, between two nationalisms.'[64] It was in this context, and lacking a significant support base, that they supported a national convention at which 'race relations' could be discussed away from the party political arena. The SAIRR conference was an initial attempt to find some common ground between the UP and perceived ANC 'moderates'. Despite the lack of agreement the conference called on the SAIRR to 'explore the possibility of convening further inter-racial conferences preliminary to a National Convention'.[65]

The SAIRR's 'dress rehearsal' affected the CoP campaign in two ways. Firstly, eight days after leaving Adams College, Z K Matthews proposed the CoP, pointing to the SAIRR initiative as an idea the ANC should take over. Secondly, the immovability of even conservative African leaders on the question of universal suffrage served to deter leading white liberals from participation in the CoP. In a supporting memorandum Matthews wrote that NP 'despotism' was forcing anti-Nationalist whites to revise 'policies and programmes which have outlived their usefulness'.[66] Matthews cited the formation of the LP and 'the changed outlook of the Labour Party' as evidence that '[t]he time is long overdue for a thoroughgoing re-examination of the place of different sections of the population in the South African body politic.'[67]

If the SAIRR conference revealed to liberals the ideological gap between themselves and the ANC, it did the same for the ANC members present. Matthews warned that the SAIRR convention, by restricting itself to established political organisations and working to a (conservative) liberal agenda, would not adequately reflect South African conditions.[68] The congresses advised the SAIRR that it was 'most appropriate' that they had taken over the proposed convention since the issue was one '… which is primarily and in the first place the concern of the non-European people themselves, who are most directly affected and who form the majority of the population'.[69]

Finally, Congress leaders pointed to the United Nations Commission on racial affairs in South Africa, which had called for 'a round-table conference of members of different ethnic groups of the Union'.[70] Yusuf Dadoo argued that the CoP 'lays the basis for a further extension of co-operation to include all national groups' in tune with domestic and international calls for a national convention: the CoP, he concluded, 'answers the historical need of the time'.[71]

White factionalism

Congress was flexing its new-found muscle by taking over from the SAIRR moves to organise a national convention, but it hoped that other organisations interested in the idea would join it in the CoP. Invitations to co-sponsor the CoP were sent to the SAIRR and the Liberal and Labour parties, and invitations to participate went to all political organisations in the country, including the United and Nationalist parties. In discussions with the LP and SAIRR, Congress members emphasised the importance of adequate white participation, both to strengthen non-racialism and to make the CoP truly representative.[72]

On the eve of the congress, however, SACOD's NEC noted that 'all other national bodies, who claim to hold the key to the future of South Africa, have abandoned the field to the Congress Alliance' and (correctly) predicted that 'it is now clear that the Congress of the People, for all the time, will be coupled in people's minds with the Congresses'.[73] From the Cape, Jimmy Gibson, having 'originally been in favour of co-sponsorship, with a view to the Liberal Party gaining control of the Congress of the People', but having been outmanoeuvred by SACOD, suddenly claimed to be 'aware of many factors which render our participation … undesirable' – including supposed secret (and never revealed) information and the fact that 'the COP was now in the hands of Communist elements'.[74] Despite the fury of the Transvaal LP the party withdrew, leaving sponsorship and participation restricted to the Congress movement and its allies, such as the Federation of South African Women (FSAW).

Former LP members, and commentators such as Janet Robertson, have argued that the LP refused to co-sponsor the CoP because the party was only invited to implement a pre-existing plan over which it was offered no control.[75] The communist bogey is frequently cited to explain and/or justify the LP's decision. Such claims belie the open approach of the Congress Alliance to white liberals in 1954 and ignore the real motive for non-participation, which was both anti-communism and political arrogance, reflected in the LP notion that it could somehow take control of the CoP and, when this failed, persuade the ANC to drop the idea in favour of an LP alternative.

Elements within the ANC were clearly encouraged by the proposed SAIRR–Labour Party–LP national convention and the rapprochement between the congresses and the LP. Luthuli, a year after rejecting joint ANC–LP membership, spoke of the LP 'between whom and ourselves there exists a warm and sympathetic understanding and friendly co-operation on specific issues where our policies agree'.[76]

The LP and other organisations invited to co-sponsor the CoP were offered equal representation with the four congresses on the NAC (which co-ordinated the campaign) and on regional CoP structures. The invitation stressed that only the broad outlines of the campaign had been settled. ' "Let us speak together of freedom." This sums up the conception we have of the range and purpose of the Congress of the People ...'.[77]

For some liberals, the concept was 'grandiose', the documentation 'sentimental and wordy', and the idea 'startlingly unrealistic'.[78] The invitation, left open until the first day of the congress, emphasised the flexibility of CoP arrangements, thus highlighting the influence non-Congress organisations might exert. Perhaps there was some political sleight of hand; if so, it has remained hidden even to hostile critics, police and Treason Trial lawyers. Certainly the LP saw a conspiracy at work.

The CoP campaign aimed to unite formal organisations with popular sentiment through the creation of a nationwide network of local communities, the development of a 'Freedom Consciousness' in ordinary people and by granting them control over the contents of the Freedom Charter. It would also confront whites with the core demands for (unqualified) equality and freedom. This programme might have been uncomfortable for many – though by no means all – LP members, and a conspiracy (real or imagined) allowed them to exit with good cause.

All organisations were invited to participate in the mobilisation taking place around the CoP and to compete for support for their views. As the NAC stated:

> We do not intend to put a preconceived 'Charter' before a hand-picked 'Assembly'. We seek rather to canvass the entire country, asking ordinary people everywhere, in every walk of life, to say in their own words what they need to make them happy.[79]

Aware of liberal hostility to universal suffrage, extra-parliamentary action and other central tenets of the Congress movement, the NAC stressed that organisations would be able to influence the CoP and the Charter by participating in the NAC; moreover, they would remain ideologically free.

> In extending this invitation, we make it clear that acceptance of the 'Call' and participation on the National Action Council does not in any way bind your

organisation to accept our views – or any other views – of what is freedom. You will remain free to put forward and campaign for your own views.[80]

The CoP campaign was intended to operate in both black and white political arenas. Elections were seen as a means of generating white support by posing a challenge in a medium central to white political practice. An unsigned article in the Springbok Legion's *Fighting Talk* argued that whites were commonly seen as 'mummified in their attitudes of prejudice and racial isolation, and that nothing will ever change them'; the reverse, it was argued with wild and entirely misplaced optimism, was true:

> Every new democratic forward movement of the Non-White people, contrasting so sharply with every new Government inroad on our peace and liberties, brings more Europeans to the point of breaking with the traditions of race discrimination and oppression. The Defiance Campaign did so, leaving in its wake the Congress of Democrats, the Liberal Party and a more thoroughly democratic Labour Party. The Congress of the People campaign can do it again, on a wider scale.[81]

By staging national elections to the CoP, it was argued, 'it can be made impossible for them [whites] to stay out'.

> Will it be possible for those who repeatedly advise the non-European people to be 'restrained' and who criticised the Congress movement for its rash impetuosity to allow election contests in European areas to go by default to the only European body thus far committed to support the Congress of the People, the S.A. Congress of Democrats? I believe not.[82]

In the face of both the logistical difficulties of staging such elections and a growing awareness of the legal dangers of talking of electing 'a new Parliament – a people's Parliament'[83] the idea of national elections was dropped in mid 1954.[84]

Congress leaders hoped that the LP and the SAIRR in particular would become full participants in the CoP, which represented a second approach from Congress leaders to white liberals following their refusal to join the Congress of Democrats in 1952, and a further attempt to broaden the Congress Alliance. Commitment to a non-racial future had emerged as the guiding principle of the Congress Alliance by the early 1950s. As Albert Luthuli stated,

> I have said it in the past, and I repeat it here that to me Afrika is a land for all who are in it who give it undivided loyalty, whatever their racial origin might

be. I believe in and work for the acceptance of the conception of all in Afrika being known as Africans …[85]

That concept, as we have seen, was by no means universally accepted within the Alliance. Congress leaders stressed to the LP and the SAIRR that their participation in the CoP was essential to maintaining and building non-racialism.[86]

The SAIRR and LP were also approached for more immediate reasons. The participation of prominent public figures such as Alan Paton, Margaret Ballinger and Donald Molteno could be expected to restrain the repression the CoP anticipated. Moreover, as the LP's Marion Friedman noted after meeting NAC representatives,

> [t]he original sponsors are extremely anxious to get the Liberal Party in as sponsors – they made it quite clear that they wished us to come in so that we could have a hand in what was being decided. Furthermore it is evident that in receiving our support they believe, and probably rightly too, that other organisations will then be more willing to come in.[87]

SACOD and the Congress Alliance

The South African Congress of Democrats set itself three main goals: 'To prove itself the most zealous guardian of our people's rights; to permit no attack from the government to pass unchallenged; to forge a militant unity of all South Africans for Democratic rights for all'.[88]

SACOD was a tiny activist organisation with an average membership of 250, but with a public profile – and influence in Congress – that belied its size.[89] It was a political home for the white left and for former CPSA members as well as socialists from the trade union movement, Springbok Legion activists, churchmen such as Trevor Huddleston and Padre du Manoir, academics and others. It issued a large amount of anti-apartheid propaganda, ran campaigns in the white areas on a wide range of issues, by means of letters to the press, and collected signatures for petitions at tables in the streets and at public meetings. SACOD members also edited and wrote for progressive newspapers, which were sold door to door.

Its members suffered a high degree of repression: by 1954, for example, forty-two of the ANC's estimated 30 000 members had been banned and forty of SACOD's 200 or so members.[90] The NEC noted that SACOD's story 'could almost be the story of the bannings'.[91] Funds were raised through subscriptions, the sale of SACOD literature, and cake and book sales, but finances were always precarious: in 1954 SACOD had a liability of £256.8.11; four years later, income and liabilities balanced out at £213.5.7 apiece.[92]

As part of the multiracial Congress Alliance, SACOD had a 'special mission to convert white South Africans'.[93] Although completely misguided where whites were concerned – whites wanting to break away from apartheid were unlikely to seek the company of left-wing, often ex-communist-party whites – this remained Congress orthodoxy throughout the struggle against apartheid. Max Sisulu, some decades later, tried to explain the challenge lying at the core of Congress's multiracialism:

> The peculiarity of the South African situation is that people live in segregated areas, and in order to mobilize we've got to go where the people are. It is a lot easier, for example, for an Indian to go and mobilize the Indians in his area, or a white amongst the whites. You can't, as an African, go and mobilize the whites – it's impossible. Part of the process of struggle is that you recognize obstacles and you find ways of bypassing them. How do you do it? You don't do it by sitting back and saying, 'We don't recognize these boundaries, we don't recognize race.' You actively fight against racism: that is the essence of non-racialism.[94]

But this philosophy had developed over decades of struggle and a growing global argument about the salience of race as a construction rather than a biological given. In the 1950s, things were quite markedly different. Throughout that decade SACOD struggled to find a point where it could marry the energy of working on campaigns with the black congresses and in black areas with the tedium of working with whites in suburbia.[95] Although some of its members rejected the call to work with whites, they remained involved in the organisation because it provided the opportunity of 'going into the townships as a Congress member'.[96]

The formation of SACOD and the call for whites to work among whites occasioned a major dispute within the white left. The organisation's members were drawn from the ranks of those who, 'by long campaigning for what were formerly ridiculous and scorned ideas, have planted the seed of progressive and radical outlook in South Africa'.[97] Such work, however, had focused on and been located within the black community. As SACOD national secretary Ben Turok noted, white radicals entered a tradition of working in the townships instead of the white areas: 'Even the Congress of Democrats, although it constantly reassessed its role and its duty to work among the whites, nevertheless a tradition had been established – and tradition in politics is a very powerful thing.'[98]

Whites who rejected apartheid – for whatever reason, ideological or humanitarian, simply did not want to work with conservative or racist other whites. Their LP counterparts, with their non-racial organisational structure, did not have to, but whites in SACOD had a powerful symbolic role to play and most did so – under sufferance.

In trying to work with whites SACOD faced both internal differences and external hostility. Attempts to work in alliance with other organisations operating in white areas largely failed because of the suspicion with which SACOD was regarded by those, particularly in the Liberal Party, who were hostile to communists.

SACOD members were active in the Western Areas protest committees formed in the white suburbs of Johannesburg, organising the despatch of thousands of postcards to city councillors, opposing the removals while sending speakers 'Sunday after Sunday after Sunday' to Sophiatown.[99] It also supported moves to form a broad committee of representatives from the LP, UP, Torch Commando, Labour Party and the churches to co-ordinate opposition to the removals.

However, its moves to gain representation on the committee for the black congresses were blocked by other organisations, who feared that it had a hidden motive, and the committee collapsed.[100] A member of the SAIRR noted that at a Congress meeting in Johannesburg the registration of delegates was 'clearly in the hands of C. O. D. – no Non-Europeans at registration tables'.[101] Lacking further evidence of SACOD dominance the SAIRR reporter nonetheless elliptically concluded: 'My own impression that whole line of action dictated by people, probably C. O. D., whose one aim is to heighten resentment.'[102]

Members of SACOD, the LP and the SAIRR were drawn largely from the same stratum of middle-class white professionals, with a smattering of unionists and others, and a host of personal and professional relationships cut across organisational hostilities. An analysis of SACOD and LP membership lists reveals a similar preponderance of lawyers, academics and other professionals, and both organisations found the English-language universities to be their major recruitment area.

SACOD also included a number of highly able working-class whites, some of whom had been CPSA members.[103] Many on both sides had been radicalised by the Second World War and by the Army Education Service (AES). LP members were largely brought into the political arena by the post-1948 growth of anti-Nationalist sentiment; SACOD members had, in large part, been active in the 1940s in organisations such as the CPSA, the Springbok Legion, and the trade union movement. Describing the hostility between the LP and SACOD, LP member Ernie Wentzel noted: 'We were suspicious of the COD because in varying degrees we believed it to be Communist controlled or influenced, but our differences were also of temperament and emphasis. We were less radical than they were; less involved with the Congress movement.'[104]

As a small body shunned by other organisations working in white areas, SACOD could not, on its own, demand attention: its influence derived from its position as a partner in the Congress Alliance. Where Congress's strength was less evident SACOD's influence waned. The organisation's Cape secretary, Bernard Gottschalk, noted that 'the crux of the matter is joint Congress weakness, which allows other groups to avoid us at present'.[105] SACOD's NEC, based in Johannesburg, reminded members of their place in the Congress movement. Where the congresses were strong, as in Durban and Johannesburg, SACOD members plodded through their political work in white areas while providing (far more energetic) technical, legal, administrative and other assistance to the congresses. In both cities SACOD was represented on joint Congress committees.

In Cape Town, where the ANC was relatively weak and some leading members were sympathetic to the LP, relations were more difficult. Cape members were reminded that while '… of course you must maintain contact with the Congress and co-ordinate your work … we hope you do not think that COD can build S.A.C.P.O or the A.N.C. Apart from assisting them when they ask for assistance, there is little that C.O.D. can do to strengthen them organisationally.'[106]

It was in Cape Town that the tradition of working in black areas was most pronounced. The Cape Town branch reported that, of a book membership of eighty, '15 can be called upon to do regular active work', of whom only four were prepared to do door-to-door work in white areas. Gottschalk stated: 'So long as there is resistance to this primary form of activity, so long will we remain small and isolated.' In contrast, 'the best aspect' of SACOD's work in Cape Town was the introduction of study classes run by its members and attended by ANC, SACPO and South African Congress of Trade Unions (SACTU) members.[107] This tradition of working in townships rather than white suburbs also helps explain, in part, the enthusiasm of the more radical, younger Liberal Party members in the Cape for the Pan Africanist Congress (PAC) once it was launched. It gave them an immediate black ally, hostile to (white) communists, and, after the march of thousands into Cape Town in March 1960, an ally that promised a genuinely mass base, something the ANC could not do in Cape Town.

In Johannesburg the work of SACOD members was largely restricted to local branch activities. Senior members, however, were represented on national and provincial Congress Alliance consultative committees, participation that generated grassroots criticism, with members arguing that SACOD's lack of growth resulted from 'the failure of leading members to take over the responsibilities of secretaryship';[108] as the SACOD journal *Counter Attack* noted, 'Too many of us spend far too much time at Committee meetings … a few less meetings and we might have won still more support by having more time canvassing among the people.'[109]

Operating as it did with shaky finances (in the years before anti-apartheid organisations were supported by donor funds), participating in a wide range of campaigns and maintaining a highly visible public profile, SACOD was over-stretched.

> We have sprung from one campaign to another without consolidating our work, without reviewing our potential, and making the necessary plans to cope with new contacts. Area work has been haphazard and unplanned … Much has to be done with small numbers, over-burdened with too many meetings and little time for careful analysis.[110]

It is questionable whether any amount of analysis would have generated a larger white membership for this left-wing, activist ginger group. SACOD was at its most active (and enthusiastic) when involved in assisting other congresses in campaigns. Leading members were integrated in Alliance structures; branch members, however, 'plodded along' in campaigns in the white areas.[111] As a result SACOD welcomed the CoP campaign, which was both non-racial and promised to integrate a larger number of SACOD members into Alliance structures.

Analyses of the role of SACOD almost universally repeat the claim that its members dominated the Congress Alliance. According to national chairperson Pieter Beyleveld, later to give evidence against his comrades in the trial that led to the conviction of Bram Fischer and thirteen others charged with membership of the Communist Party and conspiracy to commit sabotage, SACOD was '… a loose association of like-minded people, bound together by a common belief in the necessity for and the desirability of a democratic society based on the equality of all citizens regardless of race or colour'.[112]

Beyleveld noted that SACOD did not have 'an all-embracing programme and policy on everything that happen[s] here and abroad, to which every member must owe allegiance publicly, or resign'. Rather, consensus extended to the struggle for equal rights and the primacy of the ANC in that struggle; thereafter SACOD members had 'diverse political allegiances' and included communists, anti-Soviet (and anti-CPSA/SACP) socialists, non-socialists, Christians and others. According to NEC member Helen Joseph, who described herself as 'almost anti-communist' in the early 1950s,[113] the fact that a number of former CPSA members (as well as SACP members, unbeknown to their colleagues) joined SACOD was 'not surprising'. It was the only organisation to which they could belong that unequivocally supported equal rights.[114]

Most research on SACOD makes an *a priori* assumption that the organisation provided 'earnest Marxists' with an entrée to the Congress Alliance.[115] (SACOD was probably too austere for less earnest Marxists.) Such assertions reflect the Cold War phobias of the time in which they were written – but are no less ahistorical – or just plain wrong – as a result. They do not account for the role of black communists in the ANC, SAIC and SACPO, somehow seeing communist plotting as a white predilection, to be practised upon a presumably unsophisticated black audience.

They are premised on the prominence and activities of SACOD itself and commentators have chosen to ignore SACOD members who had never joined the CPSA, who had left or been purged from the party before it disbanded, or who were generally hostile to it. The latter category included Trotskyists, former CPSA members, and ANC supporters such as Helen Joseph. Joseph was a rarity: SACOD was a small in-crowd of frequently bitchy, 'more left than thou', committed activists, whose anti-communism sprang from further left perspectives than the CPSA had espoused.[116]

Commentators have gone to extreme lengths to attack SACOD's role in the 1950s. Gerhart has commented that the:

> … dozens of … favors, large and small, which radical whites on account of their relative wealth and influence were able to offer their African allies, inevitably created a debt which Africans could repay only by lending their support to the

pet causes of the white left – the peace movement and propaganda efforts on behalf of the Soviet Union and China. It seemed a small price to pay.[117]

Gerhart argues that for those 'most promising ... in their sympathy towards the ideas preached by some of the COD's earnest Marxists' there was 'a special bonus' – paid trips to Eastern Europe. She concludes that black support thus engendered 'hardly constituted a commitment on any issue close to the immediate struggle in South Africa'.[118] Condescension drips from her pen.

Mary Benson argued that SACOD members used their position in the Congress Alliance to 'forc[e] forward ... extraneous issues' such as the Korean War. In contrast with Gerhart, Benson claims that such issues were 'sharply divisive'.[119] The support of black communists and nationalists for such issues is not commented upon. Rather, Gerhart argues that SACOD set a 'definition of political "reality" [which] distracted Africans from making their own objective assessment of where black interests lay'.[120]

In 1967 Edwin Munger took this perspective to its extreme, arguing that SACOD, 'a lily-white organization', was 'the leader of the Congresses'. According to Munger, 'SACOD from time to time manipulated the upper echelons of the A.N.C., sometimes by the simple means of giving a hungry man a job at £20 per month.'[121]

Tom Lodge, while not offering a detailed discussion of SACOD, analyses the organisation in terms of its positive effects on the Congress Alliance, noting that SACOD members were 'highly experienced in the fields of political and trades union organisation'. Their high political profiles derived not from the machinations of multiracialism but from their abilities – many of them had been active for decades in black politics. Lodge described SACOD members as '... highly experienced politicians with considerable intellectual ability. Whatever their colour one would expect such people to play a dynamic role.'[122]

SACOD and the Congress of the People

The CoP galvanised SACOD members in a non-racial campaign, gave concrete form to relations between the congresses and drew white liberals into a closer working relationship with the Congress Alliance. It was for these reasons, not for those claimed by various commentators, that SACOD immediately endorsed the CoP campaign, describing it as 'political job number one for the future'.[123]

SACOD was represented on the NAC and on provincial committees and was the only white organisation to co-sponsor and fully participate in the campaign. During the campaign its membership peaked at some 500 nationally, with the organisation described as 'a tower of strength in the whole preparatory work' for the CoP and its members involved at all levels of the campaign as well as in the congress itself.[124] The campaign harnessed SACOD's full energies, bringing its members out of the exclusively white suburbs and sending them into black areas as well. Ben Turok, appointed CoP organiser for the Western Cape, was 'deeply involved in the townships'.[125]

Demands were not collected on an organisational basis but by teams of organisers of all races and SACOD members participated enthusiastically in the process, spoke extensively in the townships, provided transport and produced propaganda for the CoP. In the Cape its members worked in rural and urban areas, holding late-night meetings in shantytowns and villages.[126] At the CoP itself SACOD members built the staging and provided a lighting system. As Helen Joseph put it, 'the whites did the dirty, hard, donkey work'.[127]

Rusty Bernstein co-ordinated a committee which analysed demands received for inclusion in the Freedom Charter, while Helen Joseph and Ben Turok introduced clauses of the charter at the Kliptown meeting. Whites also participated through membership of the South African Congress of Trade Unions and FSAW. There were 112 whites among the 2 884 delegates at the CoP itself and the Freedom Charter's unequivocal commitment to a non-racial future that included whites (quoted above) bore testimony to their role.

The campaign also saw SACOD and SACPO fully integrated into the ANC–SAIC Alliance. When it ended, SACOD's NEC concluded:

> The Congress of the People has cemented the Alliance of the Congress more firmly than ever before, with each section now being recognised and accepted not just as an ally but as a full partner with equal responsibilities. Here is being forged the future Alliance of the South African people ...[128]

As noted above, however, SACOD faced internal resistance to work in white areas. Even as the Freedom Charter would assert the oneness of South African identity its members were being corralled into white suburbs, and many bridled at the prospect. The intention was that during the campaign the NAC would co-operate with white organisations at a national level; SACOD's task was to canvass white support for the CoP, elect white volunteers and make '... the European population Congress-of-the-People conscious, and ... [win] the most enlightened and democratic of them for the Congress'.[129]

With the organisation's members already fully involved in collecting demands from black areas, its leaders called for a 'many-sided campaign' in the white areas, including house-to-house canvassing, 'chalking and sticking' of CoP slogans, writing letters to the press, arranging meetings with other organisations and organising talks on the CoP.[130] SACOD branches in Johannesburg and elsewhere accordingly began a selective canvass of white areas, which elicited both support for the CoP and some new members for SACOD. An internal document noted: 'The response has been better than expected. Why? Because we have been so out of touch with our section of the public that whatever would have happened, we would have been surprised.'[131]

Much of the reluctance of SACOD members to carry out work among whites related to the perception that building non-racialism necessitated the demonstration to blacks of white commitment to democracy. Such work, however, was not without its problems. Luthuli warned SACOD that while state persecution should be expected, 'even worse than this you may find yourself suspected of ulterior motives by some of the people you are trying to liberate'.[132]

CoP national organiser Thembekile Tshunungwa, reporting on a tour of the Western Cape, described the 'extreme confusion' that arose when SACOD members were found '... taking a lead in the ANC meetings ... a politically raw African who has been much oppressed, exploited and victimised by the Europeans sees red whenever a white face appears'.[133]

Walter Sisulu, however, later noted:

Most Africans come into political activity because of their indignation against Whites, and it is only through their education in Congress and their experience of the genuine comradeship in the struggle of such organisations as the Congress of Democrats that they rise to the broad, non-racial humanism of our Congress movement.[134]

The same point has been made by Congress activists, black and white, for decades. Nationalism – even racism – was just below the surface, easy to reach; non-racialism, however, had to be fought for, day by day, and was based on the need for deep-seated trust. The same challenge as faced the SACOD activists would later face South Africa as a country.

There was extensive debate about ways of bringing whites into the anti-apartheid struggle in considerable numbers. Most of the debate, however, was stuck at the theoretical level, where inevitable internal contradictions (it was hoped) would forcibly egress liberal whites from their laager into the anti-apartheid camp, followed by others. Some argued that mass white support for the Congress movement would follow as the government was forced to 'pander to [the] prejudices' of its support base – reactionary elements in South African society – and would thereby alienate 'the less reactionary sections'.[135]

Theoreticians in SACOD and the congresses argued that 'apartheid is an inhibiting factor in the economic development of South Africa ... what progress has taken place ... has been in spite of racial discrimination and not because of it'.[136] In the light of this some SACOD members argued that the organisation would not win mass support but that whites would join 'as the contradictions of fascism become more economically apparent'.[137] White support would also grow because apartheid had '... a logic of its own, which cannot be kept in a carefully separate and "Non-European" camp ... The destruction of the liberties of the Non-European is the forerunner of the destruction of liberty for the European.'[138]

There was little difference between the way whites in the Liberal Party and those in SACOD analysed the situation. Both believed capitalism would ultimately force apartheid into a corner and 'true democrats' of all colours would rally to support the 'rational' option, democracy. Either way, white support was not going to be won by hard slog in the suburbs. Rather, whites would be forced into the democratic camp by systemic contradictions. Working in suburbs to sell cakes and raise consciousness seemed a long way from liberation and, in the meantime, SACOD members continued to work in the townships whenever possible, as did Liberal Party members.

The Liberal Party and the Congress of the People

In July 1954 the Liberal Party was invited to co-sponsor the CoP. The invitation arrived at the height of the internal battles taking place at the 1954 National Congress, which left the party deeply divided and close to collapse. Congress delegates, clearly motivated by the possibility of forging closer working links with the congresses, voted for full participation in the CoP, and the LP publicly endorsed both the congress and the proposed Freedom Charter, while leaving the question of co-sponsorship open to discussion with the NAC. [139]

Participation in the campaign immediately increased contact between the LP and the Congress movement. A Liberal Party delegation met the NAC and Piet Beyleveld addressed the LP National Committee. A CoP newsletter advised regions that 'wherever possible the co-operation of Liberal Groups must be sought', while the NAC was to involve the LP at a national level. [140] LP members attended NAC meetings as observers, while the party debated co-sponsorship, reporting the visibly less hostile reception granted to the LP, and stressing that SACOD members were not controlling the CoP campaign. LP members were also elected to CoP committees in the Transvaal and the Cape. [141]

Support for participation in the CoP came largely from those party members who argued that the LP had to develop a black support base if it were to become a 'real political force'. [142] But the CoP became subsumed in the party-wide dispute between progressive and conservative elements.

The progressives argued that the CoP offered an opportunity to overcome Congress hostility while allowing the LP to take the fight against communism into the Congress structures: in effect, accepting the NAC's challenge to canvass popular support for the LP programme in competitive co-operation with the Congress movement. Durban LP member Ken Hill, supported by Selby Msimang and other black party members in Natal, argued that through the CoP the LP should work to:

> ... strengthen the liberal forces at work in the movement and to oppose quite openly the communist and the nationalist (non-White) forces. There are considerable communist influences at work but there is also much genuine liberalism amongst the non-White leaders. This ... would involve at once a struggle with the Congress of Democrats which would be intense and would certainly

be bitter and unprincipled on their side … We must not be afraid of … trying to convert everyone we can to liberalism.[143]

At the same time, however, conservative elements in the party became increasingly hostile to the CoP. Despite evidence that SACOD was not controlling the campaign, leading LP members stressed that behind the CoP lay the hidden hand of communism, in the shape of SACOD members. Meetings with Congress members centred on the 'hidden motive' behind the request for LP co-sponsorship.[144] Conservative LP members characterised the creation of the corps of 'freedom volunteers' as a means of 'causing agitation and frustration', and LP involvement in an extra-parliamentary campaign was described as 'frightfully dangerous'.[145]

That danger was exacerbated, it was claimed, by the fact that the LP would not be able to exercise a controlling influence in the CoP because of SACOD, whose members were seen as desiring 'the kudos as fighters for freedom and democracy for themselves alone' and who 'will try to damage [the LP] if they can'.[146] Conservative members argued that the party would be rendered powerless if it participated in the CoP and painted a picture of an LP duped by communists and the victim of 'disturbances which the Party could not control'.[147]

Not surprisingly, the disputes over the CoP divided the party along similar lines to those over the franchise and other issues. Moves to change the party's 'Principles' were led by the Transvaal Provincial Committee and a minority in the Cape division, where Native Representative candidate Jimmy Gibson sat on both the National and Executive Committees. Gibson and Peter Hjul, his election agent, were elected to Cape CoP committees while the 1954 elections were under way; as Hjul noted, 'it would have been a very silly thing for us politically to have rejected it … we were highly suspicious, of course, of what was behind the whole movement'.[148]

Following Gibson's electoral defeat by SACOD candidates, he informed party leaders that his support for the CoP had waned: 'in the absence of [LP] co-sponsorship, the CoP had taken a direction he could no longer support'.[149] Gibson recommended that the LP take no part whatsoever in the final congress. His supporters circulated a memorandum designed to win support for the withdrawal from the CoP, which claimed that CoP organisers:

> … are interested in power. They will use any weapon they can find to further their ends. Most of these men are white. They include lawyers who use the grievances of the African people to make their names as 'fighters for the people', deliberately fighting hopeless legal cases to establish themselves, and getting paid handsomely for it. They include men and women who set up bogus organisations as cover for the normal Communist aims …[their aim is] to rig control of the machinery of the Congress, making it a pure Communist front organisation.[150]

The call from Cape progressives for a withdrawal from CoP structures because of communist influence gained widespread support among party leaders. Alan Paton wrote to National Committee members in September 1954 asking 'whether we are struggling or whether we are moving into a common front'.[151] Conservative party leaders declared themselves 'frankly frightened' of the combination of communist dominance and a black extra-parliamentary campaign.[152] A number of LP members called for the resuscitation of the SAIRR national convention, 'with organisations rather than "the people" represented',[153] and the party's chairperson, Oscar Wollheim, finally suggested: 'We may possibly suggest a joint delegation to discuss the whole business with [Justice Minister] Blackie Swart – I mean ourselves, the Institute, Labour and Federal parties.'[154]

Behind the anti-communist rhetoric lay two prime concerns. The first was the LP's absence of control either over the CoP or over the final form the Freedom Charter would take. Wollheim noted: 'it boils down to whether we can achieve real leadership in the C.O.P or not'.[155] The second was the party's internal struggles – in the Transvaal particularly, the CoP had become subsumed in these struggles.

By 1955 party conservatives had rallied sufficient support to withdraw the LP from the CoP[156] and in June the Executive Committee (with Gibson's support) ruled that the LP should send neither a message nor observers.[157] Angry objections to this clear breach by the Transvaal of National Committee and national congress policy were ignored and, in a private letter, Gibson explained that the reason for his changed position on the CoP was '… not so much that I am concerned about what we [did] about the C.O.P. The real question at issue was whether or not this was a suitable issue on which to defy the Executive.'[158]

After Margaret Ballinger's threat to resign as party leader, progressives were under pressure to maintain party unity in all three provinces. Gibson argued that as the radical voice on the National and Executive committees, he was in a weak position: 'Any open defiance can merely split the Party and serve little purpose … it hardly seems to me desirable to force a split in the Party. But even if it were desirable this issue can not be considered important enough.'[159]

The Liberal Party's non-participation has been ascribed to the fact that the party was offered no influence over a plan that was, in any event, pre-set. Rewritten in (self-serving) fictional form by Alan Paton, the withdrawal of the LP was cause for regret by (a fictional) Albert Luthuli, who states, in an imaginary conversation, 'it's a pity you didn't come to Kliptown. You could've saved us from putting in all the Marxist doctrines.'[160] The real Albert Luthuli, however, noted that the LP '… grumbled rather that we had got things going and only then invited them in. We found their complaint odd, since all we had done was to define what we, the sponsors, were inviting them to join us in.'[161]

Much existing commentary neglects the CoP campaign in favour of speculation about the extent to which the (more or less earnest) 'white Marxists' of SACOD were able to control the nature of the final Freedom Charter.[162] Janet Robertson, for example, has claimed that '[t]he communist-controlled C.O.D. appeared to have a dominant role in preparations for the Congress … the extent to which the communists engineered the preparations for the Congress and prearranged the terms of the Charter itself is difficult to assess.'[163]

In most cases, commentators, quoting the views of LP members, question the veracity of Congress's claims that the charter emerged from the demands of the people.[164] This refutation ignores the fact that the LP was an actor on the same political stage as the Congress Alliance, in some areas competing with the congresses for support, membership and prominence, in others opposing mass-based extra-parliamentary campaigns. The views expressed by LP members are those of an interested party to events rather than objective assessments made by disinterested commentators.

The LP's withdrawal from the CoP and the fact that it was not one of the wide range of organisations (including the Labour Party) who sent messages of support to the Kliptown meeting, served to renew Congress's hostility, which had begun to wane. In northern Natal, where LP–ANC co-operation was at its closest, ANC members were reported to have 'attacked the Liberal Party as a bourgeois organisation interested only in advancing the interests of highly-educated and well-to-do Africans'.[165] Albert Luthuli warned the party: 'Africans will judge you by what you do for them, not by your ideologies.'[166] Pointing to 'fundamental deficiencies' in the LP's programme, Luthuli noted that, 'as a Congressman I cannot conscientiously work in an unqualified alliance with the Liberal Party'.[167]

The Congress of the People campaign cemented the Congress Alliance and entrenched a non-racial South Africa as its guiding vision. In the circumstances, and given the ongoing strength of African nationalism within Congress, this was a brave move and one which came at considerable cost to the ANC, as we read below. The Freedom Charter marked the culmination of the search for a unifying ideological statement, which had marked the resistance movement throughout the turbulent 1940s and 1950s. For white radicals the non-racialism of both the Freedom Charter and the Alliance was 'our most cherished possession, and must be guarded and strengthened'.[168] Their work, with that of whites in SACTU and FSAW, ensured that the Freedom Charter unambiguously endorsed the vision of a non-racial and democratic future South Africa.

Chapter 9

The Freedom Charter and the politics of non-racialism, 1956–1960

The ten years from the end of the Second World War to the Congress of the People in 1955 were dominated by nationalism and its instrumental value as a mobilisation tool. But the South African resistance movement differed from anti-colonial national liberation movements elsewhere in Africa because of the acceptance by black nationalists, socialists, liberals and others of the permanence of whites and the complexities of developing a national liberation struggle based on broad racial co-operation rather than racial exclusiveness. Multiracialism – separate racially based organisations co-operating in a single alliance under African leadership – evolved from attempts to marry African nationalism and racial co-operation. Awkwardly, the multiracial Congress Alliance had a non-racial future as its goal, while smaller competing organisations such as the Liberal Party (LP) had both a non-racial structure and a non-racial goal.

By 1955 the Congress movement had attained the organisational unity necessary to implement the Congress of the People campaign and codify its non-racial vision in the Freedom Charter. The theory of internal colonialism, which appealed to white liberal intellectuals as much as to the new South African Communist Party (SACP), was, in part, a solution to the challenge of how an African nationalist movement (with supporters from all race groups) in a global context dominated by decolonisation should deal with the local white population, which was both large (by African standards) and permanent.

The ANC's endorsement of the Freedom Charter was followed by the arrest of 156 Congress Alliance members of all races on charges of treason. The resultant power vacuum was used to good effect by Africanists opposed to the non-racial nature of the charter and to the Alliance. Africanists, like the Liberal Party (LP), focused their attacks on the South African Congress of Democrats (SACOD), which they characterised as an organisation of white communists who dominated the African National Congress

(ANC) and wrote the Freedom Charter to further communist aims via (presumably) nationalisation and other clauses.

By couching their attacks in predominantly anti-communist rather than anti-white terms Africanists won the support of a significant section of the Liberal Party, as well as that of some former Communist Party members and other left-wingers, who called for the pursuit of class struggle by means of a single, mass-based non-racial congress. At precisely the moment that non-racialism was entrenched in the ideology of the Congress movement, if not reflected in its organisational form, wide-ranging disputes broke out over the politics of racial co-operation.

From this concluding and brief review of political developments between 1956 and 1960 it is clear that racially separate organisations working together, under African leadership, for a future non-racial democracy, as outlined in the Freedom Charter, failed to resolve many of the disputes that had marked the Congress movement in the late 1940s and early 1950s. The multiracial structure of the Congress Alliance came under increased strain – from those wanting SACOD's 'earnest white Marxists' removed from influence, from those demanding 'One Congress', liberals demanding 'colour blindness' and others – and by the end of the decade Africanists had split from the ANC, claiming it had sold out on African nationalism; progressives had split from the United Party (UP) and taken the more conservative LP members and supporters with them, claiming that the UP and LP had sold out on core tenets of liberalism; while the state grew ever more repressive and turned an increasingly menacing gaze on its opponents, some of whom, both from the Congress Alliance and from the Liberal Party,[1] – turned to armed resistance.

The ANC and the Freedom Charter

In 1955 a peaceful route to a non-racial future still seemed possible. The Freedom Charter was a lyrical statement of nationalist and social-democratic demands, stressing the (peaceful) transfer of power and privilege from the white minority to the population as a whole to the benefit of all.[2] As Albert Luthuli put it, the Charter was,

> ... line by line, the direct outcome of conditions which obtain – harsh, oppressive and unjust conditions. It is ... thus a practical and relevant document. It attempts to give a flesh and blood meaning, in the South African setting, of such words as democracy, freedom, liberty ... The Freedom Charter is open to criticism. It is by no means a perfect document. But its motive must be understood, as must the deep yearning for security and human dignity from which it springs.[3]

The charter differed from previous ANC statements of principle most clearly in its method of production. 'The people' had replaced the 'distinguished university graduates' as the ANC's legitimating base. Moreover, where *Africans' Claims* and the Programme of Action dealt with specifically African demands the Freedom Charter began by stating that 'South Africa belongs to all who live in it, black and white' and was phrased entirely in non-racial terms. The charter restated demands for equality in all spheres of political, social, educational and cultural life, and for land redistribution. It had a distinctly social-democrat flavour, with greater emphasis on economic transformation than previous policy documents. *Africans' Claims* had called for the removal of economically restrictive laws but the charter went further:

> The national wealth of our country, the heritage of all South Africans, shall be restored to the people;
> The mineral wealth beneath the soil, the banks and monopoly industry shall be transferred to the ownership of the people as a whole.

The economic clause of the Freedom Charter has frequently been taken by critics to denote the hidden hand of communist authors; as a result, comment focused to a considerable extent on speculation about the document's authorship.[4] To ask who wrote it obscures the way in which the document – the fruit of almost two years of campaigning – was produced. SACOD member Rusty Bernstein (who drafted the charter) has noted:

> Most commentators focus ... on the matter of 'who wrote the Charter?' The question is wrongly conceived; the people 'wrote' the Charter, in the sense of deciding its contents. The demands collected in their thousand are the matrix of the Charter, its text in extenso; Congress sub-committees classified, grouped and sorted, I crafted the classified matter into a fairly uniform shape and verbal style.[5]

Bernstein recalled how crafting the charter was '... delayed ... to the last moment largely because no-one had any idea about how it was to be done. We had neither precedent nor plan. The Working Committee decided that it was "just a writing job" and handed it on to me.'[6]

But in the anti-communist fervour of the 1950s (as throughout the Cold War), (communist) conspiracy was always an easier tool for critics than cock-up, and came to dominate much discussion of the charter then and later. Bernstein 'crafted' a document from what he recalled as 'literally thousands' of demands written on 'scraps of paper, backs of envelopes, pages torn from school exercise books, and often the backs of our own handbills'.[7] Regional structures of the various congresses held meetings in 1955 in order to analyse the demands that had been collected, many of them summaries of meetings or discussions rather than succinct 'demands', and to discuss what the final charter should look like; resolutions from these meetings were sent to CoP headquarters in Johannesburg.

Calls for nationalisation and land redistribution were included in 'Demands of the People', a summary of demands collected by SACOD, alongside others such as 'We shall not move' or 'Life too heavy', all of which were submitted by the South African Coloured People's Organisation (SACPO) for inclusion.[8] According to Bernstein:

> There were fewer demands on macro-economic matters than others, because who other than the students or the commercially oriented puts the 'capitalism/socialism' issue in the forefront of their demands. The formulation in the Charter on these issues derived from 'demands', but from *few* demands. The issue of the land and its redistribution proposals are [va]gue, representing again the paucity of demands actually collected from the reserves and the rural cultivators … If I had 'written' the Charter as unthinking commentators often suggest, I would surely have had something more specific – nationalisation, collectivisation, confiscation or whatever to suggest. The formulations are the best we could devise.[9]

Focusing on authorship obscures the nature of the Freedom Charter and its purpose. The charter was intended to build inter-Congress and broader consensus by expressing, without qualification, the common aspirations of South Africans – and thereby re-uniting the Congress movement with its constituency, which had diminished after the Defiance Campaign.

However, while the charter provided a single ideological statement to which all the congresses could adhere, its endorsement by the ANC triggered a damaging dispute that ultimately led to a split and to the formation of the Pan Africanist Congress (PAC).

Opposition to the Freedom Charter

A meeting of the joint Congress executives in July 1955 unanimously endorsed the Freedom Charter and called on 'the peoples of South Africa, of all races and creeds to strive for the realisation of the principles embodied in the *Charter*'.[10] Luthuli described the charter as 'a practical document which leans towards Socialism, having regard to the practical situation that obtains'.[11] Z K Matthews, more conservative and apparently less enamoured of the contents, merely stated: 'Being the chief person responsible for the idea of the Congress of the People, I am happy that it has gone through successfully.'[12]

ANC endorsement of the charter was delayed because the 1955 annual conference was an elective conference; the charter was adopted at a special conference called in March 1956.[13] In the intervening nine months the charter was subject to attack by disparate elements, led by Africanists within the ANC, who described themselves as 'sea-green incorruptibles' and the true inheritors of African nationalism as set out in the Programme of Action.[14] Africanists argued that the struggle in South Africa was a straightforward anti-colonial battle between 'the conquered and the conqueror, the invaded and the invader, the dispossessed and the dispossessor'.[15] As such, Africanist antipathy focused on the charter's non-racialism: 'African Nationalists have repeatedly and forcibly made their standpoint clear, namely the Kliptown Charter was not, and is not the Charter of the African people, for the simple reason that the African is not prepared to forfeit his claim to his fatherland …'[16]

According to leading Africanists (and later leading PAC members) Peter Raboroko and Zeph Mothopeng, the Freedom Charter blamed black oppression on 'the system', whereas '[t]he truth is that the African people have been robbed by the European people'.[17]

The non-racialism of the charter was, to Rusty Bernstein, 'the least controversial paragraph',[18] but, as he noted, there was an overt clash between then popular anti-colonial slogans such as 'Africa for the Africans' and the charter's assertion that 'South Africa belongs to all who live in it, black and white'. For the Africanists it was just that non-racialism that reflected the interests of whites and Indians, and they described ANC leaders as 'clients receiving economic benefits from the "Marshall Aid Plan" of the C.O.D. and the S.A.I.C'.[19]

The Africanists did not launch a racist attack on all the non-African congresses or offer criticism of specific clauses in the charter; rather, they claimed that ANC leaders had 'made a catastrophic blunder by accepting foreign leadership by the whites', and made SACOD the main target of attack. In this manner anti-white and anti-communist sentiments commingled quite comfortably.[20] The Freedom Charter, Africanists argued, had been written by SACOD and did not reflect African aspirations. 'The Kliptown Charter did not emanate as a finished document from the A.N.C. It emanated as such from the Vodka Cocktail parties of Parktown and Lower Houghton … The black masses who met at Kliptown were merely pawns in the game of power politics.'[21]

ANC leaders were characterised as 'lackeys, flunkeys and functionaries of non-African minorities',[22] particularly the 'Curse Of Democracy', the Congress of Democrats.

> In 1953 C. O. D. was born. Who her parents were and who the midwife was we unfortunately do not know. But rumour persists that she is the product of an incestuous union … The C. O. D. controls and dominates the A.N.C. … We declare, here and now, that we shall never submit to C. O. D. domination.[23]

These attacks on SACOD resonated with existing anti-white sentiment but also fell on fertile ground among LP members, who had long attacked SACOD as a communist front. LP anti-communism was strengthened in 1956 when journalists Patrick Duncan and Jordan Ngubane, bound by what Alan Paton called 'an almost fanatical anti-communism', joined the party.[24] Both were Africanist sympathisers: Ngubane was a delegate to the inaugural conference of the PAC in 1959, while Duncan later became the only white member.

Duncan was an erratic and unpredictable figure who talked of 'pamphleteering South Africa by plane' and rejected a proposed boycott of South African minerals in favour of boycotting frozen lobster tails, which, he argued, 'would be very telling'.[25] He brought a vicious Cold War anti-communism to the LP and to the newspaper *Contact*, which he edited, claiming that SACOD members 'proudly, unashamedly, backed the communist cause'.[26] A *Contact* policy memorandum dedicated the newspaper to 'support for the democratic front, but never of COD'.[27]

Whites opposed to apartheid were tiny in number and punched far above their weight. But, as in most liberation struggles, battles against rivals were fought with a special bitterness and intensity.

Duncan and Ngubane launched a series of public attacks on SACOD and the Freedom Charter in *Contact*, and in *Indian Opinion*, to which Ngubane contributed. Duncan considered the charter 'unexceptionable … But it was the creation of communist-minded people, not of the African National Congress.'[28] Ngubane similarly accepted that the charter was not a communist document – having presumably changed his mind from earlier days when he identified it as the new communist 'line' – but argued that its very broadness was intended 'to condition the African people for the purpose of accepting communism via the back door'.[29] One way or another, communism would be found in the Freedom Charter by those who wanted it there.

On joining the LP Jordan Ngubane noted: 'The atmosphere inside the Party is that of well-intentioned, sincere and decent people unconsciously awed by the fearful complexity of race problems. We act as though the evils we oppose are amenable to reason of the type we respect.'[30] He appealed to liberals to 'tak[e] Liberalism to the man in the Location' and party leaders sought to radicalise the LP in order to effect this – white suburban council elections were unlikely to succeed in doing so.[31]

The LP travelled a long political and ideological road from 1953 until it disbanded in 1968 and it should be judged on that basis, not solely by the blinkered and hysterical anti-communism of some members, any more than by the conservatism of others. LP leaders praised the 'truly democratic nature' of the Freedom Charter[32] but rejected its 'socialist provisions' as 'not compatible with the Party's declared policy'.[33] By 1960 the latter was no longer true: the LP endorsed a draft land policy which talked of confiscation and collectivisation, and a welfare-state economic policy;[34] black strikes and boycotts were accepted because 'no other methods are available to them' and the LP criticised those who described such methods as 'agitation'.[35] LP Chairperson Peter Brown stated: 'What we want here … is to see the Universal Declaration of Human Rights become the law of the land in South Africa.'[36] No wonder the UP's final few liberals found the Liberal Party too radical.

In 1959 the LP and the ANC jointly organised the first month-long overseas boycott of South African goods. The move generated considerable opposition from conservative LP members; according to Peter Brown, 'one had reached the point where one felt enough accommodation had been made' and a number of conservative members left for the Progressive Party.[37] LP leaders in Natal and the Transvaal saw the party as 'an organised articulate pressure-group among both whites and blacks',[38] maintaining liberal values in the ANC by co-operating with it while opposing the closeness of the ANC and SACOD. According to Brown '… it is only by being more active that we can hope to persuade Africans in particular that what we offer is better than what COD has to offer'.[39] But, as we have seen, the LP spoke with many voices.

To the party's activists in the Cape, 'COD was Communist Party'[40] and ANC leaders in the region were described as 'little more than faceless images of their COD bosses'.[41] To a degree this reflected the weakness of the Cape ANC and its leadership (as well as its small support base) compared with that in other parts of the country. It also reflected the long history of white communists organising in townships, in factories and so on. But that is background: the anti-communism of the LP in the province had a fervour all of its own. Led by Duncan, the Cape rejected the relative closeness of LP–ANC relations elsewhere in the country, which they described as 'the rather humiliating attempt to horn in on other people's parties'.[42] Duncan argued:

> The Liberal Party has no hope of achieving support or even favour in the eyes of the African masses by such co-operation so long as what Eddie Roux calls 'the dynamic activities of the Reds' inside the A.N.C. continues … in politics the major factor remains power, and … there is no substitute for the Liberal Party making its own way and developing its own membership if it wishes to win the respect of South Africa. I believe that our stand as a Party, i.e. non-racial, South African and anti-communist, is so powerful a position that if we use energy and skill we can put all differing movements on to the defensive.[43]

Duncan claimed that the influence of white communists in SACOD had 'changed the character of the A.N.C.' to the point at which it had 'ceased to be a body of Africans, led by Africans and quite independent of White control';[44] he welcomed Africanist attacks on SACOD as 'the comeback against Communist control'.[45] LP leaders criticised Duncan's 'one-man guerrilla war against the COD' and warned of the dangers of over-emphasising communist influence within the ANC. In 1959 Duncan published an 'Open Letter to Chief Luthuli', appealing 'to him to use his eyes, and to see where he is allowing his Congress to be led'.[46] The letter generated calls for Duncan's expulsion from the LP, and raised questions about his possible links with American agencies that funded anti-communist bodies.[47]

The Freedom Charter and Alliance politics

Attacks on the Freedom Charter were bound up with hostility to SACOD and its supposed bastardisation of African nationalism for communist ends. These attacks came to a head at the 1956 ANC Special Conference. Extracts were read from a letter by former

President-General Alfred Xuma, who argued that ANC leaders had 'turned their backs on the African National Congress Nation-building Programme of the 1940s' in favour of the Freedom Charter, which served to 'defer and confuse the Africans' just and immediate claims'. Xuma believed the ANC had:

> ... lost its identity as a National Liberation Movement with a policy of its own and distinct African Leadership. One hears or reads statement by the 'Congresses' and one hardly ever gets the standpoint of the African National Congress ... One and all must realise no one else will ever free the Africans but the Africans themselves.[48]

Africanist disruption of the Conference led to a lengthy dispute over the accreditation of delegates and, with 'ranks ... closed against what was regarded as obstructionism', the charter was adopted with little debate.[49] Africanists accused 'the Chameleon National Organisation called the Congress of Democrats' of controlling conference proceedings[50] and concluded: 'We are merely being made tools and stooges of interested parties that are anxious to maintain the status quo.'[51]

After the conference Luthuli rounded on critics of the charter and the Congress Alliance. In a lengthy statement, he attacked LP critics, particularly Ngubane, for insisting that whites in SACOD dominated the ANC:

> Shall we infer from this allegation of his that in the Liberal Party he is suspicious of his fellow-members who belong to other racial groups than his own: white, coloured and Indian? If he is not, why should he insinuate that relations among the allied Congresses are governed by suspicion of one another?[52]

The ANC, Luthuli argued, was 'an omnibus liberatory movement' which included members 'with different political inclinations, but all subjecting their personal inclinations to the overriding needs of our day which are to fight and defeat apartheid ...'.[53] He noted that the ANC 'has always had amongst its ranks people who are communistically orientated'. Two CPSA members had been signatories to *Africans' Claims*, touted by the disgruntled Xuma as the 'true' African voice: 'I do not see anything red there ... or are we seeing with different spectacles?'[54]

Turning to the Freedom Charter, Luthuli noted claims by Ngubane and others that the ANC in Natal opposed the charter but had their hands forced by SACOD. Luthuli, who described himself as a socialist who, in England, would vote for the Labour Party,[55] noted ironically: 'Here, surely, is naked Communism for all to see.' He maintained that the ANC in Natal 'accepted unreservedly the principles reflected in all the main clauses of the Freedom Charter' but 'thought it unwise to have padded the Charter with variable details in an all-time charter'. In conclusion, Luthuli stated that '[t]he most that could be said about the Freedom Charter is that it breathes in some of its clauses a socialistic and welfare state outlook, and certainly not a Moscow communistic outlook.'[56]

The Freedom Charter marked the culmination of a number of processes that had marked the work of Congress from its inception, most notably the search for ideological unity and broad non-racial resistance to racial discrimination. At the end of the Congress of the People the non-racial committees which had co-ordinated the campaign were transformed into permanent consultative committees at local, provincial and national level. Racial co-operation was entrenched in both the ideology and practice of the movement. Having attained broad ideological consensus with the adoption of the charter by all the congresses, the ANC's leaders called for widening resistance to the Nationalist Party through alliances with non-Congress organisations.

However, in its call for the development of a united front with the Liberal and Labour parties, the churches, the Black Sash and other anti-apartheid bodies, the Congress movement did not emphasise the charter, believing that, since most of these organisations were white, they would be 'at present … not prepared to accept the challenging vision of the Charter'.[57] Instead, the basis of unity was to be opposition to racism and the NP government. Congress leaders remained immovably (and, it has to be said, somewhat inexplicably) optimistic that there existed '… a steadily growing number of serious thinking White South Africans who … may not care to be associated with our Freedom Charter [but] are aware that the future of this country lies in the policy of equal rights …'.[58]

There was a discernible shift in attitude among some whites, who opted to work in the extra-parliamentary field. The Liberal Party radicalised its policies and worked closely with the ANC in northern Natal and patchily elsewhere. Also in Natal the Anti-Republican League organised public meetings in protest against plans to transform South Africa into a republic. The Black Sash staged their solemn, silent protests, organised cavalcades to present petitions to Parliament and 'haunted' Cabinet ministers.[59]

At parliamentary level tensions within the United Party increased and, in August 1959, twelve UP MPs resigned to form the Progressive Party, following which they held extensive talks with Africanists and Congress leaders.[60]

Whites from a wide range of organisations attended a Multi-Racial Conference (MRC) in 1957 organised to 'discuss and explore the steps which can bring about friendly and effective co-operation among the different racial groups in our country'.[61] The 350 participants and more than 300 observers, including UP and NP members, participated in commissions, all of which condemned apartheid.

At the same time, a small number of prominent Afrikaners publicly distanced themselves from various aspects of apartheid. The group included Professor L J du Plessis, a founder member of the Afrikaner Broederbond (Brotherhood), a secret society formed to further Afrikaner nationalism, who criticised Prime Minister Hendrik Verwoerd and called for greater inter-racial contact.[62] In addition, informal discussions were held between Congress leaders and members of the South African Bureau of Racial Affairs (SABRA), a body of Afrikaner intellectuals formed in 1948 to research and prepare the public for the greatest possible racial separation. The discussions were a response to a resolution passed at the 1958 SABRA conference, calling for a second multiracial conference.

All organisations operating in white politics expressed hostility towards and refused to co-operate with SACOD. SACOD, in turn, criticised white organisations for refusing to acknowledge black demands for full equality, and insisted that the principles of the Freedom Charter 'are the only basis on which the Nationalists can be defeated'.[63] It is pointless to try to assess whether it was SACOD or its critics that was more pig-headed.

Africanist attacks on SACOD and the charter won support from some, both in the LP and elsewhere. SACOD members were intensely loyal to the Congress movement – at one level they derived their legitimacy from it, at another it allowed them full expression of their opposition to apartheid and their desire for equality and enabled them to cross the colour bar personally and politically. Their loyalty held when tested by banning, house arrest and exile, by detention without trial, torture and murder. But SACOD – like white left organisations in the 1980s – was hostile to its less radical, more liberal rivals, who sought Congress's approval, and was dogmatic in its rigid adherence to the Freedom Charter, which its members had done so much to help bring into being. In short, it was intensely loyal but also a liability at times. In August 1956 Luthuli privately questioned the efficacy of '… making the Freedom Charter the basis for co-operation with any other group in the future. Why should we tie ourselves so fast to the Congress of Democrats? We should form a Freedom Front as wide as possible.'[64]

Luthuli's comment was followed by public statements from senior Congress figures arguing that the Freedom Charter should not be the sole basis of unity. Campaigning under the slogan 'The Nats Must Go!' the alliances pursued by the congresses were largely concerned with winning white support.[65] Joe Matthews argued that '[a]s the Nationalist's oppression becomes worse, the call for a united front composed of all genuine opponents of Apartheid becomes ever more insistent' and as a national liberation movement it was 'historically correct … to rally the people on the widest possible scale'. He continued:

> But should the Charter be the main programmatic condition for the United Front? Should we insist that all allies must accept the Charter? We must bear in mind that the essence of a united front policy is that it is always based on *Opposition* to dictatorship rather than common adherence to long term objectives and aims. To expect the policy of United Front to go beyond the defeat of the Fascists is mere wishful thinking … to accept the Charter means to be on the progressive camp. To be a part of the United Front requires a different generalisation.[66]

Broad-based alliance politics became the flavour of the day and the National Consultative Committee (NCC) called for a non-charter-based united front, arguing that not all anti-Nationalists supported the charter, but 'we are allies against the same main enemy …

this *unity*, growing every day and in every struggle … is the key to victory'.[67] The announcement of a general election for April 1958 further focused Congress's attention on white politics.

In turn, SACOD, clearly under pressure, criticised 'the sectarian attitude of our members' and called on them 'to get together with other organisations on the basis of mutual respect for each other's differences and the right of organisations to a separate membership and existence'.[68] SACOD, always small, was further weakened by banning and house arrest orders imposed on its members, while many of its leaders were among those arrested and put in the dock in the marathon Treason Trial. Loyal cadre it may have been, but the organisation offered no leverage or even contact with those in or near power in white political circles. Its members were committed and highly capable activists, but few provided Congress with any means of contact or communication with the upper echelons of the white power structure.

In 1958 the Congress Alliance attempted to implement the united front strategy. At the same time, however, the ANC was suffering from internal power struggles in both the Cape and the Transvaal. With senior Congress figures banned or appearing in the Treason Trial, less experienced activists were elected to provincial committees. In the face of continued Africanist dissent the Transvaal Provincial Committee tried to force its decisions on the 1957 provincial conference and demanded its re-election *en bloc* as an act of support for the trialists.[69]

Africanist opposition in the Western Cape, where the ANC was weak, led to the emergence of two rival executive committees (one 'loyalist', one Africanist), which co-existed throughout 1958.[70] At the same time both SACOD and the ANC struggled with internal disagreements over attempts to form alliances with liberal white organisations. As was the case in the late 1940s and 1950s disputes over a range of issues – the racist attacks of Africanists, anti-communism, the alliance strategy, and the efficacy of national as opposed to class struggle – came to be fought out over the question of the form racial co-operation should take.

1959–1960: The politics of non-racialism

The 1950s were dominated by nationalism. Liberals, socialists and others opposed to apartheid were forced to re-orientate their ideological and strategic standpoints in relation to the ANC as it emerged as the representative African political organisation, and to the increasingly brutal NP government. ANC leaders, noting that 'fighters for freedom in this country are continually being drawn from all sections of the population',[71] amended the militant African nationalism of the Youth League to facilitate building a broad anti-apartheid front.

By the late 1950s, however, those hostile to the ANC and/or the Congress Alliance – including LP members, former CPSA members, Trotskyists, Africanists, and a variety of maverick individuals – attempted to capitalise on the power vacuum in the ANC. Although their long-term objectives differed markedly, all focused hostile criticism on the same immediate target: the preponderant influence SACOD members were accused of wielding over the ANC through the multi-racially structured Congress Alliance. By simultaneously ignoring black communists and insisting that SACOD was a front for white communists, a disparate array of forces identified the abolition of multiracialism with the excising of communist influence. The ANC, however, repaid SACOD's loyalty and stood by the organisation.

While by the end of the decade the forces hostile to SACOD were focusing their attacks on the multiracial structure of the Congress Alliance, Congress itself continued to emphasise the *organisational form* that would allow Africans to lead the struggle of all races for equality for all. No doubt, decades-long loyalty to white communists – whose unqualified support for black freedom predated and outstripped that of white liberals – was also a factor. But so, too, was sensitivity to nationalism – to the anti-white (and anti-Indian) hostilities that lay fairly close to the surface (as we have seen), to the need for full African leadership in the face of energetic support from other race groups with better resources and better access to resources.

The same black pride (and the failure of white anti-apartheid activists to take it into account) that would ultimately split the Black Consciousness Movement from what were regarded as patronising white liberals in the National Union of South African Students (NUSAS) and elsewhere, also existed in the ANC.

But the drive for African control was overlaid with ideology and politics. ANC leaders argued that multiracialism was critical to ensuring that the struggle was, and was seen to be, African-led; and that each race group had a better entrée to its own areas, languages and cultures than did other race groups – however exciting Kotane's 'path of least resistance' may have been for white activists. But from outside, and from within the ANC, came a growing series of attacks on multiracialism, claiming (entirely wrongly) that it had been designed by white communists in SACOD to secure a disproportionate influence over the ANC. Multiracialism, in short, was seen as a (white) communist ploy; it was in fact a nationalist manoeuvre to maintain the goal of non-racialism under African leadership and avoid claims that whites, Indians or coloureds were in any way leading it or the ANC.

To drive the point home there emerged a growing discourse of 'race blindness', a forerunner of later thinking about race. But the closeness between much contemporary analysis and what was happening in this particular group five decades ago should not blind the reader to the fact that the proponents of non-racialism had a very clear political project in mind, much as the multiracialists did. The attack on multiracialism, led by Patrick Duncan and *Contact*, argued that:

Non-racialism and multi-racialism are two very different things. The non-racialist sees each human being as first and foremost a human; less important facts about him are education, his race, etc. But the multi-racialist, like the out-and-out racialist, sees each human being first and foremost as a member of a racial block.[72]

Contact's lead was followed by former members of the Non-European Unity Movement, (NEUM) close to Duncan and his anti-communist coterie, who published *The Citizen*, a fortnightly newspaper in the Western Cape. *The Citizen* asked: 'Where is this country, "Non-Europe", from which four of every five South Africans would appear to have come?'[73] Multiracialism was criticised for transplanting apartheid into the Congress Alliance; in this, the criticism echoed much more that would be thrown at the ANC over time. But the real target of attack, once again, was SACOD:

> It is multi-racialism – a gratuitous concession to apartheid – which is at the root of all other evils in Congress … And it is precisely the multiracialism of Congress which enables the 'Whites-only' Congress of Democrats to dominate the Congress 'racial' alliance and to subordinate its struggle against oppression to the interests of 'sympathetic', 'White' patronage.[74]

It took a degree of wilful misliteration to insist that by sitting on joint co-ordinating committees SACOD led the ANC by the nose while shoving communism down its throat. Nonetheless, the view was widely repeated and widely supported.

In an ironic twist, in the late 1950s multiracialism came to be seen by a wide range of forces as the creation of white communists who sought to direct the ANC. It suited those wanting to oust whites from positions of leadership or influence; those wanting communists out of the way; those wanting a single, class-based liberatory body; and yet others. As a result, attacks on multiracialism commingled with anti-communist and anti-SACOD sentiments, among others. One critic of the Congress movement argued enthusiastically:

> The phenomena of Stalinist multiracialism originally arose as an adaptation to the NEUM. Thinking Non-Europeanism to be the rising force the Communist Party, at that time of largely 'white' composition and predominantly 'white' orientation, with characteristic opportunism abandoned its old 'non-racial' organisational form in favour of working in and building racial organisations, to be aimed at making political capital out of the stirring 'black masses'.[75]

Attacks on SACOD and multiracialism were led by the Africanists, whose criticisms had a legitimacy that was absent from those of whites. Following the expulsion of Potlako Leballo and James Madzunya from the ANC for expressing hostility to white domination of Congress via SACOD, Africanist hostility to SACOD was extended to include the entire ANC leadership, and a showdown appeared inevitable. In a leader article, *Bantu World*, which championed the Africanist cause, wrote of the ANC leadership:

> They speak of Alliance with the C.O.D. and with the so-called Indian and Coloured Congresses, when in fact it is these very alliances which makes them work against African Nationalism. It is the C.O.D. together with the Indians and Coloureds who have expelled the African Nationalists from our own home, the A.N.C. We must, therefore, dismiss these foreigners from our A.N.C. and with them the present leadership. All of them must march out for we have no time to pick and choose between them.[76]

The mounting attacks attracted Cape-based ex-communists Joe Nkatlo and John Gomas, both of whom had become increasingly vocal critics of the Communist Party and increasingly sympathetic to the Africanists.[77] Nkatlo stated: 'I accept being called an "Africanist" if it means an "African" who refuses to be politically subservient to "European" leadership and who refuses to entrust his destiny to some "European" careerists who exploit him.'[78]

Patrick Duncan recruited into the LP Nkatlo and former NEUM members grouped around *The Citizen*. He also began talks with the (tiny) NEUM, noting that 'it may be that this will lead to a fusion' which would 'immensely strengthen the party'.[79]

In 1958, in an attempt to resolve disputes with the Africanists, ANC conferences were held in the Transvaal and the Western Cape. The attempt failed: three Western Cape branches broke away from the ANC, while both sides brought 'strong-arm stewards' to press their case at the Transvaal conference.[80] Transvaal Africanists left the ANC, stating: 'We are launching out on our own as the custodian of A.N.C. policy as formulated in 1912 and pursued up to the time of Congress Alliance.'[81] Duncan welcomed the break, noting with characteristic reserve that if it led 'to a national rejection of the COD alliance by the ANC ... it will in South African terms be as important as was the rejection of the Communists by the Chinese in 1927'.[82]

A year later the Pan Africanist Congress (PAC) was launched, with university lecturer and former member of the ANC Youth League Robert Sobukwe as its president. PAC speakers argued that the ANC was led by a 'white pseudo-leftist directorate', as a result of which it had '... betrayed the material interests of the African people. They have sacrificed these interests upon the political altar of an ungodly alliance, an alliance of slave-owner, slave-driver and slave.'[83]

An Africanist former Youth League colleague of ANC Secretary-General Oliver Tambo appealed to him to return to the policies of the league:

> It was and it still is the first duty of an African Nationalist, to destroy a Communist in every possible way. Right from the founding of the A. N. C. Y. L.

it was the principle and practice to annihilate Communists under all situations and circumstances … African Nationalists, then as now, believed strongly that Communists had no interest in African Freedom, except to use us as pawns of Russian foreign policy, and as revolutionary expendables …[84]

At the centre of PAC hostility lay SACOD, which, it was argued, had forced on the ANC a policy which 'consider[s] South Africa and its wealth to belong to all who live in it, the alien dispossessor and the indigenous dispossessed, the alien robbers and their indigenous victims'.[85] It is virtually impossible to separate out issues of race, class, ideology and political manoeuvring. Africanists were in it for Africanists. Trostskyists and other 'ultra-leftists' were in it for historical reasons – to oppose perceived (former) Communist Party influence – and to unhook liberation from the two-stage theory of revolution, which required a nationalist to precede a socialist revolution. Liberals were in it for these and other reasons. What welded them all together was hostility to the multiracial structure of the Congress Alliance, even though it was, itself, a creation of ANCYL nationalists.

'One Congress' or 'One Class Struggle'?

Attacks on SACOD reached a point where a participant in the third SACOD national council meeting in May 1959 'asked if we did in fact lead the A. N. C. by the nose'.[86] By the end of the 1950s the organisation was badly weakened: Transvaal chairperson Vic Goldberg and fifty-one members, roughly one-fifth of its total membership, had been banned. The organisation was also weakened by 'continual disagreements among ourselves as to the role we have to play', which stemmed from 'the fact that many members have not accepted the original role of the C.O.D.'.[87] The disagreements flowed, in part, from frustration at having to attempt to win white support, described by one member as 'slow, slogging and tenacious political work amongst our mentally depressed brethren, the Europeans'.[88] SACOD's internal problems were exacerbated in the late 1950s by a resurgence of calls for the prosecution of class struggle. As in the late 1940s these calls were couched in the language of non-racialism or 'One Congress'.

Baruch Hirson, a university lecturer later imprisoned for sabotage, noted that members of the Socialist League of Africa, a small Johannesburg Trotskyist group, joined SACOD because 'we were terribly isolated, a small handful of people'; within the organisation members 'could put a socialist line and win friends'.[89] SACOD was a forum in which battles within the white left were fought out and, ironically, where the anti-communism of the LP and Africanists was mirrored by the Trotskyists and others who loathed the Communist Party and scorned communists for 'abandoning' class in favour of national struggle. Like other ideological disputes in South Africa in the 1950s the locus of this one was the form racial co-operation should take.

Within SACOD the strictures of working with whites generated incessant complaints and frustration. As part of the alliance strategy pursued after 1956, SACOD was called on to 'broaden out or stagnate';[90] to tone down its dogmatic adherence to the Freedom Charter in favour of forming alliances with other organisations working in the white areas.

Further removed from grassroots black work, SACOD members were reported to be 'bored to tears' with 'an almost incessant round of jumble sales'.[91] Disagreement about the organisation's role was given a dramatic focus by Cape member Ronald Segal, the flamboyant editor of *Africa South*. Segal was invited to address the 1958 Workers Conference on the economic boycott; in place of his speech, however, he called for a single non-racial Congress. According to Segal, 'I took a pound out of my pocket and I said – "I hereby apply to join the ANC – will you accept me?" And there was a tumultuous "Yes! Yes!".'[92]

Within a year SACOD's student branch, based at the University of the Witwatersrand, voted to disband itself and form a non-racial youth congress which would include African and Indian students.[93] SACOD members in Johannesburg made moves to organise African domestic workers. The Cape Town branch questioned whether alliances were important enough to water down policies. 'This we are putting a stop to. If our policy is right and we offend – then we can't help it. Being broad, we have decided, means nothing more than working with other organisations and individuals on agreed issues while disagreeing – and not working together – on others.'[94]

SACOD saw attacks on multiracialism from non-Congress members as the actions of those 'never friendly to us [who] have now found a stick with which they hope to beat us, a "policy" with which they hope to sow dissension'.[95] They were right: the LP's Peter Hjul noted that criticism of multiracialism was 'our point of argument – I wouldn't say it was a huge ideological point of difference but it was a very good stick to beat the Congress movement with.'[96] Within SACOD calls for 'One Congress' resulted in part from dissatisfaction about working with whites, and from calls for broad alliances. The organisation's leaders pointed out that all SACOD members would rather belong to a non-racial body but that 'there were many obstacles in the way of this', the most obvious being the unchanging opposition from ANC and SAIC leaders. 'Change', they argued, 'would only be possible when the other Congresses were strong and confident enough' to instigate it.[97]

Calls for a non-racial Congress, however, were soon given a class content by left-wing SACOD members, who argued that by pursuing alliances and concentrating on electoral politics, liberal ideology had 'already seeped deeply into the movement'.[98] In a series of broadsheets and in the pages of *Counter Attack*, building alliances was equated with neglecting the militant organisation of blacks and with 'treating S.A.C.T.U. [the South African Council of Trade Unions] as an unwanted foster-child',[99] both assertions neatly aimed to get a reaction from the communists in the organisation. Hirson, writing under a pseudonym, argued that the planned ANC anti-pass campaign should emphasise:

... that passes are part of the capitalist system ... The passes are one link in the chain that binds us: Again and again it is necessary to explain that in fighting to break these links in the chain of oppression, our objective is to get rid of the whole chain. Our goal, which we must keep ever in sight, is to change the whole social system in South Africa.[100]

Vic Goldberg, writing in *Counter Attack*, argued that SACOD's work among whites should focus on organising white workers rather than forming alliances with middle-class intellectuals in the LP and elsewhere. Goldberg, strongly echoing Danie du Plessis of nearly a decade earlier, argued that the organisation of the working class – regardless of race – should be the first priority of the liberation movement. Class politics, he argued, could not be pursued in a multiracial alliance: 'We are agreed that whites and non-whites are inter-dependent in the developing of this country, in the struggle for freedom this must be even more applicable.'[101]

The supporters of class struggle also fought against the ideology of the South African Communist Party, particularly the theory of internal colonialism through which socialists were called on to work with and for the national liberation movement. That battle was also fought over calls for non-racialism, which resonated with existing frustration about SACOD's role in the alliance. Goldberg argued that South Africa was a capitalist country, exploited by and for local capitalists; as such, all had a stake in a common struggle. However,

[i]f we conceive of white South Africa being a colonial power and non-white South Africa being the colonial people, then the struggle can only be likened to one of national liberation. In this context, it is obvious however that the Africanist position of 'Africa for the Africans' would be correct and that a black versus white struggle would be the one progressives should support.[102]

In response, SACOD and ANC leaders argued that they all supported the ideal of One Congress.

Every Congress leader of today would be willing – and even eager – to belong to and join a multi-racial [sic] Congress. But political success in the fight against race domination is not to be won by the leaders alone. For success, leaders need the masses. Are the masses ready for a multi-racial [sic] Congress? Would the tribes people of Sekhukhuneland or the dock labourers of Durban feel that a multi-racial [sic] body was 'their' organisation, as they today feel about the A.N.C.?[103]

ANC leaders argued that however attractive a single congress might appear, 'would there not immediately be a need felt amongst Africans for a purely African organisation to put forward the views of Africans?'[104] This was borne out by the formation of the PAC, whose founders argued that the new organisation was made necessary 'following the capture of a portion of the black leadership by the white ruling class'.[105]

Multiracialism had given rise to what Ben Turok described as a 'quite horrendous' build up of committees, with a large degree of wastage and duplication of effort.[106] The local, provincial and national consultative committees, which lay at the heart of claims that SACOD dominated the ANC, had begun to break down by 1958. The committees had been given no executive powers precisely in order to avoid the encroachment of one congress in the affairs of another; because of their lack of power, however, the committees had 'fallen short of what was desired' and were largely replaced by joint meetings of Congress's executive committees.[107]

To the class content being injected into calls for one congress, however, Congress leaders responded with a defence of the two-stage theory that underlay 'colonialism of a special type'. On the one hand it was argued that similar debates over class and national struggle had taken place when SACOD was formed, but 'ideological questions were put aside … for the sake of unity on the main questions before us in the country'.[108] At the same time, an anonymous SACOD member argued that 'the winning of full democracy … is an essential stage in the progress of the popular movement', whereas critics sought to:

> … skip the historic stage of the achievement of full democracy in South Africa, and 'go it alone' towards the final break down of all economic restrictions on the working class. In this [they] should realise that [they] would lose the co-operation of broad masses of the population not particularly affected by or desiring such an economic change.[109]

Towards the future

Disputes over non/multiracialism grew throughout 1959 and were covered in a variety of Congress journals. In part they represented a resurgence of disputation over the place of class struggle in a decade dominated by nationalism. Combined with the hostile attacks of the PAC and LP, however, disputes over the form the struggle should adopt and the goals for which it should aim were blurred.

Debate was soon overtaken by events. The Sharpeville and Langa massacres in March 1960 led to the declaration of a state of emergency and the banning of both the ANC and the PAC. The LP briefly inherited the political centre stage in South Africa and ran successful campaigns against black spot removals in Natal and against the first Transkeian elections in 1962. But it also attracted the repressive attention of the state and by 1964 most of its leading activists – more than seventy of them – were banned. The party disbanded in the face of the Political Interference Act of 1968, which prohibited non-racial political parties.

In 1961 the ANC and SACP jointly formed Umkhonto we Sizwe (Spear of the Nation) and began a campaign of sabotage. By the time the ANC was forced into underground and military activity, however, the unity of organisations representing all races in South Africa in the struggle against apartheid had been integrated in its practice and ideology. At the third ANC consultative conference in Morogoro, Tanzania, in 1969, individual membership of the organisation was opened to all races. However, while non-racialism was finally adopted by the ANC in exile, multiracialism continued to guide the form of legal organisations opposing apartheid within South Africa until 1990.

From the time the ANC emerged as a leading element in the resistance movement in South Africa, it faced an array of problems relating to the nature of the struggle for equality and the form it should take. At the base of those problems – ideologically, politically and otherwise – lay the country's white population. The ANC leadership accepted the permanence of whites in the country, while seeking to mobilise and organise Africans. Multiracialism was the mechanism by which the ANC sought to do this, while co-operating with organisations representing other race groups.

The rise of the ANC initiated political discussion and debate among liberals, socialists and others outside of the organisation who opposed segregation and apartheid. All were forced to acknowledge African nationalism, and to amend their theory and practice accordingly. As a result, the 1950s was a decade of both mass struggle and ideological and strategic debate, as liberals and socialists sought to influence the programme of the ANC. The disputes which followed the rise of the ANC – over the place of class struggle, the efficacy of parliamentary action, and others – were fought about the form that racial co-operation should take, and the place of whites in the struggle against apartheid. The failure to resolve the issue adequately then lives with us all in South Africa today.

Notes

Introduction

1   Preamble to the Freedom Charter, taken from J Cronin & R Suttner 1986, *30 Years of the Freedom Charter*, Johannesburg, p 262.

2   The Constitution of the Republic of South Africa 1996, p 1 (preamble).

3   From the title of a book on non-racialism: J Fredrickse 1990, *The Unbreakable Thread – Non-racialism in South Africa*, Johannesburg.

4   H Bernstein 1991, 'The Breakable Thread', *The Southern African Review of Books* 3, March/April, pp 20–21, quoted in N Ndebele 2002, 'The African National Congress and the policy of non-racialism: a study of the membership issue', *Politikon* 29(2), p 145.

5   W C Sellar & R J Yeatman 1931, *1066 and All That: A Memorable History of England, Comprising all the Parts you can Remember, Including 103 Good Things, 5 Bad Kings and 2 Genuine Dates*, London.

6   Warren Beatty in *Bulworth* (Twentieth Century Fox 1998).

7   M Mbeki 2009, *Architects of poverty: Why African Capitalism needs Changing*, Johannesburg, p 6.

8   J Glover 1999, *Humanity: A Moral History of the Twentieth Century*, Johannesburg.

9   The salience of 'Colonialism of a Special Type' under post-apartheid conditions which have indeed seen hundreds of thousands – or millions, depending on which source is used – of whites flee the country, remains a topic to be investigated.

10   Quoted in *Business Report*, 4 March 2009.

Chapter 1 Whites and the ANC, 1945–1950

1   D O'Meara 1983, V*olkskapitalisme: Class, Capital and Ideology in the Development of Afrikaner Nationalism, 1934–1948*, Johannesburg, ch 15.

2   Quoted in O'Meara, ibid, p 230.

3   UG-48: The Native Laws Commission 1946–1948 (the Fagan Commission), paras 18-28.

4   A Stadler 1979, 'Birds in the Cornfield: Squatter Movements in Johannesburg 1944–1947', *Journal of Southern African Studies*, October, pp 93-123.

5   A Stadler 1981, 'A Long Way to Walk: Bus Boycotts in Alexandra 1940-1945', in P Bonner (ed), *Working Papers in Southern African Studies* 2, Johannesburg, pp 228-57.

6   O'Meara, *Volkskapitalisme*, op cit, p 228.

7   P Lewsen 1987, *Voices of Protest: From Segregation to Apartheid 1838-1948*, Johannesburg, pp 15-40.

8   South African Institute of Race Relations 1949, *Handbook on Race Relations in South Africa*, Cape Town, p 3.

9   From Simons and Simons 1983 (eds), *Class and Colour in South Africa 1850-1950*, London, p 556.

10   Quoted in A Paton 1971, *Hofmeyr*, Cape Town, p 277.

11   CPSA 1945, 'What Next? A Policy for South Africa', p 11.

12   C Burns 1987, 'An Historical Study of the Friends of the Soviet Union and the South African Peace Council', Honours Thesis, University of the Witwatersrand.

13   Quoted in B Bunting 1987 (ed), *Moses Kotane: South African Revolutionary*, London, p 109.

14   Ibid, p 115.

15   Fabian Colonial Bureau Papers, Rhodes House, Oxford: FCB 94/1.38: J Lewin to R Hinden 19 August 1942.

16   W K Hancock 1968, *Smuts: The Fields of Force*, Cape Town, p 476.

17   Resolution: 1942 ANC Conference, in T Karis 1977, *Hope and Challenge*, California, p 199.

18   'Africans' Claims in South Africa', in Karis, *Hope*, op cit, p 210.

19   *Die Transvaler*, quoted in R Vigne 1997, *Liberals Against Apartheid: A History of the Liberal Party of South Africa, 1953-1968*, London, p 28.

20   'Africans' Claims', op cit, p 218.

21   T Lodge 1983, *Black Politics in South Africa since 1945*, London, pp 24-45.

22   Xuma's *Preface* to *Africans' Claims*, op cit, p 210.

23   Bunting, *Kotane*, op cit, p 486.

24   Paton's biography of Hofmeyr is arguably his best book; for the continued reverence of Hofmeyr, see Vigne, *Liberals Against Apartheid*, op cit.

25   Quoted in Hancock, *Smuts*, op cit, p 486.

26   E Webster (ed) 1979, *Essays in Southern African Labour History*, Johannesburg, p 209.

27   Margaret Ballinger Papers, William Cullen Library, University of the Witwatersrand: A410/B2.14, NRC resolution, 14 August 1946.

28   Quoted in E Walker 1957, *A History of South Africa*, London, p 760.

29   *The Guardian* 5 December 1946, p 5.

30   *The Guardian* 8 May 1947, p 4.

31   *The Guardian* 9 January 1947, p 1 & CPSA 1947 Annual Conference resolution.

32   ANC Papers, William Cullen Library, University of the Witwatersrand: AD1189/5/Fa/17: 'Statement issued by the Joint Meeting of African and Indian Leaders', Durban, 6 February 1949.

33   ANCYL March 1944, 'Congress Youth League Manifesto', in Karis, *Hope*, op cit, pp 304-5.

34   Potlako Leballo 1957, 'The Nature of the Struggle Today', *The Africanist*, December, quoted in T Karis & G Carter (eds), *From Protest to Challenge* vol 3, Stanford, pp 503-4.

35   W C Sellar & R J Yeatman 1931, *1066 and All That: A Memorable History of England, Comprising all the Parts you can Remember, Including 103 Good Things, 5 Bad Kings and 2 Genuine Dates*, London.

36   The biographies of many members of the SACP, Trotskyist groups and others, which are included in the bibliography, show how some of these battles remained as immediate – and poisonous – in post-apartheid South Africa as they had been in the earliest days of apartheid.

37   Interview with Hymie Basner (n.d.), Institute of Commonwealth Studies, London, transcript pp 10-11.

38   SAIRR, *Survey of Race Relations 1946-1947*, p 22.

39   The most readable account, though sadly restricted to passing references, is in Harold Strachan's 2004 *Make a Skyf, Man!*, Johannesburg.

40   L Bernstein 1999, *Memory Against Forgetting: Memoirs From a Life in South African Politics, 1938-1964*, London, p 88.

41   See H Sapire 1989, 'African Political Mobilisation in Brakpan in the 1950s', seminar paper, African Studies Institute, University of the Witwatersrand.

42   G M Carter and T Karis, 'South African Political Materials: Co-operative African Microfilm Project (CAMP) Reel 3A:2:CC1:62/2: 1944 CPSA Central Committee Report, pp 2-4.

43   Bunting, *Kotane*, op cit, pp 110-11.

44   A Lerumo (pseud Michael Harmel) 1987 (ed), *Fifty Fighting Years: The South African Communist Party 1921-1971*, London, p 82.

45   Quoted in Bunting, *Kotane*, op cit, p 31.

46   CPSA, 'What Next?', op cit.

47   *The Guardian* 4 January 1945, p 1.

48   Lerumo *Fifty Fighting Years*, op cit, p 74.

49   The CPSA–ANC conflict is discussed in Chapter 3.

50   See D Everatt 1991, ' "Where there is no freedom the people perish": The Freedom Charter in historical perspective', in N Steytler (ed), *The Freedom Charter and Beyond: Founding Principles for a Democratic South African Legal Order*, Cape Town, pp 21-43.

51   CAMP Reel 3A:2:CC1:62/2: Central Committee Report to the 1944 CPSA Conference, p 4.

52   *The Guardian* 4 January 1945, p 6: CPSA Conference Resolution.

53   *The Guardian* 28 August 1947, p 5.

54   *The Guardian* 8 April 1948: People's Assembly: Manifesto.

55   *The Guardian* 29 July 1948, p 5.

56   *The Guardian* 29 April 1948, p 5.

57   People's Assembly: Manifesto, op cit.

58   Ibid.

59   Karis, *Hope*, op cit, pp 399-400.

60   Ibid, p 117.

61   Ibid, p 338.

62   M Legassick 1972, 'The Rise of Modern South African Liberalism: Its Assumptions and its Social Base', Institute of Commonwealth Studies: Societies of Southern Africa in the 19th and 20th Centuries, seminar paper, p 30.

63   P Lewsen, 'The Cape Liberal Tradition', quoted in Vigne, *Liberals against apartheid*, op cit, p 4.

64   Donald Molteno Papers, University of Cape Town: BC579 D1.1: D. Molteno: 'Memorandum on the Position of the Natives Representatives in the Senate and the House of Assembly', (n.d. 1943) p 6.

65   *Common Sense* was the journal of the Society of Christians and Jews, founded by R F A Hoernlé.

66   J Burger (pseud Leo Marquard) 1943, *The Black Man's Burden*, London, pp 95-96.

67   Ibid, p 96.

68   J H Hofmeyr Papers, William Cullen Library, University of the Witwatersrand: A1/Lm6: E H Brookes 1946 (article, n.d.), 'The Dilemma of the South African Liberal', p 4.

69   E H Brookes 1949, 'The Man of the Country', *The Forum*, 3 December, p 14.

70   Molteno, 'Memorandum', op cit, p 6.

71   Ibid, p 7.

72   Legassick, 'Liberalism', op cit, p 30.

73   O'Meara, *Volkskapitalisme*, op cit, ch 15.

74   Hofmeyr Papers: A1/Db3: J H Hofmeyr to J Smuts, 16 September 1946.

75   Brookes, *Dilemma*, op cit, p 3.

76   As Gerhard Mare has pointed out (personal communication), this is a fair approximation of what the National Party eventually would, in the future, have to settle for.

77   See A Ashforth 1981, 'Structures of State Ideology: A Study of some Commission Reports on the "Native Question" in South Africa', MPhil Thesis, Oxford, pp 81-83.

78   Leo Marquard Papers, Jagger Library, University of Cape Town: BC587 C71.2: L Marquard to J H Hofmeyr, 25 September 1946.

79   Ballinger Papers: A410/F3.5: M Ballinger: Presidential Address, 1953 Liberal Party Conference, p 4.

80   Brookes, *Dilemma*, op cit, pp 4-5.

81   Ballinger Papers: A410/B2.14.16: M Ballinger: 'Memorandum on the Adjournment of the Natives' Representative Council', 22 August 1946, p 1.

82   Ballinger Papers: A410/B2.14.16: M & W Ballinger to Z K Matthews, 3 September 1946.

83   *The Guardian* 12 June 1947, p 1.

84   Ibid.

85   Hofmeyr Papers: Aa1822: E H Brookes to J H Hofmeyr, 9 August 1946.

86   Hofmeyr Papers: Aa1838: E H Brookes, 'Racial Tension in South Africa' (article), 3 December 1946, p 2.

87   Ibid.

88   Hofmeyr Papers: A1/Db3: J H Hofmeyr to J C Smuts, 16 September 1946.

89   S Marks 2005, 'Worlds of Impossibilities?', in A Dubow and A Jeeves (eds), *South Africa's 1940s: Worlds of Possibilities*, Cape Town, p 276.

90   *The Guardian* 22 January 1948, p 3.

91   *The Guardian* 8 January 1948, p 1.

92   *The Guardian* 15 January 1948, p 1.

93   ANC Papers: AD1189/6/ha/8: 'Appeal to All African Voters: Boycott the Coming Elections': leaflet, 23 October 1948 (emphasis in original).

94   *The Forum* 30 July 1949.

95   *The Guardian* 10 November 1949, p 3.

96   Ibid.

97   J Ngubane in *The Forum* 15 April 1950, p 29.

98   Hofmeyr Papers: A1/Lj7: E H Brookes: 'Presidential Address' SAIRR, 1949, p 11.

Chapter 2 The emergence of white opposition to apartheid, 1950–1953

1   Duma Nokwe, interviewed by Janet Robertson 1971, *Liberalism in South Africa*, Oxford, p 88.

2   T Moll 1987, 'Growth Without Development: The South African Economy in the 1950s', paper presented to 'South Africa in the 1950s' Conference, Queen Elizabeth House, Oxford, p 6.

3   *Agenda* 2 January 1953; the Hofmeyr Society is discussed in Chapter 6.

4   Leo Kuper 1952, 'The Background to Passive Resistance', *Race Relations Journal* XX.

5   Quoted in *The Forum* 8 December 1950, p 6.

6   *Rand Daily Mail* 27 April 1950, p 7.

7   L Thompson 1949, *The Cape Coloured Franchise*, South African Institute of Race Relations New Africa Series, Johannesburg.

8   See T Karis and G Gerhart 1977, *Challenge and Violence*, California, pp 10-11; Robertson, *Liberalism*, op cit, pp 48-51.

9   M Fridjhon 1983, 'The Torch Commando and the Politics of White Opposition, South Africa 1951-1953', seminar paper, African Studies Institute, University of the Witwatersrand; T Lodge 1983, *Black Politics in South Africa since 1945*, London, p 61.

10   Patrick Duncan Papers, University of York: DU8.9.8: Notes of interview with Jack Hodgson (COD founder) October 1953.

11   BC587 E11.1.1: L Thompson: 'The First Weeks: A Survey of the Work of the Civil Rights League' (CRL, n.d.), p 2.

12   *The Guardian* 9 September 1948, p 1.

13   Marquard Papers, University of Cape Town: BC587 E2.88: L Marquard to P Brown, 27 December 1964.

14   BC587 E11.1.1: L Thompson (nd)1948, 'The First Weeks: A Survey of the Work of the Civil Rights League', p 2.

15   T Karon 1983, 'Vryheid nie op 'n "Skinkbord" nie: The Coloured People's Congress and the National Democratic Struggle in the Western Cape, 1951–1962', Honours Thesis, University of Cape Town.

16   *The Guardian* 15 February 1951, p 11.

17   Marquard Papers: BC587 H2.2: L Marquard: Citizens' Rally speech, 14 September 1948.

18   Marquard Papers: BC587 E11.2: CRL: 'Programme', (n.d.) 1948.

19   Marquard Papers: BC587 E2.88 L Marquard to P Brown, 27 December 1964.

20   CRL: 'Programme', op cit.

21   Ibid.

22   See, e.g., Oscar Wollheim Papers, University of Cape Town: BC627 M1.2: Oscar Wollheim's speech launching the East London CRL branch, (n.d.) 1948.

23   G Lewis 1987, *Between the Wire and the Wall: A History of South African 'Coloured' Politics*. Cape Town, p 267.

24   *The Guardian* 27 May 1951, p 31.

25   *The Guardian* 23 April 1951, p 1.

26   *Rand Daily Mail* 26 April 1951, p 2.

27   *The Guardian* 31 May 1951, p 1.

28   See Fridjhon, op cit.

29   *The Guardian* 24 June 1948, p 1.

30   *The Evening Post* 14 April 1951.

31   Quoted in E Walker 1957, *A History of Southern Africa*, London, p 838.

32   Joel Mervis 1952, 'The Torch Commando', *The Forum* May, p 7.

33   Interview with Len Lee-Warden 1987, transcript, p 8.

34   *The Guardian* 20 September 1951, p 7 (South West African branch statement).

35   A Hepple 1966, *South Africa: A Political and Economic History*, London, p 128.

36   Ibid; Interview with Len Lee-Warden, p 8; *The Guardian* 9 August 1951.

37   *The Clarion* 2 August 1952, p 4.

38   ANC Papers, University of the Witwatersrand: AD1189/5/G3 and SAIRR: 'The Government and the A.N.C.', March 1952.

39   Kuper, 'Background', op cit, p 29.

40   CAMP Reel 12A:2:XM65:47/9: J M Matthews to Z K Matthews 2 October 1952.

41   C J Driver 1980, *Patrick Duncan: South African and Pan African*, London, pp 92-94.

42   Quoted in A Sampson 1956, *Drum: A Venture into the New Africa*, London, p 137.

43   *The Cape Argus* 28 November 1952, p 1.

44   The six defiers were author Freda Troup, dentist and later COD member Percy Cohen, Bettie du Toit of the Textile Workers' Union, students Sydney Shall and Margaret Holt; and anthropologist Selma Stamelman.

45   Cecil Williams, Springbok Legion chairperson, in *The Clarion* 17 July 1952, p 1.

46   *The Forum* October 1952, 'Equal Rights For All Civilised People', signed by Margaret and William Ballinger, Edgar Brookes, Leo Marquard, Trevor Huddleston, Arthur Keppel-Jones, Julius Lewin, Donald Molteno, Mabel Palmer, Alan Paton, Saul Solomon, Rabbi Louis Rabinowitz, Bishop Reeves, Ellen Hellman, Winifred Hoernlé, George Gale, Harold Hanson, J B Webb, Hugh Parker, C Coblans, M MckMalcolm and J S Marais.

47   Ibid; for the importance of this statement, see P Brown 1985, 'The Liberal Party: A Chronology with Comment', paper presented to the Liberal Party Workshop, Institute for Social and Economic Research, Rhodes University; Robertson, *Liberalism*, op cit, p 86.

48   *The Forum* October 1952, op cit.

49   E M Forster 1951, *Two Cheers for Democracy*, Middlesex.

50   J Cope 1965, *South Africa*, London, pp 54-55; Carter and Karis, 'South African Political Materials: Co-Operative African Microfilm Project' (CAMP) Reel 12A:XM65:47/6: J M Matthews to Z K Matthews 22 August 1952.

51   Cope, *South Africa*, op cit, p 54.

52   Ibid, p 55.

53   CAMP Reel 12A:2:XM65:47/16: J M Matthews to Z K Matthews, 30 November 1952.

54   *The Guardian* 25 December 1947, p 2.

55   Walker, *History*, op cit, p 810.

56   Quoted in S Kavina 1972, 'The Political Thought and Career of Hon. Dr. Edgar H. Brookes of South Africa', DPhil thesis, Bombay University, p 156.

57   *The Cape Argus* 16 May1950, p 2.

58   A W Hoernlé 1950, 'Liberalism Versus Communism', *Race Relations News* XII, 8 August, p 75.

59   E R Roux 1949, *Time Longer Than Rope: A History of the Black Man's Struggle for Freedom in South Africa*, Madison, p 317; E R Roux 1943, *S. P. Bunting: A Political Biography*, Cape Town.

60   See Hymie Basner in *The Guardian* 16 January 1947, p 6 and 6 March 1947, p 2.

61   Interviews with Alan Paton, Oscar Wollheim and others; see also Ernie Wentzel (n.d.) approx. 1982 (unpublished), 'Memoirs'; Vigne, op cit.

62   Ibid, p 14.

63   Interview with Yusuf Cachalia.

64   CAMP Reel 12A:2:XM65:47/8: J N Matthews to Z K Matthews 16 September 1952.

65   Bernstein, *Memory*, op cit, p 138.

66   L Callinicos 2004, *Oliver Tambo: Beyond the Engeli Mountains*, Cape Town, p 158.

67   Interview with Yusuf Cachalia, p 1.

68   *Advance* 27 November 1952; interviews with various people (liberal and radical) who attended the meeting.

69   Brown, 'Chronology', op cit, pp 3-5; Wentzel, 'Memoirs', op cit.

70   Interview with Peter Beyleveld 1986, transcript, p 13.

71 *Advance* 27 November 1952, p 1.

72 *Daily Dispatch* 19 May 1952.

73 The Committee included Bram Fischer, Eddie Roux, Guy Routh, Jack Hodgson, Cecil Williams, Ruth First, Beata Lipman, Helen Joseph, Trevor Huddleston and Padre du Manoir. The last three were not former CPSA members.

74 Bernstein, *Memory*, op cit, p 139.

Chapter 3 Multiracialism: Communist plot or anti-Communist ploy?

1 The role of the SACP is discussed in detail below.

2 In March 1955 the South African Congress of Trade Unions (SACTU) joined the Alliance. SACTU was (in theory) a non-racial organisation comprising members of all race groups. This seemed not to cause any ideological problems for the otherwise multiracial Alliance.

3 Unless quoting from the time, 'non-racial' refers to an organisational form that allowed people of all races to be equal members (e.g., the SACP, the Liberal Party) and 'multiracial' refers to the Congress Alliance, where races were kept in separate organisations that had a co-ordinating committee to manage their collaboration.

4 Quoted in J Frederikse 1990, *The Unbreakable Thread: Non-racialism in South Africa*, Johannesburg, pp 24-25.

5 Not to be confused with the 'Non-European Unity Movement' or other formally consti-tuted unity movements.

6 Nelson Mandela in *The Guardian* 29 July 1948, p 5.

7 Figures from T Lodge 1983, *Black Politics in South Africa since 1945*, London, p 75.

8 Helen Joseph 1983, *Side by Side*, London, p 75.

9 *The Africanist* December 1955, in Karis and Gerhart 1977, *Challenge and Violence*, California, pp 207-8.

10 See below; see also Jordan Ngubane in E Feit 1967, *African Opposition in South Africa*, California, p 136.

11 Bus Apartheid Resistance Committee 1956, *The Attitude of the Propaganda Committee to the Behaviours of SACPO and COD*, pamphlet, quoted in *New Age* 21 August, p 8.

12 SC. 10-53: 'Report of the Select Committee on the Suppression of Communism Act Enquiry: Central Committee Report to 1950 CPSA Annual Conference' (hereafter 1950 Central Committee Report).

13 Bunting, *Kotane*, op cit, p 159.

14 Lerumo, *Fifty Fighting Years*, op cit, p 82.

15 1942 Annual ANC Conference Resolution, in Karis, *Hope*, op cit, p 199.

16 ANCYL 1944, 'Congress Youth League Manifesto', March, in Karis, ibid, pp 300-308.

17 Notes of ANCYL drafting committee, in Karis, ibid, p 100.

18 Buntin, *Kotane*, op cit, p 110.

19 Sapire, 'African Political Mobilisation', op cit, p 6.

20 Ibid, p 7.

21 Interview with Lionel 'Rusty' Bernstein 1988.

22 *Inkululeko* January 1940, p 2.

23 Bunting, *Kotane*, op cit, p 111.

24 Ibid, p 31: Comintern Resolution on South Africa 1928.

25 *New Nation Supplement* 27 October-2 November 1989, p 7.

26 Interview with Rusty Bernstein.

27   CPSA 1943, *The Foundation of Socialist Teaching from the Manifesto of 1848 to the 1928 Programme*, Pretoria.

28   'Democracy In Action! Proceedings of the Johannesburg District Annual Conference of the Communist Party: March 1945', Johannesburg, p 30; repeated at the 1947 conference.

29   CAMP Reel 3A:2:CC1:62/2: 'CPSA Executive Committee Report: National Movements of the Non-Europeans, 6 December 1943', p 2.

30   CPSA, 'Democracy', op cit, p 7.

31   Ibid, p 6.

32   Ibid.

33   Ibid, p 7.

34   CAMP Reel 3A:2:CC1:14/2. 1941. 'Programme of the Communist Party of South Africa' (draft), p 7.

35   *The Guardian* 9 January 1947, p 1: 1947 CPSA Annual Conference.

36   *The Guardian* 24 June 1948, p 5: CPSA Central Committee Statement.

37   1950 Central Committee Report, op cit.

38   Anton Lembede 1946,'Policy of the Congress Youth League', *Inkundla ya Bantu* May.

39   ANCYL, Manifesto, op cit, pp 304-5.

40   Ibid, p 306.

41   Ibid, p 308.

42   Ibid.

43   Lembede, op cit.

44   A P Mda to G M Pitje 10 October 1948, in Karis, *Hope*, op cit, p 321.

45   Lembede, *Policy*, op cit, p 318 (emphasis in original).

46   ANCYL, Manifesto, op cit, p 308.

47   Lembede, *Policy*, op cit.

48   Karis, *Hope*, op cit, p 103.

49   See, inter alia, Karis, *Hope*, op cit, pp 98-110; Lodge, *Black Politics*, op cit, ch 1; P Walshe 1987, *The Rise of African Nationalism in South Africa*, Johannesburg, ch XIII; Bunting, *Kotane*, op cit, ch 8. By contrast, ANC historian Francis Meli 1988, *South Africa Belongs To Us*, London, does not mention the conflict.

50   ANCYL 1948, 'Basic Policy of Congress Youth League', in Karis, *Hope*, op cit, p 330.

51   Quoted in Frederikse, *Unbreakable Thread*, op cit, p 27.

52   1950 Central Committee Report, op cit.

53   ANCYL, Manifesto, op cit, p 308.

54   Lembede, *Policy*, op cit.

55   Ibid, p 323.

56   Ibid (emphasis in original).

57   A P Mda 1949, 'Statement to the Youth League of Congress', *Inkundla ya Bantu* 27 August.

58   A P Mda 1951, *The Analysis*, in Gail Gerhart 1978, *Black Power in South Africa*, California, p 130 and n 7.

59   Ibid.

60   Quoted in Bunting, *Kotane*, op cit, p 31.

61   ANCYL, Manifesto, op cit, p 308.

62   Quoted in Bunting, *Kotane*, op cit, p 35.

63   ANCYL, Policy, op cit, p 330.

64   1950 Central Committee Report, op cit.

65   *The Guardian* 9 January 1947, p 1: 'Report on CPSA Annual Conference'.

66 '1949 CPSA Central Committee Report', in Bunting, *Kotane*, op cit, p 155.

67 See, e.g., Lodge, *Black Politics*, op cit, p 29.

68 ANC papers: AD1189/5/Fa/17. Joint Declaration of Cooperation 9 March 1947.

69 See Karis, *Hope*, op cit, pp 106-7.

70 Lembede, *Policy*, op cit.

71 ANCYL, Policy, op cit, p 329.

72 CPSA 'National Movements', op cit, p 4. Proposal 1: 'We should strive for one organisation for each of the three racial groups. Unity among these groups should be based on the basis of a joint Committee, both on a national and regional scale.'

73 1950 Central Committee Report, op cit.

74 *The Guardian* 29 July 1948, p 5.

75 Ibid.

76 ANCYL, Manifesto, op cit.

77 ANCYL, Policy, op cit, p 327.

78 A P Mda to G M Pitje 24 August 1948, in Karis, *Hope*, op cit, pp 319-320.

79 ANCYL, Manifesto, op cit, p 307.

80 1944 CPSA Central Committee Report, in Bunting, *Kotane*, op cit, p 112.

81 Walshe, *African Nationalism*, op cit, p 357.

82 Quoted in Karis, *Hope*, op cit, p 429, n 4.

83 Interviews with Rusty Bernstein and Ben Turok 1988.

84 Ben Turok. 2003, *Nothing but the Truth: Behind the ANC's Struggle Politics*, Johannesburg & Cape Town, p 40.

85 Interview with Rusty Bernstein.

86 Interview with Ben Turok.

87 Interview with Fred Carneson.

88 For ANC–CPSA clashes over the 1950 Defend Free Speech Convention, see Lodge, *Black Politics*, op cit, ch 2.

89 Of the seventeen-strong 1950 Central Committee ten were white. For an acknowledgement of criticism of the racial composition, see Treason Trial collection: AD1812 Ev1.1.6: Jack Simons (n.d.) 1954, 'Economics and Politics in South Africa', lecture, p 8.

90 Interview with Ben Turok.

91 Interview with Fred Carneson.

92 Throughout the 1950s each time the newspaper was banned a new one with a new name popped up to replace it.

93 Interview with Ben Turok.

94 Interview with Ben Turok, Amy Thornton and others.

95 Treason Trial collection: AD1812 Ev2.2/Et.1: Kenny Jordaan:,'What are the National Groups in South Africa?', p 4: Forum Club: 'Symposium on the National Question' June 1954. See also *Discussion* (Forum Club journal) for the relevant period.

96 Interview with Fred Carneson.

97 Treason Trial collection: Jack Simons 'Economics and Politics', op cit, p 18.

98 Ibid, p 7 (emphasis added).

99 Ibid, p 18.

100 1950 Central Committee Report, op cit.

101 Ibid.

102 See Karis, *Hope*, op cit, pp 408-9.

103 1950 Central Committee Report, op cit.

104   Karis, *Hope*, op cit, p 409.
105   *The Guardian* 29 July 1948, p 5.
106   Interview with Rusty Bernstein.
107   Nelson Mandela 1953, Transvaal ANC Conference speech, in Bunting, *Kotane*, op cit, p 187.
108   J Matthews 1951, ANCYL Presidential Address, in Walshe, *African Nationalism*, op cit, p 361.
109   Ibid.
110   CAMP: Reel 12A:2:XM65:47/15: J Matthews to Z K Matthews 20 November 1952.
111   Ibid: See Karis, *Hope*, op cit, p 103.
112   See, e.g., Danie du Plessis 1954, 'The Situation in South Africa Today', *Viewpoints and Perspectives* (Journal of the Johannesburg Discussion Club) 1(3) February, p 41.
113   Matthews, *Address*, op cit, p 349.
114   A P Mda 1949, 'African Nationalism: Is it a Misnomer?', *Inkundla ya Bantu* 27 August.
115   J K Ngubane 1950, 'Post-Mortem on a Tragedy', *Inkundla ya Bantu* 20 May, in Karis, *Hope*, op cit, p 441.
116   Ibid, p 442.
117   Karis, *Hope*, op cit, p 408.
118   Ibid, p 409.
119   Walshe, *African Nationalism*, op cit, p 359; see also, Gerhart, *Power*, op cit, p 117.
120   Interview with Ben Turok, p 20.
121   Danie du Plessis 1954, 'Notes on Certain Points Raised in the Discussion', *Viewpoints and Perspectives* 1(3), p 44.
122   Du Plessis, 'Situation', op cit, p 41.
123   Interview with Rusty Bernstein.
124   Eddie Roux 1953, 'Notes on Discussion 16 September 1952', *Viewpoints and Perspectives* 1(a) March, p 14.
125   Du Plessis, 'Situation', op cit, p 41.
126   Rusty Bernstein 1953, 'The Role of the Bourgeoisie in the Liberatory Struggle', *Viewpoints and Perspectives* 1(2) January, pp 31-33; Michael Harmel 1954, 'A Note by the Speaker', *Viewpoints and Perspectives* 1(3) February, p 38.
127   Bernstein, 'Bourgeoisie', op cit, p 32.
128   Ibid.
129   Harmel, 'Note', op cit, p 38.
130   Lodge, *Black Politics*, op cit, p 29.
131   Interview with Fred Carneson.
132   Harmel, 'Note', op cit, p 37.
133   Harmel, 'Imperialism', op cit, p 34.
134   Bernstein, 'Bourgeoisie', op cit, p 32.
135   1950 Central Committee Report, op cit.
136   Ibid.
137   Harmel, 'Imperialism', op cit, p 33.
138   1950 Central Committee Report, op cit.
139   Ibid.
140   Bernstein, quoted in Du Plessis, 'Notes', op cit, p 46.
141   Simons, 'Economics', op cit, p 3.
142   Du Plessis, 'Situation', op cit, p 42.

Chapter 4 From CPSA to SACP via CST: Socialist responses to African nationalism, 1952–1954

1   Vigne, *Liberals against Apartheid*, op cit, p 23.
2   Treason Trial transcript AD1812: Volume 57/11480.
3   *Advance* 8 April 1954, p 4.
4   Treason Trial transcript AD1812: Volume 57/11654.
5   Karis and Gerhart, *Challenge*, op cit, p 13.
6   SACOD was the national white Congress, absorbing COD, which had been a Johannesburg-based founding member. However, once SACOD was formed it was referred to (by friend and foe) interchangeably as both SACOD and COD; and from this point on in this text, I do the same. I have tried to use 'SACOD' where possible, since this is historically correct, but many quotations from the time refer to COD.
7   Robertson, *Liberalism*, op cit, p 165.
8   See, e.g., E Feit 1971, *Urban Revolt in South Africa 1960-1964*, Evanston, p 268.
9   See Karis, *Hope*, op cit, p 422; Karis and Gerhart, *Challenge*, op cit, p 13.
10   There were, of course, others in these categories; the better-known individuals are cited here to illustrate the point.
11   Quoted in Bunting, *Kotane*, op cit, p 165.
12   See, e.g., Lodge, *Black Politics*, op cit, pp 34, 87; and Karis, *Hope*, op cit, p 404.
13   See Bunting, *Kotane*, op cit, pp 165-7; Lerumo (Harmel), *Fifty Fighting Years*, op cit, pp 82, 87-8; Simons and Simons, *Class*, op cit, pp 605-9.
14   As is apparent from Sheridan Johns's recent piece, 'Invisible Resurrection: the Recreation of a Communist Party in South Africa in the 1950s', *African Studies Quarterly* 9(4) Fall 2007, pp 1-19, which reviewed the biographies and other post-apartheid accounts of the period and found … 'nothing new'.
15   Quoted in Karis, *Hope*, op cit, p 443.
16   Ibid.
17   Interview with Rusty Bernstein 1988; see also Bunting, *Kotane*, op cit, p 166.
18   Interview with Rusty Bernstein, p 45.
19   Bernstein, *Memory*, op cit, p 122.
20   Ibid.
21   Quoted in Bunting, *Kotane*, op cit, p 164.
22   Lerumo, *Fifty Fighting Years*, op cit, p 82.
23   Ibid.
24   Interview with Rusty Bernstein.
25   SACP 1962, *The Road to South African Freedom*, p 40. The quotation is reproduced, inter alia, in Bunting, Lerumo, and Simons and Simons.
26   Bernstein, *Memory*, op cit, p 123.
27   Interview with Rusty Bernstein.
28   *The Cape Times* 8 May 1950.
29   Ibid.
30   Interview with Rowley Arenstein 1987.
31   Bernstein, *Memory*, op cit, p 124.
32   Interview with Rusty Bernstein.
33   Lerumo, *Fifty Fighting Years*, op cit, p 82.
34   Simons and Simons, *Class*, op cit, p 608.
35   Interview with Rowley Arenstein.

36   A term used during interviews with CPSA members Rusty and Hilda Bernstein, Rowley Arenstein, Fred Carneson, Ben Turok and others.
37   Interview with Hilda Bernstein 1988.
38   Interviews with Ben Turok 1988; Rusty Bernstein, Hilda Bernstein, Issie Heymann, Willie Kalk 1987.
39   Bunting, *Kotane*, op cit, pp 165-6; Simons and Simons, *Class*, op cit, p 607.
40   Simons and Simons, *Class*, op cit, p 607.
41   Bunting, *Kotane*, op cit, pp 165-6.
42   Interview with Fred Carneson 1988.
43   Lerumo, *Fifty Fighting Years*, op cit, p 82.
44   Ibid, p 43; Bunting, *Kotane*, op cit, p 166.
45   Interview with Willie Kalk.
46   Interview with Fred Carneson.
47   Interview with Rusty Bernstein.
48   Ibid; repeated by Willie Kalk.
49   Bunting, *Kotane*, op cit, p 166.
50   Interview with Fred Carneson.
51   Ibid.
52   Ibid.
53   Ibid.
54   Interview with Ben Turok.
55   Ibid.
56   Interview with Hilda Bernstein.
57   Interview with Fred Carneson.
58   Ibid.
59   Interview with Ben Turok.
60   Interview with Rusty Bernstein.
61   Interview with Ben Turok.
62   Interview with Rusty Bernstein.
63   Ibid.
64   Interview with Ben Turok.
65   Lerumo, *Fifty Fighting Years*, op cit, p 88.
66   P Delius 1996, *A Lion Amongst the Cattle: Reconstruction and Resistance in the Northern Transvaal*, Johannesburg.
67   R Suttner 2004, 'The [Re]constitution of the South African Communist Party [SACP] as an Underground Organisation', *Journal of Contemporary African Studies* 22(1), p 50.
68   See, in particular, Bunting, *Kotane*, op cit, ch 11: 'The Party is Reconstituted', pp 184-98.
69   Ibid, p 167.
70   Interview with Rusty Bernstein.
71   Interview with Ben Turok.
72   Karis, *Hope*, op cit, p 107.
73   R V Lambert 1988, 'Political Unionism in South Africa: the South African Congress of Trade Unions, 1955-1965', PhD thesis, University of the Witwatersrand. See especially ch 2, pp 53-100.
74   Treason Trial collection: AD1812 Ev1.1.1: Jack Simons, Lecture (to the Durban Study Circle) January 1954, p 18.
75   Interview with Fred Carneson.

76 *People's World* 2 October 1952, p 2.

77 *Viewpoints and Perspectives* (Johannesburg Discussion Club journal) 1(1) March 1953, Editorial, p 1.

78 Ibid.

79 Dr Z Sanders (pseud. Zena Susser) 1953, 'Aspects of the Rural Problem in South Africa', *Viewpoints and Perspectives* 1(1), p 36.

80 *Viewpoints and Perspectives* 1(2), Editorial, p v.

81 Lambert, 'Political unionism', op cit, p 70.

82 Ibid, p 80.

83 *The Penguin Dictionary of Sociology*, London, pp 219-20.

84 See, e.g., J Hicks 2004, 'On the application of theories of "Internal Colonialism" to Innuit societies', paper presented to the annual conference of Canadian Political Science Association, Winnipeg, June.

85 See *Viewpoints and Perspectives* 1(1) to 1(3).

86 Eli Weinberg 1954, 'Problems of Trade Unionism in South Africa', *Viewpoints and Perspectives* 1(3), February p 23.

87 Treason Trial collection: AD1812 EV1.1.6: Jack Simons 1954, 'Economics and Politics in South Africa', p 7 (lecture to the Durban Study Circle), (n.d.).

88 Ibid.

89 See Fernando Claudin 1975, *The Communist Movement from Comintern to Cominform* Part 1. London, chs 1-4.

90 Peter Hudson 1988, 'Images of the future and strategies in the present: the Freedom Charter and the South African left', in Frankel, Pines and Swilling (eds). *State Resistance and Change in South Africa*. London, p 262.

91 Ibid.

92 *Viewpoints and Perspectives* 1(3), Editorial, p 5.

93 *Viewpoints and Perspectives* 1(1), Myrtle Berman, in minutes of discussion, p 25.

94 Ibid.

95 Ibid.

96 D Holt, 'White and Black Relationships in South Africa', *Viewpoints and Perspectives* 1(3), p 14.

97 Ibid.

98 Dr G Routh, 'Class Conflicts in South Africa', *Viewpoints and Perspectives* 1(2), p 2.

99 Michael Hathorn, 'Minutes of Discussion', *Viewpoints and Perspectives* 1(1), p 14 (emphasis in original).

100 Ibid.

101 *Viewpoints and Perspectives* 1(1). Dr Z Sanders (pseud. Zena Susser) in minutes of discussion, p 15 (emphasis in original).

102 Sanders, 'Rural Problem', op cit, p 34.

103 Ibid, pp 35-36.

104 Ibid, p 36.

105 Ibid, p 37.

106 Kenny Jordaan 1954, 'What are the National Groups in South Africa?', p 4, in Treason Trial collection: AD1812 EV2.2/Et.1: Forum Club: 'Symposium on the National Question', June; Danie du Plessis, 'Notes on Certain Points Raised in the Discussion', *Viewpoints and Perspectives* 1(3), p 44.

107 Du Plessis, cited in *Viewpoints and Perspectives* 1(3), Editorial, p viii.

108 Du Plessis, 'Notes', op cit, p 44.

109   Du Plessis, 'The Situation in South Africa Today', *Viewpoints and Perspectives* 1(3), p 41.
110   Ibid.
111   See, e.g., D Holt, 'Nationalism and Internationalism in South Africa', *Viewpoints and Perspectives* 1(2), p 14.
112   Jordaan, 'National Groups', op cit, p 4.
113   Du Plessis, 'Notes', op cit, p 44.
114   Holt, 'Nationalism', op cit, p 14.
115   SC.10-53: 'Report of the Select Committee on the Suppression of Communism Act Enquiry: Central Committee Report to the CPSA Annual Conference' January 1950.
116   SACP, *Freedom*, op cit.
117   Suttner, 'The [Re]constitution of the SACP', op cit, p 8.
118   Simons. 1954, 'Lectures', op cit, 5-13 January.
119   Forum Club. 1954. 'Symposium', op cit, June.
120   CAMP Reel 12A:2:XM65:81. 1954. Joe Matthews: 'African Nationalism Today' January.
121   Treason Trial collection: AD1812 Ef3.1.2. 1953, Rusty Bernstein, 'The Road to Liberty', October, p 1.
122   Bernstein, 'The Role of the Bourgeoisie in the Liberatory Struggle', *Viewpoints and Perspectives* 1(2), p 28.
123   Ibid.
124   Ibid, p 29.
125   *Viewpoints and Perspectives* 1(3), Editorial, p 5.
126   M. Harmel, 'Observations on Certain Aspects of Imperialism in South Africa', *Viewpoints and Perspectives* 1(3), p 29.
127   Ibid, p 32.
128   M Harmel, 'A Note by the Speaker', *Viewpoints and Perspectives* 1(3), p 38.
129   Simons, 'Lecture', op cit, p 15.
130   Ibid.
131   Ibid, p 16.
132   Harmel, 'Note', op cit, p 28.
133   Ibid.
134   Ibid.
135   Ibid, p 37.
136   Bernstein, 'Bourgeoisie', op cit, p 30.
137   Simons, 'Nationalisms in South Africa', in Forum Club: 'Symposium', op cit, p 5.
138   Bernstein, 'Bourgeoisie', op cit, p 33.
139   Simons, 'Nationalisms', op cit, p 6.
140   Simons, 'Lecture', op cit, p 21.
141   L Forman, 'Nationalisms in South Africa', in Forum Club, 'Symposium' op cit, p 3.
142   Harmel, 'Note', op cit, p 38.
143   Ibid, p 38.
144   Harmel, 'Imperialism', op cit, p 34.
145   Quoted in Callinicos, *Tambo*, op cit, p 180.
146   Simons, 'Lecture', op cit, p 21.
147   Harmel, 'Imperialism', op cit, p 33.
148   Ibid, p 34.
149   Bernstein, 'Bourgeoisie', op cit, p 31.
150   Ibid, p 32.

151 Ibid, p 32.
152 Ibid, p 33.
153 Ibid.
154 Simons, 'Economics' op cit, p 9.
155 Leo Marquard 1958, *South Africa's Colonial Policy*, Johannesburg.
156 Interview with Ben Turok.
157 Ibid.
158 Ben Turok, quoted in Lambert, 'SACTU', op cit, p 74.
159 *Afrika!*, quoted in *Advance* 17 December 1953, p 1.
160 J Matthews, 'Nationalism', op cit, p 1.
161 Ibid.
162 Ibid, p 2.
163 Ibid, pp 3-4.
164 Simons, 'Lecture', op cit, p 17.
165 Simons & Simons, *Class*, op cit, p 609.
166 Interview with Miriam Hepner 1990.

Chapter 5 **The South African Congress of Democrats**

1   Duma Nokwe, quoted in Robertson, *Liberalism*, op cit, p 88.
2   Treason Trial collection: AD1812:Ef8.1.2: Lionel 'Rusty' Bernstein: 'The Road to Liberty' (SACOD Launch Conference paper) October 1953, p 2.
3   *The Forum*, Editorial September 1952, p 1.
4   Len Lee-Warden (n.d.) 1985, 'Memoirs', unpublished, p 69.
5   Carter and Karis, South African political materials (Co-operative African Microfilm project – CAMP), University of the Witwatersrand: A/1454-mfm-Reel 12A:2:XM65:47/2: J M Matthews to Z K Matthews 23 July 1952.
6   Treason Trial transcript: AD1812 Volume 95/15794.
7   Bernstein, 'Liberty', op cit, p 2.
8   Albie Sachs, quoted in Frederikse, *Unbreakable Thread*, op cit, p 57.
9   Ibid.
10 CAMP, Reel 12A:2:XM65:47/12: J N Matthews to Z K Matthews 5 November 1952.
11 *Advance* 6 November 1952.
12 *Cape Argus* 28 November 1952.
13 *Cape Argus* 9 December 1952.
14 Fabian Colonial Bureau papers, Rhodes House, Oxford: FCB 95/3.34: Eddie Roux, (n.d.) (?)March 1953, 'A Statement on the Situation in South Africa Today', p 2.
15 Interview with Yusuf Cachalia.
16 Treason Trial transcript: AD1812 Volume 57/11601.
17 See Karis, *Hope*, op cit, pp 422-424; Karis and Gerhart, *Challenge*, op cit, pp 8-14; Robertson, *Liberalism*, op cit, pp 87-89.
18 Karis, *Hope*, op cit, pp 422-443.
19 Karis and Gerhart, *Challenge*, op cit, p 13.
20 Ibid.
21 Ibid, p 8; Karis, *Hope*, op cit, pp 442-443.
22 Interview with Yusuf Cachalia; interview with Helen Joseph (elected to the interim committee).

23   Interview with Yusuf Cachalia.
24   Dan Tloome 1958, 'The Africanists and the Congresses', *Fighting Talk* August, p 9.
25   Karis and Gerhart, *Challenge*, op cit, p 8.
26   Ibid, pp 8-9.
27   Driver, op cit, chs 7 and 8.
28   Duncan papers, York University: DU 8.9.8: Patrick Duncan to Cecil Williams 12 February 1953.
29   Driver, *Duncan*, op cit, p 90.
30   Ibid.
31   Treason Trial transcript: AD1812 Volume 57/11575.
32   Interview with Guy Routh 1989.
33   Ibid.
34   Treason Trial collection: AD1812: Ef3.1.2: Jack Hodgson, (n.d.) 1953, 'Draft of the Immediate Programme of Action', p 1 (emphasis in original).
35   Ibid, pp 2-3.
36   Hodgson, 'Programme', op cit, p 1.
37   Roux, 'Statement', op cit, p 1.
38   Duncan papers: DU 8.9.7: Report of an interview with Jack Hodgson 15 October 1953.
39   Treason Trial collection: AD1812 Eu.3: Bram Fischer and Cecil Williams, Circular (to all COD members) 16 July 1953, p 2.
40   Interview with Guy Routh.
41   Ivan Schermbrucker to Irene Manderstam 10 January 1953 (private possession of author).
42   Congress of Democrats, 'Draft Constitution' January 1953 (private possession of author), p 3.
43   Hodgson, 'Programme', op cit, p 2.
44   Ibid, p 3.
45   Ibid.
46   For more on the MYS, see Turok, *Nothing but the Truth*, op cit.
47   Lee-Warden, 'Memoirs', op cit, p 69.
48   Ibid, p 70.
49   Treason Trial collection: AD1812 Es5.2: 'Rule by Sjambok' (n.d.) 1953, p 2.
50   Ibid, p 1.
51   *The Guardian* 23 August 1951, p 4.
52   *The Guardian* 20 March 1952, p 3.
53   Letter to *The Guardian* 6 September 1951, p 4.
54   Interview with Len Lee-Warden 1987, transcript, p 22.
55   Treason Trial collection: AD1812 Ev2.2/Et.1: Kenny Jordaan 1954, 'What are the National Groups in South Africa?', p 2, in Forum Club, *Symposium on the National Question* June.
56   Lee-Warden, 'Memoirs', op cit, p 71.
57   Ibid.
58   Treason Trial collection: AD1812 Eu1.3: Springbok Legion, 'Urgent and Important' (Circular to all members) 15 June 1953, p 1.
59   Springbok Legion papers, William Cullen Library, University of the Witwatersrand: A617: P Beyleveld, Chairman's Report, 1953 Springbok Legion National Conference, p 2.
60   Ibid.
61   Fischer and Williams, Circular, op cit, pp 1-2; Hodgson, 'Programme', op cit, p 1; Bernstein, 'Liberty', op cit, pp 1-2.
62   *Advance* 19 June 1952, p 4.

63 Michael Harmel 1954, 'Observations on Certain Aspects of Imperialism in South Africa', *Viewpoints and Perspectives* 1(3) February, p 29.

64 Roux, 'Statement', op cit, p 3.

65 Harmel, 'Imperialism', p 33.

66 Beyleveld, 'Report', op cit, p 1.

67 COD, *Defeat the Nationalists!*, March 1953 (pamphlet in private possession of author).

68 Ibid.

69 Lambert, 'Political Unionism', op cit, pp 84-85.

70 Hodgson, 'Programme', op cit, pp 1-2 (emphasis in original).

71 Danie du Plessis 1954, 'The Situation in South Africa Today', *Viewpoints and Perspectives* 1(3), February, p 41.

72 Treason Trial collection: ADS1812 Ev1.1.6: Jack Simons, (n.d.) 1954, 'Economics and Politics in South Africa', Lecture, p 1.

73 Du Plessis, 'Situation', op cit, p 39.

74 Fischer and Williams, 'Circular', op cit, p 1.

75 Ibid.

76 See, e.g., Dilitinzaba Mji, *Advance* 26 February 1952, p 2.

77 ANC papers: AD1189/2/Ba.1: NEC Report to the 1954 Annual ANC Conference, p 1.

78 *Drum* May 1953, p 10.

79 *Advance* 23 April 1953, p 1.

80 Ibid.

81 Z K Matthews 1953, Presidential Address ANC Annual Conference (Cape) 15 August, in Karis and Gerhart, *Challenge*, op cit, p 101.

82 A Luthuli 1953, Presidential Address, ANC Annual Conference, December, in Karis and Gerhart, *Challenge*, op cit, p 121.

83 Ibid.

84 *Advance* 23 April 1953, p 1.

85 LP papers: A/1671-mfm-Reel 1: 1953 LP Principles and chapter 7.

86 Matthews, 'Address', op cit, p 103.

87 Luthuli, 'Address', op cit, p 123.

88 Nelson Mandela 1953, 'Searchlight on the Liberal Party', *Liberation* 3, June, p 7.

89 Ibid, p 9.

90 Luthuli, 'Address', op cit, p 122 (emphasis in original).

91 *Indian Opinion* 19 February 1954.

92 *Advance* 26 February 1953, p 2.

93 Walter Sisulu, quoted in *Advance* 8 April 1954, p 4.

94 *Advance* 23 April 1953, p 2.

95 Bernstein, *Liberty*, op cit, p 4.

96 Beyleveld, 'Report', op cit, p 2.

97 Roux, 'Statement', op cit, p 2.

98 Bernstein, *Liberty*, op cit, p 4.

99 Ibid.

100 Hodgson, 'Programme', op cit, p 2; Bernstein, *Liberty*, op cit, p 1.

101 Ibid, p 3.

102 Ibid.

103 Bernstein, *Liberty*, op cit, p 2.

104 Fischer and Williams, 'Circular', op cit, p 2.

105 Bernstein, *Liberty*, op cit, p 2.

106 Ibid, p 3.

107 Anthony Sampson 1958, *Treason Cage: The Opposition on Trial in South Africa*, London.

108 Edward Feit 1971, *Urban Revolt in South Africa 1960–1964*, Evanston, p 268.

109 Robertson, *Liberalism*, op cit, p 165.

110 Douglas Irvine 1987, 'The Liberal Party 1953–1968', in Butler, Elphick and Welsh (eds), *Democratic Liberalism in South Africa: Its History and Prospect*, Cape Town, pp 127-128.

111 Gail Gerhart 1978, *Black Power in South Africa: The Evolution of an Ideology*, California, pp 115–16 (emphasis added).

112 Feit, *Urban Revolt*, op cit, p 268.

113 Karis and Gerhart, *Challenge*, op cit, p 13.

114 G M Carter 1958, *The Politics of Inequality: South Africa since 1948*, London, p 378, quoted in Karis and Gerhart, *Challenge*, op cit, p 13.

115 Albert Luthuli 1982, *Let My People Go*, London, p 126.

116 Gerhart, *Power*, op cit, p 119.

117 Ibid.

118 Interview with Yusuf Cachalia, p 2.

119 Walter Sisulu 1954, *Advance* 8 April, p 4.

120 Albie Sachs, quoted in Frederikse, *Unbreakable Thread*, op cit, p 58.

121 Hodgson, 'Programme', op cit, p 1.

122 Ibid.

123 Bernstein, *Liberty*, op cit, p 2.

124 Hodgson, 'Programme', op cit, p 3.

125 Bernstein, *Liberty*, op cit, p 3.

126 CAMP Reel 4B:2:DC2:30/22: SACOD. 1953. 'Draft Policy Statement', October, p 1.

127 Ibid.

128 Lee-Warden, 'Memoirs', op cit, p 71.

129 Ibid.

130 Ibid.

131 SACOD, 'Statement', op cit, p 2.

132 Lionel Forman, 'Nationalisms in South Africa', in Forum Club, *Symposium*, op cit, p 4.

133 Simons, 'Economics', op cit, p 3.

134 Ibid, pp 7-8.

135 Danie du Plessis 1954, 'Notes on Certain Points Raised in the Discussion', *Viewpoints and Perspectives* 1(3), February, p 47; see also David Holt in *Viewpoints and Perspectives* 1(2) June 1953, pp 14-21.

136 Du Plessis, 'Notes', op cit, p 48.

137 Ibid, p 46.

138 Du Plessis, 'Situation', op cit, pp 41-42; see also David Holt, Dr Z Sanders and others in *Viewpoints and Perspectives*.

139 Du Plessis, op cit, p 42.

140 Ibid.

141 Ibid.

142 Ibid.

143 Interview with Helen Joseph, p 3.

144 Treason Trial collection: AD1812 Ef1.5.3: Report of SACOD Founding Conference 10/11 October 1953, p 4.

145 SACOD, 'Statement', op cit, p 1.
146 Ibid.
147 Ibid.
148 Ibid, p 2.
149 Hodgson, 'Programme', op cit, p 2.
150 1954 ANC NEC Report, op cit, p 2.

Chapter 6 **The Liberal Party of South Africa**

1   Ballinger papers: A410/F3.5: M Ballinger 1953, Presidential Address: Liberal Party National Conference 11 July, p 1 (emphasis in original).
2   Liberal Party papers: A/1671-mfm-Reel 1: LP Programme, (n.d.) 1953.
3   LP papers: A/1671-mfm-Reel 3: Minutes: Pietermaritzburg Liberal Group (LG) 7 July 1952.
4   Robertson, *Liberalism*, op cit, p 165.
5   Paul Rich 1984, *White Power and the Liberal Conscience: Racial Segregation and South African Liberalism, 1921-1960*, Johannesburg, p 117.
6   Ibid, pp 98-119.
7   Martin Legassick 1977, 'Liberalism, Social Control and Liberation in South Africa', seminar paper, University of Warwick, p 14 (emphasis in original).
8   Writing to Margaret Ballinger June 1953, quoted in Vigne, *Liberals*, op cit, p 29.
9   Interview with Violaine Junod 1988, p 2. For detail about the Labour Party, see G M Carter 1958, *The Politics of Inequality*, London, pp 341-342.
10 Julius Lewin 1967, 'Looking Back at the Liberals', *The Star* 25 April.
11 African National Congress 1994, *Reconstruction and Development Programme*, Johannesburg.
12 See, inter alia, Robertson, *Liberalism*, op cit, chs 1 and 2; Legassick, *Liberalism*, op cit, pp 1-19.
13 Julius Lewin 1952, 'Strategy for Political Progress', *The Forum* November, p 22.
14 Alan Paton 1958, *Hope for South Africa*, London, p 6.
15 UG-48: The Native Laws Commission 1946-1948 (the Fagan Commission).
16 Helen Suzman 1949, 'A Digest of the Fagan Report', SAIRR; Julius Lewin, *The Forum* 2 April 1949, pp 22-23.
17 The Native Question Commission (Sauer Commission) was an internal Nationalist Party commission which provided the first programmatic elaboration of apartheid.
18 A B Xuma papers: ABX.480709b: M & W Ballinger 1948, 'Outlines of a Programme for Progress for Africans' 9 July, p 3.
19 J D Rheinallt Jones 1948, 'SAIRR Presidential Address', quoted in *Race Relations Journal* XIX, February 1952, p 48.
20 Ballinger papers: A410/B2.5.13: M Ballinger to Rev J Calata 12 August 1948.
21 Ballinger papers: A410/B.2.8.2: M Ballinger to E H Brookes 29 June 1948.
22 The Ballingers, 'Programme', op cit, p 4.
23 Molteno papers: BC579 D1.32: D B Molteno 1948, 'Segregation and Democracy' 8 January.
24 Ibid, pp 13-14.
25 Ibid.
26 Quoted in S B D Kavina 1972, 'The Political Thought and Career of Hon Dr Edgar H Brookes of South Africa', DPhil thesis, Bombay University, p 157.
27 Quoted in SAIRR *A Survey of Race Relations 1947-1948*, p 23.

28   Quintyn Whyte 1948, *Apartheid and other policies together with a suggested practical programme*, p 11.
29   Cited in Robertson, *Liberalism*, op cit, p 44.
30   See Merle Lipton 1986, *Capitalism and Apartheid*, Aldershot, pp 140-2.
31   Jan Hofmeyr, quoted in Tom MacDonald 1948, *Hofmeyr: Heir to Smuts*, Johannesburg, p 75.
32   Hofmeyr papers: A1/DC: SAIRR 1048, Memorandum to the Prime Minister 2 September.
33   Deborah Posel 1988, 'The Construction of Apartheid 1948–1961', seminar paper, African Studies Institute, University of the Witwatersrand. The practical 'faction' attempted to control urbanisation rather than eradicate it; the 'purists' saw economic integration as the death knell of white supremacy and called for complete economic segregation.
34   Cited in O'Meara, *Volkskapitalisme*, op cit, p 175.
35   Quoted in *African World*, March 1949.
36   See Posel, 'Construction', op cit, p 8.
37   Ibid, p 7.
38   The Ballingers, 'Programme', op cit, p 4.
39   Marquard papers: BC587 H2.2: Leo Marquard, Speech 14 September 1948.
40   See Rich, *White Power*, op cit, pp 120-2.
41   See Hamish Dickie-Clark in P L v d Berghe (ed., 1979, *The Liberal Dilemma in South Africa*, London.
42   Hofmeyr papers: A1/Lm6: E H Brookes (n.d.) 1946, 'The Dilemma of the South African Liberal', article, p 3.
43   Marquard papers: BC587 E2.88: L Marquard to P Brown 27 December 1964.
44   ANC papers: AD1189/5/G.3: SAIRR 1952, *The Government and the A. N. C.* March.
45   Ibid. Ds Reynecke amendments 11 March 1952.
46   Whyte, *Apartheid*, op cit, p 13; see also SAIRR 1952, *Go Forward in Faith*.
47   *Race Relations News* XIX December 1952, p 136.
48   SAIRR, *Survey 1947*, op cit, pp 13-14.
49   In March 1952 the SAIRR sent out draft copies of *The Government and the A. N.C.* The assertions made above are visible in the different responses to the draft; see AD 1189/5/G: draft and responses March 1952.
50   Fabian Colonial Bureau papers: FCB 95/2.60: SAIRR Press Bulletin 1952, 'The Defiance of "Unjust Laws" Campaign' 25 August, p 1.
51   *The Forum* October 1952, 'Equal Rights for all Civilised People'. The statement was drafted by Ballinger and Lewin; responses to a draft sent out in September 1952 are as revealing as those to the SAIRR draft mentioned above. See A410/B2.14.18: draft and replies.
52   Ibid.
53   Ballinger papers: A410/B2.14.18: G E Williamson to M Ballinger 21 September 1952.
54   See NP Minister Erik Louw in *The Guardian* 23 March 1950, p 1.
55   Ballinger papers: A410/B2.14.18: G E Williamson to M Ballinger, op cit.
56   CAMP: Reel 12A:2:XM65:47/9: J M Matthews to Z K Matthews 2 October 1952.
57   Ibid.
58   E H Brookes in *Race Relations Journal* XV 1948, p 2.
59   LP papers: A/1671-mfm-Reel 1: Minutes: SALA General Meeting 16/17 January 1953.
60   Wollheim papers: BC627D2.5: Hofmeyr Society Launch Statement September 1950.
61   Wollheim papers: BC627 D2.4: J Lewin to O Wollheim 21 March 1951 (emphasis in original).
62   *Agenda* 15, 'Liberals and Conservatives' 3 June 1951.
63   Wollheim papers: BC627 D2.4: J Lewin to O Wollheim 21 March 1951.

64   Interview with Oscar Wollheim 1987.

65   The Ballinger group had some twenty members, as did Durban and Pietermaritzburg; the SALG had 126 members by December 1952, including UP MPs Colin Eglin and Bernard Friedman.

66   Ballinger papers: A410/F3.2: Minutes, Johannesburg LG 26 November 1952.

67   The Ballinger group included Winifred Hoernlé and Ellen Hellman of the SAIRR, Louis Kane-Berman of the Torch Commando, Jack and Phyllis Lewsen, Thelma Philip, Ambrose Reeves, Trevor Huddleston, Arthur Blaxall, Julius Lewin, Arthur Kepple-Jones, Jack Unterhalter, and others.

68   Conversation with Phyllis Lewsen.

69   LP papers: A/1671-mfm-Reel 1: Minutes, SALA General Meeting 16/17 January 1953.

70   Wollheim papers: BC627 D2.11: O Wollheim to J Sutherland 9 June 1952.

71   Wollheim papers: BC627 D2.8: O Wollheim to J Lewin 8 April 1951.

72   Ballinger papers: A410/F3.2: Minutes, Johannesburg LG 28 April 1953.

73   LP papers: A/1671-mfm-Reel 1: SALG, *Newsletter* November 1952, p 1.

74   Ibid.

75   Quoted in *African World* March 1949.

76   LP papers: A/1671-mfm-Reel 3: O Wollheim to R Stratford 18 July 1953.

77   LP papers: A/1671-mfm-Reel 3: P Brown, notes for speech 21 June 1952.

78   Ibid, 7 July 1952.

79   See Paton, *Hofmeyr*, op cit, p 214, pp 230-232. See also Marquard papers: BC587 C71.2: L Marquard to J H Hofmeyr 25 September 1946, 8 June 1948, 21 June 1948.

80   See, e.g., Ballinger papers: BC345 G2.2.1a: K Kirkwood to Ballinger 21 August 1948; A410/b2.10.1: CRL to Ballinger 11 May 1950; *The Guardian* 28 April 1949; *The Forum* 30 April 1949.

81   Ballinger papers: A410/F3.2: Minutes, Johannesburg LG 28 April 1953.

82   These clauses were adopted by the SALG following comments by the Ballinger group on the SALG Programme; they were then adopted in Pietermaritzburg and elsewhere, and were included in the SALA and LP constitutions.

83   LP papers: A/1671-mfm-Reel 3: P Brown, notes for speech 21 June 1952.

84   Wollheim papers: A/1671-mfm-Reel 3: P Brown, notes for speech 21 June 1952.

85   Ernie Wentzel papers: BC627 D2.8: O Wollheim to J Lewin 8 April 1953.

86   Interview with Terence Beard 1986.

87   LP papers: A/1671-mfm-Reel 1: SALG Constitution, 'It is the object of the Group to become a political party when so decided at a general meeting'.

88   Ballinger papers: A410/F3.6: Minutes: SALA Federal Council 18 April 1953.

89   Ballinger papers: A410/F3.6: Minutes: SALA Federal Council 29 May 1953.

90   Ballinger papers: A410/F3.6: Minutes: SALA Federal Council 8/9 May 1953.

91   Ibid; see Johannesburg LG 26 November 1952.

92   Ballinger papers: A410/F3.6: Minutes: SALA Federal Council 18 April 1953.

93   *The Cape Times* 6 May 1953, p 1.

94   Ballinger papers: A410/F3.2: Minutes, Johannesburg LG, 26-4-1953; conversation with group member Phyllis Lewsen.

95   Interview with Peter Brown 1987.

96   Ballinger papers: A410/F3.6: Minutes, SALA General Meeting 8/9 May 1953; the minutes do not record names against votes, but negative mandates were held by Ballinger, Molteno and the Natal delegates; the former did not switch their votes. UP MP Colin Eglin thus voted for the LP while remaining a UP member.

97   Marquard papers: BC 587 E2.88: L Marquard to P Brown 27 December 1964. See also CAMP Reel 9A:2:XB2:96/4: Interview with M Ballinger 18 January 1964.

98   Interviews with Oscar Wollheim, Peter Brown and Jack Unterhalter.

99   Wollheim papers: BC627 D2.19: O Wollheim to A Paton 23 February 1953.

100   Ballinger papers: A410 B2.14.18: A S Paton to M Ballinger 22 September 1952 and A S Paton to Q Whyte 3 February 1953.

101   LP papers: A/1671-mfm-Reel 3: O Wollheim to R Stratford 18 July 1953.

102   LP papers: A/1671-mfm-Reel 1: Minutes: National Committee 30 June 1953 and 30 June 1954.

103   W Ballinger papers: BC347 E1.10: Johannesburg LG: 'Principles and Aims' (n.d.) 1952.

104   Wollheim papers: BC627 D2.1: R Stratford to O Wollheim 13 March 1951. A/1671-mfm-Reel 3: C Gell to R F Spence 1 August 1954.

105   LP papers: A/1671-mfm-Reel 3: C Gell to R F Spence 1 August 1954.

106   *The Forum* 16 July 1949, 'The Liberals' Policy for Natives', p 3.

107   Ibid.

108   Wollheim papers: BC627 D2.2: E Hawarden 1950, 'How to Strengthen the United Party', speech to Hofmeyr Society 1 November.

109   Ibid.

110   Ibid.

111   LP papers: A/1671-mfm-Reel 1: SALG, 'Ten Point Programme' June 1952.

112   LP papers: A/1671-mfm-F3.2: Minutes, Johannesburg LG 26 November 1952, p 2.

113   Ibid.

114   LP papers: A/1671-mfm-Reel 1: Minutes, SALG 24 June 1952.

115   Molteno papers: BC579 E1.26: SALA, 'Principles' February 1952.

116   LP papers: A/1671-mfm-Reel 3: C Gell to R F Spence 1 August 1954.

117   LP papers: A/1671-mfm-Reel 1: Minutes, National Committee November 1953.

118   LP papers: A/1671-mfm-Reel 1: Minutes, National Committee 1953–1954.

119   Ballinger papers: A410/F3.6: Minutes, National Committee 27/28 February 1954.

120   LP papers: A/1671-mfm-Reel 1: J Boerne (LP secretary) to M Ballinger 20 July 1954.

121   Marquard papers: BC587 E2.66: Leo Marquard: General Notes on the Liberal Party (n.d.) 1954.

122   Julius Lewin 1970, 'Why Liberalism Failed', *Cape Times* 28 April.

123   Interviews with Peter Brown, Alan Paton and others. See also Lipton, *Capitalism*, op cit, p 293.

124   Party treasurer Robin Spence attempted to rally such support in 1954 and was unsuccessful; sporadic attempts thereafter had similar results. See A/1671-mfm-Reel 1.

125   See Alan Paton 1988, *Journey Continued*, Cape Town.

126   A phrase used by Christopher Gell in *The Forum* September 1953.

127   Douglas Irvine 1987, 'The Liberal Party 1953–1968', in Butler, Elphick and Welsh (eds), *Democratic Liberalism in Southern Africa*, Cape Town, p 116.

128   Frederickse, *Unbreakable Thread*, op cit.

129   Ibid, p 6.

130   The only prominent black member of a liberal group was Selby Msimang in Pietermaritzburg; the SALG had four black members; liberal groups elsewhere had no black members.

131   CAMP: Reel 9A:2:XB26:96: Interview with P Brown 1964.

132   Ballinger papers: A410/F3.2: Minutes, Johannesburg LG 28 April 1953.

133   Ibid.

134 See, e.g., LP papers: A/1671-mfm-Reel 3: Pietermaritzburg LG, notes for meetings 21 June; 7 July 1951.

135 Marquard papers: BC587 E2.26: I Grant to H Meidner 10 June 1953.

136 LP papers: A/1671-mfm-Reel 3: member of the Pietermaritzburg LG to chairperson [names illegible] 9 December 1952.

137 Marquard papers: BC587 E2.62: M Ballinger to L Marquard 19 June 1954.

Chapter 7 **Overhauling liberalism**

1 T W Price 1953, 'The Liberal Party Replies', *Liberation* September; see below.

2 *The Cape Argus* (leader article) 6 May 1953.

3 LP papers: A/1671-mfm-Reel 1: M Ballinger (n.d.) 1955, 'What Does the Liberal Party Stand For?'.

4 *Advance* 11 June 1953, p 4: at the first LP public meeting, Alan Paton stated: 'Let us have 10 000 colour bars by consent if necessary, but not one imposed by one race on another.'

5 LP: 'Principles', op cit.

6 Ibid.

7 *Advance* 25 June 1953.

8 Ballinger papers: A410/F3.5: M Ballinger, Presidential Address, 1953 LP National Conference, p 2.

9 Ibid.

10 LP papers: A/1671-mfm-Reel 3: L Marquard to M Ballinger 19 June 1953.

11 Ballinger, Address, op cit, p 2.

12 Quoted in Wentzel, 'Memoirs', op cit, A35.

13 LP papers A/1671-mfm-Reel 1: Natal report to National Committee (hereafter NC) 12 November 1953. Interviews with Natal members Peter Brown, Leo Kuper and Violaine Junod.

14 LP papers: A/1671-mfm-Reel 1: Minutes: NC 30/31 June 1954.

15 LP papers: A/1671-mfm-Reel 1: Minutes: 1953 National Conference 11/13 July 1953.

16 Ibid.

17 Ibid.

18 Cape Division July 1953, 'An Electoral Policy for South Africa' (private papers of Ernest Wentzel).

19 Minutes: National Conference, op cit, July 1953.

20 LP papers: A/1671- mfm-Reel 6: Resolutions from Kensington branch to the 1953 National Conference 11/13 July 1953.

21 LP papers: A/1671- mfm-Reel 4: O Wollheim. (n.d.) 1954, 'Liberal Party Memorandum'.

22 LP papers: A/1671- mfm-Reel 1: Transvaal Report 11 July 1954.

23 The LP enjoyed parliamentary representation through the Native Representatives – Margaret and William Ballinger, Walter Stanford and Leslie Rubin. All stood as Independents in the 1954 elections, despite being members of the National and Executive Committees of the LP. In 1957 B P H ('Bunny') Curran, Eastern Cape Provincial Councillor, joined the LP after his election.

24 The Executive Committee in 1953 comprised Margaret and William Ballinger, Leo Marquard, Donald Molteno, Oscar Wollheim, Leslie Rubin, Robin Spence, Alan Paton and Professor T W Price.

25 Quoted in Robertson, *Liberalism*, op cit, p 98.

26   Quoted in Anthony Sampson 1958, *Treason Cage: The Opposition on Trial in South Africa*, London, p 102 (emphasis in original).

27   G M Naicker quoted in *Indian Opinion* 19 February 1954.

28   Dr Yusuf Dadoo quoted in *Advance* 14 May 1953, p 5.

29   LP papers: A/1671-mfm-Reel 3: J T R Gibson, Report of Meeting with Cape ANC 21 January 1954; Ballinger papers A410/B2.11: Minutes: Natal Provincial Committee (hereafter NPC) 15 October 1953.

30   LP papers: A/1671-mfm-Reel 6: Minutes: Transvaal Provincial Committee (hereafter TPC) 25 June 1953.

31   Karis and Gerhart, *Protest*, op cit, p 123: Albert Luthuli, Presidential Address to the 1953 ANC Annual Conference.

32   Ballinger papers: A410/B2.11: J T R Gibson, 'Report on the ANC Conference on Bantu Education' 9 April 1955.

33   Bunting and Alexander were banned from Parliament in terms of an amendment to the Suppression of Communism Act, which extended the definition of 'communist' to include anyone who had ever professed communism.

34   Marquard papers: BC587 E2.66: Leo Marquard (n.d.) 1954, 'General Notes on the Liberal Party' (emphasis in original).

35   Wollheim papers: BC627 D2.64: O Wollheim to G N Hauser 24 December 1956.

36   N R Mandela 1953, 'Searchlight on the Liberal Party', *Liberation* June.

37   Price, 'Reply', op cit.

38   Ibid.

39   Ballinger, 'Address', op cit, p 1; see CAMP Reel 4A:2:CL2: 41/15; Alan Paton 1953, 'Letter on the Occasion of the Launching of the Liberal Party in Cape Town' May.

40   Ballinger, 'Address', op cit, p 1.

41   Ibid.

42   Ibid, p 3.

43   Christopher Gell 1953, 'Not Yet Liberal Enough', *The Forum* September, p 16; see below.

44   Ibid.

45   See Driver, *Patrick Duncan*, op cit.

46   CAMP Reel 10A:2:XH: Interview with Peter Hjul (1964), transcript, p 1.

47   Marquard papers: BC587 E2.35: J Isacowitz to M Ballinger 18 July 1953.

48   Interview with Peter Brown.

49   Ballinger papers: A410/F3.8.2: LP: Canvasser's Notes (n.d.) 1953.

50   Jordan Ngubane 1953, 'A Native's View of the Liberal Party', *The Star* 28 August.

51   LP papers: A/1671-mfm-Reel 4: Peter Brown (n.d.) 1956, 'South African Liberals'.

52   Ballinger papers: A410/F3.8.2: LP: Canvasser's Notes (n.d.) 1953.

53   Ballinger papers: A410/F3.1: Leslie Rubin in Minutes: Cape Provincial Committee (hereafter CPC) 15 October 1954.

54   Wollheim, 'Memorandum', op cit.

55   Ibid.

56   Ballinger, 'Address', op cit, p 4.

57   Leo Kuper (LP Natal Chairperson) 1953, 'The Background to Passive Resistance', *Race Relations Journal* XX(3), p 18.

58   Nomenclature changed from conference to congress in 1954.

59   Interview with J T R Gibson 1987.

60   CAMP: Interview with Peter Hjul, op cit, p 8.

61   LP papers: A/1671-mfm-Reel 3: J Boerne to M Ballinger 20 July 1954.

62   LP papers: A/1671-mfm-Reel 5: Minutes: CPC 1-6-1955; interviews with J T R Gibson and B Pogrund.

63   Gibson, 'Report', op cit January 1954; J Boerne to M Ballinger 29 June 1954; interview with Gibson.

64   Interviews with Gibson and Hjul.

65   *Liberal News* 26 February 1954, p 2.

66   CAMP Reel 4B:2:CL2:41/23: J T R Gibson to C R Swart 6 November 1954

67   Ibid.

68   Ibid.

69   Ballinger papers: A410/F3.1: Minutes: CPC 29-7-1954. The Cape Western branch had twenty members.

70   LP papers: A/1671-mfm-Reel 5: Minutes, CPC 30 May 1954.

71   Ballinger papers: A410/B2.11: O Wollheim to M Ballinger 10 January 1954.

72   Ballinger papers: A410/B2.11: H Pittman to M Ballinger 2 August 1954.

73   LP papers: A/1671-mfm-Reel 5: Minutes: CPC 1 June 1955.

74   LP papers: A/1671-mfm-Reel 1: TPC 11 November 1954.

75   SACOD 1954, *The Threatened People*, pp 16-24.

76   LP papers: A/1671-mfm-Reel 3: correspondence between P Beyleveld and J Boerne 1953-1954.

77   *Advance* 25 March 1954, p 1.

78   Ballinger papers: A410/B2.11: M Ballinger to J Isacowitz 27 July 1953.

79   See C Walker 1982, *Women and Resistance in South Africa*, London, pp 173-5.

80   LP papers: A/1671-mfm-Reel 3: P Brown to W Stanford 27 May 1953.

81   LP papers: A/1671-mfm-Reel 4: Natal Reports 1953-1959.

82   Interview with Professor Leo Kuper 1988.

83   See LP papers: A/1671-mfm-Reel 3: P Brown to W Stanford 27 May 1953; A/1671-mfm-Reel 1: Executive Committee (hereafter EC) 8 December 1953.

84   LP papers: A/1671-mfm-Reel 4: F Bhengu to Natal LP 22 September 1954.

85   LP papers: A/1671-mfm-Reel 3: Minutes, NPC September–December 1953.

86   Ballinger papers: A410/B2.11: Minutes, NPC 15 October 1953 and January-May 1956; LP papers: A/1671-mfm-Reel 4: P N Brown to E V Mahomed 24 August 1954.

87   Ballinger papers: A410/F3.3: Minutes, NPC 5 March 1957. For details of the NNALA see Peter Brown 'The Liberal Party: A Chronology with Comment', Rhodes University.

88   LP papers: A/1671-mfm-Reel 3: M Gandhi to M Ballinger 7 June 1953.

89   Both remained politically active into the 1980s.

90   LP papers: A/1671-mfm-Reel 3: Natal Report, 30(1) 1 October 1954.

91   Ibid.

92   LP papers: A/1671-mfm-Reel 4: Natal Report 5 March 1955.

93   Ballinger papers: A410/B2.11: A Paton to M Ballinger 26 February 1955 (emphasis in original).

94   LP papers: A/1671-mfm-Reel 1: Peter Brown 1953, 'Notes' March.

95   LP papers: A/1671-mfm-Reel 3: Natal Report 30(1) 1 October 1954.

96   LP papers: A/1671-mfm-Reel 3: Minutes, NPC 7 November 1953, p 1.

97   Marquard papers: BC587 E2.71: L Marquard to A Paton 20 November 1956.

98   LP papers: A/1671-mfm-Reel 4: J Isacowitz to J Boerne 2 February 1954.

99   L Rubin and O Wollheim. (n.d.) 1953. *To Those Interested in Liberalism*, LP flier.

100   Alan Paton, *Journey*, op cit, p 121.
101   LP papers: A/1671-mfm-Reel 3: C Gell to O Wollheim 28 April 1955.
102   Ibid.
103   See C Gell 1953, 'Advice to Liberals (1)', *Evening Post* 4 July.
104   Marquard Papers: BC587 E2.23: C Gell 1953, 'Some Immediate Suggestions for Liberals', (?)June. See also above.
105   C Gell, 'Not Yet', op cit, p 13.
106   C Gell 1953, 'The Policy of the Liberal Party', *The Star* 8 July.
107   Ibid, p 14.
108   See, e.g., G Gordon 1954, 'Is South Africa Losing Its Democratic Freedom?', *Cape Times* 28 January.
109   *The Forum* May 1952, p 1.
110   Kuper, 'Background', op cit, p 18.
111   Ballinger papers: A410/B2.11: C Gell to M Ballinger 24 July 1953.
112   LP papers: A/1671-mfm-Reel 1: Minutes: 1954 National Congress 11 July 1954.
113   Ballinger papers: A410/B2.11: J Boerne to M Ballinger 16 July 1954.
114   Ballinger papers: A410/B2.11: L Rubin to M Ballinger 18 July 1954.
115   Ballinger papers: A410/B2.11: O Wollheim to M Ballinger 10 September 1954.
116   Ballinger papers: A410/B2.11: O Wollheim to M Ballinger 26 October 1954.
117   LP papers: A/1671-mfm-Reel 3: M Ballinger to J Boerne 22 July 1954. See also J Boerne to L Marquard 23 July 1954: '[Ballinger] feels that this is sufficiently wide and can be construed to contain the principle of qualified franchise'.
118   Ballinger papers: A410/C2.4: W Ballinger to C Gell 16 August 1954.
119   LP papers: A/1671-mfm-Reel 5: Minutes: CPC Special Meeting 14 July 1954.
120   Ibid.
121   Ballinger papers: A410/B2.11: H Pittman to M Ballinger 16 July 1954.
122   Ibid.
123   Ballinger papers: A410/F3.1: Minutes, CPC 29 July 1954.
124   Ballinger papers: A410/B2.11: M Ballinger to J Boerne 22 July 1954.
125   Ballinger papers: A410/B2.11: O Wollheim to M Ballinger 21 July 1954; 9 August 1954; 10 September 1954; see also A410/B2.11: M Rodger 1956, 'Notes on the Liberal Party' 19 June.
126   Ballinger papers: A410/B2.11: O Wollheim to M Ballinger 3 October 1955.
127   Interview with Oscar Wollheim.
128   LP papers: A/1671-mfm-Reel 1: O Wollheim to NC members 26 November 1954.
129   Ibid.
130   Marquard papers: BD587 E2.62 M Ballinger to L Marquard 19 June 1954 (emphasis in original).
131   Ibid.
132   LP papers: A/1671-mfm-Reel 1: Minutes: EC 26-1-1955, quoting Alan Paton.
133   Martin Legassick 1977, 'Liberalism, Social Control and Liberation in South Africa', seminar paper, University of Warwick, p 14 (emphasis in original).
134   LP papers: A/1671-mfm-Reel 4: Brown, 'South African Liberals', op cit.
135   Ballinger, Address, op cit.
136   Ibid.
137   *Advance* 11 June 1954, p 4.
138   *Advance* 14 May 1953, p 2.
139   A Paton, *Journey*, op cit, p 60.

140 Interview with Peter Brown.
141 M Ballinger 1953, 'Revival of the Liberal Tradition', *The Forum* June, p 8.
142 Kuper, 'Background', op cit, p 18.
143 C Gell, 'Policy', op cit.
144 Ibid.
145 LP papers: A/1671-mfm-Reel 3: C K Hill (n.d.) 1955, 'Liberation Movements', p 2.
146 C Gell, 'Advice', op cit.
147 Interview with Peter Hjul 1989.
148 Ibid.
149 Ibid.
150 Ballinger papers: A410/B2.11: O Wollheim to M Ballinger 2 August 1955.
151 Ibid.
152 *Advance* 5 August 1954, p 2.
153 Legassick, 'Liberalism', op cit, p 14 (emphasis in original).
154 Ballinger papers: A410/B2.11: A Paton to M Ballinger 27 December 1956 (emphasis in original).
155 LP papers: A/1671-mfm-Reel 5: Minutes: Cape Provincial Congress 17 November 1957.
156 Marquard papers: BC587 E2.71: L Marquard to A Paton 20 November 1956.
157 Ibid.
158 Ibid.
159 Marquard papers: BC587 E2.75: A Paton to L Marquard 4 December 1956.
160 Ibid.
161 Peter Brown 1959, 'The Long View', *Contact* 7 March, p 9.

Chapter 8 **The Congress of the People**

1 Albert Luthuli, *Let My People Go*, op cit, p 142.
2 Suttner and Cronin, *Freedom Charter*, op cit, p 262.
3 N Ndebele 2002, 'The African National Congress and the Policy of Non-racialism: A Study of the Membership Issue', *Politikon* 29(2), p 134.
4 H Bernstein 1991, 'The Breakable Thread', *The Southern African Review of Books* 3 March/April, pp 20-21, quoted in Ndebele, 'ANC and Policy of Non-racialism', op cit, p 145.
5 See Bernstein, *Memory against forgetting*, op cit, for a personal and illuminating description of changed policing styles from friendly to hostile at about this time.
6 Treason Trial collection AD1812 Ef.1: SACOD National Executive Committee, 'Notes on the Political Situation' 24 June 1955, p 2.
7 ANC papers: AD1189/2/Ba.1: Z K Matthews (n.d.) 1954, 'Memorandum on the Congress of the People', p 3.
8 Treason Trial collection: AD1812 Eg.1: *Call to the Congress of the People*, (n.d.) 1954.
9 The Congress of the People: Annexure A, 1954 ANC National Executive Committee Report, in Karis and Gerhart, *Violence*, op cit, p 163.
10 Ballinger papers: A410/F3.8.3: Marion Friedman to Liberal Party National Committee: Report of a meeting with the COP National Action Committee (quoting Joe Slovo) 5 August 1954.
11 Communication from Rusty Bernstein 28 November 1989.
12 Suttner and Cronin, *Thirty Years*, op cit, p 262.
13 Ballinger papers: A410/E1.5.8: South African Labour Party: Non-European Policy 10 January 1953, pp 2-4.

14   See B Reid 1979, 'The Federal Party 1953–1962: An English-Speaking Reaction to Afrikaner Nationalism', PhD thesis University of Natal.

15   Ballinger papers: A410/B2.8.10: T Huddleston to M Ballinger 19 August 1953.

16   *Advance* 17 September 1953, p 4.

17   CAMP Reel 2b:2:2DA:14/4:62: 'NAC Report to the ANC Secretary-General and SAIC Joint Honorary Secretaries' 5 December 1953.

18   *Advance* 25 March 1954, p 2.

19   Lodge, *Black Politics*, op cit, pp 69-70.

20   Gerhart, *Black Power*, op cit, pp 115-116.

21   Albert Luthuli 1953, 'Presidential Address': 1953 Natal ANC Conference, *Advance* 5 November, p 1.

22   ANC papers AD1189/2/BA.1: ANC National Executive Committee Report December 1954, p 4.

23   Neither of these campaigns is discussed in detail here. See, inter alia, Lodge, *Black Politics*, op cit, chs 4 and 5; Karis and Gerhart, *Challenge*, op cit, pp 24-35.

24   SACOD NEC, 'Notes', op cit, p 2.

25   Ibid.

26   Quoted in Community Resource and Information Centre 1985, *Until We Have Won Our Liberty … Thirty Years of the Freedom Charter*, Johannesburg, p 13.

27   Quoted in *Drum* May 1953, p 10.

28   Z K Matthews, in Karis and Gerhart, *Challenge*, op cit, pp 56-57.

29   SACOD NEC, 'Notes', op cit, p 2.

30   Z K Matthews, Presidential Address 1953 Cape ANC Conference, in Karis and Gerhart, *Challenge*, op cit, p 105 (emphasis in original).

31   *Advance* 31 December 1953, p 1.

32   Interview with Rusty Bernstein.

33   Ibid.

34   Ibid. See also ANC papers AD1189/2/Ba.1: Supplementary ANC Secretariat Report on the Congress of the People, 1954 ANC Annual Conference.

35   ANC papers AD1189/10/m.2: SAIRR (n.d.) 1954, Notes of a discussion with Yusuf Cachalia.

36   Quoted in Karis and Gerhart, *Challenge*, op cit, p 57.

37   1954 ANC Secretariat Report, in *Advance* 24 December 1954, p 1.

38   SACOD NEC, 'Notes', op cit, p 2.

39   Vigne, *Liberals*, op cit, pp 46, 48.

40   For detail on this, see D Everatt 1991, 'The Freedom Charter in Historical Perspective', in N Steytler (ed), *The Freedom Charter and Beyond: Founding Principles for a Democratic South African Legal Order*, Cape Town, pp 21-43.

41   *The Guardian* 11 January 1951, p 2.

42   Moses Kotane 1952, 'The People's Task', *Advance* 19 June, p 4.

43   Ibid.

44   NAC 1954 Report, op cit.

45   *Drum* January 1955, 'How Red Is Congress?', p 29 (emphasis in original).

46   Communication from Rusty Bernstein 28 November 1989 (emphasis in original).

47   Matthews, 'Address', op cit, p 105.

48   Ibid.

49   Luthuli, 'Address', op cit, p 1.

50   *Drum*, 'Red', op cit, p 29.
51   Joe Johnson 1955, 'Can the Congress of Democrats Win Mass Support?', *Liberation* October, p 20 (emphasis in original).
52   Ibid.
53   *Drum*, 'Red', op cit, p 29 (emphasis in original).
54   *New Age* was edited by Brian Bunting; *Fighting Talk* by Ruth First and Rusty Bernstein; Michael Harmel was on the editorial board of *Liberation*; *Counter Attack* was SACOD's internal newsletter.
55   Mandela, 'Searchlight', op cit, p 10.
56   *Cape Argus* 8 April 1950.
57   *Cape Times* 4 May 1950.
58   Ballinger papers: A410/B2.5.3: J D Rheinallt Jones to D F Malan 5 May 1950.
59   Marquard papers: BC587 H2.14: Leo Marquard (n.d.) 1952, Speech.
60   Marquard papers: BC587 E1.19: Q Whyte to L Marquard 27 March 1953. Marquard chaired; Z K Matthews participated.
61   Marquard papers: BC587 E1.26: Conference Invitation 13 May 1953.
62   Marquard papers: BC587 E1.19: Q Whyte to L Marquard 27 March 1953.
63   Marquard papers: BC587 E1.52: 'Notes on the Discussions at the Conference on Franchise Rights' 5 August 1953, p 1.
64   Alan Paton in *Advance* 11 June 1953, p 4.
65   Marquard papers: BC587 E1.49: Summary of Discussion 6 August 1953, p 1.
66   Matthews, 'Memorandum', op cit, p 1.
67   Ibid.
68   Ibid.
69   Ibid, quoting a letter from the SAIC to the SAIRR.
70   *Advance* 12 August 1954, p 2.
71   Ibid.
72   SAIRR, Cachalia discussion, op cit; Friedman to NC, op cit.
73   SACOD NEC, Notes, op cit, p 3.
74   Quoting Gibson and Ballinger from Vigne, *Liberals*, op cit, p 48.
75   Robertson, *Liberalism*, op cit, pp 164-165; Peter Brown 1985, 'The Liberal Party: A Chronology with Comment', Rhodes University.
76   Luthuli, 'Presidential Address', op cit, p 139.
77   LP papers A/1671-mfm-Reel 3: 'NAC Invitation to the LP to co-sponsor the CoP' 6 July 1954.
78   Vigne, *Liberals*, op cit, p 48.
79   Ibid.
80   Ibid.
81   *Fighting Talk* April 1954, p 4.
82   Ibid.
83   *Advance*, Editorial 8 April 1954; see also Walter Sisulu in *Counter Attack* July 1954, p 3.
84   Karis and Gerhart, *Challenge*, op cit, p 57.
85   ANC papers: AD1189/5/G4: Luthuli 1956, 'On the African National Congress' 5 June, p 11.
86   SAIRR, Cachalia discussion, op cit.
87   Friedman to NC, op cit.
88   *Counter Attack* November 1953, p 1.
89   Interviews with leading SACOD officials.

90   Lodge, *Black Politics*, op cit, p 76.
91   Treason Trial collection: AD1812 Ef1.3: Organisational Report SACOD National Conference 24 June 1955, p 1.
92   Cited in A Berman 1978, 'The South African Congress of Democrats 1953–1962', Hons thesis, University of Cape Town, pp 50, 82.
93   Treason Trial collection: AD1812 Ef1: Albert Luthuli 1956, 'Our Common Task: Message to SACOD National Conference' March, p 1.
94   Quoted in Frederikse, *Unbreakable Thread*, op cit, p 78.
95   Interviews with various SACOD members.
96   Interview with Baruch Hirson 1986.
97   Treason Trial collection: AD1812 Ef.8.1.2: Rusty Bernstein 1953, 'The Road to Liberty' October, p 4.
98   Interview with Ben Turok 1988.
99   Interview with Helen Joseph 1989.
100 *Advance* 18 March 1954, p 1.
101 ANC papers: AD1189/10/M.1.g: SAIRR 1954, Report on Transvaal CoP meeting 25 July.
102 Ibid.
103 For example, printers Len Lee-Warden and Piet Beyleveld (former Labour Party members), former miner Jack Hodgson, salesperson Issie Heyman, and electrician/builder John Matthews.
104 Wentzel, 'Memoirs', op cit, p 94.
105 Treason Trial collection: AD1812 Cf.2: B Gottschalk to Y Barenblatt 1 October 1956.
106 Treason Trial collection: AD1812 Cf.2: B Gottschalk to Y Barenblatt 20 November 1956.
107 Treason Trial collection: AD1812 Ef1.6: Cape Western Report 31March/1 April 1956, p 1.
108 Treason Trial collection: AD1812 Ef.1.6: 1956 NEC Report, p 1.
109 *Counter Attack* November 1954, p 2.
110 SACOD, Organisational Report, op cit, p 5.
111 Interview with Helen Joseph.
112 SACOD papers: AD1196/C: Chairman's Address: 1958 SACOD National Conference, p 2.
113 Interview with Helen Joseph.
114 Helen Joseph 1968, *Tomorrow's Sun: A Smuggled Journal from South Africa*, London, p 52.
115 Gerhart, *Power*, op cit, p 157.
116 For a (bitchy) left-wing view of SACOD, see Baruch Hirson 1995, *Revolutions in my life*, Johannesburg, ch 14.
117 Gerhart, *Power*, op cit, p 118.
118 Ibid, p 118.
119 Mary Benson 1985, *The Struggle for a Birthright*, London, p 202.
120 Ibid, p 122.
121 Edwin Munger 1967: *Afrikaner and African Nationalism: South African Parallels and Parameters*, Oxford, p 92.
122 Lodge, *Black Politics*, op cit, p 69.
123 *Counter Attack* February 1954, p 1.
124 SACOD NEC, 'Notes', op cit, p 3.
125 Interview with Ben Turok.
126 Interviews with Ben Turok and Amy Thornton 1987.
127 Interview with Helen Joseph.
128 SACOD NEC, 'Notes', op cit, pp 2-3.

129 CAMP Reel 4B:2/DC2:41/25: 'To all SACOD members' (circular) 6 August 1954.

130 CAMP Reel 4B:2:DC2:45/28: SACOD 1954, Congress of the People Campaign (?)November, p 1.

131 CAMP Reel 4B.2:DC2:45/31: SACOD (Johannesburg) (n.d.) 1955, 'The COP and COD', p 1.

132 Luthuli, 'Task', op cit, p 1.

133 Quoted in Lodge, *Black Politics*, op cit, p 71.

134 Walter Sisulu 1959, 'Congress and the Africanists', *Africa South* July–September, p 33.

135 Johnson, 'Mass Support?', op cit, p 20 and see above.

136 SACOD papers: AD1196/K: SACOD 1956, Speaker's Notes, p 2.

137 Dennis Goldberg 1956, 'Can the Congress of Democrats Win Mass Support?', *Liberation* March, p 7; see also Ronald Press 1956, 'Can the Congress of Democrats Win Mass Support: A Criticism', *Liberation* April.

138 SACOD NEC, Notes, op cit, p 1 and ch 5.

139 LP papers: A/1671-mfm-Reel 1: Minutes 1954 National Congress and NC meeting 9–12 July 1954.

140 Treason Trial collection: AD1812 Eg1.2.1: NAC *Newsletter* 9 November 1954, p 2.

141 Friedman to NC, op cit.

142 LP papers: A/1671-mfm-Reel 1: Minutes: NC 30/31 October 1954.

143 Ballinger papers: A410/F3.5: Ken Hill 1954, Memorandum (?)November.

144 E.g., LP papers A/1671-mfm-Reel 1: Minutes: joint Edendale/Pietermaritzburg LP meeting addressed by the NIC 12 October 1954.

145 Ballinger papers: A410/B2.11: W Stanford to M Ballinger 17 August 1954.

146 Ibid.

147 LP papers: A/1671-mfm-Reel 1: Minutes, NC 31 October 1954.

148 CAMP Reel 10A:2:XH: Interview with P Hjul 1964, p 4.

149 LP papers: A/1671-mfm-Reel 1: Minutes, Executive Committee 6 June 1955.

150 Ballinger papers: A410/B2.11: A Winch, Memorandum 18 August 1954.

151 Ballinger papers: A410/B2.11: A Paton to M Ballinger 4 September 1954.

152 Ballinger papers: A410/B2.11: O Wollheim to M Ballinger 21 August 1954.

153 LP papers: A/1671-mfm-Reel 4: P Brown to D R Calder 2 November 1954.

154 Ballinger papers: A410/B2.11: O Wollheim to M Ballinger 21 August 1954.

155 Ballinger papers: A410/B2.11: O Wollheim to M Ballinger 30 September 1954.

156 Karis and Gerhart, *Challenge*, op cit, p 61 inaccurately state that LP observers were present at Kliptown.

157 LP papers: A/1671-mfm-Reel 1: Minutes, Executive Committee 6 June 1955.

158 LP papers: A/1671-mfm-Reel 3: J T R Gibson to W van der Willigen 8 July 1955.

159 Ibid.

160 Alan Paton 1981, *Ah But Your Land Is Beautiful*, London, p 131.

161 Luthuli, *Let My People Go*, op cit, p 140.

162 Gerhart, *Power*, op cit, pp 115-116.

163 Robertson, *Liberalism*, op cit, p 165.

164 E.g., E Feit 1962, *South Africa: The Dynamics of the African National Congress*, London, p 33; D Irvine 1987, 'The Liberal Party 1953–1968', in Butler, Elphick and Welsh (eds), *Democratic Liberalism in South Africa*, Cape Town, pp 127-8; Lodge, *Black Politics*, op cit, p 72; Robertson, *Liberalism*, op cit, p 166.

165 LP papers: A/1671-mfm-Reel 4: J K Ngubane (n.d.) 1956, Report on Charlestown.

166 Quoted in *Drum* January 1955, p 29.

167 Luthuli, 'ANC', op cit, p 13.
168 SACOD NEC, Notes, op cit, p 3.

Chapter 9 **The Freedom Charter and the politics of non-racialism, 1956–1960**

1   Liberal Party members were in the majority in the National Liberation Committee, later renamed the African Resistance Movement (ARM). See Karis and Carter, *Protest*, op cit, pp 654-6.
2   All quotations from the Freedom Charter are taken from Suttner and Cronin, *Thirty Years of the Freedom Charter*, op cit, pp 262-6.
3   Luthuli, *Let My People Go*, op cit, p 142.
4   See, inter alia, Karis and Gerhart, *Challenge*, op cit, p 60; Lodge, *Black Politics*, op cit, p 72; Gerhart, *Black Power*, op cit, pp 115-16; Robertson, *Liberalism*, op cit, p 165; J Ngubane 1963, *An African Explains Apartheid*, London, p 164.
5   Communication from Rusty Bernstein 28 November 1989.
6   Bernstein, *Memory*, op cit, p 152.
7   Ibid, p 150.
8   SACOD (n.d.) 1955, 'Demands of the People' (private possession of author); interview with Ben Turok 1988; Bernstein, *Memory*, op cit, p 154.
9   Bernstein, communication 28 November 1989 (emphasis in original).
10   ANC Papers, University of the Witwatersrand: AD1189 Eo.3: Minutes, Joint Congress Executives 31 July 1955, p 3.
11   Treason Trial transcript AD1812 Volume 57/11595.
12   SAIRR Auden House Collection, University of the Witwatersrand: AD1180 Eo.3: Minutes, Joint Congress Executives 31 July 1955, p 3.
13   ZKM: Z K Matthews nd, 'Autobiography', London, p 24.
14   Peter Raboroko, quoted in M Benson 1985, *The Struggle for a Birthright*, London, p 213.
15   Potlako Leballo 1957, 'What of the Future?', *The Africanist* December, p 7.
16   Africanist Statement in *The Africanist* June/July 1958, p 6.
17   Ufford Khoruba (Raboroko) and Kwame Lekwane (Mothopeng) 1958, 'The Kliptown Charter', *The Africanist* June/July, p 15.
18   Bernstein, *Memory*, op cit, p 160.
19   Ibid, p 16.
20   Ibid.
21   Ibid.
22   Ibid.
23   Editorial, *The Africanist* June/July 1958, pp 1-4.
24   Alan Paton, *Journey Continued*, op cit, p 191.
25   Duncan papers: DU 5.2.15: P Duncan to G M Hauser 7 March 1955.
26   P Duncan to A Paton 24 November 1958, quoted in Driver, *Duncan*, op cit, p 159.
27   Ibid, p 149.
28   Duncan papers: DU 5.8.21: P Duncan to G M Hauser 20 February 1956.
29   Quoted in Karis and Gerhart, *Challenge*, op cit, p 64.
30   Ballinger papers: A410/F3.8.4: J Ngubane 1956, 'Memorandum on the African and the Liberal Party', September.
31   Ibid.
32   Alan Paton 1958, *Hope for South Africa*, London, p 76.

33   Peter Brown in *Contact* 22 August 1959, p 16.
34   LP papers: A/1671-mfm-Reel 2: Draft Land Policy adopted in 1961; and Draft Economic Policy 1960.
35   LP papers: A/1671-mfm-Reel 6: Transvaal LP Statement on the 1958 Stay-away.
36   LP papers: A/1671-mfm-Reel 3: P Brown, Speech 10 December 1959.
37   Interview with Peter Brown 1987.
38   Ernie Wentzel (Transvaal provincial chairperson), 'Memoirs', op cit, A42.
39   LP papers: A/1671-mfm-Reel 6: P Brown to J Unterhalter 30 July 1958.
40   Interview with Peter Hjul (Cape provincial chairperson).
41   LP papers: A/1671-mfm-Reel 5: P Hjul to P Brown 19 May 1959.
42   Duncan papers: DU 5.14.40: P Duncan to P Brown 20 April 1959.
43   Duncan papers: DU 5.14.38: P Duncan to P Brown 14 May 1959.
44   *Fighting Talk* February 1956.
45   Quoted in Driver, *Duncan*, op cit, p 135.
46   *Contact* 2 May 1959, p 8.
47   See Driver, *Duncan*, op cit, p 148; Paton, *Journey*, op cit, p 177.
48   Letter from A B Xuma to the ANC Special Conference March 1956, in Karis and Gerhart, *Challenge*, op cit, pp 242-245.
49   Luthuli, quoted in Karis and Gerhart, *Challenge*, op cit, pp 70-1.
50   N ka Linda 1956, 'Congress and Other Organisations', *The Africanist* April/May, p 2.
51   Leballo, 'Future', op cit.
52   ANC papers AD1189/5/GA: Albert Luthuli 1956, 'On the African National Congress' (mimeo) 5 June, p 10.
53   Ibid, p 14.
54   Ibid, p 5.
55   Anthony Sampson 1956, *DRUM: A Venture into the New Africa*, London, p 141.
56   Luthuli, 'ANC', op cit, p 8; see also ANC papers: AD1189/5/G4: Luthuli to ANC Secretary General (Oliver Tambo) 19 March 1956.
57   Moses Kotane 1957, *The Great Crisis Ahead* (*New Age* pamphlet), p 10.
58   Ibid, p 7.
59   See C Walker 1982, *Women and Resistance in South Africa*, London, pp 173-5.
60   Karis and Gerhart, *Challenge*, op cit, p 307.
61   Ibid, p 301.
62   Ibid, p 303.
63   *Counter Attack* August 1955, p 1.
64   Treason Trial collection: AD1812/57/11599: A Luthuli to Dr A Letele 22 August 1956.
65   FSAW papers AD1137 Ec3.2: NCC: To All National Executives 12 November 1957, p 2.
66   Joe Matthews 1956, 'Building a United Front', *Liberation* November, pp 19-21 (emphasis in original).
67   FSAW papers AD1137 Ec.3.2: NCC, To All National Executives 12 November 1957, p 3 (emphasis in original).
68   *Counter Attack* June 1956, p 1; see also Berman, South African Congress of Democrats, op cit, chs 4 and 5.
69   Karis and Gerhart, *Challenge*, op cit, pp 307-9.
70   Ibid, p 313.
71   Luthuli, 'ANC', op cit, p 11.
72   Editorial, *Contact* 16 May 1959, p 6.

73   'Introducing "The Citizen"', *The Citizen* 31 March 1956, p 1.
74   Kenneth Hendrickse 1958, 'The Opposition in Congress', *The Citizen* 4 March.
75   P Dreyer 1959, *Against Racial Status and Segregation: Towards the Liquidation of Multi-Racialism and Non-Europeanism*, Cape Town, p 7.
76   *Bantu World* 28 June 1958.
77   See D Musson 1989, *Johnny Gomas: Voice of the Working Class*, Cape Town.
78   Quoted in *The Citizen* 4 March 1958; see also Musson, *Gomas*, op cit, p 121.
79   Duncan papers: DU 5.14.42: P Duncan to P Brown 3 May 1959 and 30 June 1959.
80   Benson, *Birthright*, op cit, p 206.
81   Ibid, p 207.
82   Duncan papers: DU 8.9.10: P Duncan (n.d.) 1958, 'Assessment of the Victory of the Africanists in the Transvaal ANC' (mimeo).
83   Quoted in Francis Meli 1988, *South Africa Belongs To Us: A History of the ANC*, Harare, p 137.
84   Micr. Afr. 484 Reel 8: P Tsele to O R Tambo 25 May 1958.
85   Micr. Afr. 484 Reel 8: Manifesto of the Africanist Movement: Africanist National Convention 4/5 April 1959, p 2.
86   SACOD papers AD1196/D: Minutes, SACOD National Council 30/31 May 1959, p 3.
87   Ibid, p 1.
88   Treason Trial collection: AD1812 Ef.2: B Gottschalk to Y Barenblatt 17 August 1956.
89   Interview with Baruch Hirson 1986.
90   SACOD papers AD1196/D: Some Suggestions (internal discussion document) (n.d.) 1958, p 2.
91   'Organisational Problems of the S.A.C.O.D.', *Counter Attack* August 1956, p 4.
92   Interview with Ronald Segal.
93   SACOD papers AD1196/D: SACOD National Council 30/31 May 1959, p 7.
94   'Discussion Corner', *Counter Attack* December 1958, p 2.
95   'Treason Trialist' 1959, 'Other Thoughts on One Congress', *Counter Attack* May, p 9.
96   Interview with Peter Hjul.
97   SACOD papers AD1196/D: SACOD National Council 30/31 May 1959, p 7.
98   K Shanker (Baruch Hirson) 1958, 'The Congresses and the Multi Racial Conference', *Analysis* 1 January, p 3.
99   Ibid.
100 Ibid.
101 'V' (Vic Goldberg) (n.d.) 1959, 'After Conference', *Counter Attack* supplement, p 2.
102 Ibid, p 3.
103 'Trialist', 'Thoughts', op cit, p 9.
104 NEC Report to the ANC National Conference December 1959, in Karis and Gerhart, *Challenge*, op cit, p 485.
105 Africanist Manifesto, op cit, p 2.
106 Interview with Ben Turok.
107 Auden House collection AD1180 Eo 3.1.5: NCC, Report to Joint Congress Executives (n.d.) 1957, p 1.
108 'Communism and C.O.D.', *Counter Attack* January 1959, p 1.
109 'R.A.L.' (n.d.) 1959, 'After Conference: Another Viewpoint', *Counter Attack* supplement.

Bibliography

Manuscript and documentary sources:

South Africa

University of Cape Town: J W Jagger Library
BC345:   Margaret Ballinger Papers
BC347:   William Ballinger Papers
BC653:   Civil Rights League Papers
BC640:   Harry Lawrence Papers
BC587:   Leo Marquard Papers
BC579:   Donald Molteno Papers
BC354:   P A Moore Papers
BC618:   Eric Walker Papers
BC741:   David Welsh Collection
BC627:   Oscar Wollheim Papers

Rhodes University: Cory Library
PR3775:   Liberal Party of South Africa: Papers for Grahamstown and Eastern Cape Division

University of the
Witwatersrand: William Cullen Library
AD1189:   African National Congress Papers
A410:   Margaret and William Ballinger Papers
A949:   S P Bunting Papers
AD1430:   Cachalia Family Papers
AD1137:   Federation of South African Women Papers
Aa: J H Hofmeyr Papers
A/1671-mfm: Liberal Party of South Africa Papers (15 Reels)
AD1712-mfm: Liberal Party of South Africa: 'Blackspot' Removals Collection (2 Reels)

A1333-mfm:	Liberal Party of South Africa: Transvaal Division Papers
A474:	'Sailor' Malan Memorial Fund Papers
AD1188:	Pan Africanist Congress Papers
AD1169:	A S Paton Papers
AD1196:	South African Congress of Democrats Papers
AD1197:	South African Congress of Trade Unions Papers
AD1180:	South African Institute of Race Relations: Auden House Collection
AD1181:	South African Institute of Race Relations: Political Collection
A1454-mfm:	South African Political Materials (CAMP)
A1906:	Rev. Douglas Thompson Papers
AD1502:	Q Whyte Papers

England

University of London: Institute of Commonwealth Studies
Marion Friedman Papers
Ike Horvitch Papers
Peter Hjul Papers
Albert Luthuli Papers
Z K Matthews Papers
Albie Sachs Papers
Randolph Vigne Papers

M839:	SACOD Collection
M859:	Pan Africanist Congress Collection
M932:	Z K Matthews Collection
M860:	South African Institute of Race Relations: Political Party Collection

University of Oxford:	Rhodes House
Mss.Afr.s 1681:	Africa Bureau Papers
Mss.Brit.Emp.s 365:	Fabian Colonial Bureau Papers

University of York:
Patrick Duncan Papers
Marion Friedman Papers
Capricorn Africa Society Papers
'Coloured' Radical Political Movements Collection

Private collections

Helen Joseph Papers:	(including SACOD and ANC materials, speeches, correspondence, journals, Treason Trial and related materials)
Ernest Wentzel Papers:	(including Liberal Party minutes and memoranda, unpublished memoirs, and correspondence)
Len Lee-Warden:	(including pamphlets, fliers, newspapers, unpublished memoirs)

Trial records

AD1812:	Treason Trial Collection (1956–1961)
AD1901:	Political Trials Collection

AD1450:   Trials 1958–1979
AD1189:   H Wolpe and P A B Beyleveld vs Officer Commanding
                                 South African Police for the District of Johannesburg, 1954

Official publications

SC.6-52:   Report of the Select Committee on the Suppression of Communism
                                 Act Enquiry: April 1952
SC.10-53:   Report of the Select Committee on the Suppression of Communism
                                 Act Enquiry: September 1953
UG-48:   The Native Laws Commission 1946–1948

Interviews

Rowley Arenstein   Durban 1987
Yetta Barenblatt   Johannesburg 1987
Esther Barsel   Johannesburg 1987
Terence Beard   Grahamstown 1987
Hilda Bernstein*
Rusty Bernstein*
Pieter Beyleveld   Johannesburg 1986
Peter Brown   Pietermaritzburg 1986,1987
Brian Bunting   London 1988
Sonya Bunting   London 1988
Yusuf Cachalia   Fordsburg 1989
Fred Carneson   London 1988,1989
Sara Carneson   London 1988, 1989
Rodney Davenport   Grahamstown 1986
Wolf Feinberg   Johannesburg 1987
Jimmy Gibson   Cape Town 1987
Gerald Gordon   Cape Town 1989
Bill Hepner   Johannesburg 1988, 1989, 1990
Miriam Hepner   Johannesburg 1988, 1989, 1990
Anne Heymann   Johannesburg 1987
Issie Heymann   Johannesburg 1987, 1988, 1989
Baruch Hirson   London 1986
Peter Hjul   London 1989
Helen Joseph   Johannesburg 1985/6/7/8/9/1990
Violaine Junod   Coventry 1988
Willie Kalk   Johannesburg 1987
Hilda Kuper   London 1988
Leo Kuper   London 1988
David Lang   Oxford 1986
Len Lee-Warden   Cape Town 1986, 1987
Govan Mbeki   New Brighton 1987
Alan Paton   Botha's Hill 1987
Benjamin Pogrund   London 1988
Peter Rodda   London 1988
Guy Routh   Brighton 1989

Ronald Segal	Walton-on-Thames 1988
Amy Thornton	Cape Town 1987
Ben Turok	London 1988
Jack Unterhalter	Johannesburg 1986, 1987
Randolph Vigne	London 1986, 1987
Jill Wentzel	Johannesburg 1987
Oscar Wollheim	Cape Town 1987

*Interviewed by Don Pinnock (England 1988). I am grateful to the Bernsteins for permission to quote from the transcripts.

In addition, I have benefited from conversations and communication with people active during the period, including Hymie Barsel, Hilda and Rusy Bernstein, Paul and Bridget Finnemore, Phyllis Lewsen, Joe Matji, Harry Oppenheimer, Gavin Stewart, Fr Cyprian Thorpe and others.

Books, articles and pamphlets

Adam, H. 1971. *Modernising Racial Dominations: South Africa's Political Dynamics*. Berkley: University of California Press.

Adam, H. and K Adam (eds). 1971. *South Africa: Sociological Perspectives*. London: Oxford University Press.

Adam, H. and H Giliomee. 1979. *Ethnic Power Mobilised: Can South Africa Change?* London: Yale University Press.

—. 1983. *The Rise and Crisis of Afrikaner* Power. Cape Town: David Philip.

Adler, G. ' "Trying Not To Be Cruel": Local Government Resistance to the Application of the Group Areas Act in Uitenhage, 1945–1962'. *The Societies of Southern Africa in the 19th and 20th Centuries*. Collected Seminar Papers 1990, Institute of Commonwealth Studies, pp 168-185.

African National Congress. 1985. *Selected Writings on the Freedom Charter 1955-1985*. London: ANC.

—. 1994. *Reconstruction and Development Programme*. Johannesburg: Ravan Press.

Albright, D E (ed). 1980. *Communism in South Africa*. London: Indiana University Press.

Altman, P. (ed). 1975. *Bram Fischer, Q.C.* London: International Defence and Aid Fund.

Andrews, W H. 1941. *Class Struggles in South Africa*. Cape Town: no publisher.

Attfield, J and S Williams (eds). 1984. *The Communist Party and the War*. London: Lawrence and Wishart.

Baard, F and B Schreiner. 1986. *My Spirit is not Banned*. Harare: Zimbabwe Publishing House.

Ballinger, M. 1969. *From Union to Apartheid: A Trek to Isolation*. Folkestone: Bailey Brothers.

Basner, H M. 1947. *A Nation of 10,000,000: A Challenge to South Africa's Native Polity*. Johannesburg: Delta Press.

—. 'Autobiography'(unpublished). Institute of Commonwealth Studies, London.

Benson, M. 1989. *A Far Cry: The Making of a South African*. London: Penguin Books.

—. 1963.*Chief Albert Luthuli of South Africa*. London: Oxford University Press.

—. 1987. *Nelson Mandela*. Harmondsworth: Penguin Books.

—. (ed). 1985. *South Africa: The Struggle for a Birthright*. London: International Defence and Aid Fund.

—. (ed). 1974. *The Sun Will Rise: Statements from the Dock by Southern African Political Prisoners*. London: International Defence and Aid Fund.

Bernstein, H. 1991. 'The Breakable Thread'. *The Southern African Review of Books* 3, March/April.

Bernstein, R. 1999. *Memory against Forgetting: Memoirs from a Life in South African Politics, 1938–1964.* London: Viking.

Blaxall, A. 1965. *Suspended Sentence.* London: Hodder and Stoughton.

Bolnick, J. 1987. 'Proletarianism, Prejudice, Patriotism and the Party Line: White Radical Socialism in South Africa, 1915-1945' (mimeo). Centre for African Studies, University of Cape Town.

Bonner, P (ed). 1981. *Working Papers in Southern African Studies* Vol.2. Johannesburg: Ravan Press.

—. (ed). 1979. *Labour, Township and Protest.* Johannesburg: Ravan Press.

—. (ed). 1983. *Town and Countryside in the Transvaal: Capitalist Penetration and Popular Response.* Johannesburg: Ravan Press.

Brittain, V. 1980. *Testament of Friendship: The story of Winifred Holtby.* London: Virago Press.

Brokensha, M and R Knowles. 1965. *The Fourth of July Raids.* Cape Town: Simmondium.

Brookes, E H. 1949. 'The Man of the Country'. *The Forum,* 3 December.

—. 1968. *Apartheid: A Documentary Study of Modern South Africa.* London: Tinling and Co.

—. 1953. *South Africa in a Changing World.* Cape Town: Oxford University Press.

—. 1977. *A South African Pilgrimage.* Johannesburg: Ravan Press.

—. and J B Macauley. 1958. *Civil Liberty in South Africa.* Cape Town: Oxford University Press.

Brown, D. 1966. *Against the World: A Study of White South African Attitudes.* London: Collins.

Brown, P. 1961. 'The Liberal Party of South Africa'. *Contemporary Review.*

—. 1985. 'The Liberal Party: A Chronology with Comment'. Paper presented to the Liberal Party Workshop, Institute for Social and Economic Research, Rhodes University, Grahamstown, July.

Butler, J, R Elphick and D Welsh (eds). 1987. *Democratic Liberalism in South Africa: Its History and Prospect.* Cape Town: David Philip.

Bundy, C. 1979. *The Rise and Fall of the South African Peasantry.* London: Heinemann.

—. 1989. 'Around Which Corner? Revolutionary Prospects and Contemporary South Africa'. *Transformation* 8, pp 1-23.

Bunting, B. (n.d.) (?) 1958. *Apartheid: The Road to Poverty* (pamphlet). Cape Town: New Age.

—. 1987. *Moses Kotane: South African Revolutionary.* London: Inkuleleko Publications.

—. 1986. *The Rise of the South African Reich.* London: International Defence and Aid Fund.

Burger, J (pseudo: Leo Marquard). 1943. *The Blank Man's Burden.* London: Victor Gollancz.

Callan, E (ed). 1968. *Alan Paton – The Long View.* London: Pall Mall Press.

Callinicos, L. 2004. *Oliver Tambo: Beyond the Engeli Mountains.* Cape Town: David Philip.

Calpin, G H. 1946. *There are no South Africans.* London: Thomas Nelson.

Carneson, F. 1951. 'The Franchise Action Committee'. *Discussion* 1(3).

Carter, D. 'The Defiance Campaign – A Comparative Analysis of the Organisation, Leadership, and Participation in the Eastern Cape and Transvaal'. Institute of Commonwealth Studies Collected Seminar Papers on the Societies of Southern Africa in the 19th and 20th Centuries. London, 1970–1971, pp 76-97.

Carter, G M. 1958. *The Politics of Inequality: South Africa Since 1948.* London: Thames and Hudson.

Carter, G M, T G Karis and N Stultz (eds). 1967. *South Africa's Transkei: The Politics of Domestic Colonialism.* Evanston: Northwestern University Press.

Cawood, L. 1964. *The Churches and Race Relations in South Africa.* Johannesburg: South African Institute of Race Relations.

Claudin, F. *The Communist Movement From Comintern to Cominform,* Parts 1 and 2. London: Monthly Review Press.

Communist Party of South Africa (CPSA). 1944. New South Africa Series. Cape Town:
No 1: *Towards Socialism.*
No 2: *Education.*
No 3: *Away With Passes.*
No 4: *The African Worker.*
No 5: *Homes for All.*
—. (n.d.) (?) 1939. *Communism and the Native Question.* Pretoria: CPSA.
—. 1943. *The Foundation of Socialist Teaching from the Manifesto of 1848 to the 1928 Programme.* Pretoria.
—. 1944. *Communists in Conference: The 1943–44 National Conference of the Communist Party of South Africa.* Cape Town.
—. 1943. *Communist Plan for Victory.* Cape Town.
—. 1945. *Democracy in Action: Proceedings of the Johannesburg District of the Communist Party, March 1945.* Johannesburg,
—. 1945. *Victory: What Now?* Cape Town.
—. 1945. *What Next? A Policy for South Africa.* Cape Town.
—. 1950. *The Nat Attack on the Trade Unions.* Cape Town: Pioneer Press.
Community Resource and Information Centre. 1985. *Until We Have Won Our Liberty ... Thirty Years of the Freedom Charter.* Johannesburg: CRIC.
Cope, J. 1965. *South Africa.* London: Ernest Benn.
Cope, R K. 1944. *Comrade Bill: The Life and Times of William Andrews, Workers' Leader.* Cape Town: Stewart Printing.
Davenport, T R H (ed). 1978. *South Africa: A Modern History.* London: Macmillan.
Davidson, B. 1952. *Report on Southern Africa.* Bristol: Western Printing Services.
Davidson, B, J Slovo and A R Wilkinson (eds). 1976. *Southern Africa: The New Politics of Revolution.* Harmondsworth: Penguin Books.
Davies, R. 1979. *Capital, State and White Labour in South Africa 1900-1960.* Brighton: Harvester Press.
Davies, R, D O'Meara and S Dlamini (eds). 1982. *The Struggle for South Africa* Vols 1 and 2. London: Zed Books.
De Braganca, A and I Wallerstein (eds). 1982. *The African Liberation Reader* Vols 1 and 2. London: Zed Books.
De Kiewiet, C W. 1956. *The Anatomy of South African Misery.* London: Oxford University Press.
De Klerk, W A. 1976. *Puritans in Africa: The Story of Afrikanerdom.* Harmondsworth: Penguin Books.
Delius, P. 1996. *A Lion Amongst the Cattle: Reconstruction and Resistance in the Northern Transvaal.* Johannesburg: Ravan Press.
Deneson, P. 1961. *Persecution 1961.* Harmondsworth: Penguin Books.
Desmond, C. 1972. *The Discarded People.* Harmondsworth: Penguin Books.
Dreyer, P. 1959. *Against Racial Status and Segregation. Towards the Liquidation of Multi-Racialism and Non-Europeanism.* Cape Town: Citizen Publications.
—. 1959. *The Death Agony of Non-Europeanism.* Cape Town: Citizen Publications.
Driver, C J. 1980. *Patrick Duncan: South African and Pan-African.* London: Heinemann.
—. 1984. *Elegy for a Revolutionary.* Cape Town: David Philip.
Dubow, S and A Jeeves (eds). 2005. *South Africa's 1940s: Worlds of Possibilities.* Cape Town: Double Storey.
Duncan, P. 1953. *The Road Through the Wilderness.* Johannesburg: Hygrade Printers.

—. 1964. *South Africa's Rule of Violence*. London: Methuen.

Edwards, I. 1987. 'The Durban Communist Party, 1940s'. *South African Labour Bulletin* 11(4), pp 44-64.

Everatt, D. 1987. ' "Frankly Frightened": The Liberal Party and the Congress of People'. Paper presented to a conference on 'South Africa in the 1950s', Queen Elizabeth House, Oxford.

—. 1990a. 'The Development of a Liberal Programme 1948–1950'. Institute of Commonwealth Studies Collected Seminar Papers on the Societies of Southern Africa in the 19th and 20th Centuries. London, pp 141-152.

—. 1990b. 'The origins of multiracialism'. Seminar paper, African Studies Institute, University of the Witwatersrand.

—. 1990c. ' "Where there is no freedom the people perish": The Freedom Charter in Historical Perspective', in N Steytler (ed). 1990. *The Freedom Charter and the South African Legal Order*. Cape Town: David Philip.

—. 1991. 'The Freedom Charter in historical perspective', in N Steytler (ed). 1991. *The Freedom Charter and Beyond: Founding Principles for a Democratic South African Legal Order*. Cape Town: Wyvern.

—. 1992 'Alliance Politics of a Special Type: The Roots of the ANC/SACP Alliance, 1950-1954'. *Journal of Southern African Studies* 18(1).

Fagan, A H. 1960. *Our Responsibility: A Discussion of South Africa's Racial Problems*. Stellenbosch: Juta.

Feit, E. 1962. *South Africa: The Dynamics of the African National Congress*. London: Oxford University Press.

—. 1967. *African Opposition in South Africa*. California: Hoover Institute Publications.

—. 1971. *Urban Revolt in South Africa 1960-1964*. Northwestern University Press.

Feit, E and R First (eds). 1954. *South Africans in the Soviet Union*. Johannesburg.

—. 1959. *The Farm Labour Scandal*. Johannesburg: Real Printing Co.

—. 1963. *South West Africa*. Harmondsworth: Penguin Books.

—. 1982. *117 Days: An Account of Confinement and Interrogation Under the South African 90-Day Detention Law*. Reading: Penguin Books.

Fischer, B. (n.d.). *'What I Did Was Right …' Statement from the Dock*. London: Mayibuye Publications.

Forman, L. (n.d.). *Black and White in South African History* (pamphlet). Cape Town: New Age.

—. (n.d.). *Chapters in the History of the March to Freedom* (pamphlet). Cape Town: New Age.

Forman, L and E S Sachs. 1957. *The South African Treason Trial*. London: John Calder.

Frankel, P, N Pines and M Swilling (eds). 1988. *State, Resistance and Change in South Africa*. London: Croom Helm.

Fredrickson, G M. 1981. *White Supremacy – A Comparative Study in American and South African History*. Oxford: Oxford University Press.

Frederikse, J. 1990. *The Unbreakable Thread: Non-racialism in South Africa*. Johannesburg: Ravan Press.

French, K. 1982. 'Squatters in the Forties'. *Africa Perspective* 21, University of the Witwatersrand.

Friedman, M (ed). 1963. *I Will Still Be Moved: Reports from South Africa*. London: Arthur Baker.

Gann, L. 1959. 'Liberal Interpretations of South African History'. *The Rhodes-Livingstone Journal* XXV.

Gardiner, G. 1957. *The South African Treason Trial*. London: Christian Action.

Gerhart, G M. 1978. *Black Power in South Africa: The Evolution of an Ideology*. California: University of California Press.

Hancock, W K. 1962. *Smuts: The Sanguine Years 1870–1919*. Cape Town: Cambridge University Press.

—. 1968. *Smuts: The Fields of Force 1919-1950*. Cape Town: Cambridge University Press.

Harris, E E. 1955. *White Civilisation*. Johannesburg: SAIRR (SAIRR).

—. 1955. ' "Heartbreak House": The Prospect for South African Liberalism'. *Race Relations Journal* XXII, pp 33-45.

Hellman, E (ed). 1949. *Handbook on Race Relations in South Africa*. Cape Town: Oxford University Press.

Hellman, E and H Lever. 1979. *Race Relations in South Africa 1929-1979*. Johannesburg: Macmillan.

Hendrickse, K. 1958. *Towards a Modern South African Patriotism*. Cape Town: Citizen Publications.

—. 1959. *The Essence of Multi-Racialism. An Analysis of the Role of the Jewish Consciousness in South African 'Leftist' Politics*. Cape Town: Citizen Publications.

Hepple, A. 1966. *South Africa: A Political and Economic History*. London: Pall Mall Press.

Hill, C R and P Warwick. 1977. *Collected Papers* No 1. Centre for Southern African Studies, York University.

Hindson, D C (ed). 1983. *Working Papers in Southern African Studies* Vol 3. Johannesburg: Ravan Press.

Hoernlé, R F A. 1939. *South African Native Policy and the Liberal Spirit*. Johannesburg: Wits University Press.

Hommel, M. 1989. *The Contributions of the Non-European Peoples to World Civilisation*. Johannesburg: Skotaville.

Hooper, C. 1960. *Brief Authority*. London: Collins.

Horrell, M (comp). *A Survey of Race Relations. 1946–1968*. Johannesburg: SAIRR.

—. 1956. *South African Trade Unionism*. Johannesburg: SAIRR.

—. (comp). 1960. *Days of Crisis in South Africa*. Johannesburg: SAIRR.

—. 1964. *A Decade of Bantu Education*. Johannesburg: SAIRR.

—. 1971. *Action, Reaction and Counteraction: A Brief Review of Non-White Political Movements in South Africa*. Johannesburg: SAIRR.

Horwitz, R. 1967. *The Political Economy of South Africa*. Bristol: Weidenfield and Nicolson.

Houghton, D Hobart. 1976. *The South African Economy*. Cape Town: Oxford University Press.

Huddleston, T. 1956. *Naught for your Comfort*. London: Collins.

Hudson, P. 1988. 'Images of the Future and Strategies in the Present: The Freedom Charter and the South African Left', in Frankel, Pines and Swilling (eds). *State, Resistance and Change in South Africa*. London: Croom Helm, pp 259-77.

—. 1986. 'The Freedom Charter and the Theory of National Democratic Revolution'. *Transformation* Vol 1.

Hughes, K R. 1977. 'Challenges from the Past: Reflections on Liberalism and Radicalism in the Writing of South African History'. *Social Dynamics* III(1).

Hurley, D E. 1965. *A Time for Faith*. Johannesburg: SAIRR.

International Commission of Jurists. 1960. *South Africa and the Rule of Law*. Geneva.

Irvine, D. 1987. 'The Liberal Party 1953–1968', in Butler, Elphick and Welsh (eds). *Democratic Liberalism in South Africa: Its History and Prospect*. Cape Town: David Philip.

Jaffe, H (ed). 1988. *A History of Africa*. London: Zed Books.

James, W G and M Simons (eds). 1989. *The Angry Divide: Social and Economic History of the Western Cape*. Cape Town: David Philip.

Johns, S W. Fall 2007. 'Invisible Resurrection: the recreation of a Communist Party in South Africa in the 1950s'. *African Studies Quarterly* Volume 9(4), pp 1-19.

Johnstone, F A. 1976. *Class, Race, and Gold: A Study of Class Relations and Racial Discrimination in South Africa*. London: Routledge and Kegan Paul.

Joseph, H. 1963. *If This Be Treason*. London: Andre Deutsch.

—. 1966. *Tomorrow's Sun: A Smuggled Journal from South Africa*. London: Hutchinson.

—. 1986. *Side by Side*. London: Zed Books.

Kane-Berman, J. 1979. *South Africa: the Method in the Madness*. London: Pluto Press.

Kane-Bernam, L. June 1987. 'The Torch Commando: The Wheel Turns Full Circle'. *Frontline* 2(7).

Karis, T. 1965. *The Treason Trial in South Africa: A Guide to the Microfilm Record of the Trial*. Stanford: Hoover.

—. 1973. *Hope and Challenge: 1935-1952*. Stanford, Calif: Hoover Inst Press.

Karis, T and G M Carter (eds). 1972-1977. *From Protest to Challenge: A Documentary History of African Politics in South Africa 1882-1964* Vols 1-4. Stanford: Hoover Inst Press.

Karis, T and G Gerhart (eds). 1977. *Challenge and Violence, 1953-1964*. Stanford, Calif: Hoover Inst Press.

Keppel-Jones, A. 1947. *When Smuts Goes*. London: Victor Gollancz.

—. 1949. *South Africa: A Short History*. London: Hutchinson.

Kgosana, P A. 1949. *Lest We Forget*. Johannesburg: SAIRR.

Kitson, N. 1987. *Where Sixpence Lives*. London: Hogarth Press.

Kotane, M. 1957. *South Africa: The Great Crisis Ahead*. Cape Town, New Age (pamphlet), nd.

Kruger, D W. 1960. *South African Parties and Policies 1910–1960: A Select Source Book*. London: Bowes & Bowes.

Kuper, L. 1953. 'The Background to Passive Resistance' (South Africa 1952). *Race Relations Journal* XX.

—. 1957. *Passive Resistance in South Africa*. New Haven: Yale University Press.

—. 1965. *An African Bourgeoisie: Race, Class and Politics in South Africa*. New Haven: Yale University Press.

—. 1974. *Race, Class and Power: Ideology and Revolutionary Change in Plural Societies*. London: Duckworth.

Kuzwayo, E. 1985. *Call Me Woman*. Johannesburg: Ravan Press.

Lambert, R. November 1985. 'Political Unionism and Working Class Hegemony: Perspectives on the South African Congress of Trade Unions, 1955–1965'. *Labour, Capital and Society* 18(2), pp 244-77.

Lawrence, J. 1978. *Harry Lawrence*. Cape Town: David Philip.

Leatt, J, T Kneifel and K Nurnberger. 1986. *Contending Ideologies in South Africa*. Cape Town: David Philip.

Leftwich, A. 1974. *South Africa: Economic Growth and Political Change*. London: Allison and Busby.

Legassick, M. 1972a. 'The Making of South African "Native Policy", 1903–1923: The Origins of Segregation'. Institute of Commonwealth Studies Collected Seminar Papers on the Societies of Southern Africa in the 19th and 20th Centuries. London.

—. 1972b. 'The Rise of Modern South African Liberalism: its Assumptions and its Social Base'. Institute of Commonwealth Studies Collected Seminar Papers on the Societies of Southern Africa in the 19th and 20th Centuries. London.

—. 1973. *Class and Nationalism in South African Protest: The South African Communist Party and the 'Native Republic' 1928–1934*. Syracuse: Syracuse University Press.

—. October 1974. 'Legislation, Ideology and Economics in Post-1948 South Africa'. *Journal of Modern South African Studies* 1(1).

—. 1977. 'Liberalism, Social Control and Liberation in South Africa'. Seminar Paper, University of Warwick.

Legum, C (ed). 1965. *Pan Africanism – A Short Political Guide*. New York: Praeger.

Legum, C and M Legum. 1964. *South Africa: Crisis for the West*. London: Pall Mall.

Le May, G H. 1971. *Black and White in South Africa: The Politics of Survival*. London: St Giles House.

Lerumo, A (pseud. Michael Harmel). (ed). 1978. *Fifty Fighting Years: The South African Communist Party 1921–1971*. London: Inkululeko.

Levy, M. 1987. 'The Liberal Party and C.O.D'. *Work in Progress* 19.

Lewenstein, A and W Agar. 1965. *Freedom's Advocate*. New York: Viking Press.

Lewin, H (ed). 1981. *Bandiet: Seven Years in a South African Prison*. London: Heinemann.

Lewin, J. 1960. 'Dr John Philip and Liberalism'. *Race Relations Journal* 27, pp 82-90.

—. 1963. *Politics and Law in South Africa*. London: Merlin Press.

—. 1967. *The Struggle for Racial Equality*. New York: Humanities Press.

—. 1974. 'Growing up in South Africa – and London: Outline for a Memoir' (unpublished).

Lewis, G. 1987. *Between the Wire and the Wall: A History of South African 'Coloured' Politics*. Cape Town: David Philip.

Lewsen, P. 1970. 'The Cape Liberal Tradition – Myth or Reality?' Institute of Commonwealth Studies Collected Seminar Papers on the Societies of Southern Africa in the 19th and 20th Centuries. London.

—. 1980. 'Cape Liberalism in its Terminal Phase' (mimeo). African Studies Institute, University of the Witwatersrand.

—. 1987. *Voices of Protest: From Segregation to Apartheid, 1938-1948*. Johannesburg: Donker.

Liberal Party of South Africa. (n.d.)(?) 1954. *Co-operation or Chaos?* Cape Town

—. July 1954. 'Statement of Policy'.

—. (n.d.)(?) 1958. *South Africa is a Wonderful Country – Ruined by Politics!* Pietermaritzburg.

—. (n.d.)(?) 1960. *Blueprint for the Future*. Cape Town.

— 1965. *Fighting the Ice?* Pietermaritzburg.

Lipman, M. 1985. *Capitalism and Apartheid: South Africa 1910-1986*. London: Wildwood House.

Lodge, T. 1977. 'The Pan-Africanist Congress: Positive Action and the Poqo Uprising'. In C R Hill and P Warwick (eds). *Collected Papers, Centre for Southern African Studies*, York University, pp 95-113.

—. July 1978. 'The A.N.C. in the Rand Townships 1955–1957'. *Africa Perspective* 8, University of the Witwatersrand.

—. 1978. 'The Cape Town Troubles, March-April 1960'. *Journal of Southern African Studies* 4(2), pp 216-39.

—. 1980. 'The Paarl Insurrection'. *Africa Perspective* 14, University of the Witwatersrand.

—. 1983. *Black Politics in South Africa since 1945*. London: Longman.

—. 1985. 'Class Conflict, Communal Struggle and Patriotic Unity: The Communist Party of South Africa during the Second World War'. Seminar Paper, African Studies Institute, University of the Witwatersrand.

—. (ed). 1986. *Resistance and Ideology in Settler Societies*. Johannesburg: Ravan Press.

Luckhardt, K and B Wall. 1980. *Organise or Starve: The History of the South African Congress of Trade Unions*. London: Lawrence and Wishart.

MacDonald, T. 1947. *Jan Hofmeyr: Heir to Smuts*. Cape Town: Hurst and Blackett.

Macvicar, N. 1947. *Western Civilization and the Bantu*. Johannesburg: SAIRR (New Africa series no 14).

Mandela, N R. 1965. *No Easy Walk to Freedom*. London: Heinemann.

—. (ed). 1986. *The Struggle is My Life*. London: International Defence and Aid Fund.

Marquard, L. 1944. *Let's Go Into Politics*. Johannesburg: Essen and Company.

—. 1958. *South Africa's Colonial Policy*. Johannesburg: SAIRR.

—. 1960. *The People and Policies of South Africa*. Cape Town: Oxford University Press.

Marks, S. 1972. 'Liberalism, Social Realities and South African History'. *Journal of Commonwealth Political Studies* 10.

—. 1986. *The Ambiguities of Dependence in South Africa*. Johannesburg: Ravan Press.

—. 1987. *Not Either an Experimental Doll*. London: The Women's Press.

—. 2005. 'Worlds of Impossibilities?', in S Dubow and A Jeeves (eds). *South Africa's 1940s: Worlds of Possibilities*. Cape Town: Double Storey.

Marks, S and R Rathbone. 1982. *Industrialisation and Social Change in South Africa*. London: Longman.

Marks, S and S Trapido. 1987. *The Politics of Race and Nationalism in Twentieth Century South Africa*. London: Longman.

Marais, B. 1952. *Die Kleur Krisis en die Weste*. Johannesburg: Goieie Hoop Uitgevers.

Marcus, G. 1985. 'The Freedom Charter: A Blueprint for a Democratic South Africa'. Centre for Applied Legal Studies, University of the Witwatersrand, Occasional Paper No 9.

Matshikiza, T. 1985. *Chocolates for My Wife*. Cape Town: David Philip.

Matthews, Z K. 1987. *Freedom for My People*. Cape Town: David Philip.

Mbeki, M. 2009. *Architects of Poverty: Why African Capitalism Needs Changing*. Johannesburg: Picador Africa.

Meer, F (comp). 1988. *Higher Than Hope: 'Rolihlahla We Love You'*. Johannesburg: Skotaville.

Meli, F. 1988. *South African Belongs to Us: A History of the ANC*. Harare: Zimbabwe Publishing House.

Menon, K N. 1952. *Passive Resistance in South Africa*. New Delhi: Roxy Press.

Midlane, K N. 1977. 'Aspects of the South African Liberal Tradition', in C R Hill and P Warwick (eds). Collected Papers, Centre for Southern African Studies, York University.

Millin, S G. 1936. *General Smuts*: Volume 1. London: Faber and Faber.

—. 1936. *General Smuts: The Second Volume*. London: Faber and Faber.

Mitchison, N. 1973. *A Life For Africa: The Story of Bram Fischer*. London: Merlin Press.

Modisane, B. 1986. *Blame me on history*. Johannesburg: AD Donker.

Moll, T. 1987. 'Growth Without Development: The South African Economy in the 1950s'. Paper presented to 'South Africa in the 1950s' Conference, Queen Elizabeth House, Oxford.

Molteno, D B. 1958. *The Assault on our Liberties*. Johannesburg: SAIRR.

—. 1959. *The Betrayal of Native Representation*. Johannesburg: SAIRR.

Mort, S. 1987. 'Some indications of CPSA/SACP activity in the early '50s as evidenced by "Leftist" newspapers of that period'. Paper presented to ASSA Conference, University of the Western Cape.

Motlhabi, M. 1984. *The Theory and Practice of Black Resistance to Apartheid*. Johannesburg: Skotaville.

Munger, E S. 1958. *Communist Activity in South Africa*. American Universities Field Staff, 8 June.

Murray, M J (ed). 1982. *South African Capitalism and Black Political Opposition*. Cambridge: Schenkman.

Musson, D. 1989. *Johnny Gomas: Voice of the Working Class*. Cape Town: Buchu Books.

Ncube, D. 1985. *The Influence of Apartheid and Capitalism on the Development of Black Trade Unions in South Africa*. Johannesburg: Skotaville.

Ndebele, N. 2002. 'The African National Congress and the Policy of Non-Racialism: A Study of the Membership Issue'. *Politikon* 29(2).

No Sizwe (pseud Neville Alexander). 1979. *One Azania, One Nation: The National Question in South Africa*. London: Zed Press.

Ngubane, J K. 1946. *Should the Natives Representatives Council be Abolished?* Cape Town: African Bookman.

—. 1963. *An African Explains Apartheid*. London: Pall Mall Press.

O'Meara, D. 1975. 'The 1946 African Mineworkers' Strike and the Political Economy of South Africa'. *Journal of Commonwealth and Comparative Politics* 13(2).

—. 1983. *Volkskapitalisme: Class, Capital and Ideology in the Development of Afrikaner Nationalism, 1934-1948*. Johannesburg: Ravan Press.

Paton, A S. 1952. *Too Late the Phalarope*. New York: Charles Scribner.

—. (n.d.)(?) 1958 . *The People Wept: The Story of the Group Areas Act*. Durban.

—. 1958. *Hope for South Africa*. London: Pall Mall Press.

—. 1964. *Hofmeyr*. Cape Town: Oxford University Press.

—. 1973. *Apartheid and the Archbishop: The Life of Geoffrey Clayton, Archbishop of Cape Town*. Cape Town: David Philip.

—. 1975. *Knocking on the Door*. Cape Town: David Philip.

—. 1981. *Ah But Your Land is Beautiful*. London: Penguin Books.

—. 1985. *Federation or Isolation*. Johannesburg: SAIRR.

—. (ed). 1986. *Cry the Beloved Country: A Story of Comfort in Desolation*. Harmondsworth: Penguin Books.

—. 1986. *Towards the Mountain: An Autobiography*. London: Penguin.

—. 1988. *Journey Continued*. Cape Town: David Philip.

Patterson, S. 1953. *Colour and Culture in South Africa*. London: Routledge and Kegan Paul.

Polley, J A. 1988. *The Freedom Charter and the Future*. Cape Town: IDASA.

Posel, D. 1986.'The Meaning of Apartheid Before 1948: Conflicting Interests and Blueprints within the Afrikaner Nationalist Alliance'. Seminar Paper, Institute of Commonwealth Studies: Societies of Southern Africa in the 19th and 20th Centuries. London.

—. 1988. 'The Construction of Apartheid, 1948–1961'. Seminar paper, African Studies Institute, University of the Witwatersrand.

Reeves, A. 1960. *Shooting at Sharpeville: the Agony of South Africa*. London: Victor Gollancz.

Rheinallt Jones, J D. 1953. *At the Crossroads*. Johannesburg: SAIRR.

Rheinallt Jones, J D, H Brookes and M Webb. 1947. *South Africa faces UNO*. Johannesburg: SAIRR (New Africa Series No 13).

Rheinallt Jones, J D and R F A Hoernlé. 1942. *The Union's Burden of Poverty*. Johannesburg: SAIRR (New Africa Series No 1).

Rhoodie, N J. 1973. *South African Dialogue*. Pretoria: McGraw Hill.

Rich, P B. 1984. *White Power and the Liberal Conscience: Racial Segregation and South African Liberalism 1921–1960*. Johannesburg: Ravan Press.

—. 1986. 'The City of God and the Crisis of Political Faith: Edgar Brookes and the "Lie in the Soul" of South African Racial Segregation'. Seminar Paper, Institute for Social and Economic Research, Rhodes University.

Roos, N. 1956. *The Black Sash: The Story of the South African Women's Defence of the Constitution League*. Johannesburg: Rotonews.

Ross, N. 1988. 'The Torch Commando, the Natal Stand and the Politics of Exclusion and Inclusion, 1952–1953'. Paper Presented to a Workshop on Natal in the Union Period, Natal University (Pietermaritzburg), October.

Roth, M. 1986. 'Domination By Consent: Elections under the Representation of Natives Act, 1937-1948', in T Lodge (ed). *Resistance and Ideology in Settler Societies*. Johannesburg: Ravan Press.

Routh, G. 1957. *South Africa: The Facts*. London: Union of Democratic Control.

Roux, E. 1943. *S P Bunting: A Political Biography*. Cape Town: African Bookman.

—. (ed). 1978. *Time Longer Than Rope: A History of the Black Man's Struggle for Freedom in South Africa*. Madison: University of Wisconsin Press.

—. and W Roux. 1970. *Rebel Pity: The Life of Eddie Roux*. London: Rex Collings.

Rubin, L. 1959. *This Is Apartheid*. London: Victor Gollancz.

Sachs, B. 1973. *Mist of Memory*. London: Valentine Mitchell.

Sachs, E S. 1952. *The Choice Before South Africa*. London: Turnstile Press.

Sampson, A. 1956. *DRUM: A Venture into the New Africa*. London: Collins.

—. 1958. *Treason Cage: The Opposition on Trial in South Africa*. London: Collins.

Sanders, Dr Z (pseud Zena Susser). 1952. 'Aspects of the Rural Problem in South Africa'. *Viewpoints and Perspectives* 1(1).

Sapire, H. 1989. 'African Political Mobilisation in Brakpan in the 1950s'. Seminar paper, African Studies Institute, University of the Witwatersrand.

Saunders, C. 1988. *The Making of the South African Past: Major Historians on Race and Class*. Cape Town: David Philip.

Scher, D. 1979. *Dilitinzaba: He-Who-Removes-Mountains*. Johannesburg: SAIRR.

Scott, M. 1958. *A Time to Speak*. London: Faber and Faber.

Segal, R. 1962. *African Profiles*. Harmondsworth: Penguin Books.

—. 1963. *Into Exile*. London: Jonathan Cape.

Sellar W C and R J Yeatman. 1931. *1066 and All That: A Memorable History of England, Comprising All the Parts You Can Remember, including 103 Good Things, 5 Bad Kings and 2 Genuine Dates*. London: Methuen.

Simons, H J and R Simons. 1959. *Job Reservation and the Trade Unions*. Cape Town: Pioneer Press.

—. (ed). 1983. *Class and Colour in South Africa, 1850–1950*. London: International Defence and Aid Fund.

Smith, K. 1988. *The Changing Past: Trends in South African Historical Writing*. Johannesburg: Southern Book Publishers.

Smuts, J C. 1952. *Jan Christian Smuts*. London: Cassell and Co.

Socialist League of Africa. 1961. 'South Africa: Ten Years of the Stay-at-Home'. *International Socialist*, summer.

South African Communist Party. 1962. *The Road to South African Freedom*. Aldenham: Farleigh Press.

—. 1981. *South African Communists Speak: Documents from the History of the SACP, 1915–1980*. London: Inkululeko.

South African Congress of Democrats. 1954. *The Threatened People*. Johannesburg.

—. 1954. *Where the Devil Drives*. Johannesburg.

—. (n.d.)(?) 1955. *Educating for Ignorance*. Johannesburg.

—. 1955. *We Are Many!* Johannesburg.

—. (n.d.)(?) 1955. *Your Number Please!* Johannesburg.

—. (n.d.)(?) 1956. *South African Congress of Democrats: The Facts*. Johannesburg.

—. *Freedom is the Apex*. Johannesburg.

—. (n.d.)(?) 1959. *Bantustan Bluff*. Johannesburg.

—. 1960. *Face the Future*. Cape Town.

South African Institute of Race Relations. 1942. *Political Representation of Africans in the Union*. Johannesburg: New Africa Series No 3.

—. 1952. *Go Forward in Faith*. Johannesburg.

—. *The 'Western Areas' – Mass removal?*. Johannesburg.

South African Research Service 1984–1989. *South African Review* Vols 1-5. Johannesburg: Ravan Press.

Southall, R. 1982. *South Africa's Transkei: The Political Economy of an 'Independent' Bantustan*. London: Heinemann.

Spottiswoode, H (comp). 1960. *South Africa: The Road Ahead*. Cape Town: Howard Timmins.

Stadler, A. 1979. 'Birds in the Cornfield: Squatter Movements in Johannesburg, 1944–1947'. *Journal of Southern African Studies* October.

—. 1981.'A Long Way to Walk: Bus Boycotts in Alexandra, 1940–1945'. In P Bonner (ed). *Working Papers in Southern African Studies* Vol 2. Johannesburg: Ravan Press.

Steytler N (ed). 1991. *The Freedom Charter and Beyond: Founding Principles for a Democratic South African Legal Order*. Cape Town: Wyvern.

Strachan, H. 2004. *Maak a skyf, man!* Johannesburg: Jacana.

Strangwayes-Booth, J. 1976. *A Cricket in the Thorn Tree: Helen Suzman and the Progressive Party of South Africa*. Johannesburg: Hutchinson.

Stultz, N M. 1979. *Transkei's Half Loaf: Race Separatism in South Africa*. London: Yale University Press.

Suzman, H. 1949. *A Digest of the Fagan Report*. Johannesburg: SAIRR.

Suttner, R. 1984. 'The Freedom Charter – The People's Charter in the Nineteen Eighties'. Mimeo, T B Davie Memorial Lecture.

—. 2004. 'The [re]constitution of the South African Communist Party (SACP) as an underground organisation'. *Journal of Contemporary African Studies* 22(1).

Suttner, R and J Cronin. 1986. *Thirty Years of the Freedom Charter*. Johannesburg: Ravan Press.

Tabata, I B. 1974. *The Awakening of a People*. Nottingham: Spokesman Books.

Thomas, W (ed). 1974. *Labour Perspectives on South Africa*. Cape Town: David Philip.

Thompson, L M. 1949. *The Cape Coloured Franchise*. Johannesburg: SAIRR, New Africa Series No 18.

—. 1949. *Democracy in Multi-Racial Societies*. Johannesburg: SAIRR, New Africa Series No 18.

Tom, P. 1985. *My Life Struggle*. Johannesburg: Ravan Press.

Trapido, S. 1968. 'African Division Politics in the Cape Colony 1884–1910'. *Journal of African History* IX(1).

—. 1974. 'Liberalism in the Cape in the Nineteenth and Twentieth Centuries'. London: Institute of Commonwealth Studies Collected Seminar Papers on the Societies of Southern Africa in the 19th and 20th Centuries, No 17.

—. 1966. 'The South African Party System'. *Journal of Commonwealth Political Studies* 4.

Treason Trial Defence Fund. (n.d.)(?) 1958. *South Africa's Treason Trial*. Johannesburg: Afrika! Publications.

Troup, F. 1950. *In Face of Fear: Michael Scott's Challenge to South Africa*. London: Faber and Faber.

Tsotsi, W M. 1985. *From Chattel to Wage Slavery: A New Approach to South African History*. Maseru: Lesotho Printing and Publishing Company.

Turok, B. 1960. *The Pondo Revolt* (pamphlet). Cape Town: New Age.

—. 1974. *Strategic Problems in South Africa's Liberation Struggle: A Critical Analysis*. Richmond: Liberation Support Movement Information Centre.

—. 2003. *Nothing but the Truth: Behind the ANC's Struggle Politics*. Johannesburg and Cape Town: Jonathan Ball Publishers.

Van den Berghe, P L (ed). 1967. *Race and Racism: A Comparative Perspective*. London: John Wiley.

—. 1978. *The Liberal Dilemma in South Africa: Apartheid and Intellectuals*. London: St Martin's Press.

Van Diepen, M (ed). 1988. *The National Question in South Africa*. London: Zed Books.

Van Rensburg, P. 1962. *Guilty Land*. London: Penguin.

Vermaak, C. 1966. *The Red Trap: Communism and Violence in South Africa*. Johannesburg: Tafelberg.

—. 1966. *Bram Fischer: The Man with Two Faces*. Johannesburg: Tafelberg.

Vigne, R. 1997. *Liberals Against Apartheid: A History of the Liberal Party of South Africa, 1953–1968*. London: Macmillan.

Walker, C. 1982. *Women and Resistance in South Africa*. London: Onyx Press.

Walker, E A. (ed). 1957. *A History of South Africa*. London: Longman, Green and Co.

Walker, I L and B Weinbren. 1961. *2000 Casualties: A History of the Trade Unions and the Labour Movement in the Union of South Africa*. Johannesburg: SATUC.

Walker, O. 1953. *Sailor Malan: A Biography*. London: Cassell & Co.

Walshe, P. 1987. *The Rise of African Nationalism in South Africa: The African National Congress 1912–1952*. Johannesburg: Donker.

War Veterans Torch Commando. 1952. *The Truth about the Constitutional Crisis*. Cape Town.

Webster, E (ed). 1979. *Essays in Southern African Labour History*. Johannesburg: Ravan Press.

Welensky, R. 1964. *4000 Days*. London: Collins.

Weyl, N. 1970. *Traitors' End: The Rise and Fall of the Communist Movement in South Africa*. Johannesburg: Tafelberg.

Williams, D. 1970. 'African Nationalism in South Africa: Origins and Problems'. *Journal of African History* XI(3).

Williams, G. 1987. 'Celebrating the Freedom Charter'. *Transformation* 6.

Wilson, F. 1972. *Migrant Labour in South Africa*. Johannesburg: Christian Institute of South Africa.

Wolpe, H. 1972. 'Capitalism and Cheap Labour-Power in South Africa: From Segregation to Apartheid'. *Economy and Society*.

—. 1988. *Race, Class and the Apartheid State*. London: James Currey.

Wright, H M. 1977. *The Burden of the Present: Liberal-Radical Controversy over South African History*. Cape Town: David Philip.

Yudelman, D. 1983. *The Emergence of Modern South Africa: State, Capital and the Incorporation of Organized Labour on the South African Goldfields, 1902–1939*. London: Greenwood Press.

Unpublished theses

Ashforth, A. 1981. 'Structures of State Ideology: A Study of some Commission Reports on the "Native Question" in South Africa'. PhD thesis, Oxford University.

Bell, M M S. 1978. 'The Politics of Administration: The Career of Dr D. L. Smith with Special Reference to His Work in the Department of Native Affairs'. MA thesis, Rhodes University.

Burns, C. 1987. 'An Historical Study of the Friends of the Soviet Union and the South African Peace Council'. Honours thesis, University of the Witwatersrand, cited in A Berman. 1978. 'The South African Congress of Democrats 1953–1962'. Honours thesis, University of Cape Town.

Fridjhon, M. 1987. 'The Torch Commando: A Study in Opposition Politics in South Africa, 1951–1953'. BA Hons thesis, University of the Witwatersrand.

Hirson, B. 1987. 'The Making of the African Working Class on the Witwatersrand: Class and Community Struggles in an Urban Setting, 1932–1947'. PhD thesis, Middlesex Polytechnic.

Karon, T. 1983. 'Vryheid nie op 'n "skinkbord" nie': The Coloured People's Congress and the National Democratic Struggle in the Western Cape, 1951–1962'. Honours thesis, University of Cape Town.

Lambert, R V. 1988. 'Political Unionism in South Africa: The South African Congress of Trade Unions, 1955–1965'. PhD thesis, University of the Witwatersrand.

Levy, M. 1981. 'Opposition to Apartheid in the Fifties: The Liberal Party and the Congress of Democrats'. BA Hons thesis, University of the Witwatersrand.

Posel, D. 1987. 'Influx Control and the Construction of Apartheid, 1948–1961'. PhD thesis, Oxford University.

Preiss, D. 1975. 'Jan H Hofmeyr and the United Party 1936–1948'. BA Hons thesis, University of the Witwatersrand.

Reid, B L. 1979. 'The Federal Party, 1953–1962: An English-Speaking Reaction to Afrikaner Nationalism'. PhD thesis, University of Natal.

Newspapers and periodicals

Advance
African Communist
The African Drum
The Africanist
Africa South
Africa X-Ray
Agenda
Analysis
ANC Bulletin (1959)
Bantu World
Die Burger
Cape Times
Cape Argus
The Citizen (1956-1959)
The Clarion
Contact
Counter-Attack
Daily Dispatch
The Democrat
Discussion
Drum
For Peace and Friendship
The Forum
Freedom
The Guardian
Inkululeko

Inkundla ya Bantu
Liberation
Liberal Opinion
Natal Mercury
Natal Witness
The New African
New Age
Passive Resister (1946–1948)
Rand Daily Mail
Race Relations Journal
Race Relations News
Reality
Spark
Sechaba
South African Labour Bulletin
The Star
Transformation
The Transvaal Communist
Trek
The Torch
Umhlanganisi
Umsebenzi
Viewpoints and Perspectives
Work in Progress
World

Index